USE OF FORCE

A. Mark Weisburd

# USE OF FORCE

## The Practice of States Since World War II

The Pennsylvania State University Press
University Park, Pennsylvania

Library of Congress Cataloging-in-Publication Data

Weisburd, A. Mark (Arthur Mark), 1948–
Use of force : the practice of states since World War II / A. Mark Weisburd.

p. cm.
Includes bibliographical references and index.
ISBN 0-271-01679-5 (cloth : alk. paper).
ISBN 0-271-01680-9 (pbk. : alk. paper)
1. Intervention (International law) 2. War (International law)
3. International relations. 4. World politics—1945– I. Title.
JX4481.W45 1997
341.5'84—dc20 96-44645
CIP


Printed in the United States of America
Published by The Pennsylvania State University Press,
University Park, PA 16802-1003

It is the policy of The Pennsylvania State University Press to use acid-free paper for the first printing of all clothbound books. Publications on uncoated stock satisfy the minimum requirements of American National Standard for Information Sciences—Permanence of Paper for Printed Library Materials, ANSI Z39.48-1992.

*To My Parents*

# Contents

# ACKNOWLEDGMENTS

A work of this scope requires the efforts of many people. Jennie Wilhelm Mau's basic research was the foundation of the entire effort. Also providing valuable research assistance were Margaret Moloney, Heather Newton, Deirdre Coury, Scott Hudson, Michael Mulvaney, Cara Familet, Joan Howe, Christian Heindel, Mark Dorosin, Ellen MacDonald, Merlin Bass, Joseph J. Kalo IV, and Alison Brown. The North Carolina Law Foundation was generous in supporting my research over an extended period. Last to be mentioned but first in importance is my wife, Martha Petty, without whose love and support I could not have completed this book.

# Abbreviations and Acronyms

| | |
|---|---|
| ANC | African National Congress (South Africa) |
| ASEAN | Association of South-East Asian Nations |
| CAR | Central African Republic |
| CDR | Conseil Démocratique de la Révolution (Chad) |
| DK | Democratic Kampuchea |
| DPRK | Democratic People's Republic of Korea |
| DR | Dominican Republic |
| DRV | Democratic Republic of Vietnam |
| ECOWAS | Economic Community of West African States |
| EOKA | Ethniki Organosis Kyprion Agoniston (Cyprus) |
| FAN | Forces Armées du Nord (Chad) |
| FANT | Forces Armées Nationales Tchadiennes (Chad) |
| FAP | Forces Armées Populaires (Chad) |
| FAT | Forces Armées Tchadiennes (Chad) |
| FLN | Front de Libération Nationale (Algeria) |
| FNLA | Frente Nacional de Libertação de Angola |
| FNLC | Front Nationale de la Libération du Congo (Zaire) |
| FRELIMO | Frente de Libertação de Moçambique |
| FRETELIN | Frente Revolucionaria de Timor Leste Independente (East Timor) |
| FRG | Federal Republic of Germany |
| FROLINAT | Front pour la Libération Nationale du Tchad (Chad) |
| GDR | German Democratic Republic |
| GUNT | Gouvernement d'Union Nationale de Transition (Chad) |
| IAEA | International Atomic Energy Agency |
| IAPF | Inter-American Peace Force (Dominican Republic) |

| | |
|---|---|
| ICJ | International Court of Justice |
| IGNU | Interim Government of National Unity (Liberia) |
| INPFL | Independent National Patriotic Front of Liberia |
| ISZ | International Security Zone (Dominican Republic) |
| KKE | Greek Communist Party |
| LPF | Lao Patriotic Front |
| LTTE | Liberation Tigers of Tamil Eelam (Sri Lanka) |
| MPLA | Movimento Popular de Libertação de Angola |
| NDF | National Democratic Front (Yemen) |
| NJM | New Jewel Movement (Grenada) |
| NLF | National Liberation Front (South Vietnam) |
| NPFL | National Patriotic Front of Liberia |
| OAS | Organization of American States |
| OAU | Organization of African Unity |
| OECS | Organization of Eastern Caribbean States |
| OSCE | Organization for Security and Cooperation in Europe |
| PAIGC | Partido Africano da Independência da Guiné e Cabo Verde (Guinea-Bissau) |
| PAVN | People's Army of Vietnam |
| PDPA | People's Democratic Party of Afghanistan |
| PDRY | People's Democratic Republic of Yemen |
| PFLO | People's Front for the Liberation of Oman |
| PFLOAG | People's Front for the Liberation of the Arabian Gulf (Oman) |
| PLAF | People's Liberation Armed Forces (South Vietnam) |
| POLISARIO | Popular Front for the Liberation of Sakiet el-Hamra and Rio de Oro (Western Sahara) |
| PPP | Pakistan People's Party |
| PRC | People's Republic of China |
| PRG | Provisional Revolutionary Government (South Vietnam) |
| PRK | People's Republic of Kampuchea |
| RENAMO | Resistencia Nacional Mozambicana |
| RLA | Royal Laotian Army |
| ROC | Republic of China |
| ROK | Republic of Korea |
| ROV | Republic of Vietnam |
| SDAR | Saharan Democratic Arab Republic (Western Sahara) |
| SRV | Socialist Republic of Vietnam |
| SWAPO | South-West African People's Organization (Namibia) |
| UAR | United Arab Republic |

| | |
|---|---|
| UDT | União Democratica Timorense |
| UNCIP | United Nations Commission for India and Pakistan |
| UNITA | União Nacional para a Independência Total de Angola |
| UPA | União das Populaçoes de Angola |
| VWP | Vietnam Workers' Party |
| WSLF | Western Somali Liberation Front (Ethiopia) |
| YAR | Yemen Arab Republic |
| ZANLA | Zimbabwe African National Liberation Army |
| ZANU | Zimbabwe African National Union |
| ZAPU | Zimbabwe African People's Union |

# CHAPTER 1

# INTRODUCTION

## The Core Idea

Efforts to limit interstate violence through legal means have a lengthy history. Beginning at least as early as the arbitration treaties of the late nineteenth and early twentieth centuries,[1] continuing through the Covenant of the League of Nations[2] and the Kellogg-Briand Pact[3] after World War I, and culminating in the Charter of the United Nations,[4] states have several times formally limited their legal rights to use force against one another.

The conclusion of these various agreements, however, has not prevented two world wars and a host of smaller conflicts. The apparent failure of these treaties lends plausibility to the proposition that there are no effective legal limits on interstate war. According to this line of thinking, the treaties that purport to impose such limits are dead letters; their strictures have a paper validity only, with no practical effect on international relations. This circumstance, in turn, is held to demonstrate the irrelevance of international law as a mechanism for controlling states' decisions to use force against one another.

The thesis of this book is that this proposition goes too far. More specifically, there is strong reason to conclude that the international legal system limits the circumstances in which interstate force can be used, even given the frequent nonenforcement of the rules of the UN Charter. This discussion will seek to demonstrate that customary international law imposes effective, if restricted, limits on interstate war. It will do this by reviewing the hundred-odd occasions since World War II in which states have used force against other states, describing not only the uses of force but the reactions by other states to those uses of force. The net effect of these interactions is to provide the foundation for a set of operative norms regulating the interstate use of force.

## Preliminary Objections

This approach to the subject of the use of force is unconventional in public international law. To be sure, the idea that international legal rules may be derived from state practice is well established. The Statute of the International Court of Justice[5] and the writings of numerous commentators[6] make clear that the conjunction of a general practice of states with states' belief that they are legally obliged to adhere to the practice creates a legal obligation. The body of such obligations is labeled "customary international law." Even so, a focus on customary law limitations on the use of force is apt to encounter two different but related objections.

First, it is likely to be argued that the inquiry is unnecessary. In the *Case Concerning Military and Paramilitary Activities In and Against Nicaragua*[7] (the *Nicaragua* case), the International Court of Justice found itself having to decide whether customary international law imposed at least some restrictions on interstate uses of force,[8] and concluded that the limitations of Article 2, Paragraph 4 of the United Nations Charter had passed into customary law.[9] Thus, it could be argued, the court settled the matter authoritatively: customary law on this issue is identical to the law of the Charter.

The second argument against this inquiry would raise doubts about its propriety. The undertaking makes sense, after all, only if the practice of states regarding the use of force makes a difference concerning the content of the law. But various authorities assert that this is not the case. One strand of this argument would note that virtually all states are parties to the Charter of the

United Nations and thus have treaty obligations to adhere to the Charter; the validity of such obligations would, under this argument, derive from the rule *pacta sunt servanda* and would therefore be quite independent of state practice.[10]

A variant approach would argue that, even considered as customary international law, the Charter's rules are unaffected by divergent state practice. Thus, the International Court of Justice in the *Nicaragua* case asserted that "if a state acts in a way prima facie incompatible with a recognized rule, but defends its conduct by appealing to exceptions or justifications contained within the rule itself, then whether or not the State's conduct is in fact justifiable on that basis, the significance of that attitude is to confirm rather than to weaken the rule."[11]

Somewhat similar arguments have been raised by distinguished commentators. For example, Professor Oscar Schachter has stated:

> I reject the view that a new customary norm may be inferred from acts violating rules of world order. For example, acts of a state violating Article 2(4) or other similar norms regarding human rights and world order would not modify those preexisting norms. Such violations should be treated as breaches of the pre-existing rules rather than modifications of those rules. Most often a state will attempt to justify its act as falling within an exception to the preexisting rule. This type of behavior confirms the legitimacy of the norm, rather than modifying it.[12]

In a related vein Professor Louis Henkin has argued: "[Article 2 (4)], I stress, is independent of collective enforcement. The argument that, under the principle of *rebus sic stantibus*, or some variation of it, the failure of the intended enforcement system vitiates Article 2 (4), has no foundation. Clearly, that was not the intent of the framers of the Charter. No Government has claimed it. Not many scholars have argued it."[13] Later in the same article, Professor Henkin underlined the fact that even states arguably violating the Charter's rules sought to bring themselves within those rules instead of asserting their invalidity.[14]

There are a number of fairly easy responses to these positions. As to the *Nicaragua* decision, it can be pointed out that judgments of the International Court are binding only with respect to the case in which the judgments are rendered.[15] It is also relevant that the court's reasoning in that case has been questioned.[16] The arguments premised on the authority of the Charter could be considered question begging, in effect asserting that the charter's language is authoritative because it is authoritative. Alternatively, to the extent those arguments rely on the primacy of the world order goal embodied in Article 2(4), one may ask the basis for the assumption that states in fact regard that goal as primary.

These responses, however, are somewhat facile. It seems preferable to consider more carefully the question whether there is some logically necessary relationship between international law and international practice. If such necessity can be established, arguments that devalue the importance of practice in establishing international law must be incorrect.

## Practice and Law

One way to begin the inquiry into the connection between international law and international practice is to ask what it means to describe some social institution as a legal system. While the answer to that question could itself occupy volumes, at least part of the answer would be that a legal system seeks to generate and enforce rules addressing the behavior of those persons or institutions subject to it. That will seldom be the only function of such a system, but surely it is at the core. Furthermore, legal systems differ from others that seek to affect behavior by their approach to enforcement: legal systems have available to them means of coercion considered legitimate in whatever social grouping is under consideration. To be sure, legal systems may also seek to influence behavior by appeals to ideas of morality or prudence or social benefit, as religious or philosophical systems do. But religious or philosophical systems not possessing secular authority, at bottom, function only if those supposedly subject to them elect to follow the system's rules. A legal system, in contrast, does not leave its subjects free to decide whether to obey its rules; rather, its very purpose is to coerce obedience, to provide a source of strong pressure to obey the system's rules that is external to any individual subject of the system. Legal rules are not merely suggestions for prudent behavior or requests for beneficial action. They are requirements. It is, after all, a contradiction in terms to describe an entity as simultaneously "obliged" to behave in a particular fashion and free to behave in some different fashion. If a particular rule is characterized as a *legal* obligation, then the characterization must mean that the legal system does not leave those subject to the rule free to decide whether to obey it but rather employs the techniques of pressure characteristic of that legal system to ensure obedience to the rule.

Of course these observations are hardly original. As H.L.A. Hart observed in *The Concept of Law:* "Rules are conceived and spoken of as imposing obligations when the general demand for conformity is insistent and the social pressure brought to bear upon those who deviate or threaten to deviate is great."[17]

Similarly, in the international law context Myres McDougal[18] and W. Michael Reisman[19] stress that a purported legal rule cannot be deemed to exist unless accompanied upon its enunciation by indications of the intention and ability of the enunciating authority to control the behavior to which the rule is directed. As Reisman states:

> [I]t is delusory to call a statement in the subjunctive mood a prescription of law if it is not accompanied by a credible communication that those who are prescribing intend to and can make it controlling. Moreover, the communication of control intention must be continuous throughout the life of the prescription. Episodic violations of a norm, among other things, have a testing function for members of the community who wish to terminate it, pushing to see whether control intention has waned and whether the prescription may henceforth be violated with diminished likelihood of sanction or with impunity.[20]

But if it is correct to argue that legal systems seek to constrain the behavior of those subject to them, it follows that one could decide whether a given rule was a rule of a particular legal system by examining behavior regarding the rule within the system. If the rule was never violated, or if the system's rule enforcers—whoever they might be—sought to compel violators of the rule to cease their violations and repair any damage their violations had done, it would be at least possible that the rule was in fact a rule of the system. It would also be important to know, of course, the source of the rule, the reasons for obedience, and the basis for the imposition of sanctions on violators. But a rule that passes an obey-or-be-sanctioned standard is at least a candidate for inclusion among legal rules. When a rule is disobeyed and the system's enforcers display no interest in enforcing it, however, one must doubt its status as law.

But what does it mean to assert that violations of the rule must meet with some effort to enforce the rule? Clearly, one could express this idea in terms so extreme as to call into question the legal character of any legal system. For example, it cannot be true that in domestic legal systems no rule counts as law unless proven violators are either imprisoned or executed. Such an approach would mean that there was no such thing as a law of contracts, since violators of that body of law are in many legal systems seldom subjected to criminal sanctions. On the other hand, to argue that strong social ostracism should be considered a sanction in all circumstances would—in some contexts—appear to dissolve any difference between rules of law and rules of morality. If it is assumed that legal systems include elements not necessarily found in moral systems, a definition of legal sanction that collapses the difference between law and morality is surely suspect.

Although the question of defining the sanction concept thus presents dilemmas, some observations seem relatively easy to make. First, evaluations of what counts as a legal sanction presumably ought to vary depending on the structure of the social grouping whose legal system is in question. For example, in a small and relatively isolated community whose members depend greatly upon one another in a wide variety of circumstances, the significance of ostracism is presumably greater than is true in a more impersonal social grouping. Again, if members of a community have managed to get along without developing institutions capable of administering onerous sanctions, failure to impose such sanctions to enforce a particular rule would be less significant than would be true in communities in which a sophisticated sanctioning capability existed but was not used.

A completely relativistic approach to this question would seem mistaken, however. That is, if sanctions are applied to behavior in order to obtain reparation for the damage the behavior caused and to inhibit future similar behavior, the imposition of a demonstrably inadequate sanction raises doubts as to whether the behavior could be considered unlawful within that social grouping. That is true, furthermore, whether the application of ineffective sanctions in a given case reflects the inadequacies of the social grouping's sanctioning structure or instead flows from a choice not to apply a type of sanction available in the social grouping and more likely to be effective than the one actually applied.

But assessing a group's sanctioning capabilities is only one factor in considering the concept of legal sanctions. A second set of observations relates to the relative harshness of sanctions applied in a given case. We may take it for granted that a group that applies the most stringent sanction of which it is capable is at least attempting to coerce particular behavior. But what about behavior that elicits a less harsh reaction? We should surely hesitate to insist that only the most stringent sanction counts—as noted above, that would mean that no American state has a law of contracts. Nonetheless, it would appear that there is a connection between lesser and greater sanctions in that—at the margin—the effectiveness of lesser sanctions depends on the availability of greater sanctions to deal with defiant wrongdoers. For example, suppose a defendant in an American court is sued for breach of contract and loses, his adversary receiving a money judgment for compensatory damages. The sanction imposed is, in effect, an order to pay compensation. Suppose, however, that the defendant ignores the judgment, refusing to pay. The plaintiff will be able to obtain a writ of execution, requiring law enforcement authorities to seize property belonging to the defendant and sell it to raise funds adequate to pay the judgment. Of course, if strangers attempted to seize the defendant's property, he would be entitled to resist them. But if he attempts to defend his property against officials executing a judgment against him, he is liable for criminal sanctions. The requirement to compensate, that is, is backed up by a threat of forcible seizure of property, which in turn is backed up by criminal penalties for anyone defying the enforcing officials.

The importance of this observation is made clear if one envisions a different situation. Imagine, in my hypothetical contract suit, that no writ of execution was available against a defendant who did not pay a judgment. Or suppose that the writ existed but that the law permitted the defendant to resist seizure of his property for purposes of executing a judgment in the same way he was permitted to resist a robbery. In such circumstances one could not say that the rules of contract law were being enforced against the defendant. Since a sufficiently obdurate defendant could resist paying a judgment without consequences, payments actually made would represent a defendant's voluntary submission to the judgment rather than an exercise of coercion in the name of the law. But, as noted above, legal rules are not requests for voluntary compliance; they are requirements. To call a rule legal, then, is to assert that coercion is available to enforce it if necessary, even if coercion is unnecessary in most cases.

These observations on the incompatibility with the concept of law of a reliance on voluntary compliance to enforce a rule suggests a third set of issues relevant to the sanction concept. A group's determination to ask only voluntary compliance with rules that the group has the capacity actually to enforce implies that the group, at bottom, does not consider the behavior the rules proscribe as being truly unacceptable. This third group of ideas about sanctions, then, concerns their opposite: approval. Suppose a given social grouping's enforcers (which might include the whole group if it is sufficiently nonhierarchical) react to particular behavior by acknowledging its acceptability. In such circumstances it would clearly make no sense to classify such behavior as contrary to some legal rule of the group. Naturally, what counts as an acknowledgment of acceptability depends on the group in question. For example, imagine a group that recognized concepts of property rights. If a particular individual was acknowledged by authorized persons within the group's legal system to have acquired property rights through a given transaction, it would be difficult to argue that the transaction violated some rule of the group's legal system. Indeed, this observation serves to highlight the fact that it is a mistake to analyze together all cases in which a putative legal rule is not enforced. The case in which a system's nonenforcement takes the form of affirmative approval of the conduct in question is considerably less ambiguous than the case in which the system does not react to the behavior either positively or negatively.

Pulling the foregoing together, then, it can be said that what counts as a sanction in a given social grouping will depend on the grouping's sanctioning capabilities; behavior that would indicate serious social disapproval in one group may be rightly perceived as tacit approval in another. Also, it is doubtful whether a group unable or unwilling to apply to particular behavior a sanction capable of inhibiting the behavior can be said actually to have applied a sanction to the behavior. Further, it would appear that, while sanctions less severe than the harshest the group sees itself as having available do not lose their character as sanctions because of their relative mildness, they may lose that character if the group does not reinforce them with the harshest sanctions. Finally, it can be said that behavior which is treated as appropriate by the group is inconsistent with arguments that the behavior violates some rule of the group's legal system.

The foregoing helps to flesh out the concept of sanction in the obey-or-be-sanctioned standard. But the concept of obedience requires some elaboration as well. It should be stressed that application of the obey-or-be-sanctioned standard does *not* require concluding that mere disobedience to a rule proves that the rule is not a part of a given legal system. Rather, the question is not so much disobedience as the response to disobedience. If one disobeying a rule is subjected to sanctions that compel him to cease his violations and make good any harm those violations have caused, the net effect of the violation has been to reinforce the proposition that the legal system will not tolerate violations. Conversely, if a rule is treated as one that may be freely violated by those within the system charged with ensuring that rules are not violated, the rule is effectively being treated as if it were not part of the system. And if the people who make up the system treat a rule as not being part of the system, in what sense can the rule be said to be part of the system?

It is also important to underline that the foregoing discussion does not assume that a legal system must necessarily be structured in any particular way. It does not, for example, share Max Weber's assumption that law exists only if there are persons within the system especially charged with coercing obedience to rules of law.[21] Nor does it demand the existence of particular formal means of generating or enforcing the system's rules. It leaves room, that is, for systems that are very decentralized, deriving their rules from the whole of a social grouping and leaving enforcement to the members of the group; it does not preclude enforcement by means of self-help. The discussion only argues that, to be considered a *legal* system, the social institution in question must provide, somehow, for enforcement of rules in the event of their violation.

It is clear, however, that this description is incomplete. It is easy to imagine circumstances in which rules' status as law is not in question even though the rules are not enforced. Consider, for example, a situation in which law enforcement officials in a part of a particular American state fail to enforce the state's antigambling statutes. Despite the fact of nonenforcement, one would hesitate to assert that the statutes were not legal rules in the area in question. It would thus appear that enforcement is not essential to characterizing a rule as legal.

Before accepting that observation, however, it is necessary to consider why one would conclude that the hypothetical gambling statute remained a legal rule. It would appear that this follows only because of what may be called the pedigree of the rule. That is, it was created in the manner required by the system of which it is a part and has not been repealed by any method recognized in that system. More specifically, in any American state, authority to enact and repeal statutes is limited to the state's legislature. The law enforcement officers who do not enforce the statute simply are not part of the rule-creating or rule-repealing portion of the system. Within the context of the system, then, to accord rule-repealing effect to actions or omissions by law enforcement officers would be to grant them authority beyond that recognized by the legal system.

Further, the hypothetical case of nonenforcement suggested above takes place against a background in which nonenforcement of enacted statutes would be very much a departure from normal practice in the legal system in question. That is, the reluctance to treat an enacted statute as nonlaw because of nonenforcement occurs in circumstances in which enacted statutes are almost always enforced. Recognizing a statute as law merely because of its enactment, without inquiring as to enforcement, thus takes place against a background in which one could reasonably take it for granted that an enacted statute would be enforced.[22] If nonenforcement of statutes became frequent in such a system, the system itself would be in crisis, since such nonenforcement would mean that law enforcement officers were regularly ignoring the authority of the legislature of the state.

Imagine, however, a legal system structured differently from that of an American state. Assume that the system included no rigid hierarchy that limited law-making authority to only some members of the social group governed by the system. Assume that rules could be recognized as law without compliance with some set of formalities. Assume, finally, that there was also no hard distinction between situations in which members of the social group in question saw themselves as enforcing existing rules and those in which they saw themselves as creating or repealing rules. In such a loosely structured system there would be no way to accord a pedigree to a rule, since there would be no institutions with either the formal status or the history of deference necessary to make them capable of generating a pedigree. Rather, the only way to determine what rules the system treated as legal would be to determine what rules were actually obeyed or what rules were enforced if disobeyed. In such a system, then, rules that could not satisfy the obey-or-be-sanctioned standard could not be considered rules of the system.

## Practice and International Law

The foregoing section develops the idea that in legal systems lacking a hierarchical structure rules of the system can be identified only by applying an obey-or-be-sanctioned standard. The international legal system is clearly one lacking hierarchy. That system possesses no equivalent of a legislature capable of generating rules over the objection of members of the relevant social grouping, here, the states of the world. It possesses no tribunals with either compulsory jurisdiction or mechanisms for enforcing their judgments. It possesses no executive arm. It would therefore appear from the argument above that the obey-or-be-sanctioned standard would be the appropriate test for determining whether a putative rule is in fact a rule of the international legal system. If that standard is applied to international law, it follows that rules of international law are those that states either obey generally or that are the basis for sanctions against states in the event of disobedience.

The previous discussion pointed out that considering the concept of sanction involves certain complexities; that observation clearly applies in the context of international law. The structure of the international legal system, both in terms of its lack of central organs and of the great power of certain community members relative to the community as a whole, affects the sanctioning ability of that system. But while centralized sanctions are rare in international law, they exist—for example, the panoply of measures available to the Security Council under Chapter VII of the Charter of the United Nations.[23] Further, individual states have available a broad array of methods to indicate disapproval of other states' actions, from symbolic actions such as the recall of an ambassador, to refusals to proceed with negotiations important to the offending state, to economic and military sanctions. Indeed, the range of sanctions available for violations of rules of international law is great enough to make it difficult to imagine a case in which it would be literally impossible for the international legal system to enforce particular rules. And from this fact it follows that the failure of that system to impose sanctions in particular cases must reflect a choice not to make use of available mechanisms.

This conclusion does not imply, however, that it is always easy to determine whether the international system has actually subjected particular acts to sanction. This follows precisely because of the range of sanctions available for violations of international law. If the system responds to particular behavior by opting for a sanction clearly ineffective to reverse or repair the wrong the behavior has arguably done, and takes this course despite the availability of a more effective sanction, one may fairly conclude that the system has in fact acquiesced in the behavior in question. For example, consider an instance of state behavior arguably violative of Article 2(4) of the United Nations Charter, to which the Security Council responds by adopting a resolution that condemns the behavior but that includes no demands for reparation and sets in motion none of the enforcement machinery of Chapter VII. The resolution itself neither reverses the behavior nor requires reparation for it nor starts a process aimed at achieving either of these ends. Since the Security Council has available mechanisms better calculated to achieve such results than a mere condemnatory resolution, its failure to use such means could reasonably be seen as acquiescence in the act in question, despite the harsh language used to characterize it.[24]

Nonetheless, however difficult it may be to determine whether a particular act counts as a sanction in a given case, sanctions are available for violations of rules of customary international law. Given that fact and the fact of the decentralization of the system, determining whether a purported rule of customary international law in fact is a rule of law requires measuring it against the obey-or-be-sanctioned standard. That is, one must examine the actual practice of states, seeking to find out if they generally obey the putative rule and whether failures to obey the rule are met with a sanction.

The foregoing statement, however, masks at least one serious problem. It refers to the practice of states as though that term referred to a unitary phenomonon. This is hardly realistic, however. Imagine that one is trying to decide whether a particular behavior is a violation of customary international law. In so doing one must determine the relevant practice of states. It is entirely possible that some states will engage in the behavior and others will not. It is also possible that some states will behave inconsistently, engaging in the behavior on some occasions while resisting inducements to do so on others. Inconsistency could take other forms as well: for example, a state could enter into treaties forbidding behavior, or adhere to resolutions in international bodies condemning behavior, while simultaneously engaging in the behavior stigmatized in the instruments it has purported to accept. Finally, the lack of unity of practice may well pertain not simply to the behavior to be evaluated but to the reactions to such behavior by states not directly involved ("third states"). That is, when such activity takes place, some third states may not react, others may acquiesce passively (perhaps accompanying their acquiescence with condemnatory statements), others may impose sanctions on the acting state, and still others may assist it. If one is attempting to determine the legality of behavior in the face of disparate state practice, how can one proceed?

It would seem that if states differ concerning their willingness to engage in particular behavior, concerning their reaction to such behavior in other states, or both, the only conclusion possible is that the behavior would not violate international law. Supporting this conclusion requires a reexamination of the idea of "law." As argued above, a rule can be said to be part of a legal system when the system seeks to compel obedience to the rule. This means that the rule must be assumed to represent a decision by the system's legislators on behalf of the social grouping they govern. That is, the rule is a decision by whoever speaks for the community as an entity.

The international legal system, however, does not regulate a social grouping possessed of central organs authorized to speak for the grouping. Rather, the states who make up the community are simultaneously subjects of the law and legislators. Even under treaty regimes it is unusual to see states constructing arrangements according to which a state might be legally bound by decisions of other states; indeed, the only obvious counterexamples are the authority of the Security Council of the United Nations under Chapter VII of the Charter and the authority of the General Assembly of the United Nations with respect to budgetary questions.[25] The more common arrangement is that a state cannot be bound legally except by its consent expressed through a treaty or through the process of customary lawmaking, in which it is of course able to take part.

Given such a decentralized system, how can one determine whether the community has made a decision to regulate particular behavior? Presumably, one must look to the determinations of the individual members of the community on the question. And if it develops that the community is divided, the only possible conclusion is that the community, as an entity, has taken no position on the subject, so that there is no law with respect to the behavior in question. Indeed, at least as regards customary law, it would seem that labeling as unlawful behavior to which only some states object would contradict the usual description of customary law as determined by the *general* practice of states.[26]

We find, then, that customary international law is necessarily a practice-based system. And if practice determines the content of the law, it follows that the only way to discover the content of the law is to examine practice. According to this reasoning, the plan of this book—in which the content of potential rules regarding interstate uses of force will be determined by examining the cases in which states have used force against one another—makes sense.

However, the effect of concluding that practice determines the content of international law is that no rule of international law is immune to nullification by contrary practice. As noted in the earlier pages of this chapter, this conclusion is strongly rejected by highly regarded authorities, at least with regard to the law regulating the use of force. The discussion will now turn to addressing arguments that at least some fundamental rules of the international system should be considered rules of law notwithstanding divergent state practice.

## Arguments Against the Relevance of Divergent Practice

The existence of rules of the international legal system immune to erosion through inconsistent state practice would seem at odds with the structure of that system. As noted above, the rules of a highly stratified legal system may not be affected by the practice of officials not empowered within the system to modify legal obligations. In such a system a rule's creation by an institution both vested with exclusive formal power to create and modify law and with an authority that is almost always respected in fact by the other elements of the legal system gives the rule a claim to status as a legal rule, or a pedigree, strong enough to withstand enforcement deficiencies. The international legal system, however, is not such a stratified system. Rather, it is about as horizontal as one can imagine. There are no central institutions authorized to bind the individual states making up the system. Nor are there formalities that must be observed before an act can have a legal effect. Rather, any act can affect the law. As noted above, in such a nonhierarchical system it would seem almost a contradiction in terms to talk of "legal" rules that do not in practice satisfy the obey-or-be-sanctioned standard.

What arguments, then, are put forward asserting that—the foregoing notwithstanding—rules of international law may exist even though contradicted by the practice of states? There are at least three. The first attacks the description given here of the nature of legal systems by asserting that the availability of enforcement is not a key element in identifying a rule of law. The second, focusing particularly on what are deemed fundamental rules of international law, seeks to rely on the authority of particular international institutions or instruments. The third, taking a similar focus, emphasizes the importance of the rules in question. This last finds significance in states' unwillingness to admit to violations of purported rules regarding the use of force. Each of these arguments will be addressed in turn.

## *Enforceability and Law*

Professor Roger Fisher has expressed doubt regarding the necessity of the "sanction" aspect of an obey-or-be-sanctioned test to determine the existence of an international legal rule. He has pointed out that we think of law as limiting the freedom of governmental units even when the legal rule in question has been promulgated by the very government whose freedom is limited, such that application of a sanction for violating the rule would require the government to coerce itself. He also argues that coercing obedience even from subordinate governmental units can be difficult, yet we assume that such subordinate units are subject to law. If governments can be said to be bound by their own "law," he asserts, the availability of coercion cannot be a necessary element of law.[27]

Professor Fisher's observations seem to be of limited applicability. First, his point regarding the absurdity of self-coercion applies only when the entity to be constrained by the rule is the entity that promulgated it. If the entity to be bound is some subordinate unit, it is not absurd to talk of that unit being coerced by the larger entity. Certainly, such coercion has taken place. For example, the United States government employed both troops and federal marshals to enforce desegregation decrees against recalcitrant governments of southern states in the 1950s and 1960s. In the international law context it is equally possible for states collectively to enforce a legal rule against one of their number that has broken the rule.

Further, Fisher's argument puts considerable weight on the fact that governments frequently obey legal rules they have imposed on themselves, even without the threat of sanctions;[28] but surely this obedience does not demonstrate that a rule purportedly binding the government but that was regularly ignored would also count as a legal rule.

Finally, Fisher's argument seems to rely excessively on reification of the law-promulgating authority. Of course it is useful to think of governments as entities, particularly in dealing with questions relating to international relations. But governments are composed of individual human beings. To say that a government has violated a legal rule imposed on itself is to say that some individual officials have violated the law. And there seems to be no reason in principle why individual officials could not be subjected to sanctions for causing the organization of which they are a part to violate the law. Even presidents may be impeached. From this perspective, however, it seems mistaken to characterize government compliance with law as "voluntary." But if government compliance with law is not voluntary, then Fisher's arguments are simply mistaken. Professor Fisher, then, does not demonstrate the inapplicability of an obey-or-be-sanctioned standard in the international law context.

## *Authority and International Law*

Other opponents to the approach advocated in this book would argue that the institutions or instruments that have purported to establish the international legal rules regarding the use of force are too authoritative to be challenged by reference to divergent practice of states. Such arguments would insist that such pronouncements as the judgment of the International Court of Justice in the *Nicaragua* case or the General Assembly's *Resolution on the Definition of Aggression*[29] must be treated as conclusive statements of international law, unalterable except perhaps by subsequent pronouncements from the same institutions. There are, however, a number of difficulties with this position.

The fundamental difficulty with the argument is that it appears to misunderstand the concept of authority. That term is used in at least two distinct senses. It may refer to some institution or individual very knowledgeable about some subject, such that the views of this authority—reflecting this high degree of knowledge—are very likely to be correct. Thus one may speak of a particular scholar as an authority on the law of the sea, meaning not that one is somehow obliged to accept the scholar's opinions on law of the sea questions but rather that—given the scholar's knowledge of the subject—one would be foolish simply to disregard that opinion. The scholar could be considered an authority, moreover, despite the fact that the correctness of his opinion would always be subject to challenge by one questioning either the information upon which the opinion is based or the scholar's reasoning about that information.

A second meaning of authority applies that term to institutions whose position within some hierarchy requires those lower down in the hierarchy to follow the institution's view of certain subjects. For example, lower federal courts are compelled by their position in the federal judiciary to bow to the views of the United States Supreme Court regarding the proper interpretation of the U.S. Constitution. In such a case the institution's authority is a function of its status, not of the correctness of its views. Indeed, strictly speaking, it makes no sense to question the "correctness" of the views of an institution like the Supreme Court. Even if a particular Supreme Court opinion is considered by the majority of knowledgeable people to be based on ignorance of a given subject, flawed factual premises, or poor reasoning, the Court's authority is of a nature such that even its terrible opinions make law for the legal system in the United States. In that sense the Supreme Court's opinions regarding the interpretation of the law and Constitution of the United States are always "correct."

If it is argued that the International Court of Justice and the General Assembly are authorities whose views are beyond question, it must be that "authority" is being used in the second of the two senses discussed above, since, as was pointed out previously, the views of the first type of authorities are always open to question. But what is the justification for analogizing the authority of the International Court of Justice over international law to that of the United States Supreme Court over federal law or that of the General Assembly to a legislature? Neither institution is vested with such authority by its chartering instrument. The Statute of the International Court pronounces its judgments binding only in relation to the particular cases before it;[30] except with respect to budgetary questions, the UN Charter gives the General Assembly authority only to recommend and study.[31] If one is to find authority of this second kind in these institutions, then, its existence must be proven by demonstrating that the deference actually accorded them with respect to questions of international law compares to that accorded domestic supreme courts and legislatures by subordinate elements of domestic legal systems.

If one sets out to make such a demonstration, however, one immediately encounters difficulties. In domestic legal systems the deference to which reference was made in the preceding paragraph is principally that of lower courts. It makes sense to focus on the behavior of those courts in domestic systems because their judgments determine the outcomes of legal disputes in those systems. Even the outcomes of cases resolved by settlement or plea bargain are presumably influenced by predictions as to the form a judgment would likely take. The international legal system, however, is one in which the role of tribunals is very limited. Even if we assume that an international tribunal hearing a case involving a use of force would accord great weight to the reasoning of the *Nicaragua* opinion and to the *Definition of Aggression Resolution,* we must also take into account that the vast majority of cases in which the international legality of the use of force is considered do not involve tribunals. Rather, the most important determinations would be those made by officials of individual states as they decide whether to use force in particular cases and how to respond to uses of force by other states.

Thus, in the international system, proof that the International Court or the General Assembly enjoys authority analogous to that of domestic supreme courts and legislatures must focus on the behavior not of international tribunals but of states. More specifically, to claim authority for the court and assembly is to assert that states would in practice defer to the determinations of those institutions in the same way that domestic courts defer to domestic supreme courts and legislatures. But this is nothing but another way of saying that rules laid down by the court or assembly can be considered authoritative only if states actually apply them—that is, if the rules meet the obey-or-be-sanctioned standard. In short, one cannot insulate the pronouncements of the International Court or the General Assembly from measurement against the actual practice of states.

The foregoing remarks apply to both the court and the General Assembly; there are, however, additional arguments against reliance on General Assembly resolutions without regard to state practice. The General Assembly is simply a grouping of states. It is not clear why states' votes on resolutions in that body should be entitled to more weight in determining the content of international law than are the other ways in which states can make known their positions on legal questions. Indeed, it would seem that in cases of conflict between practice and General Assembly resolutions, it would be the latter that would be more suspect. As noted above, the UN Charter gives the General Assembly no law-making authority. It is clear that some states, at least, rely on this lack of authority in casting their votes in the assembly—that is, they vote in particular ways *because* they are in no way bound by their votes.[32] That being true, prudence would dictate caution in assuming that General Assembly resolutions on particular subjects in fact correspond to state practice pertaining to that subject.

We see then that there are serious weaknesses to arguments that determinations of international law should be based on pronouncements by the International Court and the General Assembly without regard to divergent state practice. What about arguments relying on the authority not of international institutions but of international instruments, particularly the UN Charter? Answering this question requires further consideration of what constitutes a legal rule.

The question Is such and such a purported rule in fact a rule of the international legal system? can be posed for rather different purposes. One might ask the question in order to evaluate some action that has already taken place. In such a case the issue is whether the rule in question was obeyed or else was the basis for sanctions at some point in the past. Suppose, however, the question is asked in order to determine the legality of some proposed course of action or to determine the state of the law at the time the question is asked. Answering the question requires predicting what rules states will generally obey and reinforce with sanctions at the time the action to be evaluated actually takes place.

It must be admitted that an emphasis on predictability of sanction as the means for identifying legal rules has been criticized. Hart, for example, argued that this approach ignores the extent to which rules guide decisions, as opposed to merely describing official actions.[33] He pointed out that it would make no sense to explain the outcome of a judge's consideration of a legal issue by reference to predictability; the judge would hardly resolve the problem by seeking to predict the result of his own analysis. Rather, he would analyze the problem, applying his legal system's rules of recognition and interpretation to determine the proper outcome based on the facts of the case.[34] Those rules, in turn, would not be likely to depend upon prediction; rather, most legal systems have more certain ways for judges to determine the content of law, for example, by interpreting statutes.

However, Hart's criticisms would not apply in the context of international law. That system's decentralized character means that the key decision makers in international legal disputes are not judges but officials of individual states. To be sure, international courts and international organizations exist. But international courts lack the means of enforcing their decrees. Similarly, international organizations have no machinery independent of the states that make them up to enforce their decisions; if rules of international law are to be enforced, states must do the enforcing. Thus, officials of individual states do not simply determine whether their own state's actions will conform to a given rule. They are also the only officials in a position to sanction the actions of other states that may violate a rule. Officials of states thus not only control the actions of their own governments but also perform a function in international law analogous to that of judges in domestic legal systems. However, those officials cannot address legal issues in the same way domestic judges do. In particular, if an official must decide whether a given action is consistent with customary law, that same official lacks the judge's relatively easy methods of determining the content of the law. Since the official's task is determining whether there exists a general practice of states accepted as law relevant to the problem, the official must seek some method of determining the attitude of the generality of states toward problems of the type being faced. Indeed, the only course open to the official is to predict whether other states with an interest in the action being contemplated will treat it as lawful or not.

Further, this reliance upon prediction affects not only officials seeking to determine the lawfulness of actions they contemplate but also officials of states faced with reacting to some other state's action. For example, suppose State A has engaged in activity to which State B objects. State B might be inclined to treat State A's action as unlawful, and respond with some appropriate sanction. However, officials of State B would have to consider the possibility that other states would consider State A's action lawful. In such a case other states would presumably refuse to impose sanctions themselves, possibly rendering State B's sanctions ineffective. Further, State B's sanctions could affect not only State A but other states. If those states disagreed with State B's assessment of the situation, State B might find itself treated as a lawbreaker. Thus, attempts to predict whether particular activities will incur sanctions from other states are necessary both to a state concerned about the legality of some action it contemplates—a state in its capacity as a subject of the law—and to a state considering the proper legal response to some other state's action—a state in its capacity as enforcer of the law. Determining the content of international legal rules, then, requires predicting state behavior. But how is one to make such predictions? In answering this question it is helpful to separate the consideration of issues governed by treaty rules from those governed by customary international law.

Consider first the question of treaty rules. Assuming that the issue is whether states will either obey a particular rule embodied in a treaty or be sanctioned if they do not, in most cases the best prediction would be that states will behave as the treaty requires. States enter into treaties only after deliberation and under circumstances designed to underline the seriousness of their undertakings. *Pacta sunt servanda* is among the most basic rules of international law, and the right of treaty parties to reparation for violation of treaties in most cases is undisputed. Indeed, so reasonable is a prediction that treaties are likely to be obeyed that it would in many cases make sense to believe that a treaty would be largely observed in the future, even after it has been violated by some parties.

It must be stressed, however, that international law has seen cases in which practice by treaty parties has so diverged from that required by the treaty that the practice has had the effect of modifying the parties' treaty obligations.[35] That is, even when a treaty purports to govern state behavior, state practice under the treaty can be a key factor in evaluating the legal obligation the treaty creates. If practice under the treaty makes it impossible to predict that states' future behavior will conform to the treaty text, that text loses its legal force.

Consider next customary international law. Since its most common definition refers to the "general practice of states,"[36] it might be assumed that the relevance of practice to predictions of future state behavior is obvious. Certainly, there is little dispute that in those cases where there is no treaty or other formal act from which customary law can derive, past and current state practice is the only available basis for prediction. Furthermore, if states have engaged in a particular type of behavior in the past, it is hardly unreasonable to assume that they will do so in the future. If they have tolerated, or imposed sanctions on, particular behavior by other states, the most prudent assumption is that those patterns will continue. And if states have had no occasion to sanction particular behavior because no state has engaged in the behavior despite inducements to do so, a state contemplating yielding to such an inducement might well see the existing pattern as a prediction that the behavior would induce sanctions. In other words, where state practice is the only possible source of legal obligation, past state practice is the best predictor of future state behavior, and thus crucial to determining the content of public international law.

The issue becomes more complicated if a treaty or other more or less formal act is relevant to a question of customary international law. Such a situation may come about easily, since rules of customary law may be derived from a treaty, creating obligations even for states not party to the treaty.[37] Suppose, then, that it is asserted that a particular treaty rule has passed into customary law. How would the rule's origin affect the use of the predictability model for determining the rule's legal status?

It is submitted that the fact that a putative customary law rule originated in a treaty is no reason not to apply the predictability model to evaluate it. This becomes clear if one considers the mechanism whereby a treaty rule is translated into a rule applicable outside the treaty context. In such a case the process involves states' acceptance of the assertion that the treaty's rule has become generally applicable, thus governing even outside contexts in which the treaty itself applies. That is, the rule acquires its extratreaty legal effect because states apply it when the treaty does not oblige them to do so—in other words, because of state practice. Since practice gives the treaty-derived rule its force outside the treaty, applying predictability analysis to such rules makes as much sense as does applying such analysis to practice-based rules derived in other ways. Indeed, as noted above, there have been cases in which changes in state practice have led to modifications in treaties themselves. If such developments are possible, it would be unusual if practice was irrelevant to the legal status of rules derived from treaties but alleged to be binding because they have become customary law. In fact, international law has seen a number of cases in which customary law has changed after the adoption of treaties purportedly declarative of custom because practice subsequent to the adoption of the treaty diverged from that which the treaty would have required.[38] Treaties, in short, cannot freeze customary law. Even when rules originate in treaties, to ask whether the rules are customary law is to ask for a prediction as to whether states will either obey them or be sanctioned for disobeying them.

In sum, then, rules cannot be said to have become part of international law unless it can be predicted that they can satisfy the obey-or-be-sanctioned standard. While, as noted above, one is entitled to presume that treaty obligations will be obeyed, state practice can nullify that presumption. Customary law rules likewise must satisfy the obey-or-be-sanctioned standard, and benefit from no presumption. This is true even if the purported rules derive from treaties.

These conclusions raise problems for the argument that the UN Charter necessarily fixes the content of international law regarding the use of force. First, as noted above, practice under a treaty can have the effect of substantially modifying the treaty's requirements. Distinguished commentators have argued that this has happened with Article 2(4).[39] Second, if what is in question is some putative customary law rule derived from Article 2(4), such a rule must be evaluated against the obey-or-be-sanctioned standard as would any other customary rule, unless such a rule would differ somehow from other treaty-derived customary rules. The question, that is, is can one fairly predict that states will either obey such a rule or be sanctioned for disobeying it? If such a prediction cannot be made, the rule does not represent customary law, regardless of its derivation.

## *"Fundamental" Rules as Law*

Suppose, however, that customary rules derived from Article 2(4) *do* differ from other treaty-derived customary rules. Professors Schachter and Henkin have in fact argued that certain norms are so central to the functioning of the international system that no degree of contrary practice could weaken them. This is particularly true, it is said, when states whose actions in fact fail to conform to the norm nonetheless seek to bring themselves within it. Both of these propositions, however, seem problematic.

How is one to determine the centrality of a norm to the functioning of the international system? Presumably the best way is to examine that functioning. If states violate the norm, and other states seem to be able to live with the violations, it is hard to see how the norm could be characterized as vital. This is not to say that the system might not function better if the norm were observed, but only to note that those who must live in the system act as though they think they can get along without the norm. If that is true, it is unclear what the basis could be for an assertion of the norm's fundamental character. Rather, it would seem that only state practice can be the basis for an assertion that a given norm is central. If that is true, however, no rule could be so fundamental as to be immune from modification or nullification by contrary state practice. The more general assertion of the immutability of "fundamental" rules thus seems to fail.

The argument that mischaracterization of violations of a rule reinforces rather than undermines the rule is simply too sweeping. Certainly, there may be cases in which rules are so well established and departures from them so infrequent that one could reasonably conclude that a rule was reinforced by a state's dishonest claim that its behavior complied with the rule. But the blanket assertion that this is always the effect of state dishonesty ignores the predictability element in determining the content of rules of international law. If State A observes that State B engages in particular behavior and is not sanctioned, State A could reasonably infer that similar behavior on its part would also not be sanctioned. This would be true even if State A observed State B mischaracterizing its behavior, assuming State A knew that states generally were aware of the mischaracterization. In such a case the logical inference would be that the world cared little about the underlying behavior, at least as long as violators kept up appearances. It is very hard to see how such an event would reinforce a rule requiring states to refrain from particular behavior. At most it would reinforce a rule that when states engage in the "prohibited" behavior, they must lie about their actions. Certainly, an observing state would have *no* basis for assuming that behavior like that of the putatively offending state would incur sanctions in the future.

Indeed, such an argument ignores the importance of third-state reactions in shaping the character of international legal rules. Imagine a situation in which a state was widely known to have engaged in putatively illegal behavior but states not directly affected by the behavior acquiesced in the illegality, for example, by shipping arms to a state widely known to have initiated an aggressive war against a neighbor. Such acquiescence in this case would imply a similar reaction in similar future cases and thus be of immense predictive importance to states contemplating similar conduct. That behavior, that is, would reinforce the impression generated by the initial "violation" that the behavior in question was not, in fact, likely to be sanctioned by states collectively or individually. And, as has been argued here repeatedly, to say that in a particular legal system certain behavior is not considered sanctionworthy is to say that it is not illegal in that system. All of this would be true, moreover, however the "violating" state characterized its action, as long as the facts were widely known. In such a case observing states seeking to determine whether conduct similar to the "violator's" would likely trigger sanctions in the future would necessarily have to take into account not only the violating state's version of the facts but also third-state acquiescence in the face of knowledge of the truth. Indeed, it is plausible to speculate that such an observing state would focus primarily on third-state reactions, since third states would be a potential source of the sanctions in which our putative observer is interested. Thus, to insist that the only legally significant element in such a transaction is the violator's dishonest labeling of its action is to reduce the evaluation of legal rules to a matter of word games, unrelated to any effort to shape conduct.[40]

Furthermore, such an approach imports unjustifiable procedural rigidities into the idea of customary law. If customary law is defined as "a general *practice* of states accepted as law," surely *practice* is the key element. If there is no general practice, there is nothing to which to attach the label "custom." To insist that divergent practice somehow does not count as undermining the general rule unless accompanied by proper words is to put form before substance in a system too decentralized to create such formal requirements.

This point would seem to refute the argument made by Professor Richard

Goodman to support the validity of a purported norm of customary law limiting states' freedom to use force against one another in the face of behavior violative of the norm. Professor Goodman asserts that such behavior cannot affect the status of the norm as a legal rule if the perpetrator of the behavior does not assert an affirmative right to engage in the behavior. This follows, Professor Goodman argues, because practice alone is not sufficient to establish a rule of customary international law; rather, practice must be informed by a belief in the lawfulness of the conduct practiced, the opinio juris requirement. Absent the enunciation of such a belief in connection with behavior violating a norm, Professor Goodman asserts, the behavior cannot change the norm. This would be true, Professor Goodman contends, even if third states generally acquiesce in the "illegal" behavior.[41]

This focus on opinio juris is misplaced. First, it assumes that it is as necessary to demonstrate a legal basis for an absence of restriction on state freedom as it is to show the existence of a rule limiting freedom. Such a view, however, assumes that any state action requires an affirmative legal basis, a position completely inconsistent with the actual degree of authority the international system exercises over individual states.[42] The argument also fails to explain how a customary law rule that does not satisfy the obey-or-be-sanctioned standard can be said to be a rule in the first place. If a norm purports to restrict states' freedom, and states' behavior shows both acts violative of the norm and acquiescence by third states in those acts, the norm simply is not a rule of law. Indeed, Professor Goodman's application of opinio juris in this context equates destroying a norm with changing it. His argument would have more force if it were argued that divergent behavior had altered a legal rule as opposed to destroying one. For example, if it were argued that divergent behavior changed the rule "In situation A, states must do X" to the rule "In situation A, states must do Y," presumably it would be necessary to show opinio juris supporting the supposed obligation to do Y. But if the only effect of the divergent behavior is to eliminate any restriction on state freedom, all that the divergent behavior has done is destroy a rule by falsifying the prediction implicit in the original rule that states would either do X or be sanctioned.

A putative rule, then, cannot survive contrary practice no matter how that practice is characterized. Professor Goodman's argument, however, points up one limitation of the analysis in this book. An examination of practice can demonstrate that a purported rule of international law is *not* in fact a rule of law because contradicted by practice. The converse, however, is not true. Proof that state behavior is consistent with a putative rule cannot prove that the rule *is* a rule of law; it can only prove that the rule *may be* a rule of law. This necessarily follows because of the opinio juris requirement. After all, a rule's legal character depends on its source as well as on obedience/enforcement. As has been frequently shown, even a rule whose violation will be met with sanction can be so illegitimate in origin that it could not be considered a rule of law.[43] To defy a mugger's demand for one's wallet is to risk coercion, but that fact does not make the mugger a legislator.

A study of state practice such as that undertaken in this book can only establish whether a particular manner of behavior is "the general practice of states"; it simply does not address the opinio juris question. Therefore, the goals of this work are limited. It can determine whether certain suggested rules are *not* rules of international law by establishing whether they are inconsistent with state practice. A demonstration that a putative rule is consistent with state practice, however, can only show that the rule *may be* a rule of law, depending on whether the opinio juris requirement is met. Since consideration of that requirement goes far beyond the scope of this work, this book does not purport to prove that rules consistent with state behavior are rules of law. Rather, it has the more modest goal of identifying rules that *arguably* are rules of law because they are consistent with state behavior.

## The Approach of This Work

This book, then, intends to show what putative rules of customary international law regarding the use of force survive the obey-or-be-sanctioned standard when measured against the practice of states. Accordingly, it recounts the facts of more than one hundred instances in which states can be said to have used force against other states during the period extending from the end of World War II through 1991. Given the length of this discussion, it will be helpful to explain why these particular uses of force were selected for discussion, how they were grouped into chapters, and, finally, why the discussion focuses on some aspects of each conflict as opposed to others.

Concerning the first issue—the principle used in selecting conflicts for discussion—the touchstone has been the international character of the conflict. That is, in what circumstances have states taken actions that could be seen as uses of force against other *states*? The events discussed thus encompass all uses of force initiated between 1945 and 1991 that could plausibly be characterized as having some international aspect—or rather all such events of whose existence I was able to make myself aware. The list includes failed efforts by colonial powers to oppose the independence of colonies; the eventual statehood of the colonies is here treated as relating back to the start of the war. It also includes a number of interventions by states in civil wars in other states, including interventions that took the form of logistic support only; some such interventions are probably omitted, since at least some were likely too small to attract notice. Also, some discrete incidents forming part of the background of conflicts judged particularly important are discussed only in connection with those conflicts.

Still other episodes are not discussed at all. Some of these events were omitted because they did not involve interstate force. This group includes wars that could best be understood as having no real international element, such as the Biafran conflict or the continuing violence in Northern Ireland. The legal problems presented by internal war are sufficiently distinct from those presented by wars with international elements to justify omitting internal wars from this discussion. This group would also include uses of force in which the target was not clearly known to the user of force. Thus, there is no discussion here of the destruction of Korean Air Lines Flight 007 by the Soviet Union in 1983, given the great confusion experienced by the Soviet authorities at the time in figuring out what they were doing and to whom they were doing it.[44] In such cases the acting state's uncertainty concerning what it is doing forces into the realm of speculation any discussion as to what that state's course of action would have been had it rightly understood the circumstances in which it was acting. Also omitted from this discussion are events not involving what is clearly a use of force—for example, behavior that was arguably a threat of force without the actual use of force, such as placing troops on alert.

The foregoing explains how particular events were selected for inclusion in this work. The next organizational decision—the basis for the arrangement of chapters—flows from the importance of prediction in international law. As discussed above, state officials seeking to determine the lawfulness of particular uses of force are compelled to predict reactions to such acts based on past reactions to similar acts. Obviously, such an official would find such an undertaking facilitated if the uses of force could be categorized according to some system. Categorization would enable the official to compare particular past uses of force with others similar to them and also would simplify the assessment of likely reactions to the use of force being addressed. A number of categorization systems are possible, but surely one that could work would be a system focusing on the relationship between the states involved in the use of force and the nature and apparent purpose of the use of force. Such an approach would permit the official to determine what duties states generally recognize toward states with whom they stand in varying kinds of relationships. Further, by avoiding categorizations based on political ideology, such an approach would make it easier to determine whether there are consistencies in state practice that transcend ideological divisions. The chaptering system employed here is intended to follow just such an approach. Its focus on the preconflict relationship between combatants and on the nature and purpose of the use of force helps address the questions, What do governments think they can do? and To whom do they think they can do it?

The discussion of chapter arrangements helps explain the last organizational issue, the form of the individual narratives. Each seeks to throw light on the question, What do states believe they can do to whom? Accordingly, each narrative addresses, first, what was done. Did the war involve an overt cross-border invasion, some less blatant use of force, external support for local guerillas, or something else?

Second, why did the state(s) involved use force? A state's motives are helpful in identifying the circumstances in which it believes force may rightly be used. They also appear to be relevant to third-state reactions to those uses of force. Related to states' motives are their justifications for using force. These can also be helpful in illuminating attitudes toward force.

Third, how did third states react to what was done? Did they acquiesce in the use of force, perhaps after verbal condemnation at the United Nations? Did they seek to show disapproval in a more concrete way, as by recalling an ambassador? Did they, alternatively, facilitate the use of force through provision of arms, or legitimize it by explicitly or implicitly accepting an arguably illegal state of affairs? This question of third-state reaction is particularly important, as it indicates the limits on state uses of force that states not immediately involved in a given conflict believe to exist.

The next nine chapters will address each of these factors and apply them to each of the conflicts being analyzed. The concluding chapter will seek to set out the inferences to which that discussion will give rise and to make clear states' post–World War II practice regarding the use of force.

## CHAPTER 2

# Classic Invasions

The first category of conflict to be considered here I have labeled "classic invasions." I use this term to mean a use of force with the following characteristics: (1) it involves a border crossing by regular troops of the state(s) initiating the use of force; (2) the border(s) crossed separate states; (3) the border(s) crossed have been recognized by the combatants for some time; (4) the purpose of the invasion is either to subjugate the state invaded, to seize a portion of its territory, or to replace an unfriendly government; (5) the invaded state did not, prior to the invasion, stand in a position of de facto subordination to the invading state, i.e., the actions of the invader(s) cannot be characterized as maintenance of a sphere of influence created prior to the invasion; and (6) the conflict cannot be seen as a continuation of earlier hostilities between the combatants that had ended without resolving the basic disputes between them. In other words the classic invasion involves the initiation of war between states with no recent history of armed conflict in order to permit the initiator to absorb all or part of its target or to subordinate it to a degree that did not exist prior to the invasion. It is thus an attempt to forcibly alter the international status quo in a very fundamental way.

## United Kingdom, France, Israel/Egypt (1956)

The first use of force after World War II that most clearly[1] meets the foregoing definition of a classic invasion was the attack on Egypt by the United Kingdom and France in 1956; Israel's part in that conflict is better described as a continuation war, as that term is defined in Chapter 5. The chain of events leading to that attack began when, in July 1956, the United States and the United Kingdom each withdrew offers they had made to Egypt to pay the foreign exchange costs of the dam Egypt planned to build at Aswan.[2] President Gamal Abdel Nasser's government responded to these actions by nationalizing the Suez Canal Company on July 26, 1956, with compensation for the shareholders of the company.[3] The United Kingdom and France almost immediately began planning joint military action in response.[4]

The motives of the two states were different. The French government strongly but incorrectly believed that Egypt was the key prop of the Algerian rebellion and was glad of the excuse to attack it.[5] The motives of the United Kingdom were more complex. It was very dependent on the Canal and believed that it simply could not afford to see it in Egyptian hands. Moreover, it felt that its prestige, and therefore its position in the Arab world, was at risk. The British government faced strong internal and external political pressure against backing down, and Anthony Eden, the prime minister, felt the need personally to stand up to Nasser, based on his experience of dealing with the European dictators of the 1930s.[6]

Over the next several months efforts were made to avert the use of force, but by October 16 the British government was convinced that this approach was fruitless.[7] Essentially, the British and French governments believed that they could not maintain their states' standing in the world, particularly the third world, without forcing—and being seen to force—Egypt to back down.[8]

France and the United Kingdom were not the only states interested in making war on Egypt. Israel also had a number of reasons to attack its neighbor. The armistice agreements concluded in 1949 after the first Arab-Israeli War had not led to peace treaties. On the contrary, relations between the two sides had deteriorated. Egypt had effectively closed the Suez Canal to

Israel, maintaining that policy in defiance of a 1951 Security Council resolution.[9] It subsequently closed the Straits of Tiran to Israeli shipping and aircraft. Likewise, beginning about 1950, groups of Arab guerillas crossed the armistice lines between Israel and its neighbors, particularly Egypt and Jordan, inflicting considerable damage and causing increasing numbers of casualties. Israel resorted to a policy of retaliation. The raids and retaliations increased over this period, worsening relations and increasing tensions.[10] The international reaction to this spiral of violence was ineffectual, being limited to what amounted to exhortations to peaceful behavior by the Security Council.[11] The situation was further complicated by Egypt's October 1955 decision to obtain a relatively large quantity of armored vehicles, cannon, and military aircraft from Czechoslovakia. The quantity of arms involved was large enough to destroy the military balance in the region. Israel assumed that the arms would be used against it, though there was disagreement within its security establishment as to how quickly Egypt would act.[12] In these circumstances Israel began to contemplate a preemptive war against Egypt.[13]

As the French had considered a strike against Egypt, they also conceived the idea of cooperating with Israel in their attack. They eventually convinced the British to accept the idea as Britain and France finalized their plans for a forcible response to Nasser's seizure of the Canal Company.[14] Cooperation with the British and French offered Israel the air support it would need to advance into the Sinai, while providing the Europeans with a pretext for attacking Egypt: protecting the Canal from the combatants.[15] The three powers formally agreed to proceed on October 26, 1956.[16]

Israel commenced its attack on Egypt on October 29.[17] On October 30, as prearranged, the United Kingdom and France delivered an ultimatum to Egypt and Israel, demanding that each state withdraw its forces to a distance of ten miles from the Suez Canal and that British and French troops be permitted to take up positions along the Canal.[18] Israel's troops were a considerable distance from the Canal and thus unaffected by the ultimatum; Egypt did not withdraw, believing that Britain and France were bluffing.[19]

On the same day, the United Kingdom and France vetoed in the Security Council separate American and Soviet resolutions calling on all members to refrain from the use of force in the area, for Israel's withdrawal from Egyptian territory and for a cease-fire. Egypt had claimed to be the victim of aggression, and most members of the Security Council agreed with the objective of halting the fighting and obtaining an Israeli withdrawal. However, Israel had defended its invasion as a defensive reaction to the frequent attacks on its territory by guerillas based in Egypt. France explained its veto by reference to Egypt's policy of seeking to annihilate Israel, Egypt's support of the Algerian rebels, and Egypt's seizure of the Canal.[20]

On October 31, upon expiration of the ultimatum, British and French aircraft began bombing Egyptian airfields.[21] The UN General Assembly, called into emergency session by a successful Yugoslav invocation of the "Uniting for Peace" Resolution, had on November 2 overwhelmingly approved an American resolution calling for a cease-fire and other steps to deal with the crisis.[22] On November 4 the assembly approved a Canadian resolution calling for the establishment of an emergency force to secure and supervise the cessation of hostilities.[23] Israel had secured all its objectives by November 5, and was anxious to accept the UN cease-fire, but was prevailed upon by the French, at the request of the British, not to do so; these two powers had not yet landed troops and could hardly claim to be sending in their forces to separate combatants if there was no combat.[24] By November 6, however, British and French troops were ashore, and those states accepted the cease-fire without having secured the entire Canal.[25] The Canadian resolution had called for the establishment of an international force to protect the Canal, and Britain made clear in accepting the cease-fire that it was relying on the creation of such a force.[26]

The British had decided to accept the cease-fire for several reasons. First, the intervention was no longer credible since the fighting had stopped. Further, Israel remained anxious to accept the cease-fire. Also, the Soviet Union had sent notes to Israel, France, and the United Kingdom threatening nuclear war if the fighting did not stop; while Britain and France discounted the likelihood of nuclear intervention, there was concern that some action might be taken. In any case, the Soviet threats had alarmed the United States, which had been pushing hard for an end to the fighting. In particular, the United States withdrew capital from the International Monetary Fund, blocking British efforts to shore up the weakening pound sterling; the British were told that the price for American aid for the pound was a cease-fire.[27]

The French preferred to continue the operation but agreed to the cease-fire when the British informed them that the United Kingdom was accepting the cease-fire regardless of the French attitude. In any case, it would have been difficult for the French to act independently given the integration of their forces with the British.[28]

Over the next several months further maneuvers took place regarding the withdrawal of British, French, and Israeli forces from Egypt. The British and French dragged their heels. Britain, however, was in difficult financial straits as a result of the crisis; when the United States agreed to aid Britain financially and with shipments of oil upon receiving assurances of a British withdrawal, the assurances were forthcoming. An announcement of withdrawal was made on December 3, and it was complete by December 22.[29] Israeli withdrawal was harder to arrange. David Ben-Gurion, the prime minister of Israel, made a speech on November 7 declaring that Israel would remain in the Sinai and would oppose the introduction of other troops in that area.[30] That night, however, the General Assembly overwhelmingly adopted a resolution calling for the withdrawal of all foreign forces from Egypt.[31] Furthermore, the United States threatened Israel with the loss of all aid, with UN sanctions, and with expulsion from the United Nations if it did not withdraw.[32] Ben-Gurion, who was also very concerned about the threats made by the Soviet Union,[33] thereupon reversed course, stating on November 8 that Israel would withdraw "upon the conclusion of satisfactory arrangements with the United Nations."[34]

Israel nonetheless sought to guarantee itself three objectives before withdrawing: passage through the Straits of Tiran, Egyptian nonreturn to Gaza, and creation of a buffer in the Sinai.[35] Through February 1957 it received no such guarantees and refused to withdraw; on February 11, however, the United States agreed to support Israeli passage through the Straits. On February 16 the United States threatened the end of private as well as government aid to Israel if no withdrawal was forthcoming. Finally, on the assumption that a UN force would occupy Gaza and Sharm el Sheikh, and reserving its rights in case that assumption proved false, Israel agreed on March 1 to withdraw. Its primary reliance was on American verbal guarantees that its requirements would continue to be met.[36] During this period, the General Assembly had passed several resolutions calling for Israeli withdrawal; Israel had ignored them all.[37]

As the foregoing indicates, third-party reaction to the attack on Egypt was crucial to the outcome of the Suez crisis. The actions of the United States have been described, though it should be added that the United States justified its stand throughout as required by the Charter of the United Nations. Secretary of State John Foster Dulles stressed this point in his speech at the opening of the General Assembly's emergency session.[38] So did President Dwight D. Eisenhower in a February 1957 speech criticizing Israel's refusal to withdraw from the Sinai.[39]

As noted above, the threats of the Soviet Union also were important, particularly for Israel. In addition, Jordan and Syria mobilized, and Iraq dispatched troops to Jordan; Jordan also forbade British aircraft at two British bases in Jordan to be used against Egypt and imposed an economic boycott on France.[40] Saudi Arabia and Syria broke diplomatic relations with Britain and

France, and Jordan and Iraq severed ties with France; furthermore, a portion of an oil pipeline from Iraq that was crucial to Britain was demolished in Syria by the Syrian Army, according to Britain, though the Syrian government denied responsibility.[41] The loss of this pipeline was a factor in the economic problems Britain experienced during this period.[42] The Sudan closed its airports to the United Kingdom and to France, and Nepal warned Britain against using Gurkha soldiers—recruited from Nepal—in the fighting.[43] Aside from the states engaging in what might be called sanctioning activity, Denmark, Colombia, India, Norway, Sweden, Yugoslavia, and Canada all contributed troops to the UN force that was created to facilitate the cease-fire.[44] And the heavy majorities in the General Assembly opposing the invasion apparently carried some weight, with Israel at least.[45]

The Suez crisis was a cross-border invasion by Israel, Britain, and France. Israel justified its action on the basis of self-defense; Britain and France claimed to be doing no more than protecting the Canal. Israel's motive was close to its justification, though Ben-Gurion's November 7, 1956, speech suggests territorial ambitions as well. The motives of Britain and France, however, were unrelated to their justifications, focusing on maintenance of great power status and the punishing of an upstart state. Third-state reaction was negative, forceful, and effective. No support was expressed for the invasion itself,[46] though some states tried to avoid apportioning blame.[47] The pressure from the United States and the Soviet Union appears to have been decisive in ending the shooting and in bringing about the removal from Egypt of the invading forces. Syria's destruction of the oil pipeline also had an effect. Other states' negative reactions were expressed mainly through actions in the General Assembly; few other states outside the Arab world took any direct action against the invading states.

It should also be noted that the role of the United Nations in this matter was more one of providing the means for carrying out a cease-fire and withdrawal, through the creation of an international force, than of forcing an end to the fighting. Except to the extent that world opinion as expressed in General Assembly resolutions had a coercive effect, pressure to break off the invasion came primarily outside the United Nations framework.

## Indonesia/Netherlands (1960–1962)

The conflict between Indonesia and the Netherlands over control of western New Guinea—called West Irian by Indonesia—originated in April 1960, when the Netherlands announced its intention to dispatch an aircraft carrier and two escort vessels to western New Guinea, which at that time was a Dutch colony. This action provoked great hostility from Indonesia, which claimed western New Guinea as its territory. The Netherlands did not simply counter with its own assertion of sovereignty. Rather, it took the position that the inhabitants of the region should be permitted to exercise their right of self-determination, selecting whatever arrangement they chose for their area but not necessarily being limited to choosing integration into Indonesia. Indonesia rejected the argument that the inhabitants of the area had any right to self-determination, insisting on its own claim of sovereignty.[48]

The fighting between the two sides was limited. Indonesia made unsuccessful efforts to infiltrate troops into Dutch New Guinea in November 1960.[49] In December 1961 and January 1962, Indonesia threatened war, called for volunteers to liberate West Irian, established a military district to operate as a base for that purpose, limited air traffic in the area, and began mobilizing.[50] These actions were followed by an attempted landing; on January 15, 1962, Dutch naval vessels in Dutch waters intercepted three Indonesian motor torpedo boats carrying troops and heading for Dutch New Guinea, sinking one and apparently inducing the other two to retire.[51] Over the next five months the Indonesians dropped several small groups of paratroops in Dutch New Guinea, many being immediately captured and none achieving any military success.[52]

The position of the Netherlands was weak, nonetheless. A resolution on the issue had been proposed in the General Assembly in the fall of 1961 by a group of states, mostly from Francophone Africa. The resolution had called for negotiations between the parties but had included language that assumed the applicability of the principle of self-determination to the controversy and had called for a UN investigation if negotiations proved fruitless.[53] The paragraph referring to the principle of self-determination was voted on separately, receiving a majority less than the required two-thirds (53 for, 36 against, 14 abstentions).[54] The states supporting the resolution had come principally from Europe, the Americas, and Francophone Africa; the opponents included the Communist states, the Arab states, and several Asian and African states.[55] The remainder of the resolution, with its reference to a UN investigation, also attained a majority less than that required to pass, with roughly the same breakdown in voting.[56] Furthermore, the United States was urging compromise. In February it had banned from U.S. airports Dutch aircraft carrying military personnel, and in March it offered its aid in mediating. Furthermore, the Soviet Union agreed in May 1962 to sell quantities of arms to Indonesia additional to those covered by earlier agreements.[57]

Facing a high degree of international hostility to its position, and receiving little concrete support, the Netherlands agreed on August 15, 1962, to an arrangement whereby the United Nations would administer western New Guinea from October 1962 until May 1, 1963, and then transfer administrative functions to Indonesia. Six years later a plebiscite would be held to determine whether the people of the territory wished to continue under Indonesian administration.[58] Combat resulting from Dutch resistance to continued Indonesian efforts to infiltrate had taken place throughout the negotiations.[59]

This conflict was a cross-border invasion aimed at acquiring territory. Indonesia justified its position by reference to resistance to colonialism, and that position commanded significant support. Once shooting started, the Netherlands received no help; even an ally as presumably sympathetic as the United States in essence took a position of neutrality and ended by supporting a resolution of the conflict that amounted to a complete acceptance of Indonesia's position. This stand was taken, moreover, despite the fact that the Dutch were not seeking to retain the territory but only to give its inhabitants an opportunity to resist absorption by Indonesia. Fairly clearly, the states of the world at this period were not firmly opposed even to invasions when such actions were motivated by a desire to expel any vestige of European colonialism.

## India/Portugal (1961)

The territory of Goa, on the west coast of the Indian subcontinent, was conquered by Portugal in 1510.[60] In the years following India's attainment of independence in 1947 India sought to negotiate with Portugal regarding the transfer of sovereignty over Goa to India, but Portugal insisted that Goa was not a colony but an integral part of Portugal and refused to discuss the matter.[61]

Matters continued in this vein until 1961, when several events, apparently, contributed to a change in the situation. First, at the Belgrade Conference of Nonaligned Nations in September, India was criticized for tolerating Portugal's continued presence on the subcontinent.[62] An international meeting in New Delhi the following month likewise generated pressure on India to eliminate the Portuguese presence.[63] Furthermore, the Indian government had been subjected to considerable domestic press criticism regarding its handling of its border dispute with the PRC.[64] Speeches by the prime minister and defense minister in the Lok Sabha in late November generated a press campaign against the Portuguese, which in turn produced considerable political pressure on the government to act and which apparently led to the dispatch of troops to the Goan frontier.[65] Further, tension was increased by two incidents in November in which shots were fired from an island that was part of Goa at passing Indian-flag vessels, resulting in one fatality. The situation also deteriorated because of India's claim that Portuguese authorities were intensifying repressive actions within Goa[66] and because of its December assertion that Portugal had reinforced its military contingent stationed in Goa (both charges were later shown to be false).[67]

In fact, Indian troops had received orders to begin concentrating against Goa on November 30, in line with a previously devised contingency plan for occupying that territory apparently approved by the Indian government in very late November.[68] On December 14 the troop commander was ordered to proceed with an invasion of Goa on December 18.[69] Although there was a fair degree of diplomatic activity aimed at averting a military clash during the first half of December, the invasion in fact took place on December 18 and the Portuguese had surrendered by December 20.[70]

In the ensuing UN Security Council debates India sought to justify its actions on a number of grounds. It argued, in essence, that the Portuguese had initiated hostilities by aggressive actions and by reinforcing their troops,[71] but it does not appear that these positions were strongly defended; it is also clear that they were incorrect factually, at least with respect to the claim of reinforcement. More central to India's position were arguments essentially based on the illegitimacy of Portugal's colonial title, relying in particular on General Assembly resolutions condemning colonialism.[72] Although these arguments were vigorously criticized by Western states, especially the United States, they were as strongly supported—in the Security Council and out—by Communist and third-world states.[73] A Security Council resolution that would have called upon India to withdraw its forces was vetoed by the Soviet Union, evoking a warning from Ambassador Stevenson of the United States that the posture of the Security Council amounted to sanctioning the use of force whenever it suited the purposes of the user.[74] India faced no sanctions for its invasion. After the 1974 coup in Portugal the new government there recognized Indian sovereignty over the former Portuguese territory.[75]

This case involved a cross-border invasion for the purpose of acquiring territory. It was justified primarily on an anticolonialist rationale.[76] Despite opposition from some states, the invasion was approved by many others and subjected to no sanction. It must be seen as leading to the formal incorporation of the territory at issue by the invader, since the former territorial sovereign itself has affirmatively acknowledged a change of sovereignty. This incident therefore underlines the fact that by 1961 use of interstate force directed against European colonialism was *not* seen by the generality of states as illegal.

## Somalia/Ethiopia (1975–1988)

Although the period between 1962 and 1977 was a violent one, no use of force during that time clearly satisfies the definition of a classic invasion. The 1977 invasion of Ethiopia by Somalia, however, appears to fall into that classification. The roots of that use of force date back to Somalia's achievement of independence in 1960. From that time Somalia had taken as one of its key national goals the bringing within its borders of all the territory inhabited by Somalis.[77] It defied overwhelming African opinion when, on July 23, 1964, it entered a reservation to the Organization of African Unity's resolution of two days previous under which members of the OAU undertook to respect one another's boundaries as they existed at independence.[78]

This policy led to conflict with Ethiopia, which in the nineteenth and twentieth centuries had absorbed considerable territory peopled by Somali clans, most notably the Ogaden desert.[79] The beginnings of a detente between the two states were halted in 1969 by a military coup in Somalia, which brought a socialist government to power.[80] Five years later a coup in Ethiopia led to the forced abdication of Emperor Haile Selassie and the coming to power of a military government in that state. Unlike the coup in Somalia, however, which had led to a higher degree of national cohesion, the coup in Ethiopia accentuated that diverse state's tendencies to divisiveness.[81]

Among the groups fighting against the Ethiopian central government was the Ogaden-based Western Somali Liberation Front (WSLF), to which Somalia gave substantial logistical support as early as 1975 in an effort to take the Ogaden from Ethiopia.[82] By the summer of 1977 the WSLF was making considerable progress in the Ogaden. It enjoyed a high degree of popular support and roamed freely in the countryside, though it controlled no urban areas. In late July 1977 Somalia elected to intervene, sending its own troops into the Ogaden.[83]

Somalia apparently chose this course for several reasons. Most fundamental was the irredentism described above; Somalia strongly objected to Ethiopian control of the Ogaden. Beyond this basic factor were others. First, the WSLF was doing well; Somalia saw itself as reinforcing success. Second, the military balance at the time favored Somalia. Ethiopia was fighting a very serious war against Eritrean separatists, which effectively reduced the superiority in weapons and troop strength it could otherwise bring to bear against Somalia. Further, Ethiopia had recently broken its military link to the United States and aligned itself with the Soviet Union, which had begun supplying arms. Since Ethiopian troops had been trained on American arms, this shift in suppliers temporarily put Ethiopia at a disadvantage. Conversely, Somalia could expect its military to become less effective over time, since its troops were armed with Soviet weapons and the Soviet Union had ceased to supply Somalia with spare parts for these weapons because of the deterioration in Soviet-Somali relations as the Soviets moved closer to the new socialist state in Ethiopia. There is also evidence that Somalia believed, incorrectly, that it was likely to have access to military aid from the United States and other Western states in the event of war with Ethiopia.[84]

In any case, Somali regulars went into action in the Ogaden in late July 1977. After enjoying some initial success, their advances were halted when Ethiopia received massive quantities of military aid from the Soviet Union, as well as troops from the Soviet Union and Cuba. Thus reequipped and reinforced, Ethiopia was able to go on the offensive and Somalia was unable to resist effectively. By March 15, 1978, Somalia had withdrawn its troops from Ethiopia.[85] It had only admitted their presence within that state in February 1978, asserting that they were then being dispatched to aid the WSLF deal with Ethiopia's foreign-backed offensive.[86]

This defeat did not end the fighting between the two states, but it will be useful at this point to analyze third-state reactions to the war. Preliminarily, it should be noted that no UN organ addressed this conflict. Beyond this and as mentioned, the Soviet Union and Cuba offered tremendous support to Ethiopia, though the Soviet Union made clear that it would not aid Ethiopia to cross the border and in turn invade Somalia.[87] The German Democratic Republic (GDR) and People's Democratic Republic of Yemen (PDRY) also sent troops and/or technicans to aid Ethiopia.[88] The United States withdrew an offer of arms to Somalia once it became clear that Somalia had violated Ethiopia's borders; at least part of the American motivation for this course of action was the desire of the United States to improve its position among African states, which made particularly important the widespread African perception that the Somali invasion was an unacceptable act of aggression.[89] The United States did, however, indicate that it would react differently if Ethiopia invaded Somalia.[90] The United States also criticized the Soviet Union and Cuba for intervening in a purely African conflict.[91]

Other Western states followed policies similar to those of the United States. The United Kingdom, France, Italy, and the Federal Republic of Germany (FRG) all proclaimed their neutrality and refused to provide arms to Somalia.[92] France, however, did not object when Saudi Arabia transferred sixty tanks it had purchased from France to Somalia.[93] The FRG also provided a loan to Somalia of $18 million, in gratitude for Somali aid to German troops who were permitted to free the passengers on a Lufthansa jet hijacked to Somalia in October 1977.[94]

A number of Arab governments expressed support for Somalia; further, Saudi Arabia, as mentioned above, Egypt, Syria, and Iraq provided military equipment and financial aid. Egypt also dispatched two thousand noncombat troops to Somalia and promised that both it and the Sudan would send brigades of troops, financed by the Saudis, in the event of an Ethiopian invasion.[95] The Arabs were restrained, however, by the refusal of the United States to permit those states who had obtained American arms to transfer those arms to the Somalis.[96] Iran, like the Arab states, offered Somalia diplomatic support, but it never ended oil shipments to Ethiopia and ceased supplying Somalia with light weapons after January 1978.[97] As noted above, African states generally rejected Somalia's argument that it was not obliged to respect its border with Ethiopia and regarded Somalia's actions with serious misgivings, though they were officially neutral during the war. The OAU, however, was ineffective, limiting itself to a call to both states to cease hostile activities. This approach amounted to implicit support for Ethiopia, since it was taken at a time when Somalia denied that its troops were involved and since it omitted any reference to the principle of self-determination upon which Somalia based its claim to the Ogaden;[98] it was hardly a forthright condemnation of Somali actions, however. Morocco, Mauritania, and Tunisia declared their support for Somalia, though only Morocco accepted its irredentist argument.[99] Most fundamentally, it is important to stress that, whatever statements of support states made for Somalia, the material support Somalia received was trivial compared to that provided to Ethiopia by the Soviet Union and its satellites.[100]

To return to the course of the fighting, the WSLF kept up its activities in the Ogaden after the Somali army left.[101] Ethiopia, for its part, began supporting Somali dissident groups, and Somalia complained in 1981 and 1982 of air and ground incursions from Ethiopia, the most serious taking place in June 1982. The United States responded to this situation by sending arms to

Somalia; Italy followed suit. Ethiopia throughout insisted that it was not involved with the activities of the Somali antigovernment groups.[102] Throughout this period Somalia increased its military cooperation with the United States.[103] Finally, in April 1988 Somalia and Ethiopia signed a peace treaty. Each side agreed to withdraw its troops 15 kilometers from the border and to cease aiding the other's dissidents. Effectively, these agreements ended hostilities between the two states.[104]

The period of most active fighting between Somalia and Ethiopia was triggered by a cross-border invasion undertaken in service of irredentist goals. While some Arab states were willing to express support for Somalia, there was broad opposition to its behavior. Communist states vigorously aided Ethiopia, while Western states felt obliged to cancel previously planned arms sales, at least in part because of the strong feelings of African states on the illegitimacy of the Somali action. Further, the actual support Somalia received was minor relative to its need. It is also significant that several states promised greater support if Somalia itself were invaded, while Ethiopia's allies refused to aid an invasion of Somalia. Taken together, these reactions suggest that most states could not bring themselves to aid a state that had been guilty of an effort to acquire a large block of territory from a neighboring state by force. This was true, moreover, despite the fact that at least some of the states who stayed neutral were necessarily very concerned about the long-term effects of the degree of support the victim of aggression was receiving from their ideological adversary, the Soviet Union.[105] In various ways, that is, Somalia's actions evoked international sanctions. Given this reaction, it is both puzzling and noteworthy that the mechanism of the United Nations was completely ignored as a vehicle for addressing this war.

## Tanzania/Uganda (1978–1979)

Relations between Uganda and Tanzania deteriorated after the coup that brought Idi Amin to power in Uganda.[106] In October 1978 these bad relations finally led to an invasion by Ugandan troops of the small portion of Tanzania bordering Uganda. Amin was apparently seeking an external enemy to bolster the loyalty of his army,[107] but also explicitly asserted that the area was part of Uganda.[108]

The Ugandan troops withdrew before Tanzania was able to organize a counterattack on November 14 but not before they had inflicted atrocities upon the Tanzanian civilian population and done considerable material damage during their occupation. Tanzanian authorities concluded that their territory could not be secure as long as Amin controlled the government of Uganda, given the fact that Uganda controlled the high ground along the two states' border. In January 1979 Tanzanian troops invaded Uganda, accompanied by Ugandan exile opponents of the Amin regime. By April 10 Kampala had been taken and Amin's forces routed. A new Ugandan government, the members of which had been selected at a conference organized under Tanzanian auspices and held in Tanzania, was sworn in April 11, 1979.[109] Due to the great disorder within Uganda and the inability of the new government to restore order unaided, Tanzanian troops remained in Uganda until May 1981.[110]

Tanzania justified its invasion on several grounds. It insisted that Uganda had started the war. It stressed the injustice of allowing Uganda to get away with its aggression and of forcing Tanzania to bear the cost of that aggression. It also stressed Uganda's claim to Tanzanian territory. The decision to invade ultimately reflected Tanzania's concern over the Ugandan territorial claim and over the OAU's failure to take any action against Amin. At least initially, however, Tanzania sought to skirt the issue of whether its troops had invaded Uganda.[111] Tanzania's justifications apparently corresponded to its motivations, though the continuing bad relations between the two states also played a role in the decision to invade. Also, after Tanzania's initial success had not produced the popular uprising which that state's leaders had hoped would topple Amin, President Nyerere apparently believed that a failure by Tanzania to overthrow Amin would expose the Ugandan population in the area initially taken to revenge by Amin's forces.[112]

Third-state reaction to the invasion was divided. During the fighting the United Kingdom and the FRG each provided money for refugees that permitted Tanzania to divert other funds to military uses. Algeria sent arms to Tanzania, as did Angola in token amounts. Mozambique sent a battalion of troops to Tanzania's aid, and Zambia condemned Uganda.[113] Once the new Ugandan government was installed, Botswana, Ethiopia, Mozambique, Zambia, the United Kingdom, the United States, the PRC, and India recognized it almost immediately. The European Community quickly offered economic aid, while the Soviet Union characterized the invasion as a "countermeasure."[114] On the other hand, Libya sent troops to help Amin, and PLO troops training in Uganda likewise fought alongside the Ugandans. In March the Islamic Conference provided Amin's government with $4,000,000 in economic aid.

Sudan, Nigeria, and Morocco all criticized Tanzania, though the OAU as a body took no position on the change of government, and African states persuaded Amin not to take the matter to the United Nations.[115]

This conflict was a cross-border invasion countering an earlier cross-border invasion. It led to the replacement of the government of the original invader by a government dependent on the original victim. That state justified its actions by reference to the danger posed to it by the original aggression. Third states generally acquiesced in the second invasion; no international organization even expressed verbal disapproval. It has been argued that this reaction reflected international disgust at the terrible human rights record of the Amin regime,[116] though it appears that no state explained its reaction in this way and Tanzania did not justify its action by reference to human rights concerns. Nonetheless, the contrast between the reaction to this invasion and replacement of a government with the reaction to the somewhat similar invasion of Kampuchea by Vietnam, discussed below, is striking. Given the fact that both target regimes had engaged in acts of aggression and both had terrible human rights records, the only obvious difference in the two cases is that the international community was apparently very doubtful of Vietnam's motives for its invasion, while it was more accepting of Tanzania's security concerns and believed Tanzania's action was less motivated by self-interest than was Vietnam's invasion.

## Socialist Republic of Vietnam/Kampuchea (1978–1989)

On December 25, 1978, troops of the Socialist Republic of Vietnam (SRV) invaded the neighboring state of Democratic Kampuchea (DK),[117] which was governed by the extraordinarily cruel Khmer Rouge. By January 10, 1979, the DK army had been routed and a new government had been established in Phnom Penh—the People's Republic of Kampuchea (PRK)—headed by an individual who, on December 3, had formed an anti-DK front under SRV auspices.[118] Fighting did not end with the establishment of the PRK, however. The Khmer Rouge and certain non-Communist groups kept guerilla forces in the field in the northwestern part of the country.[119] The SRV maintained tens of thousands of troops in Kampuchea to carry on the war against these guerillas.[120] After a successful 1984–85 offensive against the various anti-PRK groups, however, the SRV announced in April 1985 its intention to withdraw all its troops from Kampuchea by 1995; it moved the date up to 1990 in

August 1985.[121] In fact, Vietnamese troops had essentially left Kampuchea by September 1990.[122] Fighting continued between the PRK government and the Coalition Government of Democratic Kampuchea, as the groups opposed to it were called after 1982, until an agreement was signed October 23, 1991, under which the fighting would stop, a temporary UN administration would be formed, and elections for a new government would be held.[123]

The SRV offered several justifications for its original intervention. It insisted, falsely, that its troops had participated in the invasion as volunteers only and that troops of the anti-DK front it had formed had actually done the fighting.[124] It pointed to the numerous border incidents initiated by DK troops, to their incursions into Vietnamese territory in 1977 and 1978, and to their massing of troops on the states' common border, and claimed it was defending itself against an impending DK attack. It also claimed to have received an invitation to intervene from the PRK government. And it frequently alluded to the unquestionable brutality of the DK government in explaining its position.[125]

Certainly, security concerns in fact played an important role in the SRV's decision to replace the DK government, especially in light of the close relationship between Kampuchea and China and Vietnam's fears of the latter state. However, Vietnam's motives went beyond those it admitted. It sought to form at least a de facto federation of the states of Indochina under its leadership and had become determined to overcome Kampuchean resistance to this idea, using force if necessary. That is, it acted in part to effectively eliminate Kampuchean independence.[126]

Third-state reaction to Vietnam's action was almost uniformly negative. The Soviet Union supported the SRV at first, seeing it as a necessary ally against China.[127] It also vetoed a Security Council resolution calling for the withdrawal of foreign forces from Kampuchea; only Czechoslovakia joined it in voting against the resolution, which had been supported by the Security Council's thirteen other members and, in debate, by ten other UN members not members of the Security Council.[128] However, the People's Republic of China (PRC) justified its attack on Vietnam in February 1979 as a sanction for Vietnam's attack on Kampuchea;[129] the United States, informed of the PRC's plans in advance, did not object.[130] The General Assembly voted each year from 1979 through 1988 to seat the DK delegation rather than the PRK delegation and adopted resolutions each year calling for the withdrawal of foreign forces from Kampuchea. The Association of South-East Asian Nations (ASEAN) took a similar position. Most significantly, European Community and Japanese economic embargoes on Vietnam—imposed because of the invasion—together with the preexisting American embargo did great damage to Vietnam's economy.[131] And when the Gorbachev regime had established itself in the Soviet Union, it too pressured Vietnam to leave Kampuchea.[132] Coupled with the effects of stigmatization as an aggressor, this isolation and economic hardship was apparently what impelled the SRV to leave Kampuchea by 1990.[133]

This conflict was a cross-border invasion whereby a state sought to conquer a neighbor and install a government that it would be able to dominate. While its claims of self-defense and its stress on its opponents' brutality had merit, the international community focused on the invader's basic goal of de facto subjugation and responded with disapproval and sanctions that, ultimately, were effective. It is worth noting that the invader's final decision to withdraw followed the change in position of its superpower patron. With no strong state supporting it unequivocally, it abandoned its effort.

## Soviet Union/Afghanistan (1979–1989)

In April 1978 the government of Afghanistan was overthrown in a coup led by the People's Democratic Party of Afghanistan (PDPA), a Marxist-Leninist party. The PDPA's leader, Nur Mohammed Taraki, became president in the new government. That government soon drew opposition from rural Afghans, who formed the majority of the population and who were composed overwhelmingly of devout Muslims. Suspicion that the new government would be anti-Islamic led to the outbreak of a guerilla rebellion in June 1978. Over the next year opposition to the government grew and a number of different guerilla groups were formed. The government received military advisors and increasing aid from the Soviet Union, which had not placed much reliance on the PDPA prior to the coup. Pakistan gave aid to the guerillas, alarmed both by the Marxism of the new government and by the Soviet presence on its doorstep. This latter factor also led China to aid the guerillas.[134]

By the fall of 1979 the war was going increasingly badly for the PDPA government. Its troops were defecting to the rebels in great numbers, and its efforts at social and economic reform aroused great resentment. The government nonetheless plunged ahead with its program, relying on harshness to establish its control. Most prominent among the party leaders who supported this policy was Hafizullah Amin, the defense minister. In the fall of 1979 a power struggle between Amin and Taraki ended with Taraki's murder and Amin's assumption of the presidency. This development led the Soviet Union to begin planning to intervene. The Soviets had become convinced that Amin's harsh policies could only lead to the defeat of his government, which could in turn lead to the emergence of a government unfriendly to the Soviet Union in a state on the Soviet border. To avoid this eventuality the Soviet Union began moving troops into Afghanistan on December 19, 1979. An effort to arrest Amin on December 27 led to his death. Later that day, Babrik Karmal, leader of a faction of the PDPA more moderate than that of Taraki and Amin, proclaimed in a radio broadcast (described as originating in Afghanistan but actually coming from Soviet territory) his seizure of power and a request for Soviet assistance.[135]

Over the next seven years the Soviet Union found itself entangled in a frustrating guerilla war. Soviet troops and the Afghan army were unable to defeat the opponents of the PDPA, collectively known as the mujaheddin, despite the use of such tactics as Afghan air force bombing of Afghan refugee camps in Pakistan. Finally, in December 1986, Mikhail Gorbachev, by this time leader of the Soviet Union, informed Najibullah, who had replaced Karmal as president of Afghanistan, that the Soviet Union would be withdrawing its troops and that the PDPA government would have to resist the mujaheddin alone. In early 1988 the Soviet Union indicated that it would begin withdrawing its troops that year. This led to the conclusion of an April 14, 1988, agreement at UN–mediated talks, ostensibly between Pakistan and Afghanistan but involving the Soviet Union and the United States as well. Under that pact Afghanistan and Pakistan agreed on mutual noninterference in one another's internal affairs. The United States and the Soviet Union agreed to guarantee the pact—but also acknowledged that the United States had the right to continue providing arms to the mujaheddin if the Soviet Union continued to aid the Afghan government. The Soviet Union further undertook to withdraw its troops from Afghanistan. Its withdrawal was complete in February 1989.[136]

The Soviet withdrawal did not end the war. The PDPA held its own for some time. In late 1990, however, the United States and Soviet Union each agreed to suspend provision of arms to the side it was supporting. Continued UN efforts to mediate between the Afghan combatants failed, and the Afghan government, crippled by defections of military units, finally collapsed in April 1992. The rebel groups installed a government, but there has been much fighting among them ever since.[137]

Third-state reaction to the Soviet invasion was intense and negative. Pakistan and the PRC continued their arms supply. The United States also provided arms, first supplying Soviet-made arms with Egyptian assistance and subsequently providing Western arms such as land mines and portable surface-to-air missiles, first British and later American.[138] Iran also provided aid to mujaheddin groups.[139]

Other sanctions were imposed as well. The United States refused to ratify an important strategic arms treaty it had negotiated with the Soviet Union. A number of states imposed economic sanctions on the Soviet Union, including the United States, the United Kingdom, Canada, New Zealand, and the European Community. A number of Western and Islamic states denounced the invasion and announced diplomatic sanctions. China and Yugoslavia were also harshly critical.[140] A number of states, including the United States, boycotted the 1980 Moscow Olympic Games in protest of the invasion.[141] The 1981 Islamic Conference demanded an immediate withdrawal of foreign troops from Afghanistan.[142] Similarly, the Meeting of Foreign Ministers of Nonaligned States in that year also called for a foreign troop withdrawal.[143] Strong opposition was also expressed in the General Assembly; a resolution calling for the withdrawal of "foreign" troops from Afghanistan was adopted each year from 1980 through 1987, attracting more votes in 1987 than in 1980 (123 compared to 104). At the same time the secretary-general began efforts at mediation in 1981, which continued until a successful agreement was finally achieved, as noted above.[144]

All of these reactions had an effect on the Soviet Union's decision to withdraw from Afghanistan; negative reactions to its invasion had caused a decline in its relations with the third world, increased difficulty in negotiating arms control agreements and trade arrangements with Western states, and contributed to the PRC's refusal to improve relations. Particularly given Gorbachev's desire to reduce reliance on the use of force in international relations, the general worsening in the Soviet Union's international situation caused by its actions in Afghanistan clearly contributed to the Soviet decision to reverse its policy. The strength of the mujaheddin also contributed to the decision to leave, and that strength reflected in part aid given the guerillas by third states.[145]

This conflict was a cross-border invasion aimed at obtaining the invader's desired outcome in a civil war by installing in the invaded state a government friendly to the invading state, albeit one lacking any appreciable support in the invaded state. The invasion was justified by false claims that the invading forces had been invited to enter the invaded state. Third states reacted harshly, providing military support to guerillas fighting the invading state and cooling their relations with it as well. The invaders ultimately decided to withdraw, realizing that the diplomatic and military costs of attempting to remain were simply too high.

## Iraq/Iran (1980–1988)

By the fall of 1980 relations between Iraq and Iran were not good. The two states had been in conflict even before the overthrow of the Shah of Iran, as they had been rivals for influence in the Persian Gulf region. This rivalry had led Iran to give extensive support to a rebellion against the Ba'ath government of Iraq by Iraqi Kurds, beginning in 1973. That rebellion did not go well, however, and by 1975 the shah faced the alternatives of abandoning the Kurds or intervening with his regular army. He opted for the former, the two states concluding an agreement in Algiers in 1975 wherein the shah undertook to close his border to the Iraqi Kurds in return for Iraq's abandonment of its claim to the whole of the Shatt al Arab waterway, accepting a boundary in the middle of the Shatt. Iraq was not pleased with this arrangement, since the Shatt is its principal outlet to the sea, but accepted it.[146]

The situation further deteriorated after the fall of the shah. The new Iranian regime's frequent calls for revolts by adherents of the Shi'a sect throughout the Gulf region posed a threat to Iraq, which had a Shi'ite majority population, and to other Arab Gulf states with significant Shi'ite populations. This latter factor touched Iraq both in its claim to be the protector of the other Arab states in the area and in having the potential to affect Iraq's access to the sea if Iran should come to dominate one of the Gulf sheikdoms. Further, there were attacks on officials of the Iraqi government in April 1980, which were tied to Iran; following Iraq's repressive response to these attacks, the Ayatollah Khomeini publicly called for the overthrow of the Ba'ath government of Iraq.[147]

It was against this background that Iraq elected to attack Iran on September 22, 1980. Iraq's war aims were to regain control of the whole of the Shatt al Arab and to ease the threat to its internal security posed by the Iranian regime. It apparently proposed to attain these goals by seizing Iranian territory on the far side of the waterway; this maneuver would itself give Iraq control of the Shatt, while its possession of Iranian territory would lead either to a peace treaty on its terms as the price for a withdrawal or a coup against what it believed was a weak Iranian government, either outcome being likely to reduce the danger Iraq faced.[148]

Iraq was in fact rather frank in stating its war aims. It justified its attack by arguing that Iran had breached the 1975 Algiers agreement by failing to turn over certain territory as that agreement required and by resuming support for subversive elements in Iraq, and by asserting that it was using force in order to regain sovereignty over the whole of its territory, that is, over the portion of the Shatt conceded to Iran in 1975. It subsequently added to its justifications the claim that Iran had undertaken substantial military actions against Iraq prior to Iraq's attack, but these statements were false. Particularly informative in this connection is Secretary-General Javier Perez de Cuellar's determination, pursuant to Security Council Resolution 598, that Iraq's attack on September 22 was a completely unjustified aggression in "violation of the prohibition against the use of force" and that Iraq was responsible for the conflict.[149]

The course of the war was relatively straightforward. Iraq was initially successful in taking considerable territory in southern Iran. However, Iranian forces eventually managed to stabilize the front and then to counterattack. By the spring of 1982 Iranian counterattacks were bearing fruit, and in June of that year the Iraqis were forced to withdraw to their own territory. Iran determined to invade Iraq, for reasons that will be discussed below, and did so on July 13, 1982. Over the next five years Iran engaged in numerous bloodily unsuccessful attacks on Iraqi defensive positions, ultimately achieving only minor lodgments on Iraqi territory. In the spring and summer of 1988 Iraqi counterattacks first ejected Iranian troops from Iraqi territory and subsequently made deep inroads into Iran. In July of that year the Iranian government accepted Security Council Resolution 598, which demanded a cease-fire and withdrawals to international boundaries. Iraq did the same in the following month upon Iran's promise to engage in direct negotiations following a cease-fire. These mutual acceptances of a cease-fire ended the war.

It should be noted that during the war both sides attacked shipping in the Persian Gulf beginning in the spring and summer of 1984. Iraq directed its attacks at vessels, both Iranian and otherwise, transporting petroleum from Iran for export, such exports being crucial to the Iranian war effort. Iranian attacks were directed at third-state vessels, including especially vessels bound to and carrying petroleum from Saudi Arabia and Kuwait, both of which heavily subsidized Iraq and both of which served as transshipment points for material bound for Iraq.[150]

At the time Iran invaded Iraq it refused to consider ending the war unless Iraq paid reparations of $150 billion, President Saddam Hussein of Iraq was tried as a war criminal, and the Ba'ath party was removed as the government of Iraq. While the Iranian leadership undoubtedly had little use for that of Iraq, there is reason to believe that the decision to invade Iraq was motivated not only by the regime's proclaimed war aims but also by a desire to unify a still-divided Iran against a common foe and to extract resources from Iraq that would finance social programs in Iran without weakening the economic position of groups affiliated with the conservative clergy who dominated Iran's government.[151]

The third-state reaction to the Iran-Iraq War cannot be summarized simply, though it can be said that reactions were by no means determined by assessments of the illegality of the combatants' overall uses of force. Initially, the Security Council responded to the situation by unanimously adopting Resolution 479 of September 28, 1980, which called on both states to immediately refrain from all uses of force and urged them to accept mediation. The Security Council members argued strongly for moderation and a peaceful resolution of the dispute, the United States explicitly proclaiming its neutrality.[152] Since Iraqi forces were in the process of seizing Iranian territory at the time the resolution was adopted, the Security Council's failure to call for a withdrawal to international boundaries and its call for Iran as well as Iraq to refrain from the use of force is somewhat surprising. There is evidence that members of the Security Council had no doubt concerning the facts of the matter but that the Council's reaction was influenced by Iran's disruptive activities in the region and by the attitude toward international obligations Iran had demonstrated in seizing American diplomats as hostages.[153]

Resolution 479 was not the Security Council's last word, however. On July 12, 1982—after Iraq's withdrawal from Iran and the day before Iran invaded Iraq—the unanimously adopted Resolution 514 added a call for a withdrawal to international boundaries to its call for a cease-fire. Resolution 522 of October 4, 1982, essentially repeated Resolution 514, though welcoming Iraq's acceptance of 514. The General Assembly also adopted a resolution on October 22 calling for a cease-fire without seeking to place blame.[154] Resolutions 540 of October 31, 1983, 582 of February 24, 1986, and 588 of October 8, 1986, and the debates accompanying their adoption were similar in tone, though Resolution 582 also "deplore[d]" both "the initial acts that gave rise to the conflict" and, among other disfavored acts, "attacks on neutral shipping."[155] Resolution 552 of June 1, 1984, was more peremptory. It was adopted after the combatants had begun to attack shipping in the Persian Gulf, and it reaffirmed the right of free navigation in the Gulf, condemned attacks on ships en route to and from Kuwait and Saudi Arabia, and demanded that such attacks cease. It characterized Kuwait and Saudi Arabia as "not parties to the hostilities" and makes no mention of Iraqi attacks on third-state tankers carrying Iranian oil.[156]

It was not until the adoption of Resolution 598 of July 20, 1987, however, that the Security Council abandoned the mediatory approach in a resolution directed at the war itself. In addition to deploring the initiation of the war and attacks on neutral shipping, Resolution 598 went on to "determine" the existence of a breach of a peace, invoke Chapter VII of the UN Charter, and "demand" a cease-fire and withdrawal to international boundaries. Statements in debate made clear that this resolution, apparently in contrast to earlier resolutions, was seen as mandatory.[157]

Outside the United Nations states took an active part in supporting one or the other—or sometimes both—of the combatants. At the start of the war the Soviet Union declared its neutrality, and cut off arms supplies to both sides, though it assisted Iran in repairing its tanks. The United States likewise proclaimed its neutrality, while permitting both the delivery to Iran of arms previously ordered and the transfer to Iran by third states of American-supplied arms. During the same period Italy provided warships to Iraq, while France did the same for Iran. France also sold aircraft and artillery pieces to Iraq, however. Syria and Libya provided military supplies to Iran. Brazil supplied both sides, and Turkey, though formally neutral, permitted arms shipments to both sides across its territory. Egypt and eastern European states provided extensive military supplies to Iraq. In 1982 Syria closed one of the oil pipelines Iraq used for export, partly due to hostility to Iraq and partly due to an Iranian bribe.[158] After Iran invaded Iraq the Soviet Union resumed arms supplies to Iraq. In 1987, however, it provided Iran with Scud missiles. France continued supplying Iraq, providing the aircraft and missiles Iraq used in its attacks on shipping. Turkey assisted Iraq in keeping order in the Kurdish area of Iraq after Iraqi Kurds began permitting Turkish Kurds to operate from Iraq. The PRC provided Iran with arms during this period, including Silkworm missiles. The United States provided Iraq with intelligence information and tried to organize an embargo on arms to Iran beginning in 1984, though secretly supplying weapons to Iran in an effort to obtain freedom for Western hostages in Beirut.[159]

Certainly, one of the more striking aspects of third-state reactions to the Gulf War was the attitude of maritime states toward attacks on shipping. As noted above, the Security Council condemned attacks on ships not bound for one of the combatant countries as early as 1984. In 1987 France, Italy, Belgium, the United Kingdom, the United States, and the Soviet Union all dispatched warships to the Gulf to protect vessels flying their flags. Further, the United States permitted several Kuwaiti-owned tankers to be reflagged as American and protected them as well. Also, the United States, the United Kingdom, and France all undertook to protect third-state neutral vessels not carrying contraband. In practice this protection was directed exclusively against Iran; there was no interference with Iraqi attacks on tankers carrying Iranian oil. The policy was not formally one of absolute opposition to Iran; it was American policy to certify to Iran that vessels being convoyed by American warships carried no contraband, while other states apparently permitted search operations by the Iranian navy. Nonetheless, the character of Iranian operations led the United States to engage Iranian minelayers and boats used for attacks on shipping; it also attacked an Iranian oil platform used for military purposes.[160]

The Iraq-Iran War is particularly instructive with respect to the content of customary international law regarding the use of force between states. The facts are undisputed: Iraq invaded Iran in order to acquire territory and was driven out two years later, whereupon Iran invaded Iraq in order to overthrow Iraq's government and obtain reparations. Not only were the facts obvious at the time they occurred but the combatants were unusually frank in explaining the bases for their actions. At least the Iraqi invasion was a violation of the rules of the UN Charter, according to Secretary-General Perez de Cuellar; arguably both invasions were. Third-state reaction, however, reflected little inclination even to distinguish between the legal positions of the parties, let alone sanction a violator. As noted above, several states supplied one or the other of the combatants while that combatant was seeking to seize territory of the other; indeed, some states aided both simultaneously, even though at least one *must* have been in violation of the Charter's rules at all times. Further, the Security Council took a mediatory approach for most of the war. Similarly, the United States and Soviet Union each proclaimed "neutrality," and the Security Council in several resolutions assumed that states not involved in the fighting could be considered "neutral."

One may question the application of the term "neutral" to states such as Kuwait, which provided absolutely crucial subsidies to one of the combatants.[161] But aside from this point, there is a more fundamental problem with the application of the term in this context, as Professors Louis Henkin and Mark Janis have noted,[162] in that the concept of neutrality would appear to be inconsistent with the legal system that the UN Charter purports to establish. This follows because, under the Charter, states have an affirmative obligation to refrain from violating Article 2(4); assertions of neutrality, however, place violators and their victims on an equal footing and thus amount to acquiescence in the violation. Several commentators have argued that because the Security Council did not identify an aggressor in this case, members of the United Nations were free under the Charter to take a position of neutrality.[163] The significance of this argument for this study is twofold. First, it appears accurately to characterize state behavior during the Gulf War. Second, it undercuts the argument that the rules of the Charter are also rules of customary international law. This follows because, if the Charter's rules are customary law, and those rules make many uses of force illegal, then states have an affirmative obligation to evaluate uses of force according to the Charter's rules in all cases, as a matter of customary law and quite apart from whatever action the United Nations takes. If, however, the Charter's rules trigger no obligations for third states without Security Council action, it follows that those rules are nothing more than treaty obligations governing duties of UN members and thus irrelevant if the responsible UN organ fails to invoke them.

This conclusion is reinforced when the arguments in Chapter 1 are recalled. As pointed out in that chapter, states are the enforcers of customary law. Thus, widespread state acquiescence in particular behavior amounts to a refusal to treat the behavior as illegal by entities responsible for enforcing the law and is therefore inconsistent with the proposition that the behavior violates the law. In the Iran-Iraq War there was simply no doubt as to the character of Iraq's behavior; arguably, Iran's after July 1982 was also violative of the rules of the UN Charter. Yet several states affirmatively assisted each of the combatants while it was engaging in dubious behavior, and other states and the Security Council took the position that the legal positions of the combatants were indistinguishable. The conclusion that best fits these circumstances, then, is that neither states individually nor the Security Council as an institution saw uses of force of the character involved here as actions compelling particular responses from third states. Rather, the collective response was to treat third states as free to react or not, as they pleased—that is, free to act as though no violation of law was present that would limit the range of legally permissible reactions of third states. In short, no state acted as though either the choice of Iraq to go to war or that of Iran to prolong the war raised any legal questions.

## Argentina/United Kingdom (1982)

The war occasioned by Argentina's seizure of the Falkland Islands from the United Kingdom in 1982 also provided states with an opportunity to demonstrate their attitudes toward interstate use of force. The dispute that led to Argentina's action began with the United Kingdom's 1833 seizure of the Falklands, which are located three hundred miles east of the Argentine mainland. That seizure took place in the face of strong Argentine claims of sovereignty. It is by no means clear that the seizure violated international law as it was understood in 1833, however. Over the next 149 years Argentina frequently protested the British presence in the Falklands and reiterated its claim to sovereignty but did nothing to disturb British control. The Argentines inhabiting the islands in 1833 were replaced by British colonists, whose descendants were the only inhabitants of the islands by 1982. As of that year the United Kingdom had peaceably administered the islands for well over a century and governed a population that considered itself British.[164]

It was against this background that Argentine troops seized the islands on April 2, 1982.[165] Argentina subsequently justified its seizure by arguing that the islands were Argentine territory, British occupation therefore constituting aggression; that efforts to resolve the dispute peacefully had failed; and that Argentina had made reservations regarding the islands at the time of its adherence to the UN Charter, precluding any obligation on its part to refrain from the use of force where the islands were concerned.[166] There is no question that Argentina strongly believed in its claims to sovereignty over the Falklands.[167] Although, as will be noted below, intense diplomatic efforts were made to avoid war during the period between the Argentine seizure and the landing of British troops in the Falklands, Argentina refused to accept any formula for peaceful settlement that did not guarantee ultimate Argentine sovereignty over the islands.[168]

The United Kingdom had learned of Argentina's plans to invade in late March and had determined on March 31 to retake the islands in the event of an Argentine conquest.[169] The British government took the position that the islands were British territory, inhabited by British people, and that Britain had the right to resort to self-defense in response to Hitler-like aggression; the United Kingdom also stressed the right of self-determination of the islanders.[170]

The Royal Navy task force dispatched to retake the Falklands arrived within two hundred miles of its target on May 1. On May 21, after air attacks by the British on the islands and by the Argentines on the British fleet, and after the sinking of the Argentine cruiser *General Belgrano* by a British submarine, British troops were landed. The Argentine garrison was defeated in several engagements with those troops and surrendered on June 14, 1982. British casualties were approximately 250 killed and 1,100 wounded; the Argentines suffered 746 killed and nearly 13,000 captured.[171]

Third-state reaction to these events may be described as weakly favoring the British position, with a minority weakly favoring Argentina, all against an undertone of uneasiness at endorsement of either side's use of force.

Preliminarily, it should be noted that a number of international organizations had, prior to the Argentine seizure, taken positions favoring Argentina's claim that the British presence in the Falklands amounted to colonialism. The General Assembly had labeled the Falklands a colony in 1965 and congratulated Argentina on its efforts to secure decolonization in 1973. The Nonaligned Movement had taken a similar position in 1975 and 1976, as had the Inter-American Juridical Committee.[172]

Nonetheless, on April 3 the Security Council adopted Resolution 502, determining that there existed "a breach of the peace" in the Falklands under Chapter VII of the UN Charter and demanding the withdrawal of Argentine troops.[173] Only Panama voted against the resolution, accepting Argentina's characterization of the dispute; Poland, Spain, the Soviet Union, and the PRC all abstained, while the other permanent members were joined by Guyana, Ireland, Japan, Jordan, Togo, Uganda, and Zaire in voting for the resolution. However, on May 26 the Security Council adopted Resolution 505, which reaffirmed Resolution 502 but also called on the secretary-general to undertake a mission of good offices with a view toward ending hostilities. On June 4 a resolution that would have requested the parties to observe a cease-fire was defeated only by a British and an accidental American veto.[174]

Debates in the Security Council as the crisis progressed revealed considerable division; several speakers, including representatives of states not members of the Security Council, were clearly most concerned to avert any use of force, and some supported Argentina's position. In particular both the PRC and Soviet Union characterized the question as primarily colonial, endorsing Argentina's territorial claim and calling for a peaceful settlement. Clearly, a number of states were uncomfortable at the thought of using force to reverse Argentina's use of force.[175]

Outside the United Nations, the United States unsuccessfully sought to mediate the crisis; its attempt foundered in part on American insistence that Argentina not enjoy the fruits of aggression. Peru made two attempts to mediate. The first, which was in any case not clearly near success, ended when Argentina refused to accept a proposed solution in the wake of the sinking of the *Belgrano*. The second failed over Argentina's insistence on a guarantee of eventual sovereignty. The same issue, together with Argentina's insistence on advantageous terms in other respects, also led to the failure of Secretary-General Perez de Cuellar's mediation in mid-May.[176]

Once its effort at negotiation failed, the United States declared that Argentina was guilty of aggression, imposed economic sanctions, and provided material assistance to the British, as indeed it had begun to do earlier.[177] The European Community imposed sanctions on Argentina in April and renewed them on May 25, although Ireland and Italy refused to join in the May action, and the community generally was unenthusiastic about British military action.[178] A number of third-world states expressed a lack of sympathy for Argentina's claim to be acting against colonialism.[179] And the English-speaking Caribbean states refused to support a proposed OAS resolution on the crisis that failed to condemn Argentina's use of force.[180]

On the other hand, the Meeting of Foreign Ministers of the parties to the Rio Treaty—primarily Latin American states—adopted a resolution on April 28 recognizing Argentina's claim to sovereignty over the islands but also acknowledging the binding character of Resolution 502 and "urging," as opposed to "demanding," that the United Kingdom cease hostilities. On May 29 the same body adopted a resolution condemning Britain's efforts to retake the islands, urging the United States to cease aiding Britain and requesting the parties to the Rio Treaty to give Argentina the assistance each judged appropriate. The group never contemplated adoption of collective defense measures against Britain, but neither did it heed arguments about the primacy of the UN Charter and the obligation to adhere to Resolution 502 put forward by, among others, Mexico, Brazil, Chile, and Colombia. It adopted its May 29 resolution by a vote of 14–0–4, the abstainers including the United States, Trinidad and Tobago, Chile, and Colombia.[181]

This conflict arose from the attempt by one state to seize territory from another on the basis of a long-standing claim of sovereignty and an argument based on anticolonialism. The target state resisted, arguing self-defense and the importance of the right of the inhabitants of the territory to self-determination. Those inhabitants clearly opposed the seizure. Third states generally supported the state originally in possession of the territory in its condemnation of the seizure, and the Security Council invoked Chapter VII of the charter and demanded an end to the invasion. It is also true, however, that third states were clearly uncomfortable with the use of force to regain the territory, favoring—as evidenced by Security Council votes—a peaceful resolution of the dispute. Sanctioning the invader, that is, ceased to be a high priority for most states once hostilities became imminent. Further, an important regional bloc of states was willing to give at least rhetorical support to the invader despite the invasion, focusing on the merits of the territorial dispute.

## Iraq/Kuwait (1990–1991)

On July 16, 1990, Iraq began a campaign of pressure against Kuwait. Iraq's president, Saddam Hussein, faced a difficult situation. His personal position was shaky, in part because of the terrible condition of the Iraqi economy in the wake of the war with Iran. His demands on Kuwait therefore focused on economics: forgiveness of the debts Iraq owed Kuwait for money loaned during the war with Iran, Kuwaiti actions supporting higher oil prices, and greater aid for Iraq. Kuwait and its neighbors sought to negotiate and urged the United States—which had initially favored a strong reaction against Iraq—to tread softly. But on August 2 Saddam ordered his troops to invade Kuwait, that state having refused to accede to all of his demands.[182]

Saddam initially sought to justify his action by claiming that the Kuwaiti government had been overthrown in a coup and that the new government had sought Iraqi aid. This argument was soon abandoned because of the survival of the Emir of Kuwait and the strong negative reactions to the invasion both from Kuwaitis and from the international community. Instead, Iraq switched to a reliance on a long-standing if doubtful claim to Kuwait made by previous Iraqi governments and purported to annex Kuwait.[183] Saddam's motives for acting were the belief that Kuwait had not shown proper deference to its larger neighbor, the desire to use Kuwait's wealth to rebuild Iraq, the improvement in his domestic political position that would come from vindicating Iraq's historic claim to Kuwait, and the greater prestige and power that would flow from a successful conquest and from control of Kuwait's oil.[184]

Third-state reaction was immediate and negative. The United States, which Saddam may have expected to react mildly in light of its quiet reaction to Iraq's actions in July,[185] immediately condemned the invasion and froze Iraqi and Kuwaiti assets. Apparently, the United States was moved in part by the threat to its interests in Iraq's controlling a large fraction of the world's oil and in part by its objection to what it considered a flagrant violation of international law. The United Kingdom reacted similarly, likewise seeing the incident as a clear case of aggression violating international law. The Soviet Union also saw the invasion as clearly illegal. Against this background, on August 2, 1990, the Security Council adopted Resolution 660, which invoked Chapter VII of the charter, determined the existence of a breach of the peace, condemned the invasion, and demanded an Iraqi withdrawal. All Security Council members supported the resolution except Yemen, which abstained in the absence of instructions.[186] This was followed by Resolution 661 of August 6, imposing mandatory economic sanctions on Iraq.[187]

By late August the United States—concerned that Saudi Arabia could be attacked and that it was, in any case, vulnerable to pressure that could lead it to undercut economic sanctions against Iraq—persuaded the Saudi government to request U.S. defense assistance. Other Arab states, most notably Syria and

Egypt, also joined the American-led multinational force assembled initially for the defense of Saudi Arabia, the Arab states ultimately abandoning efforts to mediate the crisis and voting in the Arab League to condemn the Iraqi invasion.[188] Iran refrained from opposing the American deployment, despite Saddam's efforts to improve relations by agreeing to accept Iran's position on several key issues still outstanding after the Iran-Iraq War.[189] The United Kingdom and France sent troops to the multinational force, and Germany and Japan provided financial support, moved at least in part by the need to show solidarity with the United States. Further, the economic sanctions imposed by the United Nations were generally obeyed, though some holes in the sanctions led the Security Council to adopt Resolution 665 on August 25, permitting states to use force to effect a blockade of Iraq; eventually twenty-three states sent naval units to enforce the blockade.[190]

This strong international negative reaction to the invasion did not lead Saddam to withdraw his troops, however. Nor did diplomatic contacts bear fruit, Saddam making efforts to attach conditions to his withdrawal, such as seeking changes in Israel's position regarding the Palestinians and Syria's regarding Lebanon. Ultimately, the failure of other means to produce an Iraqi withdrawal led the United States to seek UN authorization to use force to expel Iraq. This was provided in Security Council Resolution 678 of November 29, 1990, which authorized states cooperating with Kuwait to use "all necessary means" to expel Iraqi forces, unless Iraq complied with all earlier Security Council resolutions by January 15, 1991. Yemen and Cuba opposed the resolution, but all other Security Council members supported it, except China, which was uncomfortable with agreeing to a use of force against a third-world state but also anxious to repair its relations with the United States, damaged after the Tiananmen Square killings. China therefore abstained in the vote on the resolution. Particularly noteworthy was the vote of the radical Ethiopian government, which was impressed by analogies to Mussolini's attack on Ethiopia in the 1930s.[191]

Continued efforts to resolve the crisis proved fruitless. The United States, the United Kingdom, France, and Saudi Arabia began a heavy aerial campaign against Iraq on January 16, 1991, the day after the UN deadline expired, but efforts at negotiation continued. Diplomatic exchanges by the Soviet Union extended into February 1991, but Saddam continued to refuse to accept unequivocally the obligations imposed by the Security Council's resolutions. Ultimately, on February 23, 1991, after learning of extremely destructive actions being undertaken by the Iraqis in Kuwait, the United States issued an ultimatum, demanding an Iraqi acceptance of the United Nations resolutions within twenty-four hours. Iraq did not meet the condition of the ultimatum, and ground troops of the multinational forces attacked on February 24. They ceased fire on February 28, the Iraqi army having been forced out of Kuwait after taking a terrible beating.[192]

It should be stressed that all states were not willing to support action against Iraq. Outside of Arab states, few third-world states supported the effort against Saddam, although India allowed United States and Australian aircraft to refuel on their way to the Gulf. Algeria, Tunisia, and Mauritania spoke out for Iraq, and Morocco, which had sent troops to aid the defense of Saudi Arabia, had to moderate its support in the face of domestic opposition. Only Argentina of the Latin states actively supported the UN effort. While the United Kingdom and France played an important role in the attack on Iraq's forces, other European states were more hesitant in their support. On the other hand, Canada and Australia sent naval and air forces to the Gulf, Germany, Japan, Korea, and a number of the Gulf states provided crucial financial support; and Turkey both rigorously enforced economic sanctions and permitted air strikes against Iraq from its territory.[193]

This conflict began with an effort by one state to subjugate another. Third states, working through the United Nations, reacted by imposing economic sanctions backed by force and ultimately by attacking the invader and forcing its troops from the victim state. It is clear that third states, or at least those leading the effort, were moved to act at least in part by the conviction that the effort at subjugation was a violation of law. The outcome of this conflict thus strongly supports the proposition that an attempt by one state to subjugate another is a violation of customary international law. It should also be noted, however, that many states were hesitant, ultimately, to support the use of force when the invader refused to bow to economic sanctions. That is, although there appears to have been very widespread agreement that sanctions against the invader were appropriate, there was much less agreement that sanctions should include the use of force if less drastic measures were inadequate to compel the invader to withdraw.

## Analysis

Examination of these ten conflicts can provide a fair degree of insight concerning the law regulating the use of force between states. Perhaps the most important point to make about these events is the most obvious: there are not many of them. As violent as the post–World War II period has been, this violence has taken the form of the classic invasion on relatively few occasions. Furthermore, in six of the ten cases the invader was subjected to significant international sanction. In the Suez, Somalia-Ethiopia, and Iraq-Kuwait cases the international negative reaction was widespread and largely responsible for the failures of the invasions in question. The international reaction was less crucial but still important in the withdrawal of the invaders in the Vietnam-Kampuchea and the Soviet Union–Afghanistan cases. Finally, the negative international reaction to the invasion was least significant in the Falklands War, serving mainly to reinforce the legitimacy of the United Kingdom's defensive response without contributing to the material success of that response to the same extent as was true of the international reaction in the cases discussed above; further, the invader in this case received at least rhetorical support from states in its region, though none from elsewhere.

Even in the Falklands case, however, the sanctions applied by third states were significant, and that was even more true in the other conflicts. In the Somalia-Ethiopia and Iraq-Kuwait wars sanctions took the form of dispatch of troops to aid the victim of the invasion. In the Vietnam-Kampuchea case sanctions included a punitive attack on Vietnam carried out by China. In the Afghan and Kampuchean cases significant arms aid was given to troops resisting the invaders; in the Somalian case arms aid upon which Somalia could normally have relied was denied. In the Falklands case logistic support was provided to the United Kingdom. In the Suez, Kampuchean, Afghan, Falklands, and Kuwaiti cases the invader was subjected to significant economic sanctions. In the Suez and Afghan cases the invaders also encountered significant diplomatic sanctions, that is, American threats to expel Israel from the United Nations because of its obduracy over Suez and Chinese and American refusals to proceed with negotiations important to the Soviet Union after the Afghan invasion. These reactions were in addition to rhetorical condemnations voiced by various international organizations.

The four cases in which no international sanctions were imposed were quite different from one another. The Indonesian campaign for West Irian was justified by Indonesia under the rubric of self-determination and accepted as such by most states outside the West. Further, even the leading Western state—the United States—was unprepared to oppose Indonesia on this matter. As will be discussed in more detail in Chapter 3, the self-determination principle—at least as applied to European rule over non-European peoples—has become so thoroughly imbedded in international law as to provide a basis for approval of uses of force. And while it is appropriate to note that the violence in effect excused by application of this principle in the West Irian case was at a rather low level, the same cannot be said of India's seizure of Goa. Yet that action as well was widely supported at the time as an application of the self-determination principle. Indeed, time and Portugal's express acceptance of the result of the invasion have legitimized India's action.

While it is not entirely clear why the Tanzanian invasion of Uganda avoided sanction, certainly there were factors present in that case which were absent in those cases in which invaders were subjected to third-state sanctions. First, Tanzania itself had been the victim of an attack by Uganda. Second, Tanzania's professed fears of future invasions were not implausible, given the character of Uganda's government. Third, Tanzania acted in a relatively disinterested way. It claimed no territory and could not be said to have installed a puppet government or to have faced significant opposition from the Ugandan people. This last factor distinguishes this invasion from Vietnam's attack on Kampuchea and the Soviet Union's on Afghanistan, both of which were understood as intended to establish the invading state's dominance over its victim. Finally, the Amin regime's terrible human rights record may have reduced international willingness to support it—although it is unlikely that this factor alone would have led to acquiescence in this invasion, given the strong opposition to Vietnam's attack on Democratic Kampuchea, with a human rights record worse than Amin's.

The Iran-Iraq War, by contrast, began with an invasion that Iraq admitted was aimed at taking territory and that the invader did not attempt to justify by reference to any argument for the use of force which commands any degree of support. The lack of reaction to that invasion thus cannot be said to reflect acceptance of some principle upon which the invader had relied. It could be said, therefore, to support an argument that such invasions are not contrary to customary international law. Certainly, states' reactions to that conflict are hard to reconcile with the idea that it was seen as raising crucial legal questions.

It must also be noted, however, that third states' great suspicion of Iran likely contributed to their nonresponse to the Iraqi invasion. Iran was widely believed at the time to intend to revolutionize the entire Gulf region. While there was no indication that Iran was planning a conventional attack on any of its neighbors, there was considerable evidence that it was seeking to undermine the governments of several of them, including Iraq. Given the great international interest in stability in the Gulf, it is perhaps not surprising that third states claimed to be neutral or even assisted an attack on a state believed to threaten that stability, even when the attack was itself an attempt to gain territory.

In the first chapter of this work it was argued that a postulated norm cannot be considered a rule of law within a given legal system unless those entities subject to the system either obey the proposed rule or are sanctioned when they disobey it. Applying that standard, it would appear that a norm prohibiting states from carrying out classic invasions against one another could be a rule of law. As noted above, such invasions are relatively uncommon. Further, on the ten occasions on which they did occur, the invaders were subjected to significant sanctions in six. In the Indonesian and Goan cases the invaders were not sanctioned, but those invasions were seen as justified by an exception to limitations on the use of force recognized for wars directed against European colonialism. In the Tanzanian case there were also no sanctions, but that invasion could reasonably have been seen as an exercise in self-defense. Only the Iran-Iraq War triggered no significant negative sanctions (aside from those in response to attacks on noncombatant shipping) while falling outside any category of justified use of force, and even in that case one may speculate that the perceived dangerous character of the victim state was relevant to the international response to the use of force.

We thus see only four classic invasions in the period 1945–91 that triggered no international sanctions, and three of those invasions were seen as excusable by large numbers of states. Even by a rigorous application of the obey-or-be-sanctioned standard, then, it would seem that a rule prohibiting such invasions is consistent with the practice of states.

It should also be noted, however, that even in these cases there was generally great reluctance on the part of third states to resort to or even acquiesce in forcible coercion of the invader. Third states were willing to resort to force to aid the victim of an invasion only in the Somalian, Kampuchean, and Kuwaiti cases. In the Somali case only the superpower patron of the target state took such action, and in Kampuchea the Chinese punitive action fell far short of forcing a Vietnamese abandonment of its invasion. Even in the Kuwaiti case the use of force came only after months of efforts to avoid the use of force, and without the support of significant states. In the other cases third states apparently never contemplated using force against the invaders (with the possible exception of the Soviet reaction to the Suez invasion), and in the Falklands War third states even sought to dissuade the victim state from using defensive force.

We can thus summarize the status of classic invasions as follows. A rule prohibiting such invasions meets any reasonable test of legality in a decentralized legal system. Even so, states have shown some hesitancy in insisting on adherence to this rule when the alternative to acquiescence in a rule violation was a significant use of force.

CHAPTER 3

# Wars for the Independence of European Colonies

The uses of force discussed in this chapter are those in which hostilities were undertaken in order to end European control of colonized areas. They include internal wars between colonial powers and insurgent groups in colonies that led to the independence of the colony in question. They also include conflicts in which existing states found themselves on the opposite sides of anticolonial conflicts, playing important or even controlling roles.

## France/Syria (1945, 1946)

In 1946 Syria raised before the first meeting of the United Nations General Assembly its unhappiness at the continued presence of French troops in its territory. As the League of Nations mandatory power in Syria, France had exercised a high degree of political control of that region, which it had agreed in 1943 to give up.[1] It had, however, delayed both the evacuation of its own forces and the surrender of command of locally recruited troops. France saw this military presence as a lever to pry from the Syrian government treaties that would confirm special privileges for France in an independent Syria. France argued that its historical connections to the area and its "cultural mission" entitled it to a preeminent position in the region, which the proposed treaties were intended to secure.

When in May 1945 France revealed the texts of the proposed treaties, as well as its intention to maintain the military situation until the treaties were concluded, severe public disorder broke out in Syria. French troops responded violently, bombarding populated areas with artillery and air strikes. In late May the British—whose troops were also stationed in Syria as a war measure—intervened to separate the combatants. Subsequently, the French agreed to remove their troops and pass over command of locally raised units, but the process was still moving slowly as of January 1946, despite ongoing French-British negotiations on the subject. Syria and Lebanon raised the issue of the continued presence of French troops at the General Assembly, and after considerable discussion France agreed to an unconditional withdrawal. Syria and Lebanon were supported in their position by the Soviet Union as well as by other Arab states, while France's allies did not support France's position.[2]

The use of force in question here was France's delay in withdrawing its troops from Syrian territory despite Syrian demands that they leave. It should be noted that Syria's argument was not so much that the original entry of France was somehow unlawful, as that its continued presence was no longer tolerable. France's motive for acting was its desire to preserve, in effect, some of the benefits of its status as the equivalent of a colonial power. Third states, including France's closest allies, agreed with Syria, and France gave way.

Thus in this case we see a state in a situation analogous to that of a colonial power dragging its feet at implementing a change in status to which it had earlier agreed. With no real support for its desire to salvage some vestige of its privileges, France gave way.

## France/Vietnam (1945–1954)

On September 2, 1945, Ho Chi Minh, leader of the Viet Minh, proclaimed the independence of Vietnam. The new state was understood to include the areas named by France, the colonial ruler until displaced by Japanese conquest, as Tonkin, Annam, and Cochin China. But French forces, with the assistance of British troops who were in the area to receive the Japanese surrender, took power from the Viet Minh in Saigon later that month. In October the French began their effort to reassert control in Cochin China.[3] In 1946 France and Ho Chi Minh's government reached an agreement that envisaged a continued connection between France and Vietnam, but the agreement was never implemented in Cochin China, where fighting continued.[4] A modus vivendi reached in September of 1946 was likewise never implemented, as the French continued their efforts to subdue Cochin China and refused to yield authority to the Vietnamese. With the French bombardment of Haiphong on November 23, 1946, the situation began to deteriorate rapidly. When in December the French commander in Tonkin demanded that the Viet Minh disarm its militia, the Viet Minh responded with an attack on Hanoi, and fighting began in earnest.[5] By the spring of 1947 the military situation was at an impasse, with the French in control of the cities and communications arteries and the Viet Minh controlling everything else.[6]

Politically, the French had come to insist that the only acceptable outcome was for Vietnamese independence within the French Union, which would have left France in control of defense and foreign relations; on March 18, 1947, the French National Assembly rejected the 1946 agreement with the Viet Minh as inconsistent with the design of the French Union as defined in the French Constitution.[7] This position was at bottom tied to what was seen as France's vital national interest in maintaining its greatness, which in turn required maintenance of its empire.[8]

During this period few states outside the region expressed much interest in the problem. At the 1947 Asian Relations Conference in New Delhi, Vietnam and Indonesia joined in urging other Asian states to take various actions to assist their respective struggles for independence, such as raising before the United Nations the matters of the two independence struggles and providing material support. They received a lukewarm reception, however, Prime Minister Jawaharlal Nehru of India explaining that material support could not be provided without broadening the area of conflict.[9] India did, however, forbid French aircraft bound for Vietnam to land in its territory.[10] The Soviet Union likewise declined to take much interest in the Vietnamese, and the British saw the matter as a purely French concern.[11] The United States was also disinclined to do more than express a wish for peace, its traditional anticolonialism colliding with its interest in supporting France, which was seen as a key factor in Western Europe.[12] A September 1947 Viet Minh letter to United Nations Secretary-General Trygve Lie received no reply.[13]

Developments in late 1949/early 1950 changed the pattern of the war. The Viet Minh—in which the Communists had played a more and more obvious role—recognized the People's Republic of China in late 1949; the PRC accordingly recognized the Viet Minh government in early 1950, as did the Soviet Union.[14] This led to assertions by the United States that the Viet Minh were revealed to be Communists rather than nationalists,[15] and to quick recognition by the United States and United Kingdom of the "Associated States" of Vietnam, Cambodia, and Laos once France had ratified treaties granting these states a severely limited independence in February 1950.[16] This was followed in May 1950 by American promises of military and economic aid for France and the Associated States;[17] by 1954 the United States was paying 80 percent of France's military expenditures.[18] This was consistent with American concern, expressed as early as 1949, with Communist aggression in the region; such behavior by the Chinese Communists, Secretary of State Dean Acheson said at the time, would violate the principles of the UN Charter.[19] When the question of American military intervention began to be raised in 1954, however, President Eisenhower consistently resisted the idea.[20]

The Viet Minh's move to underline their Communist ties also led to a change in emphasis by the French government. By 1953 the French too were taking the position that the war must necessarily be controlled by the "great Communist powers" and thus could not be seen as involving nationalism.[21] For purposes of domestic politics, however, French governments continued to stress the importance to France of maintaining control of the area, though over time this position evolved, with greater stress on an inclusive idea of the French Union and less on the importance of colonialism.[22]

But Viet Minh association with the PRC did not lead only to increased American aid to France and a change in French justifications for the war; it also led to increased Chinese military support for the Viet Minh, apparently based on ideological affinity.[23] In 1950 the Viet Minh took advantage of this development by increasing the scale of their operations.[24] With PRC support, especially the provision of heavy artillery, the Viet Minh were able by 1954 to greatly undermine the French position in northern Vietnam and finally to force the surrender of the French post at Dien Bien Phu on May 8, 1954.[25]

By this time a conference had been convened at Geneva to address the problems of Indochina.[26] The United States had come to characterize the problem simply as one of Communist aggression, ultimately directed by the

PRC and the Soviet Union.[27] In the spring of 1954 Secretary of State Dulles called for "united action" to prevent the Russians and Chinese from imposing themselves in Indochina,[28] and attempted to form an anti-Communist alliance to protect the Associated States. However, proposed members France, Australia, and the United Kingdom rejected the idea.[29] Further, several neutral Asian states (India, Pakistan, Burma, Indonesia, and Ceylon) were at that time calling for a cease-fire and an end to colonialism.[30] Against this background the Geneva participants (each of the Associated States, the Viet Minh [now the Democratic Republic of Vietnam, or DRV], France, the United Kingdom, the Soviet Union, the PRC, and the United States) produced an agreement. Under the Geneva Accords (which the United States and the "State of Vietnam" refused to sign) fighting was to stop and Vietnam was to be divided at the seventeenth parallel until national elections were held to reunify the country in 1956. An international commission composed of Canada, Poland, and India was established to oversee the cease-fire and the elections.[31] In effect, the DRV had acquired international status,[32] while the State of Vietnam, which had earlier been recognized by thirty-five states,[33] was formally deprived of control of the part of its territory above the seventeenth parallel (albeit an area where its control was weak in any case) and required to submit to an election on the future of the rest.[34]

In summary, the First Indochina War can be seen as an effort by France to reestablish its control over Indochina through the device of establishing local governments it dominated in important respects. It also included decisions by the PRC to provide significant support to the Viet Minh and by the United States to shoulder much of France's financial burden. France justified its actions initially by reference simply to its own interests. By the end of the war it was casting its position as one of defending the idea of the French Union against "nonnationalist" adversaries, but it is doubtful that its original self-interested motive ever ceased to carry weight. The United States was moved by an uncomplicated anti-Communism, perceiving the problem primarily as one of aggression at the behest of larger Communist states. The PRC also seemed to be heavily influenced by ideological factors.

Third-state reactions to the conflict varied over time. First, as long as the struggle was perceived as a nationalist rebellion, most of the rest of the world did not care to get involved. Second, once the issue was seen as one involving Communism, interest in aid to France grew greatly among Western states, as reflected in aid from the United States and in diplomatic recognitions of the Associated States. The United States, in particular, characterized the war as involving aggression linked to the Soviet Union and the PRC, though this label apparently had more to do with American assumptions of the unity of Communism than with a dispassionate analysis of the facts on the ground. Even the United States, however, was unwilling to commit its own armed forces. At the same time PRC aid to the Viet Minh also increased.

It is also interesting that uninvolved states tended to concentrate more on ending the conflict than on determining which party was the aggressor and proceeding accordingly. Issues regarding the legality of the use of force apparently drew the attention of no disinterested states. Finally, the lack of any role for the United Nations is striking. Indeed, by 1954, when Thailand proposed to put Indochina on the Security Council's agenda, there was opposition based on the fear that actions in the Council, e.g., a Soviet veto, could somehow interfere with the Geneva Conference.[35] That is, the body nominally responsible for implementing the charter's rules was seen as more likely to play a negative than a positive part in ending the First Indochina War.

## Netherlands/Indonesia (1945–1949)

This conflict again involved a colony's struggle for independence. Under Japanese auspices the Republic of Indonesia proclaimed its independence from the Netherlands on August 17, 1945.[36] The initial Allied occupying troops, however, dismissed the leaders of the Republic as collaborators. For its part the Netherlands—convinced that its economy depended on its links to Indonesia—sought a return to the prewar status quo.[37] The situation in the country was very disorderly, and there were clashes between supporters of independence and British Commonwealth occupation troops in late 1945, as well as fighting between supporters of independence and Dutch forces.[38] However, negotiations between the Indonesians and the Dutch produced an agreement on October 14, 1946. It soon began to break down, however, undermined by mutual suspicion and the Dutch belief that the Netherlands could not do without Indonesia's resources.[39] On July 20, 1947, the Netherlands began aggressive action, ultimately setting as its goal the elimination of the Republic.[40]

Third states took varying positions over this period. Throughout, France and Belgium maintained that the question was purely a Dutch internal affair and thus outside the jurisdiction of the United Nations.[41] Initially, other states also were unwilling to act, and when the Security Council first considered the Indonesian situation in early 1946, it did nothing.[42] Over time, however, the Republic picked up support. The Arab League recognized it in November 1946,[43] and the United States and United Kingdom gave de facto recognition in April 1947.[44] Despite objections from Belgium, France, and the Netherlands, the Security Council effectively recognized the Republic in August 1947 by adopting a resolution addressed to the Netherlands and to "the Republic of Indonesia."[45] States also expressed support for Indonesia more directly. The United States blamed the Netherlands for the fighting. The United Kingdom suspended shipments of arms and provision of training to the Netherlands, limiting the effect of its action to the Netherlands East Indies. India promised aid to Indonesia. Australia maintained its recognition of Indonesia and joined India in appealing for UN action. The Arab states protested to the United Nations and demanded its intervention.[46]

These reactions had an effect. On August 1, 1947, the Security Council called for an immediate cease-fire.[47] When the cease-fire call was not heeded, the Security Council established a Good Offices Committee to help achieve a settlement.[48] The Good Offices Committee was able to work out an agreement in January 1948, permitting Dutch forces to remain in designated areas but also calling for a plebiscite.[49]

Again, however, the conflict was not settled. Finally, in frustration, the Netherlands again attacked on December 18, 1948, arresting the leaders of the Republic.[50] The result was an outpouring of condemnation. The United States suspended Marshall Plan aid to the Netherlands East Indies.[51] The U.S. Congress considered ending arms sales to the Netherlands for use in Europe, and a resolution to terminate all Marshall Plan aid to the Netherlands was introduced in the United States Senate.[52] A conference of Asian states called on the United Nations to assure transfer of sovereignty to Indonesia by 1950 and to bring about an immediate Dutch withdrawal.[53] India and Ceylon closed their airports to Dutch aircraft,[54] and India, Australia, and the Arab League demanded a cease-fire.[55] This culminated in a Security Council debate in which the United States, India, the Soviet Union, Australia, Burma, and Norway all labeled the Netherlands' actions as illegal.[56] The Security Council called first for a cease-fire and finally demanded release of the arrested leaders of the Republic and steps by the Netherlands to transfer sovereignty, the latter resolution being unanimous except for a French abstention.[57] The Council refused, however, to condemn Dutch actions as aggression.[58]

The Netherlands finally gave way. The Security Council accepted its proposal for a round table conference to end the conflict in March 1949.[59] Negotiations with the Indonesians resumed, and the Netherlands transferred full sovereignty to the Republic on December 27, 1949.[60] Although the Soviet Union condemned the agreement as unequal, it was generally welcomed at the Security Council.[61]

Like the First Indochina War, this conflict involved a colonial power's effort to reestablish its control over a colony in which a well-organized independence movement was in a position to take power. The motives of the Netherlands, like those of France in Indochina, partook of an important element of self-interest. Third-state reaction to the two conflicts was very different, however. Perhaps because of the absence of any plausible Communist connection, the states of the world generally opposed the actions of the Netherlands, going so far as to label those actions as illegal. Furthermore, states acted. The United Nations forced a Good Offices Committee on the Netherlands. Steps were taken that had the effect of hampering the Dutch war effort. Beyond these, the United States threatened an action—a cutoff of reconstruction aid to the Netherlands itself—that could fairly be seen as a sanction. Even here, however, the most extreme actions were avoided. The Netherlands was neither labeled an aggressor nor faced with threats of force. When the Dutch proposed negotiating an end to the war, the states of the world, speaking through the Security Council, ultimately decided to allow that approach, in essence leaving it to the parties to resolve their problems. Still, the approach taken to this conflict could reasonably be seen as one focusing on legalities.

## France/Tunisia (1952–1956)

In 1881 France established a protectorate over the North African state of Tunisia.[62] Though Tunisia remained formally independent, France effectively took control of the country.[63] By the beginning of the twentieth century, however, Tunisian nationalism had begun to develop; that sentiment continued to grow as the century advanced.[64] By 1950 it was hoped by many Tunisians that France would grant independence; while France did introduce reforms after that date, they were of a much less sweeping character than had been expected. The result was disorder and terrorism perpetrated by Tunisian nationalists and brutal efforts at repression by French authorities.[65] This situation continued until about 1955, the terrorism fading away after France had granted to Tunisia complete internal autonomy on July 31, 1954.[66] In 1955 France granted independence to another protectorate, Morocco, which led to demands in Tunisia for equal treatment. Such demands strengthened the hand of more radical political elements in Tunisia. To forestall the radicals, on March 20, 1956, France granted complete independence.[67]

Third-state reaction to Tunisian developments was largely verbal. In the spring of 1952 Afghanistan, Saudi Arabia, Burma, Egypt, India, Indonesia, Iraq, Iran, Pakistan, the Philippines, and Yemen sought Security Council discussion of the situation, arguing that the violence in Tunisia, coupled with arrests of Tunisian public figures by the French, endangered international peace and security. They further argued that colonialism was unjustifiable.[68] The Soviet Union, Chile, Brazil, and the Republic of China all favored Security Council discussion of the matter, stressing the importance of protecting small nations and, in the case of the Soviets and Chileans, attacking the idea of colonialism.[69]

The majority of the Security Council refused to place the matter on the agenda, however, and the eleven concerned states, joined by Syria and Lebanon, took the matter to the General Assembly.[70] France refused to participate in the debate, arguing that the subject was within its domestic jurisdiction and in any case covered by existing treaties between France and Tunisia. The First Committee of the General Assembly defeated a sweeping resolution by the thirteen states who had first raised the matter that would have labeled the situation in Tunisia detrimental to the equal rights of all nations and to the development of friendly relations among nations and a threat to international peace and security. It also would have called on France to establish "normal conditions and normal civil liberties" in Tunisia and would have established a Good Offices Committee to facilitate negotiations between France and Tunisia. The assembly adopted instead, by a vote of 45–3–10, a resolution proposed by eleven Latin American states expressing confidence that France would further the development of free institutions in Tunisia and expressing the hope that negotiations would continue, with a view toward bringing about self-government for Tunisia.[71] The General Assembly did not act again on the Tunisian issue.[72]

This matter can be seen as yet another ultimately unsuccessful effort by a colonial power to preserve its position. In this case third-state reaction was limited to verbal rejections of the legitimacy of colonialism by some states. It is noteworthy that the resolution the General Assembly ultimately adopted, in urging negotiations between the parties with a view toward self-government, followed the precedent of the Indonesian matter in placing a colonial power and its colony on an equal footing.

## France/Morocco (1953–1956)

In April 1947 the Sultan of Morocco gave a speech in Tangier carefully criticizing the French protectorate of his country.[73] He thus associated himself with the Moroccan nationalist movement, whose goal was that state's independence from France.[74] Over the next six years Moroccan nationalists gained support among their people and the sultan became, more and more clearly, a spokesman for them. French officials in Morocco, wishing to maintain their control of the country and not effectively controlled by the French government, finally decided to remove the sultan, forcing his abdication on August 20, 1953.[75]

By October 1953 the Moroccans had begun to respond with terrorism. France's harsh repression and efforts at reform were insufficient to eliminate either violent opposition or the nationalist feeling that underlay it. On the contrary, support for independence and the deposed sultan waxed as time passed, becoming especially violent on the second anniversary of his removal from the throne, August 20, 1955. The French government attempted various expedients, including the employment of large military forces, but was unable to regain control. France was compelled finally to free the sultan from his exile in Madagascar and fly him to Paris, where he entered into successful negotiations with the French government.[76] He returned to Morocco on November 16, 1955, and resumed his position; France formally acknowledged Moroccan independence on March 2, 1956.[77]

Actions taken by the United Nations, where the question was raised as early as 1951, had little effect on the situation. In 1952 the same bloc of thirteen states which in that year had raised the question of Tunisia also brought up that of Morocco, seeking a resolution from the General Assembly that would recognize Morocco's sovereignty and call on France and Morocco to negotiate a settlement consistent with that sovereignty. France argued that the matter fell within its domestic jurisdiction, and the United States, the United Kingdom, and a few other states also questioned the jurisdiction of the United Nations in this matter. The First Committee nonetheless took the matter up, narrowly defeating the thirteen states' resolution, instead adopting a Latin American resolution essentially identical in its thrust to that adopted with respect to Tunisia.[78] This resolution was adopted by the General Assembly by a 45–3–11 margin on December 19, 1952, with the only change being that the assembly replaced a paragraph in the First Committee's draft referring to "bringing about self-government for Moroccans" with one referring to "developing the free political institutions of the people of Morocco" with due regard for legitimate rights under international law.[79]

After the deposition of the sultan in 1953 the thirteen states who had raised the Moroccan matter in 1952, joined by Liberia and Thailand, sought to take the issue to the Security Council, but only five members of the Council (the

Soviet Union, the Republic of China, Chile, Lebanon, and Pakistan) agreed. The United States and the United Kingdom opposed the idea, arguing that no threat to international peace existed. The United Kingdom also agreed with France that the matter fell within France's domestic jurisdiction.[80] The matter was subsequently taken up by the General Assembly, but a First Committee resolution that would have "urg[ed] that the right of the people of Morocco to free democratic political institutions be ensured" failed, obtaining a majority of less than the required two-thirds. A number of states explained their opposition to the action by reference to doubts as to the United Nations' competence in the matter. It is nonetheless interesting that the states supporting the resolution were mainly African, Asian, Communist, and North European, while those opposing it included European states with colonies, the United States, and most Central and South American states.[81] Arguably, many of the states supporting France were concerned primarily with maintaining the solidity of the Western alliance against Communism.[82] The United Nations did not act further on the Moroccan matter, the General Assembly in 1954 and 1955 passing resolutions noting the parties' intentions to negotiate and expressing confidence in a satisfactory solution.[83]

Outside the United Nations, however, third-state actions had a more direct impact on the situation. Spain, which maintained a protectorate over northern Morocco, criticized the deposition of the sultan and continued to recognize his position; it also refused to hand over to French authorities nationalists escaping to the Spanish zone.[84] More concretely, secret radio stations began broadcasting to terrorists from the Spanish zone,[85] and gunrunners operated from there as well.[86] Further, nationalist bases were established in the Spanish zone, apparently with the acquiescence of Spanish authorities.[87] Radio Damascus, Radio Budapest, and Radio Cairo all provided strong propaganda support for the nationalists,[88] and Egypt also permitted the nationalists to establish offices and training facilities in its territory.[89] Egypt further complained to ambassadors of NATO members that France's actions were hostile to all Arabs and involved the use of NATO weapons.[90]

This conflict resembled others in which France had sought to maintain its colonial position. A factor that distinguishes it from others, however, is that the nationalist side received from non-Communist third states aid that went beyond support in the United Nations. Spain and Egypt, most prominently, provided concrete assistance. Further, the rejection by Asian, African, and Communist states of the relevance of the Charter's domestic affairs limitation to matters of colonialism was a portent of the future.

## France/Algeria (1954–1962)

In October 1954 a group drawn from the indigenous inhabitants of Algeria—Arabs and Berbers—began a war to obtain Algeria's independence from France.[91] The Front de Libération Nationale (FLN) and the French authorities carried on an increasingly brutal struggle for nearly eight years, the two sides each taking straightforward positions: France considered Algeria an integral part of the French Republic and saw itself as fighting for its own territorial integrity,[92] while the FLN sought independence.[93] The FLN ultimately prevailed; France recognized Algeria's independence on July 3, 1962.[94] The French government, in the person of President Charles de Gaulle, was finally moved to take this step by the ultimate impossibility of ruling Algeria against the wishes of the Algerians, by the weakness and war-weariness of France, and by the strongly negative reaction of the rest of the world to France's efforts to maintain its position.[95]

Third-state reactions to this war reflected increasing international discomfort with France's efforts to retain control of Algeria and a corresponding acceptance of the legitimacy of the FLN's struggle. More specifically, several states extended quite concrete assistance to the FLN, others expressed verbal support for the principle of self-determination, and still others—including France's allies—took a more neutral position but opposed actions taken by France to sanction the states actively aiding the FLN. No state expressed unqualified support for France.

To discuss the foregoing in more detail, Egypt provided to the FLN a headquarters, propaganda support, and some arms.[96] Tunisia, Libya, and Morocco permitted the transit of arms for the FLN through their territory,[97] with Tunisia in particular also providing sanctuaries for FLN troops.[98] Yugoslavia, Soviet satellites, and the PRC all provided arms aid.[99] The Arab League provided large sums of money.[100] A number of states, then, made clear their support for the FLN in unambiguous ways.

The rhetorical support for the FLN is illustrated by developments in the United Nations, where support for Algeria—grounded on the importance of the principle of self-determination[101]—increased over time. The Security Council rejected a 1956 request by thirteen African and Asian states to discuss the situation in Algeria; the United Kingdom, Belgium, and Cuba accepted the French argument that the matter fell within France's domestic jurisdiction, while the United States, Peru, and the Republic of China felt that a discussion would be useless.[102] In the General Assembly events progressed as follows:

1955, item deleted from the agenda; 1956 and 1957, matter discussed but General Assembly adopts innocuous resolution; 1958 and 1959, First Committee adopts resolution recognizing Algeria's right to self-determination, but resolution fails to obtain required two-thirds vote in General Assembly; 1960, General Assembly recognizes Algeria's right to independence and self-determination.[103] It is noteworthy that the switch in position between 1959 and 1960 occurred because twenty of the twenty-two states that had opposed the 1959 resolution favoring self-determination in Algeria either voted for or abstained from voting on the similar resolution in 1960.[104]

The willingness of uninvolved states to support those third states actively aiding the FLN is illustrated by the reaction to the French bombing of the Tunisian town of Sakhiet Sidi Youssef on February 8, 1958.[105] France justified the raid by reference to the town's status as an FLN base and the fact that French aircraft, operating over Algeria, had been fired upon from Sakhiet.[106] This characterization apparently had some validity.[107] Nonetheless, the United States, the United Kingdom, Italy, and Lebanon all criticized the raid. Further, after France and Tunisia had accepted an offer of good offices by the United States and United Kingdom, the two mediators' proposed solution did not require Tunisia to alter its sanctuary policy but did urge France to remove troops based in Tunisia.[108] Notwithstanding the implicit rebuke to France and the acceptance of Tunisia's stance, France agreed to the outlines of the British-American approach.[109]

Aside from these developments, there was a gradual falling off of support for France. After 1957 the United States ceased to support France on the matter in the United Nations.[110] When President John F. Kennedy, a supporter of Algerian independence, took office in 1961, he increased pressure on France.[111] Several of France's NATO allies were among those states switching in 1960 to a position of nonsupport of France in the General Assembly after having supported her in 1959.[112]

The Algerian conflict, in summary, was France's last effort to retain a territory the rest of the world considered a colony. By the end of the war it had become clear that many states were prepared to support struggles like that of the FLN and that other states were unwilling to label such support unlawful. Conversely, there was a decline in the willingness to treat as permissible France's efforts to defend its position. Particularly in light of the explicit reliance upon the principle of self-determination by the FLN's supporters, it would appear that many states came to approach this matter on the assumption that even provision by outside states of crucial assistance to fights for self-determination was not illegitimate.

## United Kingdom/Cyprus (1955–1959)

The United Kingdom began to rule Cyprus in 1878;[113] Turkey, which had conquered the island in 1571,[114] recognized the 1914 British annexation of the island in the Treaty of Lausanne of 1923.[115] From the beginnings of the British administration of the island, however, the hierarchy of the Eastern Orthodox Church on Cyprus, which formed the leadership of the Greek Cypriot community, strongly supported "enosis," or union of the island with Greece;[116] Cypriots of Greek ethnicity made up 80 percent of the population, the ethnic Turkish population constituting the remainder.[117] Enosis was not only very popular among Greek Cypriots but also in Greece. Successive governments of Greece therefore moved from halfhearted endorsement of the idea in 1947 to strong advocacy of union by 1954.[118] This evolution led to a reaction from Turkey, which stated on April 21, 1951, that it could not allow any change in the sovereignty of Cyprus; it called for continued British rule.[119] The United Kingdom for its part wished to retain control of the island, seeing the basing facilities there as vital to its ability to protect its interests in the eastern Mediterranean.[120]

It was against this background on April 1, 1955, that a guerilla organization called EOKA began a campaign of terror and sabotage on Cyprus intended to force the British to accept enosis.[121] The leader of the Greek Cypriot community was the head of the Cypriot Church, Archbishop Makarios; it was he who ordered EOKA to commence operations.[122] With the aid and cooperation of the government of Greece, though not really under its control, EOKA's campaign continued until 1959.[123] Initially directed against the British and those Greek Cypriots identified with them,[124] its targets were broadened to include the Turkish Cypriot community,[125] as that group and Turkey itself increased their opposition to enosis and called for partition of the island.[126] Turkish Cypriots also used violence as the situation deteriorated.[127]

By 1959 the United Kingdom had reassessed its strategic needs and concluded that its interests did not require total control of the island.[128] Greece and Turkey finally concluded that it simply was not possible for either of them to obtain its preferred solution, reached a compromise, and then obliged their respective Cypriot communities to go along.[129] In February 1959 the three states reached an agreement that required the granting of independence to Cyprus, with all three states guaranteeing that independence. Also, under the agreement the United Kingdom was granted sovereignty over two large air bases on the island, while Greece and Turkey were each allowed to station small bodies of troops there. Finally, the constitution sought to protect the Turkish Cypriots by guaranteeing to them certain powerful government positions, as well as a proportion of government jobs and seats in the legislature. Upon conclusion of the agreement EOKA declared a cease-fire.[130]

Third-state reaction in this matter was somewhat muted, mainly taking the form of inconclusive debates in the General Assembly. Although the assembly discussed the Cyprus matter in 1956, 1957, and 1958, and considerable support was expressed for the general principle of self-determination, the complexities of the situation and alliance politics led that body to do no more than adopt innocuous resolutions.[131] Outside the assembly the most interested states were the United States and its NATO allies, who were concerned about the deterioration in relations between the United Kingdom, Greece, and Turkey, all members of NATO. These third states stressed their impartiality and called for negotiations.[132]

This conflict began as an effort by a colonial power to retain a strategically important colony in the face of demands from the larger of the colony's two communities for self-determination in the form of union with another state. That state aided, though it did not entirely control, the ensuing insurrection. The struggle was unusual in that another outside state also had an interest in a portion of the population, and the ultimate resolution involved an agreement between the sponsors of the two communities within the colony. Third-state reaction was generally supportive of self-determination but had little effect on the outcome of the dispute.

## Portugal/Angola Nationalists (1961–1974)

The war to obtain Angola's independence from Portugal can be dated from an unsuccessful attempt to free political prisoners from Portuguese prisons on February 4, 1961.[133] This event was followed by widespread violence in the northern portion of the country, characterized by attacks on Portuguese civilians by rebels and attacks on Angolan civilians—including attacks in areas not previously involved in the conflict—by the Portuguese armed forces. The Angolans were more or less led by the União das Populaçoes de Angola (UPA), an organization drawn primarily from the BaKongo people and headed by Holden Roberto.[134] After 1962 the operations of the UPA—merged into the Frente Nacional de Libertação de Angola (FNLA)—were limited to the area inhabited by the BaKongo, along the Angola-Zaire border.[135] A second nationalist organization was also operating against the Portuguese, the Movimento Popular de Libertação de Angola (MPLA), composed of people from the capital, Luanda; members of the Kimbundu people, a highly assimilated group; and mestiços.[136] The MPLA's operations were limited to the eastern regions of Angola and had declined to a very low level by 1974.[137] In 1966 a third group, the União Nacional para a Independência Total de Angola (UNITA), was formed by Jonas Savimbi, a former subordinate of Roberto's; UNITA was drawn mainly from peoples of southern Angola—the Chokwe, Ganguela, Ovimbundu, and Ovambo.[138] By 1974 UNITA's efforts were focused more on building its political strength among the people of Angola than on combat.[139] Indeed, by that year the military situation in Angola was essentially stalemated, with neither side having the prospect of being able to defeat the other.[140]

Then, on April 25, 1974, the Portuguese government was overthrown in a leftist coup.[141] In August the new government, supported by antiwar sentiment in Portugal,[142] pledged to transfer power to the people of Angola;[143] it had established tacit cease-fires with UNITA and the MPLA by the end of July and signed a cease-fire with the FNLA on October 12, after the latter had spent the previous three months strengthening its military position in the northern part of the country.[144] The nationalist war against Portugal was over at that point. The consequences of the conflicting ambitions of the three nationalist groups will be discussed in Chapter 6.

During the war Angolan nationalists received extensive support from other states. Zaire provided bases for both the FNLA and the MPLA early on.[145] Algeria provided arms and training.[146] Zambia provided a key base for the MPLA.[147] The OAU provided both diplomatic and financial support, as did individual African states. The Soviet Union provided large quantities of arms for the MPLA, while the PRC gave smaller amounts of aid to UNITA. India and the Scandinavian countries also provided money and other forms of aid. While the United States, the United Kingdom, France, and the Federal Republic of Germany continued to support Portugal, that position was decidedly in the minority.[148]

Portugal's increasing isolation was reflected in votes in the United Nations. In 1962 a General Assembly resolution condemning Portugal's colonial war and requesting Security Council sanctions and an end to arms supplies to Portugal was adopted by a vote of 57–14–18, with 11 states not voting. That is, nearly half of the members of the General Assembly had not voted for the resolution, and Portugal's NATO allies had either voted against or, in the case of Greece, Norway, and Denmark, abstained.[149] By 1973 a resolution using even stronger language, in that it added calls for representation of Angolan liberation movements in international fora dealing with Angola and called on states to provide material assistance to those movements, was adopted 105–8–16, with 6 states not voting. By this point, of the members of NATO only France, the United Kingdom, and the United States voted with Portugal; Belgium, the FRG, Italy, and Luxembourg abstained, and the rest of NATO either voted against their ally or did not vote.[150]

In 1969 Zambia brought to the Security Council a complaint regarding Portuguese incursions from both Mozambique and Angola. Portugal responded by complaining of the bases provided to nationalist groups by Zambia. The debate in the Security Council, in which states not members of the Council participated, was striking for the lack of interest in Portugal's arguments. Rather, speaker after speaker stressed that the only important issue was Portugal's failure to accord the right of self-determination to its African possessions. The debate culminated in the approval of a resolution condemning Portugal by eleven votes to none, with four states abstaining.[151] No state, apparently, considered relevant the question of the extent of Zambia's aid to Portugal's enemies. Rather, self-determination was a trump.

The case of Angola provides more evidence of the decreasing legitimacy of efforts by colonial powers to retain control of distant territories. Portugal sought to retain its colony, not to expand. The reaction of several third states was to aid the nationalist movements fighting against Portugal and to condemn Portugal for not giving up. By the time of the 1974 coup Portugal had few defenders left, while the states that had provided arms, training, and bases to Portugal's opponents encountered little negative international reaction and enjoyed considerable support.

## Portugal/Guinea-Bissau (1961–1974)

The history of Portugal's efforts to retain control of its colony of Guinea-Bissau is in broad outline identical to that of the Angolan war of independence. In Guinea-Bissau the fighting began in 1961, led by the Partido Africano da Independência da Guiné e Cabo Verde (PAIGC).[152] Throughout, the PAIGC received extensive support from Guinea-Bissau's neighbors, Senegal and the Republic of Guinea, the latter providing not only bases but even artillery support for PAIGC troops.[153] The Soviet Union, Cuba, Czechoslovakia, Algeria, the PRC, Ghana, and the Republic of Guinea provided arms, training, or both.[154] However, the PAIGC was unable to prevail militarily; indeed, its situation deteriorated after 1968 due to improvements in Portuguese tactics, strategy, and political action among the population.[155] Rather, the independence sought by the PAIGC came to Guinea-Bissau as it did to Angola as a result of the 1974 military coup in Portugal: the new government simply handed power over to the PAIGC.[156]

The international outlook on Portugal's actions in Guinea-Bissau was identical to that taken toward its actions in Angola. As noted above, third states provided the PAIGC with extensive concrete support. And, as with Angola, the attitude displayed toward Portugal was unremittingly condemnatory, while great solicitude was shown for states aiding the PAIGC. Complaints of Portuguese incursions by Senegal and the Republic of Guinea were made to the Security Council several times during the fighting. On each occasion Portugal responded with complaints of the support those states were giving the PAIGC. On each occasion the debate treated the Portuguese charges as irrelevant and either criticized Portugal or adopted resolutions condemning her outright.[157] It should be stressed that such condemnations were possible only because *no* permanent member was willing to oppose these resolutions. Indeed, it is noteworthy that Portugal denied all connection with a 1970 raid on Conakry, the capital of the Republic of Guinea, which in fact apparently involved both Portuguese troops and opponents of the Guinean government and was aimed at both that government and the PAIGC.[158] In 1973 the General Assembly went so far as to "recognize the independence" of Guinea-Bissau by a vote of 93 to 7, with 30 abstentions—all Western and Northern European states, all NATO members, Australia, New Zealand, Japan, and some Latin American states either abstaining or joining the few "no" votes.[159]

Thus, the history of the war in Guinea-Bissau reinforces the impressions created by events in Angola. Efforts to defend colonial empires aroused extreme hostility and considerable concrete opposition and were denounced as illegitimate and defended by no one. Assistance to nationalist groups—even to the extent of active military help—was seen by most states as raising no questions under international law, while arguably defensive reactions by metropolitan powers against states aiding nationalist groups were condemned as illegitimate and accorded no active support, without regard to the degree or nature of the assistance rendered to the nationalists. Even Portugal hesitated to claim the right to attack states providing active aid to the groups it was fighting.

## Britain/South Yemen (1963–1967)

On October 14, 1963, a group organized by the United Arab Republic (UAR)—then prosecuting its war in Yemen—determined to initiate an armed struggle to eliminate British rule in southwestern Arabia, an area also known as South Yemen and including the port city of Aden. The motives of the rebels and their Egyptian supporters were straightforward: as Arab nationalists they were strongly opposed to the continued British presence in the area. Their political orientation, furthermore, led them to oppose as well the traditional Arab rulers upon whom British rule was based. Also, the plans of the UAR—operating as it was in support of the Yemeni republican government—were facilitated by Yemen's long-standing objection to the United Kingdom's presence in the area and Yemen's claim to the areas under British protection. Britain's opposition to the insurrection was based on motives the mirror image of those of its opponents. That is, it wished to oppose Arab nationalism, support traditional Arab rulers—whose states it had sought to organize into a Federation of South Arabia—and maintain its influence in the region.[160]

The course of the war was straightforward, if depressing for the British. The traditional rulers to whom Britain was committed were opposed by Arab tribesemen living in some of South Yemen's more remote regions and by more modernized Arab nationalists concentrated in Aden. Concessions to those groups to win their loyalty would have undermined the rulers to whom the British were committed. Britain was therefore forced to rely purely on military means to deal first with a rural insurgency that appeared in 1964 and subsequently with a terrorist campaign in Aden. Its situation was further complicated by its 1964 announcement of its intention to grant independence to the Federation of South Arabia in 1968, seeking only to retain a base in Aden, and its subsequent February 1966 announcement of the abandonment of the plan for an Aden base and of its unilateral abrogation of its defense arrangements with the traditional Arab rulers in the area.

The effect of these announcements was to greatly discourage Arab cooperation with Britain, since the prospect of British loss of control of the federation and subsequently of Britain's complete departure from the area meant that Arabs who assisted the British would be vulnerable to retaliation after the British had left. This impression was reinforced in July 1966, when Britain declined to retaliate for an air attack from Yemen on one of the federation's states, despite the terms of the protectorate agreement with that state. The United Kingdom instead referred the matter to the Security Council, which refused even to investigate, the net effect being an erosion of British credibility.

The perhaps inevitable decline in the British position was accelerated by its government's determination to pull out as fast as possible. By August 1967 the positions of the traditional rulers had been completely undermined, and nationalists had taken power in their states; British troops had by this time been withdrawn into Aden in preparation for their final departure. By November 1967 one group had emerged preeminent from infighting among the nationalists, and the British negotiated the final details of their withdrawal with that group. The British left on November 29, 1967.[161]

Third states apparently did not consider the war in Yemen a matter of high priority, but their reactions were anti-British to the extent that they existed. Thus, when in 1964 Britain retaliated for air attacks from Yemen on states of the federation with an air attack on a Yemeni fort, the Security Council's reaction was to adopt a resolution condemning reprisals, deploring specifically the British attack and deploring generally "all attacks and incidents in the area" without mentioning Yemen.[162] Incidentally, the United Kingdom abstained in voting on the resolution, which must thus represent one of the few cases in which a permanent member of the Security Council permitted that body to adopt a resolution critical of itself. The General Assembly called for self-determination for South Arabia by a very large majority,[163] and dispatched an ineffectual mission to the area to recommend practical steps toward that end.[164] These multilateral reactions, though negative from Britain's perspective, had little ultimate effect on the outcome of the conflict. Much more significant, of course, was Egypt's role in assisting the nationalists. The Soviet Union and the PRC also supplied the nationalists with weapons.[165] By and large, however, third states other than the nationalists' allies contributed little.

This war can be summed up as an effort by a colonial power to maintain its position in its colony, opposed by a nationalist group with outside assistance fighting for self-determination. The nationalists won, in large part because the colonial power decided, relatively quickly, to abandon the fight. Moreover, the United Kingdom took no military action against Yemen or Egypt, despite heavy Yemen-based Egyptian involvement in supporting the insurgents; indeed, it acquiesced in a Security Council resolution deploring its "reprisals." Noninvolved third states were disapproving of the effort to maintain the colonial relationship but did little to affect the outcome of the fighting. Specifically, none of the parties encountered third-party sanctions, either for aiding or for resisting the self-determination effort.

## Portugal/Mozambique (1964–1974)

The war for the independence of the Portuguese colony of Mozambique began with small attacks by guerillas of the Frente de Libertação de Moçambique

(FRELIMO) against Portuguese military and administrative posts on September 25, 1964.[166] It continued until a cease-fire was signed in Lusaka between FRELIMO and Portugal on September 7, 1974, establishing a FRELIMO-dominated transitional government to administer the country until independence, which became effective on June 25, 1975.[167] During the ten years intervening between the war's first shots and the Lusaka Accords, the conflict remained a guerilla struggle. FRELIMO was able over time to shift its operations from northern Mozambique to the western part of the country, and finally to the central regions. By 1974 FRELIMO was creating high levels of insecurity among the white settlers in central Mozambique, especially through its use of land mines. More fundamentally, its steadily widening areas of operation demonstrated that the Portuguese were unable to contain it, containment being Portugal's strategic goal.

FRELIMO thus possessed the strategic initiative, and knowledge of this fact and of the corollary—that Portugal was not winning the war despite the losses it was suffering—helped to demoralize the Portuguese military. This demoralization, in turn, contributed to the April 25, 1974, military coup in Portugal. Initially, the new Portuguese government hoped to preserve some link to Mozambique and proposed to end the conflict through a cease-fire and elections in which FRELIMO would be but one of several parties. FRELIMO responded to this situation by greatly increasing its operations in the central portion of the country. The Portuguese troops in Mozambique, realizing that the war was likely to end soon in negotiations with the guerillas, refused to fight. By the summer of 1974 a de facto truce existed. The Lusaka Accords followed.[168]

Third-state reaction was crucial in this as in the other liberation wars in Portuguese colonies. FRELIMO relied on bases in Tanzania and, to a lesser extent, Zambia; without these bases it could not have functioned. It received arms and training from the PRC, the Soviet Union, the GDR, Tanzania, and, early on, from Egypt and Algeria. Malawi was of some small assistance toward the end of the conflict, but by and large was of little help, depending as it did on Portugal for access to the sea through Mozambican ports. FRELIMO also benefited, at least in its morale, from recognition by the OAU and the United Nations, though the former was of little material help.[169] The previous discussions of United Nations support for the nationalists in Angola and Guinea-Bissau apply equally to Mozambique; indeed, resolutions by UN organs tended to lump the three areas together.

It should be noted that Portugal generally refrained from retaliating against Tanzania and Zambia for their support for FRELIMO, aside from some cross-border raids in "hot pursuit" and some shelling of Tanzanian areas close to the river that formed Mozambique's northern border. This is true despite Zambia's economic vulnerability, depending as it did on Mozambican ports for access to the sea. Portugal apparently feared the loss of income it would suffer if it curtailed Zambian use of Portuguese rail lines, and it also feared the loss of whatever leverage its control of those lines gave it. Its avoidance either of military action against or of serious efforts to subvert Tanzania and Zambia also reflected fear of the international repercussions of such action.[170]

Portugal was not without international assistance. Due to its reliance on bases in the Azores and the Cape Verde Islands, the United States provided Portugal with a degree of economic assistance and small quantities of military aid. France and the Federal Republic of Germany were relatively important suppliers of arms to Portugal, and Belgium also sold arms to the Portuguese (these sources of support began to dry up after 1971, however, when FRELIMO's propaganda began to make itself felt in Western Europe). South Africa, moved by ideological solidarity and a sense of a common enemy, provided weapons, training, and may have contributed its paramilitary police to the Portuguese cause. Rhodesia was of particular help. Beginning with the pursuit of Zimbabwe African National Union (ZANU) guerillas in 1971, joint operations between Portugal and Rhodesia became more common in the next three years. Rhodesian units during that period were operating against FRELIMO as well as against ZANU, at least in part because those two organizations were likewise cooperating closely. Rhodesian cooperation with Portugal dropped significantly, however, after the 1974 coup in Portugal.[171]

This colonial conflict generally resembles others discussed in this chapter. The colonial power was subjected to considerable rhetorical criticism and received relatively little outside support except from other pariah states. The guerillas received crucial support from states adjacent to the colony, which states the colonial power was reluctant to attack in part because of the likely international reaction. FRELIMO also received arms and training from the Communist powers. The end of the war thus cannot be said directly to reflect international condemnation of Portugal; rather, it resulted from the guerillas' battlefield success and Portugal's resulting demoralization, that success in turn depending more on international actions aiding the guerillas than on actions aimed directly against Portugal. Portugal's reluctance to act against states aiding its enemy nonetheless illustrates an element of most colonial wars. Specifically, it demonstrates the degree of legitimacy accorded efforts to aid insurgencies such as FRELIMO's by means short of direct intervention in support of the insurgents. And the history and result of this conflict underline the fact that, by the mid-1960s, the legitimacy of wars against European colonialism was receiving increasingly wide recognition.

## South Africa/Namibia (1966–1989) South Africa/Cuba, Angola (1977–1989)

Namibia's struggle for independence from South Africa and the international aspects of Angola's postindependence civil war became so intertwined that it is not possible to address either conflict without considering the other. This portion of the discussion, therefore, will examine both.

The starting point is the beginning of the fighting in Namibia in 1966. South Africa had been in formal control of that area since 1920, when it received a League of Nations mandate to govern what was then known as South-West Africa.[172] After World War II South Africa refused to place the territory under the United Nations Trust Territory system, seeking instead to incorporate it; the United Nations refused to accept this arrangement and became increasingly critical of the manner in which South Africa was discharging its mandate.[173] Finally, in 1966 the General Assembly voted to terminate the mandate;[174] the Security Council reaffirmed that vote in 1970 and also labeled South Africa's acts after the termination of the mandate illegal and requested states to refrain from all acts implying recognition of South Africa's authority over Namibia.[175]

None of this activity affected South Africa's behavior in Namibia. The people of South-West Africa began to resist various aspects of South African rule in the 1950s; in 1961 the South-West African People's Organization (SWAPO) determined to engage in armed resistance, beginning training in the UAR.[176] In 1966 it put that decision into practice. Its armed activities were low-level, however, eventually coming to focus on minelaying in northern Namibia by guerillas operating from Zambia.[177] Increasing South African pressure on Zambia, however, led to increasing Zambian pressure on SWAPO, culminating in SWAPO's shifting its bases from Zambia to Angola in 1975. This shift recommended itself in part because of the close relationship between SWAPO and UNITA, one of the Angolan nationalist organizations contending for power in that country in the wake of Portugal's departure.[178]

The SWAPO-UNITA alliance was soon to dissolve. As will be discussed in more detail in Chapter 6, in 1975 South Africa entered the civil war in Angola on the side of UNITA, seeking to block the Marxist MPLA. In return, UNITA turned on SWAPO, providing South Africa with intelligence on SWAPO's movements and the location of its camps. For its part, the MPLA sought allies against UNITA in southern Angola, and therefore cultivated SWAPO, permitting the latter to establish bases in Angola. Both UNITA and SWAPO benefited from this arrangement. UNITA received arms and training from South Africa at bases in Namibia, while SWAPO was able to increase its military operations in Namibia because of the Angolan bases.[179]

Over the period 1977–88 the violence on both sides escalated. SWAPO's increased effectiveness led to a reaction by South Africa, whose troops attacked SWAPO bases in both Angola and Zambia. South Africa also increased its support to UNITA, both because it hoped to use UNITA to pressure the MPLA government to cease aiding SWAPO and because UNITA was a useful ally against SWAPO. In the early 1980s South African forces began attacking Angolan government forces within Angola because of that state's efforts to defend its southern border; a more effective Angolan border defense would have hindered South African raids against SWAPO bases.[180] South Africa's motives went beyond the tactical, however, since it was greatly concerned by the Marxist character of the Angolan government, and particularly by the large numbers of Cuban troops stationed in Angola in support of the MPLA; much of South Africa's attitude toward Angola was shaped by its apprehensions of the Cuban presence there.[181] Despite these motives, however, in early 1984 South Africa agreed to pull its troops out of Angola, pressured by the United States; in return it was agreed that SWAPO would not enter a cease-fire zone covering part of the border. Despite SWAPO violations of this agreement, which it had in any case not joined, South African troops pulled out by May 1985.[182]

They returned soon. UNITA had greatly increased its activities beginning in March of 1984, seeking to pressure the Angolan government to deal with it in the context of the regional settlement that UNITA expected was in the offing. The MPLA responded with an offensive against UNITA's base areas in the fall of 1985; strengthened by large shipments of Soviet arms and Soviet planning, the offensive made considerable progress. At that point, however, South Africa reinforced UNITA with mechanized troops from its regular army and with extensive air support, which the Angolans were not prepared to counter. The Angolan offensive was routed.[183] In the following year Angola reaffirmed its intention to attack UNITA, and the Soviet Union made clear that it would ensure Angola an ample supply of weapons. The United States, however, made antitank and antiaircraft missiles available to UNITA,[184] the two superpowers thus making possible a higher level of violence.

Another Soviet-supplied (and commanded) Angolan offensive against UNITA was repulsed in 1987 with South African help; UNITA and South African forces pursued the Angolan troops to their base and besieged it for several months. The Angolans, reinforced by Cuban troops, held, and South Africa and UNITA abandoned the siege in May 1988. In the meantime Cuba had begun to move sizeable forces toward Angola's Namibian border, South Africa countering by reinforcing its troops there. The two sides managed to avoid contact until June 26, 1988, when South African units patrolling north of the Namibia-Angola border attacked a Cuban unit, inflicting casualties. Cuba responded with an air attack on the dam at Calueque,[185] a facility within Angola but very important to the Namibian economy and therefore guarded by South Africa.[186] After these clashes both South Africa and Cuba paused; each was aware of the danger in confronting the other, and neither was eager to accept the risk such a confrontation would entail. Their mutual reluctance to meet head-on contributed to the peace settlement reached later in 1988.[187]

Discussion of the peace settlement requires consideration of the responses of third states to the fighting in the region, since they proved to be crucial. Of course, the depth of international reaction to South Africa's continued occupation of Namibia is well known. As noted above, the General Assembly and the Security Council had labeled its presence illegal as early as 1970. The number of symbolic actions by UN organs and condemnatory General Assembly resolutions on the subject were legion. It is safe to say that almost every state in the world expressed tremendous opposition to South Africa's retention of Namibia. But the contribution of these UN actions to the ultimate settlement was limited. Some progress was made in the late 1970s by a "contact group" composed of Canada, the Federal Republic of Germany, France, the United Kingdom, and the United States—the Western members of the Security Council in 1977. These states had devised a plan for Namibia's ultimate independence that was embodied in Security Council Resolution 435 and accepted in principle by South Africa in April 1978.[188] But acceptance in principle by South Africa did not lead to acceptance in practice; on the contrary, South African foot-dragging and obfuscation prevented the implementation of Resolution 435.[189]

Then, in 1981 the United States altered its policy. Previously, it and the other contact group states had approached the problem as one involving nothing more than independence for Namibia. The Reagan administration, however, changed that focus; it proposed to link independence for Namibia with a Cuban withdrawal from Angola. Each would be the quid pro quo for the other. The advantage to this strategy was seen to be, first, the removal of an important Communist asset in southern Africa and, second, the sweetening of the deal as far as South Africa was concerned, offering it a concrete gain in exchange for its surrender of Namibia.[190] Accordingly, the United States began a seven-year diplomatic campaign that finally bore fruit in 1988. By this time the Soviet Union, reluctant to bear the costs of continuing war, was helpful, and Cuba and South Africa had become receptive to an accommodations as each became concerned about the consequences of confronting the other and each experienced a certain war-weariness. Cuba, Angola, and South Africa therefore agreed to an arrangement broadly similar to the original linkage idea—Namibian independence pursuant to Resolution 435 in return for Cuban withdrawal from Angola.[191] South Africa and Angola also agreed, respectively, to end material and logistic support for both UNITA and the African National Congress, the group fighting apartheid within South Africa itself.[192] The agreement was signed on December 22, 1988; implementation of the plan for establishing Namibian independence was set for April 1.[193]

Implementation was at first complicated by SWAPO's abortive efforts to infiltrate troops into Namibia in violation of the peace plan. That matter was resolved, however,[194] and events in Namibia then proceeded relatively smoothly; elections were held in November 1989, and Namibia became formally independent in March 1990.[195]

Events in Angola have moved less smoothly. Fighting continued between the MPLA and UNITA, supplied respectively by the Soviet Union and the United States. By April 1990, however, the stalemate in the fighting had been reestablished and Portugal had begun a mediation effort. With assistance from the United States and the Soviet Union the process finally led the two Angolan combatants to reach an agreement, which was signed May 31, 1991.[196] That agreement has since broken down.[197]

In summary, it can be said that the fighting in Angola involved intervention by Cuba to support an ideological ally in a civil war and intervention by South Africa partly for the same purpose and partly to limit the aid Angola could give to SWAPO. The Namibia conflict, on the other hand, was yet another fight for self-determination by the people of an African state, with South Africa opposing that result and attacking guerilla bases deep within neighboring states to prevent it. South Africa had no real justification for its actions beyond its anti-Communism and its desire to retain Namibia. Its behavior in both conflicts was frequently criticized and subjected to mostly symbolic sanctions—in contrast to those imposed for other reasons, for instance, apartheid. In the end, however, it was not sanctions that led to South Africa's departure from Angola and Namibia; it was, rather, a combination of its reluctance to bear continued high military costs and a willingness on the part of other states to recognize

South African interests in seeing Cuba's presence in Angola eliminated. That is, *pace* the various United Nations resolutions, it was not possible simply to treat South Africa's actions as illegitimate; it was necessary, rather, to acknowledge that South Africa could not be compelled to leave Namibia and to come up with a quid pro quo for its departure.

As for the other states involved, Zambia and the other African states supporting SWAPO grounded their actions on their support for self-determination. Cuba and the Soviet Union assisted the MPLA for similar reasons, reinforced by ideological affinity. Ideology led the United States to aid UNITA and to sympathize with South Africa's anti-Communism, but the United States also put weight on self-determination, as shown by its efforts on behalf of Namibian independence. The United States and the Soviet Union, by providing UNITA and the MPLA, respectively, with arms after 1988, could have been seen as intervening in Angola's civil war but were not subjected to sanctions. Indeed, formal international sanctioning mechanisms seem to have been much less important in settling this pair of related conflicts than were persistent diplomatic efforts—though those efforts were facilitated by the availability of international support for implementing the agreements.

## Rhodesia/Zimbabwe Civil War (1966–1979)

On November 11, 1965, the British colony of Southern Rhodesia declared itself independent of the United Kingdom.[198] Its government, completely dominated by the 3 percent of the population composed either of white immigrants or descendants of earlier white immigrants,[199] took this step to shield itself from the United Kingdom's pressure to reorganize the government so as to permit the colony's indigenous black population, amounting to about 97 percent of the total, to exercise a degree of control commensurate with its numbers.[200] Although guerillas seeking majority rule had actually begun to operate a few years before 1965, the start of the war is dated from April 28, 1966, when a group of guerillas from the Zimbabwe African National Liberation Army (ZANLA), the military arm of the Zimbabwe African National Union (ZANU), were attacked by Rhodesian security forces.[201]

The military aspect of that struggle falls into three phases. In the first, lasting into 1968, the guerillas unsuccessfully sought to directly confront Rhodesia's troops.[202] From 1968 until 1972 ZANLA was training its forces at camps in Tanzania and in the field with FRELIMO, the group fighting for

Mozambique's independence from Portugal. Finally, in December 1972 ZANLA returned to operations within Rhodesia, or Zimbabwe as the area was called by its African inhabitants, those operations continuing until the crisis was settled in 1979.[203]

At all times, however, this conflict involved more than the contending parties within Zimbabwe. The United Kingdom, which had sought to block any Rhodesian effort to declare independence without providing for majority rule, imposed increasingly stringent economic sanctions on Rhodesia in 1965 and 1966. In April 1966 the United Kingdom also prevailed upon the Security Council, which had earlier condemned the declaration of independence, to authorize the U.K. to use force to block oil shipments intended to reach Rhodesia from reaching the port of Beira in Portuguese-controlled Mozambique. In December 1966 the Security Council labeled Rhodesia's declaration of independence a threat to international peace and security; it also imposed an embargo on the purchase from Rhodesia of a number of its most important exports and on the supply to Rhodesia of petroleum products and military equipment, aircraft, and motor vehicles. In May 1968 these mandatory sanctions were broadened to forbid essentially all economic contact with Rhodesia and much travel to that entity.[204] Furthermore, the General Assembly adopted by large margins a number of resolutions condemning Rhodesia during the course of the conflict.[205]

These sanctions, standing alone, did little to advance the cause of majority rule in Rhodesia. On the contrary, Rhodesia's economic situation in 1974 was considerably better than it had been in 1965, and the morale of the white community was very high.[206] At least in part this failure of economic sanctions reflected the refusal of certain states to adhere to them. South Africa, Portugal, and, to a lesser extent, Malawi, ignored the sanctions, continuing to trade with Rhodesia and, more important, continuing to permit the transit through their territories of goods and commodities imported and exported by Rhodesia. South Africa, in fact, dispatched both police forces and regular troops to aid Rhodesia, withdrawing the former during an unsuccessful effort to improve its relations with other African states. Zambia, Botswana, Zaire, the FRG, and Australia continued to trade with Rhodesia, alleging economic necessity; it is clearly true that at least Zambia and Botswana would have suffered tremendous hardship if they had observed the embargo, and Zambia in fact did suffer when it closed its border with Rhodesia in 1973. The United States determined in 1971 to import from Rhodesia certain minerals deemed to be strategic, notwithstanding its earlier votes to embargo trade, then returned in 1977 to observing the embargo. And Switzerland and Gabon also had economic relations with Rhodesia during the period of the embargo, the former justifying its position by reference to its nonmembership in the United Nations.[207] Furthermore, the United Kingdom and the United States vetoed Security Council resolutions that presumably would have increased the effectiveness of the embargo by imposing sanctions on South Africa and Portugal.[208]

Despite this record, third-state reaction to this conflict was crucial to its resolution. In the first place, third states were vital to the guerillas. As noted above, ZANLA trained in Tanzania. Zambia also provided base areas.[209] The PRC provided arms and training to ZANLA, while the Soviet Union gave similar help to ZANU's rival, the Zimbabwe African People's Union (ZAPU); Ghana, Egypt, and Cuba also provided training.[210] Most crucial, Mozambique—having attained its independence in 1975—not only provided a friendly base area for the guerillas but also in 1976 closed its border with Rhodesia, greatly complicating that entity's supply problems and accelerating the reversal of Rhodesia's improved economic performance that had begun with the 1973 oil crisis. This reversal was exacerbated by increased guerilla activity and the withdrawal of the South African police, all of which combined to increase the costs of the war while interfering with Rhodesia's economic efficiency.[211] Indeed, the assistance given the guerillas by various of the states bordering Rhodesia at times gave those states a strong voice in determining the guerillas' actions.[212] None of this activity by outside states evoked sanctions from states not involved in the fighting, although the Rhodesian government retaliated against its neighbors' efforts to aid the guerillas, most notably by launching the Resistencia Nacional Mozambicana (RENAMO) insurgency against the government of Mozambique, as discussed in Chapter 6.

Aside from third-state efforts at supporting the guerillas, third-state influence led ultimately to the settlement of the conflict. Initiatives by the United States and the United Kingdom had led to the Rhodesian regime's acceptance of the principle of majority rule and kept alive the idea of negotiation.[213] American refusal to countenance British recognition of the Rhodesian regime in 1979 after Rhodesia had made certain essentially cosmetic constitutional changes helped to dissuade the Thatcher government from recognition, as did Prime Minister Margaret Thatcher's own experience at the Commonwealth Conference in Zambia in 1979.[214]

Instead, Britain convened a conference between the guerillas and the Rhodesian government that in December 1979 ultimately led to a settlement, the key terms of which included a constitution with extensive protections for minorities and free elections that would lead to majority rule and would be supervised by the British.[215] The Rhodesian government's willingness to agree to this arrangement resulted at least in part from the cumulative effect of the economic sanctions discussed above, as well as from the realization that the military aspect of the conflict was stalemated, though also because it was convinced that it could win a fair election.[216] South Africa, which had become less willing to bear the costs of supporting Rhodesia, contributed to its accepting this outcome.[217] Similarly, the guerillas were influenced to attend the conference partly by their awareness that they were unlikely to win a military victory in the near term but also because of pressure from Zambia, Mozambique, and Tanzania, the former two in particular being anxious for an acceptable settlement due to the damage their economies were suffering.[218] Indeed, Mozambican pressure was what apparently led to the guerillas' final decision to accept the settlement, though the military factors and their confidence in their own electoral prospects also contributed.[219] Finally, the United Kingdom's management of the negotiations also contributed greatly to their success.[220]

In summary, then, this was yet another conflict involving an effort by an indigenous people to attain independence from European colonialism; it differed from other, similar struggles in that the principal opposition to self-determination came not from the colonial power but from local European-derived inhabitants. The outcome was essentially a victory for the principle of self-determination and was greatly facilitated by third-state pressure exerted on the side of the indigenous peoples. At the same time, however, it should be noted that third-state support for the guerillas was by no means unanimous throughout the conflict and that the final result was due at least in part to a willingness on the part of the guerillas to accept a settlement, several elements of which were included to induce, rather than coerce, the assent of their opponents. The outcome in this case is generally in line with others involving self-determination in the context of European colonialism; however, in reflecting some concern for the interests of those opposing self-determination, the result in this case, as in that of Namibia, shows a certain international unwillingness to push to the limit of its logic the idea of the "illegality" of opposition to self-determination.

## South Africa/Botswana, Zimbabwe (Zambia, 1985, 1986)

The uses of force described here took place during the course of a nationalist war similar to that in Rhodesia/Zimbabwe involving force directed against guerilla bases in neighboring states by a white minority government. In March 1985 South African civilians were killed near the border of Botswana, apparently by opponents of the South African government. An arms cache was discovered by South African authorities in the same vicinity in April 1985. Against this background, South African armed forces raided Gaborone, the capital of Botswana, on June 14, 1985, attacking houses South Africa claimed were the nerve center of the African National Congress's (ANC's) Botswana operation. South Africa insisted that ANC guerillas were operating from Botswana and asserted that its actions were taken in self-defense. Botswana acknowledged giving asylum to refugees from South Africa but denied that any guerillas operated from its territory.[221]

Third-state reaction to this incident was negative but limited. The United States condemned the raid and temporarily withdrew its ambassador from South Africa; the United Kingdom also condemned the action. On June 21 the Security Council adopted a resolution of condemnation, further demanding that South Africa compensate Botswana for the damage done by the raid. However, the resolution imposed no sanctions, and both the United States and the United Kingdom, in voting for the resolution, made clear that they did not see it as contemplating action under Chapter VII of the UN Charter or indeed as having specific consequences under that instrument.[222]

A similar incident took place on May 19, 1986. This time South Africa raided into Zimbabwe and Zambia as well as Botswana, again insisting that it attacked only targets connected with ANC guerilla operations. It again asserted that it acted in self-defense, comparing its raids to the American bombing of Libya earlier that year in response to a terrorist incident in Berlin. The states attacked asserted that most of the targets had no links to the ANC and insisted that in any event they permitted no ANC guerilla bases on their territory.[223]

Again, third-state reaction was limited. The United States rejected any parallel between its attack on Libya and South Africa's raids, implicitly disagreeing with the proposition that anything done in the states attacked by South Africa could be compared to Libya's involvement in terrorism. The United States also expelled the South African military attaché and recalled its own from Pretoria. Canada likewise recalled its ambassador to South Africa, and Argentina broke diplomatic relations. The European Community and the United Kingdom strongly condemned the raids, as did the Soviet Union. At least part of the reaction, apparently, reflected outrage at the timing of the raids, which came while Commonwealth mediation efforts were in progress. However, no sanctions beyond the diplomatic steps described above were imposed. A Security Council resolution that would not only have condemned the raids but also imposed mandatory economic sanctions was vetoed by the United States and the United Kingdom. These states objected to mandatory sanctions, as did France, which abstained.[224]

Both of these incidents were raids by a state experiencing a guerilla war against what it alleged were guerilla bases located in neighboring states. The target states denied harboring guerillas. Rhetorical condemnation of the raids was strong, and relatively minor diplomatic sanctions were imposed in each case. In neither case, however, were even the states most outraged at the raids prepared to impose more serious sanctions on the raiding state except in the context of UN action, which was unavailable due to the rejection of this course by two permanent members of the Security Council.

## Analysis

The fifteen uses of force discussed in this chapter each involved efforts by inhabitants of areas colonized by Europeans to throw off European rule. Thirteen of the cases were struggles for independence; one was an effort to force an elite of European and European-descended settlers to acknowledge the rights of a local majority; the last was an incident in a similar conflict. In each of these cases outside states provided significant material support for the anticolonial side. Also relevant to this discussion are the invasions of Western New Guinea by Indonesia and of Goa by India, discussed in the last chapter. Considering all these cases, it can be said that the thrust of state practice indicates that it is not unlawful for states to provide basing facilities, military training, and military supplies to insurgents fighting against European colonialism. Nor does state practice support the proposition that it is unlawful for states to invade colonies in order to acquire sovereignty over them, provided that such an invasion can plausibly be characterized as ousting Europeans from an area over which the invader ought to be seen as having a sort of residual sovereignty. Indeed, state practice gives some support to the argument that it is unlawful for a colonial power to resist a war against its own rule.

To understand these conclusions it is helpful to recall that putative rules of law are being tested against the obey-or-be-sanctioned standard. That is, to determine whether uses of force directed against European colonialism are unlawful, it is necessary to pose two questions. Have states generally refrained from aiding anticolonial insurgencies and from using force against European colonialism? Have those states who have engaged in these activities been sanctioned in any significant way? Since the answer to both questions is "no," the only possible conclusion is that such activities cannot be seen as illegal.

Consider aid to insurgent groups first. A number of states have provided such aid on a number of occasions. This happened in the First Indochina War, in the Moroccan and Algerian wars of independence, in EOKA's war against the British in Cyprus, in the independence struggles of Portugal's colonies in Africa, in the fighting to eject Britain from South Yemen and South Africa from Namibia, and in the civil war in Zimbabwe. Further, the states providing such aid have never been sanctioned by third states for doing so. Indeed, even the states fighting against the insurgents have seldom sought to sanction the states aiding their foes. Aside from the French attack on Egypt in 1956, the abortive Portuguese cooperation in an attempted coup in Guinea, the support of UNITA by South Africa and the support of RENAMO by Rhodesia, states contending against such insurgencies have limited their military actions in third states to attacks on insurgent bases. And three of these four cases are ambiguous in their effect, since both France and South Africa had reasons to attack Egypt and Angola, respectively, aside from their aid to insurgents, and since Portugal sought to deny its involvement in Guinea. Generally, the structures of states aiding anticolonial insurgents have not been attacked by the states opposed to the insurgents. The fact that many states have aided guerillas without encountering any sanction even from the guerillas' opponents strengthens the proposition that assistance to such insurgencies is not unlawful.

This conclusion is reinforced by third-state reaction to invasions justified as directed against European colonialism. As discussed in Chapter 2, both India's seizure of Goa and Indonesia's effort to acquire West Irian were justified as opposing colonialism, and both were legitimized. Third states assisted Indonesia in its efforts, and even Portugal eventually acquiesced regarding Goa.

Finally, the reactions of third states to at least some efforts by colonial powers to retain their colonies cast doubt on the legality of such undertakings. The Netherlands encountered threats of significant sanctions because of its efforts to reimpose its rule on Indonesia. The negative reaction to France's bombing of an FLN base in Tunisia, the pressure put on the Netherlands to accommodate Indonesia's desire for West Irian, the relative tentativeness of the United Kingdom's effort to retain its position in South Yemen, the concerted effort by leading Western powers to get South Africa out of Namibia, and the fact that South Africa's attacks on neighboring states harboring ANC forces were apparently directed almost exclusively against the ANC's bases all lend some support to this position, quite apart from that provided by the rhetoric of General Assembly resolutions on the subject.

In sum, states have aided anticolonial insurgents and invaded colonies without encountering sanctions from third states, or even from the colonial powers in question. Uses of force aimed at ousting European colonial administrations in favor of indigenous governments cannot, then, be said to be unlawful; similarly, aid to groups undertaking such uses of force is not unlawful.

It should also be noted, however, that an important element of the international reaction to several of these conflicts was to urge negotiation. Thus, the United Nations did not initially oppose the Netherlands' behavior in Indonesia; it first sought to assist negotiations between Indonesia and the Netherlands. Similarly, third-state intervention by way of assisting negotiation between the parties was important in ending the fighting in the First Indochina War, the West Irian dispute, the Namibian conflict, and the Rhodesia/Zimbabwe civil war. It is also significant that, except in the West Irian case, none of these negotiations was simply a face-saving exercise to disguise a capitulation by the side opposing self-determination. In each case third-state participants in the negotiation acknowledged certain interests of that side as legitimate and aided that side in salvaging something from the conflict. This recognition of certain interests of some of the states opposing self-determination suggests that, while resisting a struggle for self-determination is of questionable legality, the international community is unprepared to totally disregard the interests even of states engaged in such an undertaking.

CHAPTER 4

# POSTIMPERIAL WARS

When empires break up, many questions regarding the political status of their component parts may be left unsettled. New entities, formerly colonies, may quarrel over territory, or even over one another's right to exist. Neighbors of former colonies may challenge the legitimacy of erecting a state in the territory formerly colonized. Similar issues may arise when the entity that has dissolved is not a colonial empire but a multinational state. This chapter examines wars that have arisen out of imperial dissolution. Each of them involves what could be called an invasion. Unlike the classical invasions described in Chapter 2, however, the borders crossed in these wars had no long history of acceptance by the states that violated them. On the contrary, they bounded recently created entities that, according to the invaders, were either illegitimate or else not fairly entitled to all the territory they claimed.

# India/Pakistan (1947–1948)

As of October 1947 the Maharajah of Kashmir had not yet decided whether to accede to Pakistan or India, the two states formed upon the end of British colonial rule in India the previous August. Most of the maharajah's subjects were Muslims, creating an interest on the part of Pakistan, which had been established as a homeland for Muslims. The maharajah himself was Hindu, however.[1]

On October 22, 1947, the Maharajah was overtaken by events. His state was invaded by Muslim tribesmen responding to reports of mistreatment of Kashmiri Muslims by Hindus; the invaders were also interested in loot. The tribesmen received some assistance from Pakistani officials but were not controlled by them.[2] Unable to repel the invasion, the maharajah sought aid from India. India refused to assist Kashmir, however, unless Kashmir acceded to India; accordingly, the maharajah acceded on October 27, 1947. Though India had apparently made no plans covering such an eventuality, it began an immediate airlift of troops to Kashmir.[3] At some point over the next few months, and no later than February 1948, the Pakistan Army was deployed in Kashmir to aid the tribesmen and the so-called Azad Kashmir Army, a group of Kashmiris opposed to the maharajah. Neither side was able to drive the other out of Kashmir, and a cease-fire negotiated with the assistance of the United Nations Commission for India and Pakistan (UNCIP) took effect January 1, 1949, with both sides maintaining positions in Kashmir.[4]

The formation of UNCIP was the outcome of the Security Council's consideration of the matter, which had been triggered by an Indian request for Security Council assistance on January 1, 1948. Throughout this period India's position was that upon the maharajah's act of accession, Kashmir became part of India. India further claimed that the original invasion had been assisted and controlled by Pakistan, which was therefore guilty of a hostile act. Pakistan countered that the actions of the tribesmen and others opposed to the maharajah had been spontaneous and inspired by massive violations of the human rights of Kashmiri Muslims.

Against this background third-state reactions focused on stopping the fighting rather than on fixing legal responsibility.[5] The Security Council created UNCIP in a January 20, 1948, resolution in which all members of the Security Council agreed that the best solution to the crisis would be for the combatants to work the problem out between themselves.[6] The Council subsequently adopted a resolution on April 21, 1948, to which both combatants had earlier agreed. It envisaged solving the crisis by a withdrawal of the invading tribesmen, followed by a reduction in the number of Indian troops, followed by a plebiscite to determine the ultimate fate of Kashmir.[7]

Upon its arrival in the subcontinent, UNCIP discovered that its task was more complicated than it thought because of the presence of the Pakistan Army in Kashmir.[8] Although, as noted above, it was able to achieve a cease-fire, it was unable to attain its further objectives due to the obduracy of India and Pakistan. Pakistan, which justified the deployment of its army by reference to the need to prevent an Indian invasion of Pakistan, stem the flow of refugees into Pakistan, and prevent India from taking all of Kashmir by force, insisted that it would withdraw its forces only simultaneously with an Indian withdrawal, denying absolutely the legality of India's claim to Kashmir.[9] This position contradicted both the thrust of the Security Council's resolution of April 21, 1948, and UNCIP's modification of it of August 13, 1948; the former called for the tribesmen to leave before any Indian withdrawals began, having been drafted in ignorance of the Pakistan Army presence, while the latter explicitly required that Pakistan withdraw first because the Pakistani presence was a change in the situation from that which had been represented to the Security Council.[10] The Indian side maintained its position, and an impasse was reached, UNCIP finally deciding that it was unable to resolve the matter.[11] While the United Nations provided an observer force to help maintain the cease-fire,[12] the matter was not brought to any final resolution. As will be seen below, the dispute contributed to further hostilities in 1965.

The facts of this dispute are fairly clear. Pakistan aided an invasion of an area it wished to control, while India—seeking control of the same area—extracted an accession agreement as the price of assistance against the invaders. The presence of Indian troops, in turn, led Pakistan to send in its troops. Both sides claimed self-defense, with Pakistan relying as well on claims of human rights violations to at least mitigate the seriousness of the original invasion, and also claiming it sought only to prevent an Indian conquest based on an illegal accession.

In this case the Security Council's actions seem representative of the views of third states generally, and those actions focused almost entirely on ending the fighting without much emphasis on identifying the wrongdoer. To be sure, the implication of the Security Council's action was that it questioned both states' positions—Pakistan had to withdraw first, while India's claim to Kashmir would have to be tested in a plebiscite—but it made no explicit judgments. Far from imposing sanctions, it urged the combatants to settle the matter, and when they did not, the Council did not seek to impose a solution. It appears that the rest of the world mainly sought to halt hostilities; once that objective was achieved, there was little interest in addressing the underlying dispute, let alone in assessing blame.

## Israel/Arab States (1948–1949)

On February 18, 1947, the United Kingdom, treating the United Nations General Assembly as the successor to the League of Nations for purposes of supervising League of Nations mandates, referred to the General Assembly the question of the disposition of its mandate in Palestine.[13] The assembly had not resolved the matter when the United Kingdom announced in September 1947 that it would complete its withdrawal from Palestine by May 14, 1948.[14] Constrained by the British decision, the General Assembly voted on November 29, 1947, to partition the mandate into two states: one for the Jewish inhabitants and one for the Arabs.[15]

This plan aroused great opposition among Arab states, though the goals of those states conflicted. King Abdullah of Transjordan planned to occupy the areas designated as Arab, as well as some Jewish areas, and then reach a settlement with what was left of the Jewish state.[16] Syria wanted to occupy northern Palestine. The Grand Mufti of Jerusalem, with the support of Syria and Lebanon, sought to establish a Palestinian state, expelling the Jews. And Egypt's main goal was to block King Abdullah.[17] These states, however, shared a mutual hostility toward the proposed Jewish state. They thus agreed in October 1947 to establish a military committee to aid Palestinian Arabs, and in December 1947 they decided to frustrate actively the General Assembly's planned partition by arming, training, and dispatching groups of volunteers to Palestine.[18] Fighting began between Jews and Arabs in November 1947 and by February 1948 had begun to grow more and more serious as more units of Arab volunteers arrived.[19] The Jews for their part evolved a plan to go on the offensive when possible, in order to link Jewish-held areas and take the high ground.[20]

On May 11, 1948, Lebanon, Syria, Iraq, Jordan, and Egypt, though still in disagreement as to ultimate goals, finalized plans to invade the Jewish areas of Palestine on May 15, the day after the formal end of the British mandate. On May 14 the Jewish residents of Palestine proclaimed the existence of their new state, called Israel. The next day the Arab states invaded as they had planned.[21] They justified their intervention as intended to restore order and prevent the spread of fighting to their territories.[22]

The war that followed falls into four chronological periods. Hostilities were halted June 11 when all combatants accepted a truce that the Security Council originally had called for on May 29; under the Council's resolution failure of any party to accept the resolution's terms would lead the Security Council to address the crisis under Chapter VII of the UN Charter, empowering it to compel compliance.[23] Fighting resumed with an Egyptian breach of the truce on July 8, 1948; both sides had earlier rejected a plan put forward by the UN mediator, Count Bernadotte of Sweden, that would have required important territorial concessions from all combatants except Transjordan, which would have gained significantly.[24] The second round of fighting ended July 18, pursuant to the terms of a Security Council resolution of July 15, which provided that failure to accept its terms would be treated as a breach of the peace under Chapter VII of the UN Charter.[25] Israel renewed its attack in the Negev region on October 14, after provoking an Egyptian breach of the truce; this fighting was ended on October 22, pursuant to another Security Council cease-fire mandate.[26] Arab attacks in northern Israel provided a pretext for similar operations in that region.[27] The Security Council subsequently adopted a resolution calling for withdrawals of troops to their positions as of October 14,[28] but Dr. Ralph Bunche, the new mediator, agreed that the resolution would be satisfied by Israeli withdrawal of mobile forces only, while leaving garrisons in place.[29] On December 23, 1948, Israel renewed its attacks on Egyptian troops in the Negev, taking full control of that region and entering Egyptian territory. This latter development triggered an ultimatum from the United Kingdom, which cited its Treaty of Friendship with Egypt and demanded Israeli withdrawal from Egyptian territory. Israel acceded to this demand, but the untenable position of Egypt's troops in the Gaza Strip led Egypt on January 6, 1949, to agree to armistice talks with Israel, pursuant to the Security Council's call for an armistice on November 18, 1948.[30] Armistice agreements with the other combatants, except for Iraq, were concluded during 1949.[31] The net effect of the war was Israeli control, within the armistice lines, of considerably greater territory than had been allotted to it under the original partition plan.[32] The armistice did not, however, end conflicts between Israel and the Arab states.

The part played by third states in this war was varied. The United Kingdom, apparently concerned for its relations with the Arab states,[33] opposed treating the Arab invasion as a breach of the peace requiring the invocation of Chapter

VII of the UN Charter. It stressed the past ineffectiveness of such efforts to invoke the mandatory provisions of the charter. It was joined in this position by Belgium, China, Canada, and Argentina, as well as by Syria and Egypt. An odd coalition of the United States, the Soviet Union, France, Colombia, and the Ukraine unsuccessfully pushed for action under Chapter VII.[34] However, after Israel's October 14 offensive the United Kingdom and China sought to bring their resolution requiring a pullback to pre-October 14 positions under Chapter VII.[35] The Soviet Union and its Ukrainian satellite consistently supported invocation of Chapter VII, apparently equating Arab success with the continuation of Western imperialism in the area.[36] The United States also argued strongly for Israel; however, as noted above, while it sought to invoke mandatory provisions of the United Nations Charter against the Arab states, it never suggested any sort of enforcement action. There is evidence that American reluctance to introduce United Nations forces into this matter reflected its desire to exclude Soviet troops from the Middle East;[37] further, the United States faced domestic political pressure not to use its own troops.[38]

In sum, then, this conflict began with a cross-border invasion of an entity established by the United Nations. The hostilities continued until the invaded party, Israel, had greatly improved its security situation. The Arabs' justification—restoring order—was not generally believed at the time, and certainly not recognized in the UN Charter. And the actual motives of the invaders involved no more than ethnic animosity and a desire for territory. Israel's plea of self-defense was not denied but triggered relatively little support.

Third states were not prepared to act strongly to deal with this situation. The United Kingdom, indeed, took a relatively indulgent attitude toward the Arabs, while other states—though supporting Israel in greater or lesser degrees—provided little concrete assistance. To be sure, the Security Council's resolutions apparently aided in bringing about the various cease-fires, and its representative, Ralph Bunche, made a great contribution toward concluding the eventual armistice.[39] But apparently because of regional interests, in the case of the United Kingdom, and a combination of Cold War politics and a reluctance to use force, in the case of other states, no serious consideration seems to have been given to enforcement of Charter rules with respect to the invasion itself. It should be noted, however, that the United Kingdom *was* apparently willing to use force once the Israelis crossed the well-established boundary between Egypt and Palestine, and that the United States—though issuing no ultimata—backed the British demand for an Israeli withdrawal. There was thus some contrast between reactions to violations of Israel's brand-new borders and violations of Egypt's well-established boundaries.

## Korean War (1950–1953)

In 1945 troops from the United States and the Soviet Union entered the peninsula of Korea to accept the surrender of Japanese troops stationed there and to administer the country. Adopting the 38th parallel as a convenient administrative division, the two powers took responsibility for the southern and northern halves, respectively, of the former Japanese colony.[40] The occupying states originally had planned to work together to establish a provisional government for the whole of the peninsula.[41] As relations between the two occupying powers and between Korean factions in the north and south worsened, it became apparent that the cooperation necessary to establish such a government was not possible.[42] The United States therefore proposed in the UN General Assembly that the United Nations appoint a temporary commission to oversee elections to be conducted throughout the country for the purpose of unifying it. The General Assembly adopted a resolution to that effect on November 14, 1947.[43]

The commission accordingly attempted to carry out its function but was not permitted to enter North Korea. Elections were held May 9, 1948. The commission certified them as valid in those areas in which it had been able to observe them, and a Korean assembly was subsequently formed.[44] This assembly, elected solely from the south, approved a constitution for the Republic of Korea (ROK), which claimed authority over the whole peninsula. In October 1948 the General Assembly recognized the ROK, though not indicating whether its authority was recognized over the whole of the country or over the south only. Its application to join the United Nations was vetoed by the Soviet Union, but it was admitted to other international organizations.[45] Meanwhile, the Communists in the north had proclaimed the existence of the Democratic People's Republic of Korea (DPRK), also claiming the whole of the peninsula. Its application to join the United Nations was also rejected.[46]

The Soviet Union announced that its forces would complete their withdrawal from Korea by December 1948. It aided the DPRK in building powerful armed forces, however, and left an advisory force of three thousand.[47] The United States withdrew its forces, except for its military mission, in mid-1949,[48] leaving behind an ROK military inferior in several respects to that of the DPRK.[49] This imbalance was noteworthy in light of the ruthless and strongly nationalistic characters of the leaders of the two Koreas, Kim Il Sung of the DPRK and Syngman Rhee of the ROK,[50] and more particularly because of the bad relations between the two entities: the DPRK had supported a considerable guerilla force in the south starting in 1948, while at least some border incidents were initiated by ROK forces.[51]

The attitude of the United States toward these developments was ambiguous. The Truman administration had proposed legislation extending various kinds of aid to Korea, and it maintained a military advisory command there to assist in training the ROK armed forces.[52] However, it had also given various indications that it did not attach high priority to the defense of the ROK, most notably in a speech by Secretary of State Dean Acheson on January 12, 1950, indicating that the ROK was outside what the United States considered its "defense perimeter" in the Pacific.[53]

This was the background of the massive invasion of the ROK launched by DPRK forces on June 25, 1950.[54] Although American authorities assumed at the time that the invasion had been ordered by Stalin,[55] and there is reason to believe that the Soviet Union was informed of and approved of Kim's plans,[56] it is entirely possible that the invasion was a DPRK initiative, although undertaken with Soviet acquiescence.[57] Its motive presumably would have been the reunification of Korea.[58] It should be noted that the DPRK stated on June 26 that the ROK had attacked first, but UN observers on the scene utterly rejected that claim, insisting that the DPRK had initiated hostilities.[59]

As noted above, the United States viewed the invasion as a Russian initiative and felt obliged to respond to what it saw as a Cold War probe.[60] Its chosen vehicle was the United Nations. The Soviet Union was at that time boycotting meetings of the Security Council; accordingly, the United States was able to secure Security Council adoption of resolutions on June 25, June 27, and July 7 determining that the DPRK attack was a breach of the peace, recommending that members of the United Nations furnish troops to aid the ROK and that those troops be placed under American command, and requesting the United States to appoint the commander.[61] Of the ten members of the Security Council present, the United States, the United Kingdom, France, the Republic of China, Cuba, Ecuador, and Norway supported each of the resolutions. Egypt and India also supported the June 25 resolutions but abstained on the next two, while Yugoslavia voted against the second resolution and abstained on the other two.[62]

The United Nations effort attracted considerable support; sixteen states eventually contributed combat units, and five others supplied medical support.[63] Other states opposed the action: Czechoslovakia,[64] Poland,[65] Egypt,[66] and most notably the Soviet Union and the PRC. The Soviet Union vigorously attacked the actions of the United States, asserting that the war had been started by the ROK with the support of the United States and condemning the

UN actions as illegal.[67] The PRC had also verbally condemned the American action,[68] but its response went beyond words.

The aid given by United Nations forces had reversed the course of the war; by October the DPRK forces had been forced north of the 38th parallel, and United Nations forces had followed.[69] On October 7, 1950, the General Assembly adopted a resolution calling for the reunification of Korea. This decision was taken, apparently, partly because of the danger of a renewed invasion by the DPRK if operations were halted at the 38th parallel and partly because of an American desire to seize what appeared to be an easy opportunity to eliminate a Communist state.[70] However, as American troops advanced close to the Yalu River, the border between Korea and China, the PRC launched a massive attack that forced United Nations forces to retreat in some disorder to the 38th parallel.[71] The PRC described its troops as volunteers—that is, as not acting under government orders in their Korean operations.[72] In fact, it was the government of the PRC that had chosen to act,[73] for several reasons. First, it saw the American forces in North Korea as a threat to China, possibly the beginnings of an attack on China. Second, it was concerned by the possible demise of another Communist state. Finally, it may have believed that the fallout from its inflicting a defeat upon the United States would advance its own goals.[74]

After the retreat to the 38th parallel the war essentially stabilized. The United States obtained General Assembly condemnation of the PRC in February 1951, but the first indication of a possible halt in the fighting came in June of that year, when the Soviet Union indicated an interest in resolving the conflict peacefully. It appears that the Soviet Union put pressure on the PRC and DPRK to open peace talks in July 1951.[75] The talks took two years to bear fruit, apparently because of the reluctance of the PRC and DPRK to agree to end the fighting. For reasons that remain speculative—possibly including the PRC's desire to focus on domestic questions, the impact of the death of Stalin, changes in the UN negotiating posture, and fear that the newly elected American president Eisenhower would use nuclear weapons against them—the PRC and DPRK finally did agree to an armistice in July 1953.[76]

In summing up the Korean War some facts are fairly clear. The DPRK carried out a cross-border invasion to reunify Korea. Despite knowing the facts, several states, including most important the Soviet Union and the PRC, lent it verbal support, albeit ostensibly on the basis of its clearly false claim of self-defense. Conversely, many other states reacted strongly against the invasion, providing military assistance to the ROK under the rubric of the United Nations and the leadership of the United States. These states, in turn, set out to eliminate the DPRK as an entity and carried this effort to the point that the PRC—at least in part due to fears for its own security—intervened to aid the DPRK.

Several comments about this conflict are in order. First, it resembles a classic cross-border invasion by one state of another. But while it is certainly not implausible to think of the two Koreas as being separate states, given the fact that each possessed the various indicia of statehood, it is important to keep in mind that neither was a long-subsisting, well-established entity. On the contrary, each was a recent creation, taking the form it did due to almost accidental circumstances attending the end of World War II and of Japanese colonialism. Neither had existed for as long as two years. Indeed, neither saw the continued division of the Korean peninsula as legitimate.

It is also striking that important states took opposing positions on the legalities of the matter. To be sure, the public positions of all states were consistent: all claimed to be supporting the victim of an attack, and the difference was simply over deciding which of the Koreas was the victim. However, there was in fact no basis for doubting that the DPRK was the attacker and also good reason for believing that the Soviet Union and the PRC knew the facts, whatever their public statements might be. Therefore, the impression necessarily created for the world was that the Communist great powers were at least verbally supporting a state they knew to have launched an attempt at conquest. It should also be noted that the PRC never acknowledged ordering its troops into Korea, suggesting a reluctance to formally defy the United Nations. Also, its actions have at least some overtones of self-defense. Its persistence in fighting after any threat to its borders was removed, however, raises questions concerning whether its goals were purely defensive.

Assessment of these actions must also take account of the actors' understanding of the way in which other states would view their actions. As noted above, prior to the invasion the United States had indicated in various ways that it would accommodate itself to the eventual demise of the ROK. This American posture has been analyzed by strategic theorists as possibly weakening Soviet incentives to discourage an invasion by suggesting that such an invasion would be relatively costless.[77] These American signals could also be seen as having legal significance, however, in the sense that they suggested that an invasion would not be met with any serious American sanction. As was argued in Chapter 1, a key way for states to identify a legal prohibition is to determine which of their actions is likely to provoke a serious response from third states. American indications that an attack on Korea would not evoke a serious response therefore can be seen as signals that such an attack was something with which the United States could live—that is, not an illegal action. Of course, the signals did not correctly characterize American attitudes toward an invasion of the ROK, but they could nonetheless have been important in any pre-event assessment by the DPRK and the Soviet Union as to whether the United States would consider an invasion intolerable.

The decision of the UN forces under American leadership to, in effect, eradicate the DPRK is also worth comment. To be sure, the DPRK could fairly have been characterized as an aggressor, but even so, its destruction as a state was a fairly extreme goal. It appears that the goal was, to a great extent, ideologically driven. Ideology thus played an important role in the Korean War in the sense that states supported their ideological allies vigorously. At the same time it is important to note that ideology did not completely overwhelm other considerations affecting states' reactions to this conflict. The initial decision to attack may have been affected by American signals that such an attack would not provoke an American response—that is, that the attack would not trigger sanctions. Communist states supported the DPRK but, except for the PRC, did not commit troops. The PRC, further, did not send in troops until it appeared that its own security was threatened. On the United Nations side, states not aligned with the United States provided some aid to the ROK. And the United Nations limited its operations to the Korean peninsula even after the PRC's intervention. In short, ideology played an important role in some states' choices to involve themselves in the Korean fighting, but more neutral factors were not irrelevant.

## Somalia/Ethiopia (1960–1964)

Beginning in 1960 border clashes broke out between Somalia, which became independent in that year, and Ethiopia. The fighting became particularly bad in January 1964. The dispute arose because the Ogaden region of Ethiopia was inhabited by ethnic Somalis, and Somalia argued that these persons should be permitted to vote in a referendum on whether their region should join Somalia or remain part of Ethiopia. The 1964 fighting met with widespread disapproval, the United States and the Soviet Union both urging peace. Neither superpower sought to use its foreign aid as leverage in this regard, however (the United States was providing aid to both states, while the Soviet Union had promised arms for Somalia). Somalia had originally complained of Ethiopia's behavior to the United Nations but withdrew its request for a Security Council meeting to permit the OAU to address the matter. That body called for a cease-fire, and agreement on an end to hostilities was reached March 30, 1964, with Sudanese mediation. Somalia continued to argue, however, that it should not be bound to accept its borders with Ethiopia, dissenting from the OAU's resolution of July 21, 1964, calling on all African states to respect national borders as they existed at independence.[78]

This conflict at this point took the form of a border dispute, though it arose from a Somali claim to much of Ethiopia and from its rejection of the obligations to accept the borders as they stood. Perhaps because it involved only small-scale fighting, the conflict aroused little interest outside Africa. Even in Africa the focus was on mediation to end the fighting rather than on identifying and sanctioning a wrongdoer. The underlying dispute did not, however, end with the agreement of March 1964.

## Somalia/Kenya (1963–1984)

In 1963 fighting broke out between Somalia and Kenya. Somalia had irredentist claims to a portion of northern Kenya inhabited by ethnic Somalis, claims similar to those it had made regarding the Ogaden region of Ethiopia. The low-level fighting continued until halted by a 1967 agreement mediated by President Kaunda of Zambia under the auspices of the OAU. The agreement's ambiguous language did not really resolve the underlying dispute, permitting each side to read it as favoring its own position, but the situation remained calm for ten years.

In 1977, however, more border incidents took place, with Somalia denying its involvement and denying any interest in Kenyan territory while insisting on its right to protect ethnic Somalis living in Kenya. The situation continued to deteriorate into 1980, with Kenya and Ethiopia jointly demanding in December of that year that Somalia accept the borders between the states as they existed and Somalia denouncing the demand. In June 1981, however, bilateral Kenyan-Somali talks began to improve relations, and by 1984 Somalia had closed the office of the so-called Northern District Liberation Front, which had been headquartered in Somalia, and had returned the Front's members to Kenya pursuant to an amnesty. In essence, Somalia abandoned its claim.[79]

Third states apparently took very little interest in this conflict, aside from the OAU mediation of 1967. Again, it will be noted that the reaction to this border fighting by those states who were interested was to press for mediation rather than to sanction either side. And it appears that there was even less third-state interest after 1967, aside from that of Ethiopia, which was essentially a party to the dispute.

## Indonesia/Malaysia (1963–1966)

In September 1963 Indonesia began a campaign of "confrontation" against the newly formed state of Malaysia.[80] Malaysia was created by merging the independent state of Malaya, formerly a British colony, with three other areas that were in 1963 still British colonies: Singapore, Sarawak, and Sabah, the last three all located in northern Borneo, the southern part of which was Indonesian territory. It was planned that the new state would retain links to the United Kingdom; in particular, it was envisioned that the two states would conclude a defense agreement that would permit the British to retain military bases within Malaysia.[81]

By 1963 Indonesia had come to strongly oppose the creation of Malaysia, claiming that it represented simply a new form of colonialism and would perpetuate British dominance of the peoples involved; colonialism was anathema to Indonesia, and the belief that Malaysia's creation would carry forward colonial relationships made Indonesian opposition almost inevitable.[82] Indonesia maintained this position even after a UN team, dispatched by Secretary-General U Thant at the request of Malaya, Indonesia, and the Philippines, had determined that the merging of the various colonies with Malaya to form the new entity was consistent with the wishes of the majority of the population of the affected areas.[83] On September 15, 1963, Indonesia rejected the conclusions of the United Nations and stated that it would withhold diplomatic recognition of Malaysia when it was proclaimed the next day.[84]

Over the next two years Indonesia carried out small-scale military operations against Malaysia. Prior to September 1963 it had provided military training to small groups of inhabitants of the northern Borneo territories who were opposed to the creation of Malaysia; after that date Indonesia began to use its own troops to carry out guerilla operations in northern Borneo.[85] As it became clear that those operations were not likely to be successful, due to the lack of popular opposition to Malaysia in the areas in which the guerillas sought to operate, Indonesia's military focus broadened to include the Malay peninsula. In the late summer and early fall of 1964 Indonesia attempted a number of seaborne and airborne landings on the peninsula, each effort involving relatively small forces that were neutralized fairly quickly.[86]

Small-scale fighting continued until the fall of 1965, when Indonesia began to scale back the confrontation after the failed coup by Indonesian leftists in October 1965 and the ensuing antileftist reaction that ultimately led to President Sukarno's effective loss of power.[87] The new Indonesian regime thought it imperative to end the confrontation so as to regain access to essential foreign aid from Western states, such aid having been greatly reduced since September 1963.[88] Against this background an agreement formally ending the controversy was signed August 16, 1966; all it required of Malaysia, in return for an end to the fighting, was that the decision of the inhabitants of northern Borneo to affiliate with Malaysia be "reaffirmed" in general elections, which condition presumably was satisfied by the holding of the next elections in those areas when they would normally be due.[89]

Throughout this episode Malaysia received a great deal of support from the United Kingdom, whose military forces did most of the fighting.[90] Australia, Canada, and New Zealand also provided military aid.[91] Furthermore, after Indonesian paratroop landings on the Malay peninsula in the fall of 1964, the Security Council voted 9–2 in favor of a Norwegian resolution that would have deplored the landing and called on the parties to respect each other's territorial integrity, the resolution failing adoption because of the veto of the Soviet Union. In the debate prior to the vote Indonesia had argued, essentially, that anticolonialist principles justified its use of force against Malaysia and precluded any obligation on its part to respect the territorial integrity of an entity it considered an extension of colonialism. Only the Soviet Union spoke in favor of the Indonesian position, and only Czechoslovakia joined the Soviet Union in voting against the Norwegian resolution, even Morocco and the Ivory Coast joining the majority.[92]

The Second Conference of Nonaligned Countries, held in Cairo in October 1964, rejected Indonesian efforts to amend resolutions calling for respect for established frontiers and abstention from the use or threat of force against the integrity of other states, thus endorsing a position contrary to that Indonesia was taking toward Malaysia.[93] Aside from these actions, the United States ended significant elements of its foreign aid program to Indonesia in September 1963.[94] France banned arms sales to Indonesia in December 1963 at Malaysia's request.[95] As noted above, the loss of Western aid influenced Indonesia's decision to end its confrontation policy after the change of regime following the events of October 1965.

At the same time Indonesia's policy was supported by the Soviet Union, as shown by Soviet behavior in the Security Council in 1964. The Soviet Union also supplied arms to Indonesia,[96] as did Czechoslovakia.[97] The PRC, too, supported Indonesia.[98] Pakistan declined to take sides.[99] The Netherlands concluded an aid agreement with Indonesia in 1964.[100] Japan stressed "educating" rather than "threatening" Indonesia, fearing that harsh actions would lead to Sukarno's fall and a Communist takeover.[101] Even the United States took a position similar to Japan's, seeing a need to "save President Sukarno from himself and Indonesia from Communism,"[102] and involving itself in an unsuccessful effort to negotiate an end to the crisis. And while American economic aid to Indonesia was greatly reduced after September 1963, it was not eliminated.[103] For that matter, despite characterizing Indonesian behavior as "aggression,"[104] the United Kingdom never attacked Indonesian territory during the conflict and only contemplated that step at the time of the assaults on the Malay peninsula in 1964.[105]

Summing up this conflict points up its unusual character. It involved a small-scale cross-border invasion for vague goals. Indonesia justified its actions entirely on the basis of anticolonialism, essentially rejecting the argument that it was obliged to refrain from the use of force, since Malaysia posed no military threat to it. Several third states aided Malaysia, and others imposed economic sanctions that eventually contributed to a change in Indonesia's policy, albeit only after the government that had launched the confrontation policy had been displaced. At the same time, however, important states supported Indonesia's position and gave it significant help, and even states opposing its actions were reluctant to press it too hard, apparently fearful of alienating its government. International reaction to Indonesia's behavior, then, seems to have been a bit muddled. Steps were taken to oppose it that eventually bore fruit, but one gets the impression that even the states that were sanctioning it were attempting to use kid gloves. States as important as the United States and Japan supported mediatory efforts,[106] apparently seeing preservation of their links with Indonesia as a policy goal comparable in importance to that of blocking its assault on Malaysia rather than as one that had to be put aside in order to stigmatize Indonesia's conduct.

## Armenia/Azerbaijan (1988–?)

In 1923 the government of the Soviet Union detached an Armenian-inhabited region later called Nagorno-Karabakh from Armenia and attached it to Azerbaijan, both Armenia and Azerbaijan being constituent republics of the USSR. Beginning in 1965 the people of Nagorno-Karabakh began to agitate for reunification with Armenia. In 1987, as the regime in the Soviet Union relaxed, inhabitants of Nagorno-Karabakh pressed their claims, supported by Armenia, which was experiencing a nationalist upsurge. Azerbaijan was likewise becoming strongly nationalist, however, and was opposed to any change in the status of the disputed territory. Violence between Armenians and Azeris, centering on possession of Nagorno-Karabakh, began in early 1988. The government of the Soviet Union at first sought to restore order but was unable to do so in the face of the passions on both sides and its own increasing weakness.

After the disintegration of the Soviet Union, Armenia and Azerbaijan both became members of the United Nations and sought mediation from both that body and the Conference on Security and Cooperation in Europe (now the Organization for Security and Cooperation in Europe, OSCE). The Security Council did not become deeply involved, refusing in April 1993 to adopt a Turkish-proposed resolution that would have condemned Armenia for aggression; instead it urged both sides to cease fire and withdraw from captured territory. Its subsequent resolutions demanded an end to hostilities and condemned the occupation of various areas of Azerbaijan, but they neither extended the Council's condemnation to any state or group nor invoked Chapter VII of the Charter. Turkey sought to aid the ethnically related Azeris and provided training for that state's troops. Karabakh declared its independence from Azerbaijan in 1992. Armenia provided Karabakh with large quantities of weapons, including heavy weapons, and there was evidence that Armenian troops became involved in the conflict. In 1994 Russia sought to intervene in a peacekeeping role and was able finally to convince Armenia, Azerbaijan, and Nagorno-Karabakh to agree to a cease-fire in May 1994 at a point at which Azerbaijan had lost control of 20 percent of its territory, including all of Nagorno-Karabakh.[107] The cease-fire was renewed in July of 1994,[108] and has continued in force to the date of this writing, but no settlement of the conflict has been reached, despite diplomatic efforts by the United States, Russia, and the OSCE.[109]

This conflict is a territorial dispute between two states that have only recently ceased to be portions of a larger entity. That larger entity, in turn, played a role in creating the dispute that currently divides the combatants. Third states—except for the principal successor state to the larger entity—have, by and large, sought to avoid involvement in this conflict, offering mediation services or championing one side or the other on the basis of ethnic ties but otherwise standing aloof. The United Nations likewise has not involved itself deeply.

## Wars in Former Yugoslavia (1991–?)

In late June 1991 Slovenia and Croatia, two constituent republics of Yugoslavia, announced their secession from that state. The central government of Yugoslavia, dominated by the Republic of Serbia, refused to acquiesce in that secession and ordered the Yugoslav Army to restore central authority. By late July the army had determined to withdraw from Slovenia, and fighting ceased in that republic. Ethnic Serb inhabitants of Croatia, however, insisted on their right to secede from an independent Croatia and affiliate with Serbia. Very bitter and brutal fighting between Croatian forces, on the one hand, and Croatian Serbs and the Yugoslav Army, on the other, took place until a cease-fire finally took hold in early January 1992. The United Nations thereupon deployed a peacekeeping force to help maintain the cease-fire.[110]

Serbia, which by the end of 1991 had clearly come to dominate what was formerly "Yugoslavia," justified its actions initially by its efforts to preserve the integrity of the state. As it became clear that Yugoslavia would not survive, and as the brutality of the Yugoslav Army's operations in Croatia became clear, Serbia sought to deny what was not seriously in question, that it was actively engaged in the Croatian fighting.[111]

Third states sought to ameliorate the conflict without becoming directly engaged, but as time passed they increased their pressure on Serbia. The European Community dispatched monitors to the war zone to help oversee the evanescent cease-fires. More concretely, the Security Council imposed a mandatory arms embargo on Yugoslavia in September 1991, indicated its willingness to establish a peacekeeping force in appropriate circumstances in December 1991, and established such a force in February 1992.[112] The European Community, the United States, and other states also imposed economic sanctions on Yugoslavia in November 1991, deciding to remove those sanctions from all the Yugoslav republics except Serbia and its ally Montenegro in the following month.[113]

But while the situation in Croatia was stabilizing, that in the neighboring republic of Bosnia-Herzegovina was deteriorating. That republic proclaimed its independence on March 3, 1992, and was admitted to the United Nations on

May 22, 1992. However, the independence proclamation had been based on the results of a referendum boycotted by ethnic Serbs, who declared later in March 1992 the existence of their own "Serbian Republic of Bosnia-Herzegovina" and their desire to affiliate with Serbia. Fighting between Bosnian Serbs, supported by the Yugoslav Army, and the primarily Muslim supporters of the government of the new republic became intense. After May 1992 Serbia sought to deny that its troops were involved in the fighting and claimed that it had ended all support for the Bosnian Serbs in August 1994. However, these assertions were treated skeptically by observers, who saw the conflict as a manifestation of an aggressively nationalist Serbia seeking to include within its borders as much territory as possible. Indeed, there were reports of significant Serbian help reaching the Bosnian Serbs as late as June 1995. Thus assisted by Serbia, the Bosnian Serbs enjoyed considerable military success; by the end of 1994 they controlled approximately 70 percent of the territory of Bosnia-Herzegovina.[114] In the late summer and early fall of 1995 this situation changed. Initially, Croatian government forces broke the cease-fire in that state, driving the Croatian Serb military from positions it had occupied in western Croatia since 1992. The Croatian advance continued into Bosnia-Herzegovina; the joint effort of the Croatian forces and of the troops of the government of Bosnia-Herzegovina drove Bosnian Serb forces from large portions of the territory they had occupied with Bosnia-Herzegovina, reducing the proportion of Bosnia-Herzegovina controlled by the Bosnian Serbs to about 49 percent.[115]

Third-state reaction to the carnage in Bosnia-Herzegovina was, in one sense, vigorous. The Security Council imposed mandatory economic sanctions on Serbia on May 30, 1992, and continued to increase the pressure, imposing still more stringent sanctions on April 17, 1993. It repeatedly condemned Serbian violations of humanitarian law in Bosnia-Herzegovina and established an international tribunal to prosecute violations of that law. It also authorized UN forces in Bosnia-Herzegovina to oversee deliveries of relief supplies and forbade the flight of fixed-wing aircraft over that state, authorizing armed enforcement of this prohibition.[116] Threats of air strikes by NATO in early 1994 forced Bosnian Serb forces to end their bombardments of Sarajevo and Gorazde and withdraw their heavy weapons from the vicinities of those towns.[117] After the Bosnian Serbs had renewed the shelling of Sarajevo in the summer of 1995, actual air strikes by NATO and artillery bombardment by units under United Nations command induced the Bosnian Serbs to pull their heavy weapons back from Sarajevo and to end their blockade of that city.[118]

In addition, however, the United Nations, the European states, and the

United States consistently supported peace plans that effectively required Bosnia-Herzegovina to sharply alter its internal structure, with a weakened central government and a high degree of autonomy for the areas controlled by the Bosnian Serbs. Thus, in 1993 Bosnia-Herzegovina was urged by mediators from the United Nations and the European Community to accept a peace plan that would turn it into a confederation of Serbian, Croatian, and Muslim entities joined by a very weak central government.[119] In 1994 the United States, Russia, the United Kingdom, France, and Germany proposed a plan under which only 51 percent of Bosnia-Herzegovina would be subject to the direct control of the government of Bosnia-Herzegovina; the remaining 49 percent would fall under the authority of the Bosnian Serbs, who would exercise a high degree of autonomy.[120] The Security Council not only supported this plan but imposed sanctions on the Bosnian Serbs when they refused to accept it.[121] In 1995, after the Croatian/Bosnia-Herzegovinan military successes and the NATO/UN air strikes and artillery bombardments described above, the parties to the conflict finally accepted in principle a resolution of the conflict generally adhering to the 1994 proposal.[122] This was followed by a cease-fire on October 12, 1995,[123] and the formal conclusion of peace accords on November 21, 1995.[124] In response to these developments the United Nations Security Council suspended its sanctions against Serbia in November 1995,[125] and also suspended sanctions against the Bosnian Serbs in February 1996, upon their compliance with the initial requirements of the peace accords.[126]

In short, because of the success of the Bosnian Serbs, supported to at least some extent by Serbia, in using force in circumstances the Security Council had condemned, the United Nations, the United States, and the leading states of Europe came to support a peace plan under which Bosnia-Herzegovina was obliged to acquiesce in the loss of full sovereignty over a portion of its territory. Except for the NATO ultimata and uses of force that brought about an end to the bombardments described above, neither the Security Council nor individual states, other than Croatia, were willing to use force against either Bosnian Serb forces or the Serbian military.[127] Indeed, it is interesting that the International Tribunal that the Security Council has established is empowered only to hear cases involving violations of humanitarian law; it has no authority to hear cases involving crimes against peace.[128]

The Croatia and Bosnia-Herzegovina conflicts developed from the dissolution of the multinational state of Yugoslavia. Whether they are seen as international wars because of the formal status of the combatants, or as civil wars between parts of the former Yugoslavia, or as civil wars between groups within Croatia and Bosnia-Herzegovina, they arose in circumstances similar to the other episodes described in this chapter. Third states responded with condemnations of violence, with arms embargoes intended to limit the fighting, with mediation assistance and humanitarian aid, with stringent economic sanctions for Serbia, and with threats of and, on one occasion, the actual use of force to end particularly brutal attacks on populated areas. This approach in the case of the Croatian fighting facilitated a cease-fire. In the case of Bosnia-Herzegovina it appears to have led to the effective partition of that state in an arrangement formulated by powerful states and endorsed by the United Nations. The United Nations and several of its leading members, that is, are essentially urging surrender on a member state victimized by a use of force arguably violative of the Charter. The members of the United Nations have not, to be sure, simply acquiesced in this development. But in the final analysis states not parties to the conflict have been willing to threaten and use force only to limit violence. They have been unwilling to go beyond economic sanctions to protect the territorial integrity of a state whose existence within the borders it claims has been a matter of violent controversy with its neighbors from the moment it proclaimed its independence.

## Analysis

The eight conflicts discussed in this chapter share only one characteristic: all arose from the disorder and disagreement that accompanied what could be called the breakup of empires, either through the attainment of independence by colonies or mandated territories, or through the disintegration of multinational states. They differ, however, in their timing relative to the breakups that produced them. The war between the Koreas and the clashes between Somalia and its neighbors followed by several years the end of their colonial status. The other five conflicts began either at the time of the breakups in question or relatively shortly thereafter. These conflicts also differ in their level of violence. Only low-level fighting was involved in the Somali-inspired episodes discussed in this chapter and in the Indonesia-Malaysia "confrontation." The other five uses of force, in contrast, were full-scale wars.

Despite these differences, third states have reacted to postimperial conflicts—except for the Korean War—in remarkably similar ways. With respect to the fighting in the Middle East, Kashmir, the Caucasus, and East Africa, the international community appeared uninterested in identifying an aggressor and applying sanctions accordingly. Rather, third states responded to these conflicts by trying to convince the parties to stop fighting. In the Indonesia-Malaysia matter third states applied economic sanctions against Indonesia and provided defensive assistance to Malaysia. However, severe sanctions were not applied, and even states applying sanctions clearly saw negotiation as the preferred method of ending the conflict. Similarly, in the former Yugoslavia the dominant approach by third states has been to try to bring about agreements among the combatants. More stringent economic sanctions have been applied in this conflict than in those discussed above, and force has been threatened to protect civilian populations, but third-state force was actually used to protect civilians on one occasion only, and the prime focus has been on mediation.

These reactions are significant for two reasons. First, it was clear in most of these cases which state or states had first used force. Second, the last two incidents described in this chapter have coincided with the end of the Cold War. The failure of third states to respond to these situations with force, therefore, cannot be said to reflect factual confusion; nor does it seem attributable to some Cold War–related ineffectiveness of the Security Council, given the similarity in reactions before and after the end of that competition. Nonetheless, in these seven cases third-state reaction has focused on ending the fighting rather than on sanctioning a wrongdoer.

Continuing to leave Korea aside for the moment, one might ask why this is so. Even if the East African problems are dismissed as too small scale to justify a strong reaction, the same cannot be said of the other five conflicts. I would suggest, however, that this reluctance to treat the initiation of these wars as simple rule violations reflects the fact that none of these uses of force can fairly be characterized as challenging a previously stable status quo. The Somali actions were too small to be true threats to their neighbors, while the other five serious wars erupted at a time of fundamental change in the regions in which they took place. In essence, the attackers in these wars challenged the legitimacy of entities whose right to exist or to claim disputed territory was not fortified by time. In each case, of course, the victims of the attacks were formally full-fledged members of the international community, entitled to all the rights of established states. In practice, however, the states of the world have simply not been willing to demand the same respect for brand-new entities as they do for long-subsisting governments. Certainly, there is a striking contrast between third-state reactions in the cases discussed in this chapter and the reactions to the wars examined in Chapter 2. The uses of force in Chapter 2, however, each involved a clear and serious challenge to a stable status quo; those in this chapter did not.

I believe this distinction helps explain the international reaction to the

Korean War. To be sure, that reaction was in part ideological, as the United States felt compelled to respond to what it perceived as a challenge from Stalin. But it should also be noted that, unlike the other very violent conflicts discussed in this chapter, the Korean War did not break out very shortly after the combatants ceased to be colonies. On the contrary, the Republic of Korea had been in existence for nearly two years before it was attacked. That is, a stable status quo had begun to emerge in the Korean peninsula at the time of the attack by the DPRK. I would suggest that the fact of the ROK's relatively established character increased the ideological stakes for the United States and led to a reaction different from that which would have taken place if an attack had come prior to the ROK's demonstration of its relative solidity. Conversely, the willingness of the Soviet Union to acquiesce in the attack arguably reflected that state's assumption that the United States did *not* see the situation in the Korean peninsula as stable but rather as one that was still in flux, providing no status quo to defend.

In short, the contrasting international reactions to the wars described in Chapter 2 and those discussed in this chapter suggest that an important determinant of the response to a use of force is the extent to which that use of force can be seen as upsetting a previously stable situation. Leaving aside anticolonial wars, which trigger the self-determination principle, it appears that the less stable the international status quo challenged by a resort to arms, the more likely states are to forgo efforts to identify and sanction a lawbreaker, preferring instead to urge the combatants to come to an agreement. That is, where force is used in an unstable situation, third states will seek to bring the disputants to the point of creating a basis for stability rather than insisting unequivocally on the nonuse of force. The remaining chapters of this book will lend support to this proposition.

CHAPTER 5

# Continuation Wars

Not all wars result in the resolution of the disputes that give rise to them. International hostilities have often been terminated by agreements focused primarily on ending bloodshed. Some such agreements also attempt to address the problems underlying the fighting but do so by means that fail to satisfy the goals of some or all of the combatants while leaving them with the means to undermine the agreements in order to attain their goals. Not surprisingly, such agreements sometimes break down, giving rise to second and third rounds of fighting in what can be seen as wars continuing the original hostilities. This chapter examines such continuation wars. Each of the conflicts it discusses involves either an invasion or a civil war but differs from the wars described in Chapter 2 and Chapter 6 in that it carries forward an earlier use of force. All the wars described in this chapter can be considered as resumptions of one of the wars discussed either in Chapter 3 or in Chapter 4.

# United States, Republic of Vietnam/Democratic Republic of Vietnam (1961–1975)

It is somewhat arbitrary to date the Second Indochina War from 1961, given its links to the First Indochina War. However, actions that would define the character of the war were taken by both sides in 1961, and that year therefore seems a reasonable starting point for this discussion.

Necessarily, however, the story of the war begins earlier. As noted in Chapter 3, the First Indochina War had ended with the Geneva Accords of 1954, which divided Vietnam into two zones, the northern under the administration of the Communist side and known as the Democratic Republic of Vietnam (DRV), and the southern under the successor government to the French-established State of Vietnam. According to the agreement, each side was to "regroup" its partisans in its zone and elections were to be held in 1956 to resolve the question of unification of the country. However, in 1955 the government in the southern zone refused to consult with the DRV regarding the 1956 elections, and in October of 1955 it promulgated a constitution establishing itself as the Republic of Vietnam (ROV).[1] Both the Soviet Union and the PRC acquiesced in this result;[2] indeed, the Soviet Union deleted the discussion of Indochina from the 1955 Geneva foreign ministers' meeting and proposed in 1957 that both the DRV and ROV be admitted to the United Nations.[3] The DRV was thus left alone with its goal of reunification of the two zones of Vietnam.[4]

Although between 5,000 and 10,000 of the 90–100,000 Viet Minh troops who had fought in the south had been left there even after the regroupments of 1954, the Vietnam Workers' Party (VWP), as the Communist Party ruling the DRV was called, resolved at first to limit its efforts toward reunification to political action.[5] By 1959, however, the ROV government's efforts at repression had been successful enough to jeopardize greatly the position of VWP cadres in the south. In that year the party elected to allow limited armed action by its members and established military units in the DRV and in Laos to facilitate infiltration into the ROV.[6] A number of armed attacks took place in 1960, with the VWP guerillas enjoying considerable success.[7] In 1960 the VWP established the National Liberation Front of South Vietnam (NLF),[8] a group that—despite propaganda to the contrary—was controlled by the VWP from its founding.[9] In the following year the People's Liberation Armed Forces (PLAF) was founded to coordinate the activities of the various armed groups that southern party units had established.[10]

Two points should be made at this juncture. First, significant numbers of the PLAF's troops were southerners who had gone north after 1954 and were returned to the south by the VWP after its decision to revive armed struggle; a majority, however, were locally recruited.[11] Second, while there is no question that there was significant opposition to the rule of the ROV's President Diem that contributed greatly to the success of the PLAF, it is equally clear that the struggle was not a simple upwelling of resentment at Diem's oppression, real though it was, but rather was throughout controlled by the directives of the VWP.[12] This point is of some importance, since during the Vietnam War it was argued by some that the NLF should be seen as an organization independent of the DRV, which it apparently was not.[13]

The results of the VWP's decision to resort to armed force were, from its perspective, positive; by late 1961 the situation of the Diem government was very bad.[14] This situation in turn raised a dilemma for the United States, which had provided military aid and training to the ROV since 1955 and had ensured, when establishing SEATO, that the ROV could request that alliance's aid even though it was not a member.[15] But in 1961 the United States was forced to decide whether and how to respond to the very real threat facing the Republic of Vietnam.

The Kennedy administration felt compelled to respond by "containing" what it saw as a new challenge launched by monolithic Communism.[16] Accordingly, President Kennedy—in a letter to Diem in December 1961—promised increased American support; this support took the form of increased troop deployments, American strength in the ROV growing from about 800 in early 1961 to about 11,000 by late 1962, the troops being training, support, and logistics personnel rather than combat units.[17] This increased level of American troops in the ROV greatly exceeded the limits on foreign troops set by the 1954 Geneva agreements; the United States sought to justify its action by pointing to the infiltration of troops and equipment from the DRV discussed above, arguing that this amounted to a breach of the Geneva Accords by the DRV.[18] The DRV responded by insisting that it played no role in the fighting in the ROV, a position it was to maintain until after its final victory in 1975;[19] however, the International Control Commission—the tripartite Indian, Canadian, and Polish body established by the 1954 accords—determined in June 1962 that infiltration from the DRV was, in fact, taking place.[20] (This 1961 American decision to greatly increase U.S. troop strength in the ROV clearly internationalized the war and is thus a convenient point from which to date the beginning of its indisputably interstate aspect.)

Until August 1964 the war continued to follow the pattern established in late

1961, that is, gradually increasing numbers of American troops sought to undergird a largely ROV counterinsurgency effort while the Communist insurgents increased in strength and effectiveness.[21] The United States encouraged a military coup that overthrew Diem in November 1963, the Americans believing the war unwinnable while Diem remained in power. However, his ouster was followed by a rapid succession of governments in Saigon, and the ROV's situation continued to decline.[22] In August 1964 the United States first engaged in overt combat, as opposed to support of ROV combat operations, when planes from American aircraft carriers attacked DRV naval installations in retaliation for the second of two attacks reportedly delivered against two American destroyers operating in the South China Sea very close to DRV territorial waters.[23] It was shortly after this incident, and before the end of 1964, that regular units of the People's Army of Vietnam (PAVN), as the army of the DRV was called, began to infiltrate into the ROV.[24] Early in 1965 the Communist command structure in the ROV was strengthened by the dispatch of officers of higher rank than those formerly in charge; the new arrivals were often northerners and their predecessors southerners, but this change reflected a need for officers that could not be met solely from the pool of those with experience in the south, not a change in command of what had always been a struggle controlled by the VWP.[25]

In the following year the United States elected to take a more active role in the war. In February it began a campaign of aerial bombardment of the DRV, initially in retaliation for particular attacks on U.S. personnel and by March as part of a campaign of pressure on the DRV.[26] The objectives of this campaign were to demoralize the DRV, to interfere with its ability to infiltrate troops and supplies into the ROV, and to induce the DRV to negotiate on terms acceptable to the United States, those terms requiring the DRV to agree to cease its war against the ROV as a condition for a halt to the bombing.[27] The aim of the campaign was not to destroy the DRV; on the contrary, the United States took pains to avoid steps that could be seen as threatening its survival, believing that the Soviet Union and the PRC would be unlikely to intervene so long as the fate of the DRV itself was not at stake.[28]

At the time the American bombing campaign began, the United States had approximately 27,000 military personnel in the ROV; in April 1965, however, the United States concluded that the military situation was so bad that the war could not be won without American ground combat units. The mission of the units first deployed was ostensibly the protection of American air bases; even those units, however, were authorized to patrol aggressively in the vicinity of the areas in which they were posted. In July President Lyndon B. Johnson decided to dispatch larger numbers of American troops whose mission went beyond defense.[29]

Over the next three years the war fell into a pattern. More American troops were sent, and they achieved some battlefield successes, to the point that American officials made optimistic public statements. However, the ROV made little progress in strengthening its political position among the population and its military became increasingly dependent on American support. The Communist side suffered severe casualties but continued to be able to conduct offensive operations and to avoid combat when necessary; its political organization in the ROV remained intact.[30]

This situation was changed by the offensive launched on January 31, 1968—New Year's Day in Vietnam—called Tet. The Communists, relying mainly on PLAF troops, launched massive attacks throughout the ROV, concentrating on urban areas. Their maximum objective was to provoke uprisings against the ROV government, forcing the downfall of President Thieu's administration and its replacement by a coalition government that would not be a satisfactory partner for the United States, forcing an American withdrawal. Failing that result, it was hoped that the United States would perceive the war as a stalemate and abandon its hopes of victory.[31]

The Tet offensive failed in its battlefield objectives; the Communist forces were unable to hold any of the urban areas they had initially seized and suffered very heavy casualties.[32] Nonetheless, Tet began the process that eventually led to the withdrawal of the United States. The Communists' ability to launch so massive an attack made a deep impression on many Americans, especially because statements on the war by American officials in the months preceding Tet had painted a very gloomy picture of the Communists' situation. Particularly when it became known that after Tet the American command in Vietnam had sought a 40 percent increase in American troop strength in Vietnam, opposition to the war began to be heard in the United States from quarters previously supportive of government policy.[33] In light of these circumstances, on March 31 President Johnson announced both his decision not to seek reelection[34] and a temporary halt to American bombing of the DRV north of 20°.[35] The DRV agreed to talks on a complete bombing halt on April 3.[36] Preliminary peace talks began in Paris in May 1968 between the United States and the DRV; after indications from the DRV that a complete bombing halt could lead to productive talks, Johnson halted all bombing of the DRV on October 31, 1968.[37] Full peace talks, involving the ROV and the NLF as well as the United States and the DRV, began in Paris in January 1969.[38]

In 1969 Richard Nixon assumed the presidency of the United States.

Initially, Nixon took the position that any end to the war must recognize the independence of the ROV, carrying forward Johnson's views on this subject. Accordingly, Nixon's first negotiating position called for withdrawals by all foreign troops, meaning troops of both the United States and the DRV. The DRV, however, had consistently insisted that all Vietnam was one state and that the ROV therefore had no claim to an independent existence.[39] In addition to determining his position in the Paris talks, Nixon announced a change in strategy on May 14, 1969; he stated that from that time U.S. forces would gradually be withdrawn, in line with the American view that all non-ROV forces should leave South Vietnam.[40]

Over the next four years fighting continued, although the American role in ground combat diminished steadily. Negotiations also continued, both publicly and secretly. In May 1972 the United States abandoned its demand that DRV troops be withdrawn from the ROV as part of any settlement. The DRV did not seize on this concession, as its troops had launched a major offensive earlier that year and seemed on the verge of victory; the offensive failed, however, in the face of massive American air attacks on Communist troops in the ROV and due to a renewal of the American bombing of the DRV. By October a deal had been reached, the DRV abandoning its demand for changes in the makeup of the government of the ROV, the agreement calling only for consultations among the Vietnamese regarding the future of the ROV.[41] President Thieu of the ROV, however, objected to the proposed agreement. It required him to consult with the NLF—now called the Provisional Revolutionary Government (PRG)—while the PAVN remained in the ROV, affirmed the unity of Vietnam, and recognized Communist political rights in the ROV; all these aspects of the agreement challenged the legitimacy of Thieu's government. The United States therefore reopened the apparently closed deal, raising doubts as to its reliability in the DRV and inducing the DRV in turn to make new demands. The peace talks broke off on December 13. President Nixon sought to break the logjam by intensive bombing of the Hanoi area in the latter half of December, which was intended both to pressure the DRV and to reassure Thieu of American support. He also threatened Thieu with a complete loss of American aid if he did not abandon his objectives. In January 1973 an agreement was reached little different from that of October. A standstill cease-fire went into effect on January 27, 1973, and the last American troops left the ROV on March 29.[42]

The war, of course, was not yet over, since all the Vietnamese combatants remained in the field. Fighting was relatively limited for the rest of 1973, as both sides jockeyed for position. But Thieu refused to implement the political elements of the peace agreement, and the DRV used this refusal as a pretext to abandon the agreement itself. Fighting intensified in 1974, and a Communist offensive in 1975 had greater success than anticipated, forcing the surrender of the Saigon government on April 30. The only American response to that last offensive was an effort by President Gerald Ford's administration to send increased quantities of war matériel to the ROV; American forces took no part in the last campaign.[43]

The positions taken by the two principal combatants in the Vietnam War were remarkably stable. As noted above, the DRV, although dishonestly denying its control of the Communist forces fighting in the ROV, consistently took the position that Vietnam was a single juridical entity and that the ROV was therefore not entitled to maintain its independence. The United States, in contrast, argued that the ROV was entitled to maintain its independence and thus to defend itself from attacks that, the United States insisted, were controlled by the DRV.[44] The motives of the two states essentially tracked their justifications. The DRV sought to reunify Vietnam. The United States sought to defend the independence of the ROV, impelled, to be sure, by a desire to contain Communism. Neither state sought to rely on international mechanisms to end the war. Neither state seriously tried to use the United Nations as a vehicle for negotiation. A reconvened Geneva Conference could perhaps have substituted for the United Nations; however, a British proposal to that effect to the Soviet Union (the two were cochairs of the conference) drew from the Soviets in March 1965 a reply in effect calling for the two states simply to endorse the DRV's position, thus torpedoing the idea.[45] Given the unlikelihood that the Soviet Union would have taken that position without some contact with the DRV, it seems likely that, at that time at least, the DRV was not seriously seeking to use the conference as a vehicle to end the war.

Third-state reactions to the war did not reflect unequivocal acceptance of the rules of the United Nations Charter; such a reaction would have led states to more strongly support the ROV, since it was the object of a use of force by the DRV aimed at destroying the ROV's political independence. Neither were those reactions governed purely by states' ideological affinities, however. Rather, they demonstrated both a general aversion to violence and a general uneasiness with opposition to a use of force with anticolonial overtones.

Since the ROV had a relatively high degree of international standing—it was recognized by about sixty states and a member of several of the UN specialized agencies[46]—simple acceptance of the Charter's rules would have led to treating it as an entity entitled to the protections of Article 2(4). This is not what happened. To be sure, the ROV received a high degree of international support beyond the aid it received from the United States; Australia, New Zealand, the ROK, and Thailand all committed combat troops in the war and suffered casualties.[47] Thirty-five other states sent other sorts of aid.[48] And, initially at least, the United States' closest allies, except for France, supported its position.[49] Even given this degree of support for the ROV, however, the international reaction to its situation can be seen as somewhat tepid.

For example, the role of the United Nations in the conflict has been described as "intermittent and marginal."[50] While the opposition of the Soviet Union and France to UN involvement necessarily precluded any action by the Security Council,[51] the General Assembly could, in theory, have acted. It did not. Further, while speakers in the General Assembly frequently addressed the subject, their views were by no means unified. On the contrary, when the subject came up during the period after the United States had begun its bombing campaign, many speakers took the position of Secretary-General U Thant, that the war should be ended by negotiations between the parties and that an end to the American bombing of the DRV—a precondition of the DRV for any negotiations.[52]—should be the first step toward bringing those negotiations about.[53] Others generally supported the idea of negotiations, though not accepting the secretary-general's formula.[54] Outside the United Nations many states were simply indifferent to the war, while the Communist states and some non-Communist states were strongly opposed to the American position; even some of the closest allies of the United States expressed misgivings about its efforts in the ROV.[55] Many states during the course of the war echoed generally the call of U Thant for a negotiated solution. Taken together, these reactions hardly represent strong support for the ROV's rights under any customary law equivalent to Article 2(4).

How can this reaction be explained? It is not a question of ideology. Ideology was not irrelevant to the war, of course, but it did not completely determine the reactions even of the leaders of the blocs. Thus, while aid from the Soviet Union and the PRC was clearly vital to the DRV's war effort,[56] and both those states were very critical of American policy, neither was willing to carry its support for the DRV too far. For example, both carried through on planned important diplomatic contacts with the United States in the spring of 1972, despite the renewal of American bombing of the DRV at that time.[57] Similarly, the United States refrained from destroying the DRV, albeit at least in part to avoid provoking a response from the Soviet Union and the PRC.

The background of the war is more important than ideology in explaining an international reaction that, over time, came to focus more on stopping the fighting than on the issues at stake in the war.[58] First, the war took place at a time when the legitimacy of wars against European colonialism was becoming increasingly accepted by most states. Of course, the ROV was not a colony, but the history of its creation, its increasing dependence on the United States as the war continued, and the frequently reported indifference or hostility of its people to its government surely contributed to doubts as to whether its establishment could be said to reflect its people's rights to self-determination. Further, the obvious links between the beginnings of the Second Indochina War and the failure to implement the 1954 Geneva Accords presumably made it easier to see the second war as a continuation of the first, and thus vested with whatever legitimacy the first war's clearly anticolonial character may have given it. In addition to the influence of the self-determination concept, the traditional relationship between the parts of Vietnam, reinforced by the 1954 accords' assumption of the unity of the country, may also have made it difficult for many states to agree wholeheartedly with the American position that the efforts of the DRV to unify Vietnam were to be equated with a Hitler-style foreign invasion. And of course some states professed to doubt the degree of DRV control over the Communist side in the war; to the extent that the war could be portrayed as purely a civil war among the people of the ROV, American claims of DRV aggression rang still more hollow. Again, some of the reaction was likely a function of the relatively graphic reporting of the great violence of the war.

In summary, then, the Second Indochina War was an effort by the DRV to complete its effort to create a united, Communist Vietnam. The United States, arguing that the ROV had the right to defend its independence and inclined by ideology to aid that defense, opposed the DRV, eventually taking control of the war from the ROV. The DRV was aided by other Communist states; the ROV and the United States likewise received considerable international aid. Third states confronting this situation faced a problem: while the ROV, an entity that met all traditional criteria of statehood, appeared to be facing an attack, its juridical status was uncertain, and the attack it was facing not only resembled an anticolonial struggle in important respects but was fairly obviously a continuation of an unambiguous colonial war. In these circumstances the international community as a whole took no firm position on the war beyond making frequent ineffectual calls for negotiations, apparently on the assumption that any outcome of the negotiations was acceptable, provided that it ended the war. American participation in the war ended because of the absence of battlefield success and the growth of American popular dislike for the war; international institutions and legal rules seemed to have had little to do with the ultimate outcome. The final victory of the DRV was achieved through battlefield success, against a background of international indifference.

## Turkey/Cyprus (1963–1967)

On December 3, 1963, Archbishop Makarios, president of Cyprus and leader of its Greek Cypriot community, announced a proposal to revise the Cyprus Constitution so as to effectively eliminate provisions designed to give special protections to the island's Turkish minority.[59] The constitution was part of a package of legal arrangements created in 1960 in an effort to resolve the problems created by the 1955–59 Greek Cypriot insurrection against the United Kingdom's colonial rule. Another element of the package was the Treaty of Guarantee between the United Kingdom, Cyprus, Greece, and Turkey. Under this treaty Cyprus promised to ensure respect for its constitution, and the three other parties guaranteed the "state of affairs" established by, among other things, the constitutional provisions that President Makarios proposed to change; further, the treaty provided that, if it was breached, each of the guarantor powers reserved the right to act unilaterally to "restore the state of affairs" established by the treaty if common action proved impossible.[60]

A few days after Makarios's announcement fighting broke out between members of the Greek and Turkish Cypriot communities.[61] Several attempts to resolve the matter over the next few months proved ineffectual.[62] Finally, on March 4, 1964, the Security Council recommended the establishment of a United Nations peacekeeping force on Cyprus; that force began to assemble and to take up its duties within a few months.[63] Prior to the arrival of the UN peacekeepers, however, Turkey had, on March 12, threatened to use force to protect the Turkish Cypriots from massacre, relying on the Treaty of Guarantee as a basis for its action.[64] In response, Secretary-General U Thant stated the next day that the peacekeeping troops would be in place soon, and the Security Council unanimously called on all states to refrain from action likely to worsen the situation in Cyprus;[65] Turkey backed down.[66] Again in June Turkey began serious planning to invade Cyprus, motivated by continuing persecution of Turkish Cypriots.[67] The United States, in response, strongly pressured Turkey not to invade; President Johnson, in a letter to Turkish Prime Minister Ismet Inönü, stressed the illegality of an invasion (though not, apparently, arguing that nondefensive uses of force are per se illegal) and threatened a cessation of military aid if an invasion took place.[68] The United States also moved naval units into the area between Turkey and Cyprus.[69] Again Turkey backed down.[70]

At this time, however, Cyprus asked Greece to send troops to help it deal with the anticipated Turkish invasion. Greece agreed, putting the troops under the command of General Grivas, who had led the terrorist group EOKA in its campaign against British rule in Cyprus.[71] Greece took this step despite the fact that it was illegal under the 1960 treaties, which permitted Greece to station on Cyprus no more than the 950 troops already there in June 1964.[72]

Grivas considered himself answerable only to Greek military authorities, not to those of Cyprus, but he quickly took command of the Cypriot national guard, the officers and senior noncommissioned officers of which were in any case seconded from the Greek army.[73] Greek and Greek Cypriot forces then began a campaign of economic blockade against Turkish Cypriot areas of the island. This culminated, in early August, in military operations against a Turkish Cypriot enclave on the northwestern coast, in violation of a promise by Makarios to the commander of UN forces. A unit of those forces in the area was unable to establish a cease-fire and removed itself to avoid getting caught up in the fighting. Apparently seeing no other means of protecting the enclave, Turkish aircraft bombed Greek and Greek Cypriot positions on August 7 and 8, killing civilians as well as military personnel; it characterized its actions as being taken in self-defense.[74] It also relied on the Treaty of Guarantee.[75]

Cyprus took the matter to the Security Council, the president of which, on August 9, appealed to Turkey to end its bombing and to Cyprus to direct its troops to cease firing. On the same day the Council approved an American resolution calling for a cease-fire and calling on all states to refrain from action that might exacerbate the situation.[76] Both sides accepted the cease-fire.[77]

The situation on the island, however, did not improve markedly; on the contrary, tension and violence, albeit at a low level, continued for the next three years.[78] More organized violence recurred on November 15, 1967, when the Cypriot National Guard, after carefully planning an attack on a Turkish Cypriot village, provoked the Turkish Cypriots within the village into firing at a police patrol and then took advantage of that pretext to execute their attack.[79] Objections by UN forces to the dispatch of the police patrol were ignored, and those forces were themselves put in jeopardy by the National Guard.[80] A cease-fire was finally established on November 16, after the village had been overrun.[81]

Turkey responded to this situation by delivering an ultimatum to Greece on November 17, threatening to invade Cyprus if the ultimatum was not satisfied and also to invade Greece if Greece resisted the invasion of Cyprus. The most important of Turkey's demands was for the withdrawal of Grivas and the Greek troops stationed on the island in violation of the 1960 treaties.[82] This ultimatum quickly led to intense diplomatic activity, though this time the target appeared to be Greece more than Turkey, even though it was Turkey that was threatening to use force. Thus, it became clear that the United States and other NATO states would not block any use of force by Turkey.[83] Greece was particularly vulnerable to American pressure, since the military coup in that state the preceding April had led to Greece's diplomatic isolation.[84] The debate in the Security Council produced generalized calls to maintain the peace, with even the Soviet Union directing its remarks more against the military regime in Greece than against Turkey.[85] Greece and Cyprus finally agreed to the troop withdrawals in early December, Grivas having been withdrawn earlier, after appeals from the secretary-general. These appeals had been arranged by Turkey and Greece to provide the Greek government with a face-saving basis for accepting Turkey's demands.[86]

The international reaction to the events in Cyprus over this four-year period is worthy of study. First, the idea of dealing with the situation by using a peacekeeping force attracted a great deal of support; in 1964, for example, nine states sent troops or police contingents to the UN force on Cyprus, and twenty-five others made financial contributions to that operation.[87]

Second, the reactions to the 1964 threats of force by Turkey were rather harsher than those occurring after its actual use of force. The United States made sharp threats when Turkey threatened invasion in June 1964, and even interposed its navy between Turkey and Cyprus. After the Turkish bombing in August, however, no sanctions were imposed on Turkey, and while a small number of states promised support for the Greek Cypriots,[88] or ended military aid to Greece and Turkey,[89] others stressed their neutrality.[90]

Finally, the international reaction to the events of 1967 reinforces the impression that there was little interest in confronting Turkey on this issue. Thus, the response to a Turkish invasion threat was not support for Greece and Cyprus but rather international diplomatic activity that conveyed to Greece that it would have to face Turkey alone if Turkey carried out its threat. Indeed, Turkey gained from the episode two of its most important demands: the removal of Grivas and Greece's troops from the island.

This international reaction is especially significant because the Turkish invasion ultimatum cannot accurately be characterized as essentially defensive. While it is true that carefully planned actions by troops under Greek command had led to the crisis, the incident that had triggered the ultimatum was over by the time the ultimatum was delivered; that is, the ultimatum could not be said to be limited simply to dealing with the particular attack made on November 15. Further, a threat by Turkey to invade not merely Cyprus but Greece as well would seem to be grossly disproportionate to the danger presented by the triggering event. Nonetheless, the international reaction could be described as neutral, if not indeed neutral on the side of Turkey.

This conflict is unusual in having five distinct parties: Cyprus, the Greek Cypriots, the Turkish Cypriots, Greece, and Turkey. Both Greece and Turkey, however, apparently saw the problem as involving only themselves and their respective communities on Cyprus, not a Cypriot state distinct from those communities; outside reaction seems most understandable if it is assumed that outside states saw the problem in that way, too. The mild reactions to Turkish uses of force make sense only if much of the rest of the world was acknowledging the legitimacy of Turkey's interest in the Turkish Cypriots, at least in the face of heavy Greek support for the Greek Cypriots and the Cypriot government. Arguably, since both the 1964 bombing and the 1967 invasion threat followed concrete escalations of violence by Greek Cypriot troops under Greek command, the rest of the world was prepared to see this situation as raising problems for Turkey analogous to those faced by a state whose nationals faced great danger in some other state. The formal statehood of Cyprus was, to a certain extent, disregarded in light of the reality of the significant interests of both Greece and Turkey in the welfare of their respective communities.

This episode presented the international community with a situation in considerable flux, involving violence in Cyprus directed against ethnic Turks by ethnic Greeks led by the Greek military, and in which Turkey's interest in Cyprus was formalized in a treaty. In such a case the rest of the world was unprepared to sanction Turkey for its actions in 1964 and 1967. Indeed, the message to Greece in 1967 that a Turkish invasion would not be blocked amounted to sanctioning the Greek government whose use of force had led to the problem. The fact that the juridically distinct Cypriot state would be the victim of the invasion was simply not considered as important as the realities of this five-cornered relationship.

## Pakistan/India (1965)

By 1965 the dispute between India and Pakistan over Kashmir had hardened into stalemate. The two sides' positions on the issues had changed little since the fighting described in Chapter 4. India continued to insist that Kashmir was part of India; Pakistan rejected this view and insisted on a plebiscite to determine the future of the territory.[91] Neither, furthermore, could compromise. For India, integration of Kashmir was vital to demonstrate the viability of the multiethnic, secular, democratic state it saw itself as being. Insistence on the retention of Kashmir also underlined the commitment of the government of India to the unity of that state in the face of various kinds of separatism. On the other hand, Pakistan was created because most Muslims in British India had come to accept two related ideas: that religious differences between Hindus and Muslims made it impossible to create a state embracing both, and that religion could serve as a basis for a Muslim state. Integration into India of a Muslim area contiguous to Pakistan both undermined the basis for Pakistan's existence and deprived Pakistan of territory it believed must necessarily be its own, given Kashmir's religious composition.[92]

Other factors complicated the matter. Partly in response to the continued security threat from Pakistan, India had taken a number of steps to integrate Kashmir over the period 1960–65, presumably raising concerns in Pakistan that the prospect of detaching Kashmir from India was becoming more and more bleak.[93] Further, India's military strength had begun to increase greatly due to its efforts to build up its forces in the wake of its defeat by the PRC in the war of 1962; the Pakistan military began to fear that this Indian buildup was eliminating any chance it might have of seizing Kashmir by force. Also, Pakistan drew sinister conclusions from that buildup, discounting the security problem the PRC posed for India.[94]

Pakistan was also apparently encouraged by the outcome of small-scale fighting in January–April 1965 between the two states in the Rann of Kutch, a disputed area on the southern part of their common border. Pakistan's higher quality weapons, recently received from the United States, performed well; the Indian military was not able to contain that of Pakistan; and third states generally took little interest.[95] Indeed, there is reason to believe that Pakistan had escalated that incident to test the effectiveness of its weapons and the ability of the Indian army to counter them.[96] This particular matter was ended by an agreement concluded between the two states on June 30, calling essentially for a return to the *status quo ante* and arbitration to determine sovereignty over the Rann,[97] but it gave Pakistan confidence as to the ultimate outcome of a conflict with India.[98]

The war between the two states began on August 5, 1965, with the infiltration across the cease-fire line in Kashmir of guerillas controlled by Pakistan and including some Pakistani troops.[99] Pakistan apparently hoped that the guerillas would spark a revolt against Indian rule and assumed that in any case India would not respond to the incursion by itself attacking across the cease-fire line.[100] Both assumptions proved false. No revolt took place,[101] and, after a large infiltration on August 14, heavily supported by Pakistani artillery, India attacked across the cease-fire line and seized some strategic ground in Pakistan-held territory.[102] It should be noted that at this time Pakistan was denying that its troops were involved; indeed, it did not admit that its troops had entered Indian or Indian-controlled territory until September 9.[103]

The Indian attack threatened the position of Pakistani and Pakistan-supported Kashmir forces. Pakistan responded on September 1 with a tank-supported assault by its regular army from Pakistani territory into southern Kashmir; the area attacked was vital to Indian communications.[104] By September 5 the Pakistan forces were close to the key town of Akhnur. To relieve the pressure caused by this attack, India elected to attack south of Kashmir, across the international border between the two states in the Punjab. India struck first toward Lahore on September 6, attacking further north on September 7; these moves had the effect of inducing Pakistan to withdraw its tanks from the attack on Akhnur to meet the threat in the Punjab.[105] Fighting in the Punjab finally ended on September 22, when both sides accepted a Security Council resolution demanding a cease-fire and a return to positions held on August 5.[106] As of the twenty-second, each occupied territory that was either clearly within the other's boundaries or had been controlled by the other in Kashmir.[107] On January 10, 1966, after mediation by the Soviet Union, both states agreed to give up the territory each had seized during the fighting and return to positions held on August 5.[108]

Third-state reaction was an extremely important factor in ending the fighting in this war. This reaction did not, however, take the form of sanctions imposed on the state deemed guilty of unlawfully using force. Rather, it manifested itself as pressure on both sides to end the fighting. In particular, the United States and the United Kingdom suspended military and economic aid to the two combatants during the fighting.[109] These actions put particular pressure on Pakistan, whose capacity to continue combat was dependent upon American resupply, thereby playing a major part in Pakistan's accepting a cease-fire on what amounted to India's terms; India was also affected, however, in that some of its tanks required British spare parts, and also because the suspension of economic aid would put pressure on its ability to simultaneously resupply its military and avoid economic difficulties.[110] The Soviet Union avoided publicly taking sides, which permitted the Security Council to function without threat of a veto; the Soviet Union, did, however, continue its supply of arms to

India.[111] Most public pronouncements by states called for an end to the fighting without apportioning blame, though Turkey and Iran offered symbolic aid to Pakistan.[112] Indonesia also offered aid to Pakistan, an American ally, both in the spirit of Muslim solidarity and on the basis of the somewhat curious argument that India, a leading nonaligned state, was inspired by American imperialism to attack Pakistan.[113]

Perhaps the most notable supporter of Pakistan was the PRC. That state had accused India of aggression against Pakistan on September 7 and 8. Its reaction to the fighting, however, was limited to a demand that India remove military installations that the PRC claimed India had constructed in Tibet, followed five days later by an announcement that India had complied with its demands. India denied both the existence of the posts and their removal. The United States had strongly warned the PRC not to use force against India, and it is doubtful that the PRC ever intended to use force, its original demand being aimed simply at putting pressure on India so as to redeem in part promises of support made to Pakistan.[114]

In the end, though, the vehicle by which the shooting was stopped was the Security Council. On September 4 that body called on each combatant to cease fire and withdraw to positions on its own side of the Kashmir cease-fire line, though its resolution did not invoke Chapter VII of the Charter.[115] On September 6 the Security Council again called on the parties to cease fire and also called for withdrawals to positions occupied prior to August 5, still not invoking Chapter VII.[116] Finally, on September 20 the Council adopted a resolution that, while still not invoking Chapter VII, did not "call upon" but "demanded" that the combatants cease fire and return to August 5 positions, also deciding to consider what steps might be taken to assist in settling the political problem underlying the conflict.[117] This last resolution followed a trip by Secretary-General U Thant to the subcontinent, during which India had indicated as early as September 15 its willingness to accept a cease-fire if Pakistan would; apparently, the Indian cabinet was concerned about the economic effects of the war and also saw an opportunity to stigmatize Pakistan if it did not accept the cease-fire.[118]

Pakistan had resisted accepting a cease-fire that called for a return to the *status quo ante*, urging that any cease-fire resolution call for the complete demilitarization of Kashmir, assumption of security responsibilities within Kashmir by UN forces, and a plebiscite in Kashmir to determine whether it would accede to India or to Pakistan.[119] The provision in the September 20 resolution promising Security Council consideration of the disputes that had given rise to the conflict was apparently included as a gesture toward Pakistan's desire to have the Council address the Kashmir question; U Thant had been convinced by his trip to the subcontinent that Pakistan would accept a cease-fire if given a face-saving way of doing so. The Security Council refused to do more toward addressing the problem, however; only Jordan urged that course, and Jordan abstained on the final vote.[120] In any case, Pakistan did finally accept this last resolution at the last possible moment.[121]

This war was a fight over territory, albeit territory that carried significant ideological importance for both combatants. Pakistan sought to detach Kashmir from India by force, although it also sought to deny its responsibility for the use of force. India's use of force was defensive, its invasion of Pakistani territory aiming only to relieve military pressure on Indian-held territory; it was not an effort to acquire land from Pakistan. Third-state reaction was strong but even-handed; clearly, the focus was on stopping the fighting, not on naming a culprit. This is striking, in a sense, since there was apparently no doubt that Pakistan had started the conflict. That is, the general lack of interest in casting blame for the first use of force did not reflect confusion as to whom to blame. Rather, it reflected an orientation that focused first of all on ending the shooting that, as a practical matter, depended on the agreement of the two sides. This view was exemplified by the secretary-general in his explanation for his decision not to release a report prepared by UN observers in Kashmir that would have demonstrated Pakistan's responsibility for initiating the fighting. He stated: "My first and primary objective has to be to see the fighting end rather than indicating or denouncing any party for starting and continuing it."[122] By and large, the rest of the world took the same approach.

## Israel/UAR, Syria, Jordan, Iraq (1967)

On April 7, 1967, unusually heavy Syrian artillery fire was directed at Israeli farmers and settlements in the vicinity of the Golan Heights. Although there had been several incidents on Israel's western border in 1966 involving artillery fire from Syria and fedayeen attacks from Syria and Jordan, 1967 had been relatively quiet until that point.[123] Israel responded by directing air strikes against the Syrian artillery positions; attempts by Syrian aircraft to oppose the Israeli planes cost Syria several MiGs.[124] This incident was followed by a marked increase in mining and mortar attacks in Israel and led to a corresponding rise in tension within that state. Israel responded by moderately reinforcing the border with Syria, and clearly had decided to retaliate locally if Syrian behavior continued; the Soviet Union, however, falsely informed Nasser, president of the United Arab Republic (UAR) (Egypt), that Israel had greatly reinforced its troops facing Syria and was planning a major attack.[125] Confronting a decline in his international standing and a Syrian request for aid, Nasser acted to relieve perceived pressure on Syria, moving troops into the Sinai peninsula on May 15.[126]

Over the next three weeks the situation escalated rapidly. Nasser elected to greatly reinforce his troops in the Sinai, to the point that they had an offensive capability. A United Nations emergency force had been deployed since the 1956 Suez crisis on the Egyptian side of the Israeli-Egyptian armistice line in the Sinai as a buffer between Egypt and Israel. Nasser ordered that force to leave Egyptian territory. He also made several statements indicating his intention to eliminate Israel. Jordan joined the preexisting military alliance between Egypt and Syria, and placed its troops under Egyptian command; Egypt correspondingly dispatched troops to Jordan. An Iraqi armored division entered Jordan, and Iraq also joined the alliance of the other three Arab states. Egyptian aircraft overflew the Israeli nuclear research facility. Most significantly, after the departure of the United Nations force from Sharm el Sheikh, overlooking the Straits of Tiran, Nasser announced the closing of those straits to Israeli shipping. As Israel's only outlet to the Red Sea, the straits were seen by Israel as essential, and Israel had made clear that it would regard such a closure as an act of war.[127]

Third-state reaction during this period exacerbated the crisis. The Soviet Union unequivocally blamed Israel for the increasing tension. France, traditionally Israel's ally, took a strictly neutral position, refusing to honor guarantees it had given in 1957 regarding Israel's access to the Straits of Tiran. The United States strongly supported Israel's right to use the straits and tried to organize an international effort to physically challenge and thereby eliminate the Egyptian blockade. However, the United States also urged caution, and its effort to organize a blockade running force had clearly failed by June 4.[128]

Against this background, on June 4 Israel elected to go to war. Its reasons were, first, that the increasing concentration of Arab troops on its borders indicated an intent on the part of the Arab states to attack Israel and, second that it could not tolerate the closure of the straits. Its decision also reflected (1) the failure of international efforts to break the blockade or otherwise defuse the crisis; (2) the conclusion that, legally speaking, Egypt's closure of the straits was an act of war to which Israel was legally entitled to respond; and (3) the belief that its action would be supported diplomatically by the United States and that the Soviet Union would not intervene militarily in the war.[129]

The war began on June 5 with a preemptive air strike against Egypt's airfields, completely destroying the Egyptian air force. Israel initially justified its actions before the United Nations by claiming, falsely, that it had been attacked first, though it subsequently reinforced this argument by stressing both the character of the Egyptian blockade as an act of war and the very dangerous situation in which Israel found itself on June 5.[130] By June 8 Israel had destroyed Egypt's army in the Sinai, seizing the entire peninsula including the east bank of the Suez Canal.[131] On the fifth, Israel had informed Jordan that it would not be attacked if it refrained from attacking. Nonetheless, Jordan, apparently impelled by a sense of solidarity and misled by Egyptian reports of a great defeat for Israel, attacked Israeli forces in the vicinity of Jerusalem and launched an air raid. Israel responded with air raids that destroyed Jordan's small air force and with army operations that led to Israel's capture of all of Jordan's territory west of the Jordan River, including the Old City of Jerusalem.[132] It should be noted that Israel's decision to advance to the Suez Canal reflected in part operational considerations and in part a desire to obtain a secure boundary with the UAR, while the decision to capture the Old City of Jerusalem reflected what may be called ideological concerns, that is, the great religious importance of Jerusalem to Judaism and thus to an explicitly Jewish state.[133]

The fighting between Israel, on the one hand, and Jordan and Egypt, on the other, essentially ended by June 8. On June 6 and June 7 the Security Council of the United Nations had adopted resolutions calling for a cease-fire in the conflict; Israel accepted on June 7, subject to acceptance by the other parties to the conflict, with Jordan accepting on the seventh and again on the eighth, and Egypt accepting on the eighth, Israel having questioned Jordan's first acceptance because its armed forces had been placed under Egypt's command. It should be noted that each of these resolutions called only for a cease-fire; neither spoke of a return by any combatant to positions occupied prior to the outbreak of fighting.[134]

During this period Syria had been engaged in a limited way only, employing its air force and firing artillery from the Golan Heights at Israeli positions. It indicated early on June 9 its acceptance of the Security Council's cease-fire resolutions, but its artillery did not comply. To silence the artillery, and also to eliminate the risk of future bombardment and future threats to Israel's access to the Jordan River, whose headwaters were in the area in question, Israel elected to move against the Golan Heights later on June 9. Its forces took that position by the afternoon of the tenth, at which time both Israel and Syria accepted yet a third cease-fire resolution.[135]

Third-state reaction to this crisis was striking in a number of respects. The position of the Soviet Union and its satellites was consistent throughout the controversy; these states weighed in unequivocally on the side of the Arabs. By June 10 the Soviet Union was threatening military intervention against Israel unless that state halted its operations.[136] As noted above, the Soviet Union's false report to Egypt of a massing of troops by Israel against Syria contributed to igniting the crisis, and its attitude prior to the start of the fighting was simply to insist on Israeli restraint and to ignore Israel's requests for help in moderating the Arabs' behavior.[137] The Soviet Union also introduced a resolution in the Security Council condemning Israeli aggression and demanding that it withdraw its troops from Arab territory unconditionally.[138]

The United States was almost equally supportive of Israel. Israel's initial decision to use force reflected in part American signals that such an action would be backed. The decision to attack Syria was preceded by similar American signals.[139] Furthermore, the United States reacted to Soviet threats to halt Israel's operations by force by deciding to resist any Soviet intervention and by disposing its naval forces so as to clearly convey this intention to the Soviet Union.[140]

Other states' reactions, as reflected in UN debates, generally took one of two forms. Communist states, Arab states, and several prominent nonaligned states tended to condemn Israel unequivocally and demand immediate withdrawal from the territory Israel had taken during the fighting, the Communist states going so far as to break diplomatic relations with Israel. The second view, adhered to by the United States, Canada, Australia, New Zealand, Japan, most Western European states, most Latin American states, and much of Francophone Africa, was that it was not useful to seek to apportion blame for the crisis but rather that it was necessary to address its causes, including Israel's complaints; adherents to this view agreed with the first group concerning the inadmissibility of seizing territory by force but argued that Israeli withdrawals from Arab lands should be accompanied by Arab action to address Israel's problems.

These views were demonstrated by votes in both the General Assembly and Security Council. A Soviet General Assembly resolution condemning Israel and demanding its withdrawal from Arab lands, without reference to any action by Arab states, was defeated in a paragraph-by-paragraph vote, no paragraph attracting the support of more than 48 of the assembly's 123 members. An Albanian resolution even more harshly critical of Israel received only the votes of the Communist and Arab states. A resolution proferred by 17 nonaligned states that would have called for an immediate Israeli withdrawal, with subsequent actions to resolve the underlying crisis, received a majority of votes but less than the two-thirds majority required for passage. A resolution by 20 Latin American states that linked a request for an Israeli withdrawal to a request to the Arabs to end their state of belligerency with Israel likewise received a majority of less than two-thirds. Similarly, a Soviet resolution in the Security Council that would have condemned Israel and required its immediate withdrawal failed, only 3 states joining the Soviet Union in voting for condemnation and those plus 2 others joining the call for withdrawal; all other Security Council members abstained on both votes.[141] The only measure upon which the General Assembly could agree was a resolution calling upon Israel to rescind the changes it had made in the status of Jerusalem.[142] The Security Council, however, finally did act affirmatively, unanimously adopting Resolution 242 on November 22, 1967. That resolution stressed both Israeli withdrawal and the termination of belligerency by all states, and also affirmed the necessity to guarantee free navigation rights and to resolve the Palestinian refugee problem.[143]

This war was begun by Israel after the UAR had instituted a blockade of a strait Israel considered vital and in the belief that it was about to be attacked itself. Once it became apparent that Israel would win, its war aims expanded to include broader security, economic, and ideological goals. It justified its action on the ground of self-defense. Third-state reaction was quite divided. Prior to the opening of hostilities, third-state actions were limited to halting and ineffectual efforts to break the blockade of the Straits of Tiran and to pleas to Israel to refrain from using force. During the hostilities most states seemed to focus on stopping the fighting, with the Communists and Arab states insisting on blaming Israel and the United States acquiescing in Israel's use of force. Once the shooting had stopped, the international consensus that emerged was, in effect, that while Israel could not be permitted to retain the land seized from the Arabs, any return of the land had to be linked to satisfaction of Israel's reasonable security concerns. That is, the international community was unwilling to focus solely on the fact that Israel acquired the Arab lands by force without reference to the underlying political situation that led up to the use of force. Indeed, the United States had acquiesced in that use of force before it took place.

## Israel/UAR, Jordan, Lebanon, Syria (1967–1970)

Beginning about three weeks after the end of hostilities in the Six-Day War, fighting resumed in the Middle East. Over the next three years the combatants engaged in constant, relatively low-level combat. The fighting was particularly intense in the Sinai, taking the form of artillery barrages, air raids and aerial combat, minelaying, and raids by land forces on both sides, the Israelis employing as much as a battalion in these latter operations. In 1970 Israel, with the acquiescence of the United States, inaugurated a campaign of bombing raids relatively deep in Egypt, intended to pressure President Nasser to agree to a cease-fire and possibly to peace talks. However, when Egypt found that it could not defend itself against the raids, it did not bow to Israel's pressure. Instead, it invited aid from the Soviet Union, which provided not only antiaircraft missiles, but the troops to man them, and also dispatched units of fighter aircraft. This increased both Israeli aircraft losses and the level of risk, since it made direct Israeli-Soviet confrontations possible. Such a confrontation finally occurred in late July 1970, when Israeli and Soviet pilots clashed in a series of dogfights that cost the Soviets five aircraft and Israel none. Almost immediately thereafter Israel, the UAR, and Jordan accepted a cease-fire proposed by the United States. The Israel-Egypt front remained quiet until 1973.[144]

The level of fighting on Israel's other borders was less intense but very serious nonetheless. Arabs, mostly Palestinian guerillas, raided into Israel from Jordan and, to a lesser extent, Lebanon. The governments of the latter two states had allowed the guerillas to establish bases in their territories; they acquiesced in the raids, sometimes even assisting the raiders. There were also attacks on Israeli territory by gunfire from Jordan and Syria. Israel responded with its own gunfire and its own raids against positions it characterized as guerilla bases, using both its land and air forces. Israel also carried out commando operations, for example, the 1968 raid that destroyed several civil aircraft at Beirut airport in retaliation for an attack on an Israeli civil aircraft in Greece, Israel having concluded that the attack had originated in Lebanon.[145] The 1970 cease-fire had less effect on these other fronts, although guerilla attacks on Israel from Jordan were curtailed after the Jordanian government moved against the Palestinians in Jordan in September 1970.

Most third states reacted to these events in a limited way only. The Security Council adopted several resolutions in 1968, 1969, and 1970 addressed to Middle East cease-fire problems. Generally, they called for observation of the cease-fire and condemned violations; only Israel was condemned by name for its actions. Two points of view were expressed in Security Council debates. The Arab states, supported by the Communist states, France, and some nonaligned states, insisted that all of the violence in the area was occasioned by Israeli aggression and that the appropriate remedy was therefore action directed against Israel. The other viewpoint, expressed by Western and Latin American states, agreed that various Israeli actions were unacceptable, condemning in particular the practice of armed reprisal, but also argued that the problem could not be solved by focusing solely on the actions of one of the combatants. In no case did Security Council action go beyond verbal condemnations, more or less harsh and more or less general.[146]

Outside the United Nations the most important third-state reactions were those of the Soviet Union and the United States. As noted above, the Soviet Union reacted to the fighting along the Suez Canal by arming Egypt and dispatching its own forces to Egypt's defense. (France provided arms to Libya in the expectation that the arms would reach Egypt.[147]) The United States supplied arms to Israel and made clear its intention to continue such supplies at whatever levels were necessary to maintain a balance in the region.[148] As noted above, the United States also sponsored the cease-fire that ended the fighting on the Suez front, that cease-fire having been put forward as part of an effort to achieve a comprehensive peace in the region along the lines set out in the Security Council's Resolution 242.[149]

The fighting described in this section can best be seen as a continuation of the Six-Day War, as the Arabs continued their efforts to damage Israel, their determination strengthened by the loss of territory to Israel, and as Israel responded violently to the Arabs' actions, seeking both to deter attack and to coerce a peace. Each side justified its acts by reference to the acts of and the danger posed by the other. Third states cannot be said actually to have applied sanctions, the efforts of the United Nations having been ineffectual. Rather, third-state reactions took two forms. Some states supplied arms to the combatant they found more congenial. Also, the United States—and other states at least rhetorically—sought to bring the parties to negotiations in an effort to end the fighting by addressing the political disputes that underlay it. This second approach, that is, did not separate the use of force from the context in which it occurred and focused on preventing future uses of force by ending the basic controversy rather than on punishing past uses of force.

## Israel/Lebanon (1970–1975)

In the period 1970 through 1975 the pattern of violence along the Israel-Lebanon frontier persisted. Prior to November 1971 the Palestinian guerilla groups regarded their positions in Lebanon as secondary to their main base in

Jordan. In that month, however, the guerillas began to make the Arqub region of eastern Lebanon their primary base, having been driven out of Jordan.[150] Even so, their operations were almost entirely limited to the Israeli-occupied Golan Heights until April 1974. Israeli operations against them before that time, therefore, represented responses either to actions in the Golan Heights or to incidents of international terrorism.[151] During this period Israel did not justify its actions as reprisals; rather it argued that the targets of its attacks were terror organizations responsible for numerous attacks against Israelis and that Israel had a duty to protect its people from such organizations.[152] In other words, it claimed to be engaged in a war with the Palestinians rather than to be responding to discrete actions.[153]

The first Lebanon-originating Palestinian attack on Israel proper took place on April 11, 1974. It was followed by other raids against civilian targets, to which Israel consistently responded with force.[154] Israel continued to justify its actions by reference to the centrality of Lebanon as a Palestinian base and to Lebanon's failure to prevent the use of its territory for attacks against Israel.[155]

Throughout this period Lebanon was essentially a passive observer. In November 1969, after efforts by its army to restrict guerilla operations had provoked domestic disorder and considerable fighting between the guerillas and the Lebanese Army, Lebanon and the guerillas entered into the Cairo Agreement, according to which guerilla activity was limited to southeastern Lebanon and was required to be coordinated with the Lebanese Army. Contrary to this agreement, however, the guerillas expanded their areas of operation, and the army was unable to restrain them.[156] Lebanon reacted to Israel's retaliatory raids by denying that Palestinian activities had originated from Lebanon.[157] One may wonder, in any case, whether Lebanon was in a position to do any more than it did to restrain the Palestinians.

Third-state reaction to these raids and retaliations resembled third-state reaction to other elements of the Arab-Israeli dispute. That is, at the diplomatic level some states laid all blame for the problem on Israel, while others criticized Israel but added that Palestinian violence was also objectionable. Over the period 1970–75 the Security Council adopted eight resolutions condemning Israel by name for various violations of Lebanese territory; most of these included as well condemnations of all violence directed against innocents, which at least some Council members intended to refer to violence perpetrated by the Palestinians. A further three resolutions condemning Israel were vetoed by the United States as too one-sided.[158] Yet this almost universal focus on Israeli actions at the rhetorical level was not matched by a similar material response. Throughout this period Israel continued to face great opposition from Arab states and states sympathetic to them and to receive support from Western states, especially the United States. No states not connected with the Arabs imposed sanctions on Israel because of its attacks on Lebanese territory.

This series of events, then, amounted to a series of raids by a guerilla group from the territory of a state reluctantly acquiescing in the raids, at least in part because of an inability to do anything else, and counterraids by the state that was the guerillas' target. The latter state justified its actions as, in effect, self-defense in an ongoing war. Third states verbally condemned the counterraiding state, while making only generalized references to the guerillas' actions and none to the failure of the state wherein the guerillas were based to restrain them. In practice, however, nothing concrete was done by third states to restrain either side. Third states frequently expressed their dismay at the loss of life but seemed unprepared to take steps that would inhibit the activities of either the Palestinians or the Israelis. And, of course, one very important state—the United States—made more definitive action against Israel impossible. Third-state reaction to this constant situation of low-level war seems to have been that it was regrettable but not so intolerable as to require forceful action.

## Cambodian War (1970–1975)

As early as 1965 Prince Sihanouk of Cambodia agreed to the establishment within Cambodian territory of base areas for Democratic Republic of Vietnam (DRV) military units operating against Cambodia's neighbor to the east, the Republic of Vietnam (ROV). He also permitted the importation of supplies intended for DRV troops through the Cambodian port of Sihanoukville, which supplemented the Ho Chi Minh Trail supply lines that ran in part through Cambodia.[159] Beginning in March 1969 and continuing for the next fourteen months the United States began bombing DRV base areas in Cambodia; the United States claimed that Sihanouk had approved these attacks, and it at least appears clear that he was aware of them and did not protest them.[160] The United States undertook these operations in the belief that they would seriously hamper operations by DRV-armed forces in the ROV.[161]

In March 1970 Sihanouk's government was overthrown in a coup by his prime minister, Lon Nol. The coup took place in part because of resentment among a number of Cambodians at the large-scale Vietnamese presence in the eastern region of the country.[162] On March 13 Lon Nol demanded that the DRV abandon its Cambodian bases within two days. When this demand was not met, Cambodian military forces began to seek various kinds of support from ROV troops against the DRV troops within Cambodia. ROV troops crossed the border several times in March to assist the Cambodians; DRV forces, in the meantime, reacted to the greater pressure they faced in eastern Cambodia by shifting their operations westward, which the weak Cambodian armed forces could not prevent.[163] Lon Nol made a general request for aid against the Communists, and the United States began to provide some military equipment.[164]

During the next month the United States began to consider an invasion of the DRV base areas in eastern Cambodia. It was hoped that the invasion would disrupt DRV operations and thus facilitate continued American troop withdrawals from the ROV. A joint American-ROV attack was made on April 30, 1970. Lon Nol's first reaction was to complain that the invasion violated Cambodia's territorial integrity, although in the following month he accepted offers of military aid from an emissary sent by the American president, Nixon.[165]

Pursuant to a statute enacted after the invasion, American troops were withdrawn from Cambodia by June 30.[166] The United States continued very heavy bombing of Communist targets in that state through August 1973 and provided military aid to Lon Nol's government until its fall in 1975.[167] ROV troops remained in Cambodia for two years after the invasion and in fact engaged in operations with Lon Nol's troops even after the end of U.S. operations in Southeast Asia in 1973.[168] The DRV troops who were the original target of the invasion continued to fight, needing to retain Cambodia as a base in the face of Lon Nol's declared opposition.[169] Nonetheless, by 1973 very few DRV troops were left in Cambodia except those along the Ho Chi Minh Trail. Lon Nol's opponents by that year were Cambodian Communists, who were hostile to the Vietnamese and independent of them, except for reliance on them for logistic support.[170] Despite the aid it received, however, the Lon Nol government was unable to defend itself against the Cambodian Communists, or Khmer Rouge, and Phnom Penh fell to the Communists on April 17, 1975.[171]

Third states reacted to the events of May 1970 and their aftermath by and large in line with their overall attitude toward the Second Indochina War. Laos and Indonesia expressed understanding of the American move, though the latter also expressed regret; the United Kingdom refused to comment, and France condemned the invasion.[172] New Zealand[173] and Australia[174] supported the invasion, as did Thailand, the Republic of Korea, and the Republic of China.[175] The PRC, the Soviet Union, India, and Sweden all condemned the invasion, the latter expressing the fear that the war would be widened and escalated.[176] Italy and the FRG made no comment, while Canada expressed regret but refused to condemn the American action.[177] In short, those states whose troops were fighting with the United States in Vietnam expressed support for the move, and some other states in the region seemed to acquiesce in it, but the Western allies of the United States were apparently dismayed by the action and certainly did not express support for it, while the Communist states opposed it. After the American troop withdrawal third-state reaction to the fighting in Cambodia is very hard to separate from third-state reaction to events in Indochina generally.

At one level this reaction is puzzling, since the target of the attack was the DRV's position in Cambodia, and the attack was generally in line with the policy of the sovereign of the territory attacked. What seems to have driven the reaction, however, was not this juridical point but fears similar to those expressed by Sweden—that the war would be widened and expanded. It is also noteworthy that it was the United States rather than the DRV that was the target of criticism, even though the DRV's actions were much more direct threats to Cambodia's sovereignty than were those of the United States. Again, this makes sense if it is assumed that negative reactions were driven by fears of an expanding war; the United States had not previously operated in Cambodia, as far as was generally known, while the DRV had. The DRV's presence, however regrettable, was nothing new; that of the United States was new, and provoked a negative reaction. Finally, it should be mentioned that, criticism aside, none of the combatants in Cambodia encountered any sanctions for their behavior from states not parties to the conflict.

The Cambodian War, then, involved (1) an American/ROV attack on DRV troops in Cambodia, more or less with the acquiescence of Cambodia; (2) DRV resistance to this attack and also to hostile moves from the Cambodian government; (3) DRV support for Cambodians opposed to the government; and (4) continued American support for the Cambodian government as the conflict became, essentially, a civil war. The United States justified its initial action as defensive, in light of the link between the DRV positions in Cambodia and the war in Vietnam; the support subsequently accorded the Lon Nol government was likewise seen as a helpful adjunct to the American position in Vietnam. Apparently, the American motive was as portrayed: a desire to eliminate a threat to the war effort in the ROV. The DRV did not really justify its actions, which were to protect its position in the fighting in the ROV. Third states did not focus on the issue of identifying the state(s) using force unlawfully in this conflict; rather, they expressed concern but took no action otherwise, apparently seeing events in Cambodia as inseparable from the wider problem of the Second Indochina War.

## India/Pakistan (1971)

In early 1971 Pakistan faced a political crisis. The previous December the military government of the country had held elections to select a National Assembly that would write a constitution as a first step toward a return to civilian rule. Seats for the assembly had been apportioned on the basis of population, which meant that most seats were allocated to East Pakistan—the portion of the country separated from the rest of Pakistan by the whole of India—as it was the more populous part of the country. One of the leading contenders in the election was the Awami League, a political party localized in the east whose platform called for greatly increased autonomy for East Pakistan and stressed the party's roots in the culture of Bengal, the region from which East Pakistan had been formed when British India was partitioned in 1947. To the great surprise of the government the Awami League won all but two of East Pakistan's seats, thus garnering an absolute majority in the National Assembly as a whole and the power to write its autonomy principles into the constitution.[178]

In the months after the election, difficulties began to develop when Zulfiqar Ali Bhutto, the leader of the Pakistan People's Party (PPP), which had won 81 of West Pakistan's 138 assembly seats, insisted on concessions from the Awami League as the price of his party's participation in the assembly. The military government was sympathetic to the PPP's position and inclined to blame the Awami League for the ensuing disputes. It was also increasingly uneasy at the prospect of an Awami League government. Negotiations among the government, the PPP, and the Awami League were unsuccessful, and President Yahya Khan announced the indefinite postponement of the convening of the National Assembly on March 1, 1971.[179]

The immediate reaction in East Pakistan was a general strike and a complete disappearance of government authority. By default, the Awami League became the only authority recognized in East Pakistan. Faced with an unexpected situation, President Yahya entered into negotiations with Sheikh Mujibur Rahman, leader of the Awami League, during March. During the course of these negotiations, however, the army became doubtful about the security of its forces in East Pakistan and about the Awami League's commitment to the unity of the country. By March 23 the army command had decided to take military action against what it had come to see as a rebellion. Its operations began the night of March 25, 1971.[180]

What followed was a campaign of great violence directed by the Pakistan Army against the civilian population of East Pakistan. Seeking to repress what it considered a rebellion, the military behaved with great brutality.[181] By mid-April it had established military control over most of the province. The army had also hoped to seize the top leaders of the Awami League, but all except Sheikh Mujib escaped to India, where they organized a government for an autonomous state of Bangladesh, whose independence had been proclaimed by a Bengali military officer on March 27. A number of Bengali military and paramilitary units also escaped with their arms to India, where they became the nucleus of the Bengali resistance forces, the Mukti Bahini. Most significantly, huge numbers of refugees began fleeing to India from East Pakistan; by the end of June they numbered in the millions and were mostly Hindus, the Pakistan Army having particularly targeted Hindus in its repression.[182]

It was in these circumstances that the Indian government began to involve itself in the civil strife in East Pakistan. India's government had taken the basic decision that the country could accept no resolution of the crisis that did not lead to the repatriation of all the refugees. It came to this conclusion because of the immense economic burden posed by supporting the refugees and because the areas of India the refugees entered were politically volatile, with domestic difficulties likely if the refugees remained. Further, it concluded that in order to induce the refugees to return, an Awami League government in East Pakistan was necessary. It decided to support the Mukti Bahini to achieve its objectives, and it provided arms, training, and some cooperation from Indian troops for Mukti Bahini operations.[183] It also sought to mobilize international support for its view, hoping that Pakistan would be forced to accept a political settlement. Pakistan, however, was unwilling to deal with the Awami League, and no political solution emerged.[184] By mid-July India had apparently decided to use whatever force was necessary to achieve its goals, including an invasion if the efforts of the Mukti Bahini were not sufficient. By this time India's concerns also included the prevention of the establishment of a radical government in Bangladesh. Its goals had also broadened somewhat to include the reinforcement in status that would come from a victory over Pakistan.[185]

The Mukti Bahini began to act effectively during the monsoon season, which

refugee problem

began in June. After the monsoon Mukti Bahini operations became still more effective, at least in part because of higher levels of Indian involvement, including on occasion support from artillery, tanks, and aircraft. By November the Mukti Bahini had taken control of a number of areas within East Pakistan and along its borders.[186] In late November the Indian Army began more active operations. Instead of occasionally entering Pakistan to aid the Mukti Bahini and then withdrawing, the Indian Army made numerous small lodgments in East Pakistan. These maneuvers were in preparation for a full-scale invasion scheduled for early December. However, on December 3 Pakistan attacked first, with air strikes launched from West Pakistan and advances in Kashmir. Pakistan's leaders apparently acted in the hope of provoking international intervention and in frustration at the intractability of the problem. India responded with the invasion of East Pakistan that it had planned to launch in any case. On December 16 the Pakistan Army in East Pakistan surrendered. The fighting in the west was less dramatic; India retook the areas in Kashmir that it had captured in the 1965 war and then given up afterward, as well as territory in the vicinity of the Rann of Kutch. President Yahya accepted a cease-fire in the west on December 17.[187]

The two states' justifications for going to war differed. Pakistan insisted both that it had been the victim of aggression for months and that India was seeking to dismember Pakistan. India noted that Pakistan had initiated hostilities but stressed that the basic problem had been caused by Pakistan's repression; it also insisted that it would not agree to any solution to the problem without the input of representatives of Bangladesh and subsequently stated that it would consider a cease-fire and withdrawal only after a political settlement acceptable to the elected representatives of the people of Bangladesh.[188] Prior to the war India's leaders made clear their imperative need that the refugees leave India,[189] and during Security Council discussion of the December fighting they characterized the flooding of its territory with refugees as a species of aggression to which it was reacting in self-defense.[190]

Third-state reaction to the war was quite varied. The Soviet Union and India had gone through with the long-planned signing of a friendship treaty in August, which at Indian insistence included a clause forbidding either party to provide military aid to a state engaged in armed conflict with the other. Also in August the Indians informed the Soviet Union of their intention to use force to deal with the East Pakistan situation if no political solution emerged after a few months. When Prime Minister Indira Gandhi visited Moscow in September, she sought arms supplies, which the Soviet Union agreed to provide; the Soviet government concluded by the end of Mrs. Gandhi's visit that India intended to invade East Pakistan and decided that it would have to support that decision if it was to preserve its relationship with India. Accordingly, it accelerated its arms deliveries to India in October and gave diplomatic support to the Indian position that the Awami League must be involved in any serious political settlement of the East Pakistan crisis.[191] In the Security Council on December 5 the Soviet Union vetoed a proposed resolution that would have called for a cease-fire and mutual withdrawals; it did the same on December 13 in the voting on an American resolution that contained a similar provision.[192]

The Soviet Union was not unfailingly helpful to India, however; Poland, presumably with the acquiescence of the Soviet Union, proposed a resolution that would have required Pakistan to transfer power in East Pakistan to the representatives elected in December 1970 but that would also have required an immediate troop withdrawal and renunciation of claims to territory acquired during the war. India intended both to keep its troops within Bangladesh to help the new government stabilize itself and to retain the territory it had seized in Kashmir; passage of this resolution would have complicated its situation, but India had concluded that, if the resolution were adopted, it would have to comply. Perhaps fortunately for India, Bhutto, who was representing Pakistan in the Security Council, denounced the inaction of the Council and walked out, effectively killing discussion of the Polish proposal.[193]

In contrast to the Soviet Union, the United States strongly opposed India. American economic aid to India was suspended after the December invasion. Further, the American United Nations ambassador denounced India's actions as "aggression" and, for reasons that were not entirely clear, U.S. naval forces were sent into the Bay of Bengal during the war.[194] Some in the American government apparently feared an Indian attack on West Pakistan, and the United States reacted forcefully in an effort to prevent that development.[195]

Other third states did not react strongly to the fighting. The PRC gave Pakistan verbal support but had indicated before the fighting began that it would not intervene.[196] The General Assembly adopted a resolution calling for a cease-fire by an overwhelming vote,[197] but that action had no effect on the conflict. Perhaps the most telling third-state reaction was that, within a year of the December fighting, Bangladesh had been recognized as independent by over ninety states, including the United States.[198]

This conflict began as one involving Indian support for an insurgency in East Pakistan that it did not inspire. It developed into a full-scale invasion of Pakistan. India justified its actions by reference to the burden of caring for the mass of Bengali refugees who had entered its territory and to the necessity for the establishment of an Awami League government in East Pakistan to induce the refugees to return home. Third-state reaction was split, and no sanctions were imposed on India for its actions. It should be noted, however, that India apparently would have felt constrained to defer to a Security Council resolution requiring it to withdraw its troops from Bangladesh, indicating that India acknowledged the possibility of sanction. It should also be noted that the relatively quick and widespread recognition of Bangladesh suggests that the states of the world were not prepared to dismiss it as an illegitimate entity, which implies a sort of post hoc approval for India's actions.

## Egypt, Syria, Iraq, Jordan, Saudi Arabia, Morocco/Israel (1973)

On October 6, 1973, which in that year was the Jewish High Holy Day Yom Kippur, Egypt attacked Israeli positions on the Suez Canal and Syria attacked Israeli positions on the Golan Heights. Israel was taken by surprise, and the forces of both Arab states had some initial success, the Syrians recapturing portions of the Golan Heights taken by Israel in 1967 and the Egyptians successfully establishing a bridgehead on the east bank of the Suez Canal. Within days, however, the Israelis had gained the initiative. They counterattacked first on the Golan Heights, regaining the ground the Syrians had recaptured and then taking still more territory. In so doing they encountered troops from Iraq, Jordan, Saudi Arabia, and Morocco as well as Syria. Israel likewise counterattacked on the Suez front, succeeding in establishing a bridgehead on the west side of the canal. Israeli operations on the west side of the canal cut off some of the Egyptian troops on the east side.

In these circumstances, on October 22 Egypt and Syria accepted Security Council Resolution 338 calling for a cease-fire. The Egyptian unit cut off on the east bank of the Canal sought to break out in spite of the cease-fire, however, and Israel reacted by tightening its encirclement of those troops. Again under pressure from the United States and the Soviet Union, Israel and Egypt accepted the cease-fire on October 24, and the Yom Kippur War ended.[199] It should be noted that Resolution 338 did not merely call for a cease-fire; it also called for immediate implementation of Resolution 242 and decided that Middle East peace negotiations should begin. It should also be noted that on October 25 the Security Council adopted Resolution 340, providing for a United Nations Emergency Force for the area.[200]

The justifications Egypt and Syria gave for their attacks were false; each claimed that Israel had attacked first.[201] Their actual goals in attacking were to recapture Israeli-held territory and, more important, to trigger a crisis that would lead the superpowers to force Israel to return to its 1967 borders without requiring any Arab state to formally sign a peace treaty with Israel.[202] They also wished to eliminate any sense the Israelis may have had that the Arabs were militarily negligible; his conviction that this latter goal had been achieved was one of the reasons that Egyptian President Sadat accepted the cease-fire.[203]

Third-state reaction to this conflict was extremely important. First, Egypt's ability to launch its attack depended on the previous supply by the Soviet Union of massive quantities of antiaircraft missiles; the placement of these missiles along the west bank of the Suez Canal made Israeli air operations over the east bank very hazardous and for a time neutralized Israel's air superiority.[204] Further, on October 1 President Anwar Sadat informed the Soviet Union's ambassador that Egypt was planning to attack and might be "obliged to move fast," the ambassador responding that the Soviet Union would help.[205] Once the conflict began, the Soviet Union and the United States both organized airlifts to resupply the Arabs and Israelis, respectively, with vitally needed weapons and munitions.[206]

Superpower involvement was not limited to fueling the conflict, however. Resolution 338 was proposed jointly by the Soviet Union and the United States[207] on October 21 after the Security Council had not met since October 12,[208] and the resolution was accepted by the combatants only after pressure from their respective patrons, the Soviet Union, at least, stressing its responsibilities under Resolution 242.[209] Despite this cooperation between the United States and the Soviet Union, they narrowly averted a serious dispute. The Soviet Union had urged that the two superpowers dispatch troops to the area to ensure adherence to the cease-fire. When the United States objected to the idea, the Soviet Union suggested that it might dispatch troops unilaterally, and it did in fact put some of its airborne divisions on alert. The United States, feeling it necessary to indicate that it could not agree to unilateral Soviet action, put some troops, including some of its strategic nuclear forces, on limited alert, while publicly downplaying the significance of the dispute. The Soviets ended by accepting the American position.[210]

The actions of other third states had less immediate effect on the crisis, although one such action was very significant indeed. This was the oil price increase and production cut put into effect by several Arab oil-producing states, including Saudi Arabia, Abu Dhabi, Libya, Algeria, and Kuwait. This action was coupled with an embargo on oil shipments to states such as the

United States and the Netherlands, deemed to have been of too much assistance to Israel.[211] A number of Western European states sought to stay neutral in the conflict to avoid a similar embargo.[212] But aside from these actions and those of the superpowers described above, other states' actions with respect to the conflict were mainly symbolic, such as Ethiopia's termination of diplomatic relations with Israel.[213] There was also some objection in the Security Council from the PRC and India to excessive superpower control of the Council's actions.[214] and to the fact that Resolution 338 was not sufficiently tough on Israel, the PRC being much more strongly of that opinion than India. Despite their objections, however, neither state voted against the resolution; India voted for it and the PRC did not participate in the vote.[215]

This war was a cross-border invasion aimed as much at political as at territorial gains. Egypt and Syria attacked Israel in an effort to trigger a political process that would lead to their recovery of land lost in 1967. In Egypt's case the tactic worked; the war brought about a change in political relationships that led to Egypt's recovery of the Sinai, though not without direct dealings with Israel.[216] Third states were, by and large, irrelevant to the conflict, with the important exceptions of the United States and the Soviet Union. The two superpowers both focused on aiding their respective allies and on stopping the fighting and moving the parties toward negotiations on the political issues underlying the fighting. They did not, that is, seize on the use of force itself as a basis for sanction, each having abetted the use of force by its client. With some bad grace the rest of the world went along with the superpowers' approach; no state imposed any sort of sanction as a reaction strictly to this use of force.

## Events in Cyprus (1974)

In the period following the 1967 military coup in Greece the relationship between the Greek and Cypriot governments was altered. The Greek government came to favor partition of the island between its Greek and Turkish communities, with the Greek portion to be united with Greece. The Cyprus government, though still on record as favoring union with Greece, in fact had come to oppose union. Further, it had sheltered opponents of the Greek military dictatorship and worked in alliance with leftist parties found objectionable by the Greek government. In these circumstances Greece began a campaign of subversion against Cyprus no later than 1971, and possibly earlier.[217]

In 1971 General Grivas, the Greek officer identified with the 1964 efforts to unify Greece and Cyprus, returned to Cyprus from Greece. Grivas proceeded to found a terrorist organization called EOKA-B, named after the group he had headed in the terrorist campaign against British colonialism in the 1950s. His target this time, however, was the independent Cypriot government headed by the president, Archbishop Makarios.[218]

Grivas's campaign was unsuccessful, however, and the Greek government resorted to more direct means. In early July 1974 Makarios wrote to the nominal president of Greece, complaining of Greek support for EOKA-B and its effort to subvert his government. On July 15 the Cypriot National Guard, all of whose officers were seconded from the Greek army, overthrew President Makarios in a coup, installing in his place Nikos Sampson, a Cypriot known for his anti-Turkish sentiments.[219] After seeking British aid for joint military action under the 1960 Treaty of Guarantee and being refused, Turkish forces entered Cyprus on July 20.[220] On the same day the Security Council adopted Resolution 353, calling for a cease-fire and an end to foreign military intervention that was contrary to the sovereignty, independence, and territorial integrity of Cyprus.[221] On July 22 both the Greek military dictatorship and its puppet on Cyprus fell.[222] Between July 25 and July 30 the foreign ministers of the three Treaty of Guarantee powers—Turkey, Greece, and the United Kingdom—met in Geneva as called for in Resolution 353. They agreed to implement that resolution and to meet again on August 9, together with representatives of the Greek and Turkish Cypriots. During the intervening period, however, Turkey greatly reinforced its troops on the island. When the conference resumed, the Greek Cypriots offered a return to the constitutional *status quo ante*; Turkey, however, demanded a federal government for Cyprus, with separate Greek and Turkish subdivisions. When Greece and the Greek Cypriots asked for thirty-six hours to consider the proposal, Turkey responded by renewing its military offensive on August 14. By August 18, when Turkey proclaimed a cease-fire, it had occupied about one-third of the territory of Cyprus.[223] On February 13, 1975, the leader of the Cypriot Turkish community proclaimed the creation of the Turkish Federated State of Cyprus. That entity declared its independence in November 1983.[224]

The justifications and motives for the Greek and Turkish interventions differed. Greece falsely denied any connection with the July 15 coup;[225] as noted above, it acted due to dislike of the existing Cypriot government. Also, it appears that at least some Greek officials assumed that they could unify

Greece and Cyprus without provoking a Turkish invasion.[226] Turkey justified its initial invasion by reference to its status as a guarantor state and characterized itself as defending the independence and constitutional order of Cyprus.[227] After the resumption of Turkish military activity on August 14, however, Turkey justified its actions as protecting the interests of Turkish Cypriots, insisting that the island's government be reorganized to accord autonomy to a geographically discrete Turkish portion of the island.[228] It took this course, apparently, for reasons of nationalism and because of considerations of military strategy considered important by the politically powerful Turkish armed forces.[229]

Third-state reaction to these events was acquiescent. The United States reacted to the Greek-inspired coup by receiving the Sampson government's foreign minister and denying the involvement of the Greek government in the coup.[230] It likewise declined to oppose the August 14 Turkish advance, though in public it called for a return to the precoup status quo.[231] Despite its status as a party to the Treaty of Guarantee, the United Kingdom declined to act against the Greek coup, preferring to leave the matter to the United States.[232] After the Turkish invasion it convened the Geneva Conference and later criticized Turkey as the cause of the failure of that conference.[233] The Soviet Union's reaction to the coup was negative, but it took no action outside the Security Council. It likewise did not act against the Turkish invasion, in fact indicating its support for that action.[234] The Security Council as an institution likewise did little. Its Resolution 354 of July 23 "demand[ed]" a cease-fire and its Resolution 358 of August 15 "insist[ed]" that the parties obey its earlier resolutions and observe a cease-fire, but its Resolution 360 of August 16 merely "urg[ed]" compliance after "recording [the Security Council's] formal disapproval" of the unilateral military actions taken against Cyprus. The only sanction imposed was an embargo on arms sales to Turkey enacted by the U.S. Congress in February 1975 and ended in September 1978 without having affected the results of the Turkish invasion.[235]

These incidents involved two separate uses of force by states. The first was the Greek-controlled coup against the government of Cyprus; the second was the Turkish invasion of Cyprus. Greece did not attempt to justify the coup; its motives were apparently nationalistic and territorial. It failed to achieve its objective because of the Turkish invasion, which Turkey sought to justify under the Treaty of Guarantee as a response to Greece's action. The actual motive for the invasion, however, was presumably different, given Turkey's refusal to withdraw its troops once the failure of the coup became apparent. Rather,

Turkey's motive apparently lay in its desire to take control of a portion of Cyprus for reasons of strategy and nationalism.

Third-state reaction involved Security Council condemnations but no effort by any state other than the combatants to sanction the uses of force—except for the imposition of the American embargo, which in the circumstances was mainly of symbolic value. While the Security Council acted to maintain the United Nations peacekeeping force in Cyprus to help separate the combatants along the border between the Greek and Turkish portions of the island,[236] its resolutions became increasingly plaintive as the crisis wore on. The rest of the world was prepared to tolerate the effective Turkish seizure of over a third of Cyprus, perhaps as a way of finally eliminating the problems caused by strife between the two ethnic communities on that island.

## Interventions in Lebanon (1976–1991)

Beginning in 1976 Lebanon found itself subject to forceful interventions by foreign states more serious than the raids by Israel against Palestinian guerillas described above. Although each of these interventions was distinct from the others, their relationship to one another makes it advisable to discuss them together.

The civil war that began in Lebanon in April 1975 was an important contributor to foreign intervention. In 1975 Lebanese politics was organized on the basis of religion, with Maronite Christians dominating the system and Sunni Muslims also benefiting from it. The Druse and Shi'ite communities, however, were both limited in their access to politics and economically considerably worse off than the other communities. The Muslims agreed among themselves that continued Christian domination was unjust, as it was based on a 1932 census that showed Muslims in Lebanon outnumbered by Christians, a circumstance believed no longer to obtain. Among the Muslims, however, the Sunni were prepared to accept political changes less radical than those sought by the other communities, and they were less interested than the other communities in the government's addressing questions of social justice.

The operations within Lebanon of the Palestinian guerillas further complicated the situation. The Maronites tended to be Lebanese nationalists and saw the relatively autonomous guerilla organizations as both an affront to Lebanese sovereignty and a threat, since Palestinian activities triggered Israeli retaliation. The Muslims, however, tended to identify more strongly with Arabs generally and faulted the Christian-dominated government for not supporting the guerillas more strongly. The guerillas themselves, moreover, regarded the Maronites as a threat both to themselves and to their desire to fight against Israel.[237] Against this background, with all sides arming themselves, fighting finally broke out between Maronites, on the one hand, and Palestinians and their Druse-led Lebanese allies, on the other, in April 1975.[238]

This development affected Syria's interests for several reasons. In the first place, Syria had long seen Lebanon as rightfully part of its territory, and in fact did not have diplomatic relations with Lebanon. Second, Syria's population resembles Lebanon's in being divided by both sectarian and regional loyalties and by a skewed wealth distribution; sectarian and ideological violence in a neighboring state was therefore of concern to Syria's government, especially because that government was itself dominated by a religious minority, the Alawi. Further, if the outcome of the sectarian violence was a partition of Lebanon leading to the creation of an independent Christian state, Syria could find itself facing a new opponent. Third, Syria was avowedly Pan-Arabist in ideology and accordingly had given strong support to the Palestinian guerillas, striving to be identified as their protector; threats to Palestinian interests therefore concerned Syria. However, Syria also sought to dominate the Palestinian movement and was thus opposed to any development that might lead to greater Palestinian independence from its control. Finally, Syria was concerned about Lebanese developments as they impinged on its vulnerability to Israel; not only was Syria open to attack by way of Lebanon, but control of Lebanon by radical groups could precipitate a war with Israel at a time unfavorable for Syria but that Syria could not avoid.[239]

In these circumstances Syria first sought to mediate between the Lebanese factions, its initial positions tending to favor the leftist side in the civil war.[240] By January 1976, however, after requests from Lebanese leftist leaders, Syria went beyond mediation, sending Palestinian units under its control into the Beq'a valley, freeing other leftist units to block Christian sieges of Palestinian refugee camps that had been undertaken to secure territory in the event Lebanon was partitioned. Syria opposed partition and also felt obliged to come to the Palestinians' aid.[241]

In late January Syria proposed constitutional reforms for Lebanon that would, it hoped, end the fighting. As part of this arrangement Syria supported the limits on Palestinian guerilla activity from Lebanon established in agreements predating the civil war. Christian leaders and conservative Muslims accepted this plan. However, Syria's erstwhile allies opposed it. The Lebanese leftists thought the plan insufficiently radical, while the Palestinians objected to restrictions on their activities. Lebanese leftists went so far as to attempt to prevent the election of a new Lebanese president, despite Syria's support for and domination of the electoral process. Syria responded to this opposition by, first, dispatching Palestinian units under its control into Lebanon to aid the Christians and, finally, by intervening against the leftists with its own troops in June 1976. Syria claimed to have acted in response to appeals for aid from Christian villagers under attack from leftists. Both Lebanon's incumbent president and its president-elect denied foreknowledge of the intervention, but the former justified it as necessary to implement Syria's proposed constitutional reforms.[242]

The Syrian intervention was not immediately successful. However, by October Syria had done considerable damage to the leftists and their Palestinian allies. In particular, it launched an offensive shortly before a scheduled Arab League summit and despite the efforts of an Arab League mediator, apparently to establish its ascendancy over all the factions in Lebanon.[243]

At a minisummit convened by Saudi Arabia prior to the plenary Arab League meeting in Cairo, the Syrians were forced to accept a cease-fire. However, the net effect of the two meetings was to legitimize Syria's presence in Lebanon. This came about because the league's plenary meeting decided to replace a small peacekeeping force established in Lebanon shortly after the Syrian intervention with a much larger Arab deterrent force. The peacekeeping force had come to be composed almost exclusively of Syrian troops; the same situation developed with the deterrent force. The only real difference the league's action made was that its contributions for the support of the deterrent force helped Syria to meet expenses.[244]

Syrian troops remained in Lebanon after their entry in 1976, essentially taking control of the Beq'a region. Their goal, apparently, was to seek an end to the disorder in Lebanon while reinforcing Syria's claim to dominance. Their presence was criticized by other states, and they also encountered Lebanese opposition, as in the resistance displayed by the forces of the Christian General Aoun in the spring of 1989 and the fall of 1990. Ultimately, however, their claim to preeminence was recognized. Thus, at a May 1989 Arab League summit Syria rejected extensive criticism from other Arab states over its presence in Lebanon and refused to withdraw its troops, claiming a special relationship with Lebanon. In October 1989 the Lebanese National Assembly, meeting in Taif, Saudi Arabia, accepted a plan for ending the civil war mediated by Saudi Arabia, Morocco, and Algeria that modified the political system and permitted the Syrians to keep troops in Lebanese territory. In October 1990 Syria—having received a formal request from the newly elected president of Lebanon—crushed the forces of General Aoun. In May and September 1991 Syria and Lebanon entered into treaties confirming the presence of Syrian troops in Lebanon and requiring a high degree of cooperation between the security forces of the two states. Syria's permanent presence in Lebanon was therefore regularized.[245]

Third-state reaction to Syria's presence in Lebanon has generally been acquiescent. To be sure, a number of Arab states criticized Syria's original invasion (some even sending aid to Syria's opponents), the Arab League ended support of the Arab deterrent force in 1982, and Arab states again criticized Syria's refusal to withdraw its troops in 1989. In the end, however, the Arab League effectively endorsed Syria's presence, first with the establishment of the Arab deterrent force and later with the crafting of the Taif agreement.[246] Israel, despite earlier warnings to Syria not to invade, acquiesced in the 1976 invasion. The two states agreed—through the United States, acting as intermediary—that Syrian forces would not cross a figurative "red line," that they would remain out of a zone in southern Lebanon, that the Syrian air force would not be used against ground targets in Lebanon, and that Syria would emplace no surface-to-air missiles in Lebanon.[247] As will be noted below, the Israelis did not challenge the Syrians at all during Israel's 1978 invasion of Lebanon and, whatever their original intentions, stopped well short of an effort to expel Syria in 1982.

The Soviet Union reacted negatively to the 1976 invasion, curtailing arms supplies to Syria, but resumed its former relationship rather quickly.[248] The Soviet Union and more particularly the French took an interest in Aoun in 1989, as did Iraq; however, the final Syrian effort to crush Aoun in 1990 drew little international comment, coming as it did during the period when Western states and moderate Arab states were seeking Syrian adherence to the anti-Iraq coalition. Iran provided aid to the Shi'ite Hezbollah organization, but while this has given that group a degree of independence from Syria, the focus of the effort has not been opposition to Syria.[249] And, finally, the Taif agreement had the effect of recognizing Syria's position in Lebanon. This last point is important; indeed, it should be stressed that while individual Syrian actions, such as its firing on American aircraft in late 1983–early 1984[250] or its 1989 moves against Aoun, drew sometimes forceful negative reactions from third states, the basic fact of Syria's installing itself in Lebanon was not challenged.

Syria was not the only significant intervenor in Lebanon during this period. Israel, too, involved itself deeply in Lebanon, engaging in activities beyond the reprisals that characterized its first response to the Lebanon-based activities of Palestinian guerillas. As noted above, Israel acquiesced in the initial Syrian invasion of Lebanon, perceiving that invasion as directed against the Palestinians and thus serving Israel's interest, which was seen simply as preventing attacks on its territory by guerillas from Lebanon. Israel also reacted to the situation created by the invasion and civil war by beginning a civic action program in southern Lebanon and by creating the South Lebanese Army, a mainly Christian Lebanese entity; Israel hoped that these steps would inhibit Palestinian operations in southern Lebanon and lead to the pacification of the area.[251]

After the October 1976 cease-fire in the Lebanese civil war, however, Palestinian guerillas who had left southern Lebanon to take part in that conflict sought to return, and it became apparent that the South Lebanon Army was unable either to prevent the reentry of the Palestinians into the area or to completely prevent Palestinian operations directed at northern Israel. Fighting erupted in 1977, with Israel supporting the South Lebanon Army with aircraft, artillery, and eventually an armored incursion. Although the United States sought to establish a maintainable cease-fire in the area, hostility between the Palestinians and the South Lebanon Army led to the failure of this effort.[252] It became apparent that Israel had not succeeded in pacifying southern Lebanon.

This situation led Israel to undertake a large-scale invasion of southern Lebanon in March 1978. The pretext for the invasion was a Palestinian attack on a bus inside Israel that led to thirty-seven deaths. In fact, however, it was a response to the general security situation. The operation was designed to aid the South Lebanon Army by removing Palestinians from the area and more generally to permit the establishment of a buffer zone adjacent to the Israeli border and under the control of Israel's clients. The attack began on March 15 and by March 18 had secured the area that Israel had sought as a buffer zone.

On March 19, however, Israel resumed its advance, seizing somewhat more territory. On the twenty-first Israel proclaimed a unilateral cease-fire. Meanwhile, the Security Council had adopted Resolution 425 on March 19, calling for Israel to withdraw and for the establishment of a United Nations force in the area (UNIFIL) to police a cease-fire and aid Lebanon in restoring its authority. Israel agreed with UNIFIL authorities that UNIFIL would patrol an area north of the buffer zone Israel had established—essentially the area Israel had occupied after March 18—while the Lebanese Army would patrol the buffer zone itself. As it worked out, however, Israel handed control of the buffer zone over to the commander of the South Lebanon Army rather than to troops under the control of the Beirut government. Although that government regularized the situation by acknowledging that commander as one of its officers, Israel blocked efforts to insert Lebanese troops in the area by insisting that they remain outside certain Christian enclaves and by demanding the continuation of its civic action program. In essence, then, the 1978 operation had created a double-security belt for Israel in southern Lebanon; an outer line guarded by UNIFIL and an inner line manned by the South Lebanon Army.[253]

Third-state reaction to Israel's 1978 invasion was surprisingly mild. Israel's troops were careful to avoid contact with Syria's,[254] and Syria in turn made no effort to counter the Israeli attack. Indeed, just as Israel acquiesced in Syria's 1976 invasion, subject to its red-line conditions, so Syria's acceptance of those conditions amounted to acquiescence in Israel's security claims in southern Lebanon. Nor did other Arab states respond to the invasion, except rhetorically.[255] Further, although in the Security Council the debate on the invasion took its usual form, with the Arab and Communist states attacking Israel and Western states deploring both terrorism and reprisals, the resolution ultimately adopted both refrained from condemning Israel and implicitly acknowledged Israel's security interests in the area by establishing UNIFIL. It is striking that the Soviet Union did not veto such a resolution, despite the resolution's failure to condemn Israel and the potential of UNIFIL to interfere in Palestinian operations.[256] Essentially, the world can be seen as acknowledging Israel's concerns as manifested in the invasion.

Over the period 1978–1981 tension continued high along the Israel-Lebanon border. The buffer zone and the UNIFIL presence reduced the number of Palestinian operations but did not eliminate them. When such operations took place, the Israelis responded with air strikes and, occasionally, incursions by ground troops. By and large the third-state reaction to this situation was one of passivity, aside from debates in the Security Council. In 1980 the Council adopted a resolution condemning an Israeli ground reprisal raid, and throughout the period it expressed concern for the tension between the South Lebanon Army and UNIFIL. However, no sanctions were imposed on any of the combatants by any state, though criticism of Israel in the Security Council's debates followed well-established patterns.[257]

In the spring and summer of 1981, however, the situation in Lebanon deteriorated. In part this reflected a change in Israeli policy. First, Israel began to view the PLO's presence in the area north of the UNIFIL zone as a political as well as a security problem; it concluded that the increasingly solid PLO presence in Lebanon precluded Palestinians resident in areas occupied by Israel from settling with Israel on terms with which Israel could be comfortable. Second, Israel began to identify itself to an increasing extent with Maronite groups in Lebanon, in part out of sympathy and in part in the realization that the Maronites were the only relatively strong Lebanese group likely to act resolutely against the Palestinians. Third, Syria took steps in that period contrary to the 1976 red-line compromise, introducing surface-to-air missiles to Lebanese territory and responding harshly to Maronite provocations.[258]

It was the last of these developments that provoked the first Israeli response in April 1981, with the Israeli Air Force assisting Maronite forces under attack by Syrians; Israeli plans to attack the Syrian missile positions were canceled after the United States urged mediation. In late May–early June, and again in mid-July, Israel carried out punishing air strikes against Palestinian positions, to which the Palestinians replied with artillery and rocket fire into northern Israel. Apparently concerned by its casualties and pressured by the United States, Israel accepted a cease-fire with the Palestinians, negotiated with Saudi assistance by Ambassador Habib of the United States.[259] There was little third-state reaction to this series of events, beyond debates in the Security Council that followed established patterns.[260]

The cease-fire altered nothing fundamental, and the two sides interpreted its terms differently. Israel argued that the cease-fire required Palestinians to halt all operations against Israel everywhere in the world and did not preclude Israeli aerial reconaissance over Lebanon, while the Arabs asserted that it precluded only cross-border operations by the Palestinians and forbade Israeli reconaissance. More basically, however, the cease-fire did not speak to Israel's growing determination both to eliminate the PLO as a political force, not simply as a security threat, and to install a Maronite government in Lebanon.[261]

Israel received the pretext for an attack in June 1982, when its ambassador to the United Kingdom was shot by a Palestinian. Although the assailant apparently belonged to a group opposed to the PLO, Israel nonetheless attributed the attack to that organization and on June 5 invaded Lebanon. It asserted that its objective was clearing the Palestinians from an area extending twenty-five miles north of Israel's borders, pushing them beyond artillery range. The actual objective, however, appears to have been the destruction of the PLO,[262] and possibly the expulsion of Syrian forces from Lebanon.[263] Describing "Israel's" objectives is somewhat complicated, however, by the strong evidence that Defense Minister Sharon misled the Israeli cabinet as to the scope of the operation he intended. There is evidence that Sharon manipulated the cabinet into agreeing to advances beyond the originally announced twenty-five-mile line and actively sought a confrontation with Syrian forces, despite public statements to the contrary by Prime Minister Begin.[264]

The actual operations of the Israeli Army were rapid. The attack began on June 5, with the initial fighting involving only the Israelis and Palestinian forces. On June 8 Israeli-Syrian combat began in eastern Lebanon, but the Syrians, though suffering heavy losses of aircraft and tanks and the destruction of their surface-to-air missile batteries, were able to avoid being driven from Lebanon and agreed to a cease-fire with Israel that took effect on June 11; the United States had insisted upon this cease-fire when it became clear that Israel was not restricting itself to the twenty-five-mile, anti-Palestinian campaign it had earlier proclaimed. By June 14 Israeli forces had essentially routed the Palestinians throughout Lebanon south of Beirut and had linked up with Maronite forces, bottling up PLO and some Syrian troops in West Beirut. A cease-fire had been negotiated for western Lebanon on June 12; it was broken on June 13, each side blaming the other, and again by Israeli maneuvers to improve their positions around Beirut from June 22 through June 25, when a new cease-fire was proclaimed. Israel now made clear that it would accept nothing less than the departure of the PLO and Syrian forces from Beirut, by negotiation if possible, by force if necessary. Over the next several weeks combat continued around Beirut, as Israel sought to force the PLO to surrender. Concurrently, negotiations were taking place to find a way to peacefully remove from Beirut those PLO members beseiged there. On August 12 Israel undertook a particularly heavy bombardment, despite the knowledge that Ambassador Habib's negotiations were close to bearing fruit. The bombardment produced much negative international reaction, but a cease-fire was agreed to later that day.[265]

By September 3 the PLO's troops and high command, including Yasser Arafat, and their Syrian allies had been removed from Beirut, bound for other Arab states. This withdrawal had been facilitated by the presence of an American-French-Italian multinational force, charged with ensuring the safety of the departing troops; that force withdrew by September 12, its mission completed. On September 14, however, Bashir Gemayel, the newly elected Maronite president of Lebanon and a very close ally of Israel, was assassinated. Israeli troops moved into West Beirut on the following day, ostensibly to ensure order. Late on September 16, at the request of the Israelis, militiamen of Gemayel's Kataib party moved into two large Palestinian refugee camps, charged with searching out PLO troops who had remained behind after the general withdrawal. Before the militiamen were ordered out by Israel on the morning of September 18, these troops had perpetrated a massacre of

Palestinian civilians in the camps. The atrocity produced a worldwide outcry, which led to the reintroduction of the multinational force into Beirut beginning September 24 and Israel's withdrawal from that city by September 26. Meanwhile, on September 21 Bashir Gemayel's brother Amin—considerably less close to Israel than Bashir had been—was elected President of Lebanon.[266]

Over the following three years events in Lebanon gradually resumed their violent course. Israel and the Gemayel government, with the assistance of the United States, concluded an agreement on May 17, 1983, calling for the withdrawal of Israeli, PLO, and Syrian troops from Lebanon and the reestablishment of a Lebanese army presence in southern Lebanon, one element of which was intended to be constructed around the South Lebanon Army. Lebanese groups had resumed their civil war, however; the Muslim and Druse groups, opposed to the Maronite-dominated government, targeted both Israeli troops and the multinational force, seen as supporting the government. The Israelis responded by withdrawing from the Beirut area in early September 1983; the United States responded by authorizing its forces to act against the antigovernment groups, employing naval gunfire among other weapons. Troops of the multinational force were in turn the targets of serious terrorist attacks in October 1983, and, as noted above, American aircraft flying reconaissance missions in connection with the multinational force were fired upon by Syrian forces in November; an American air attack the following month on Syrian antiaircraft guns lost two aircraft. Ultimately, the disintegration of the Gemayel government in the face of its Syrian-backed opposition led to the withdrawal of the multinational force over the period February–March 1984.

Syrian-backed groups also prevailed in internecine fighting among Palestinian guerilla groups based in Syrian-controlled territory. Conflict began in May 1983 between Syrian-supported groups opposed to the continued leadership of Yasser Arafat and Arafat loyalists. Despite Syria's best efforts, Arafat reentered Lebanon to lead those loyal to him, but he and his troops were forced to withdraw by way of Tripoli under UN protection in December 1983. The deterioration in its position forced the Gemayel government to reach an accommodation with its opponents and their Syrian patron; the price of an agreement was the March 1984 abrogation of the Lebanon-Israel agreement of May 1983, which Syria had always strenuously opposed. Throughout this period Israeli troops remained in Lebanon south of Beirut, suffering casualties through guerilla action and terrorist attack. Unable to reach an agreement with the Gemayel government and facing increasing and vociferous domestic opposition, Israel finally opted for unilateral withdrawal, beginning its pullout in

February 1985 and completing it the following June. It left behind an enlarged and ethnically diversified South Lebanon Army.[267] Israel persisted in its efforts to maintain its security buffer in southern Lebanon; fighting in the area continues as of this writing.[268]

In considering third-state reaction to Israel's 1982 invasion it is important to distinguish between reaction to particular aspects of the invasion and reaction to the basic idea of Israel's effort to remove the PLO from Lebanon. Thus the United States pressured Israel to accept a cease-fire with Syria, permitted resolutions critical of Israel to be adopted by the Security Council in late July and August during the period of Israel's siege of Beirut, threatened sanctions after the August 12, 1982, bombardment of Beirut, and insisted on Israel's withdrawal from West Beirut on September 17, 1982.[269] On the other hand, it vetoed a June 8 resolution that threatened sanctions of Israel if it did not withdraw, vetoed another on June 26 that called for a cease-fire in the Beirut area without requiring a Palestinian withdrawal from Beirut, and vetoed a third on August 6 that would have required a cutoff of arms supplies to Israel in light of its refusal to agree to a cease-fire in Lebanon. Further, it apparently forced the removal from an August 4 resolution censuring Israel of references to Israeli atrocities and to Chapter VII of the UN Charter. In all the cases in which the United States vetoed resolutions its negative vote was the only one cast.[270] And, as noted above, U.S. mediation assisted Israel in attaining its goals of removing the PLO from Beirut and of reaching an agreement with the Gemayel government in May 1983. The United States, in short, acquiesced in Israel's policy.

The attitudes of other third states altered as Israel's broader objectives became apparent. Thus Syria sought to avoid conflict with Israel initially;[271] when it became clear that its preeminence in Lebanon was threatened, however, Syria organized resistance to Israel through the various Lebanese groups opposed to the Gemayels.[272] Similarly, the Soviet Union took no active steps against Israel during the initial stages of the fighting and provided no material support to the besieged PLO in Beirut, but began resupplying Syria in September 1982.[273] Further, it vetoed a French resolution offered in the Security Council in February 1984 to establish a peacekeeping force in Beirut;[274] presumably, had the resolution been adopted, Syria's efforts to weaken the Gemayel government would have been hampered. Finally, France and Italy contributed troops to the multinational force that made possible the achievement of Israel's objective of removing the PLO from Beirut. Other Arab states offered little support either to Syria or to the PLO during the 1982 fighting, apparently reacting to Syria's persistent efforts to exclude other Arab states from Lebanon; indeed, Arab states were initially reluctant to accept PLO troops withdrawn from Beirut.[275] Rhetorically, however, third states were harsh in their criticism of Israel, as indicated by votes in the United Nations on the subject of Israel's presence in Lebanon from 1982 through 1985.[276] After Israel's withdrawal in 1985, however, third-state reactions became more muted. Security Council resolutions criticizing Israel became less common, and the debate less predictable, perhaps because of the demise of the Soviet Union.[277]

Summarizing events in Lebanon over the period 1976–91, it can be said that that country was invaded by two states in competition with one another. Syria entered in 1976 and remained to establish its effective domination of Lebanon. Israel established the beginnings of a security zone in 1976 and has retained that zone; it also invaded twice, in 1978 and from 1982 through 1985, besides penetrating Lebanese territory on numerous other occasions on retaliatory raids. Syria's justification for its action originally was an invitation by elements of the Lebanese population, though more recently it has been more forthright in claiming a "special relationship" with Lebanon. Its motive has been establishing its dominance over Lebanon. Israel's justifications throughout have been defensive; these largely correspond to its actual motives, though during the 1982–85 period its "defensive" objective involved remaking the political map of Lebanon.

Third states have been basically passive throughout this process. Syria's initial invasion met with no strong negative third-state reaction and was effectively endorsed, ultimately, by the Arab League, which also approved of its continuing presence. Nor did particular Syrian actions in Lebanon, such as its organizing opposition to the Gemayel government in 1983 and 1984, its attacks on the PLO in 1983, or its attacks on General Aoun in 1989 and 1990, evoke any strong international response. Israel's actions have met with more rhetorical criticism than Syria's, and certain of them, such as its siege of Beirut in 1982, have come close to triggering sanctions from the United States. But American support has prevented third states from reacting strongly to Israel's actions, though it is not clear they would have been inclined to do so in any case, as suggested by the weak reactions to the 1978 and, initially, the 1982 invasions. Further, other third states have acquiesced regarding some of Israel's objectives in Lebanon, both the establishment of UNIFIL and the creation of the first multinational force, in effect acknowledging certain of Israel's security concerns. In Syria's case it appears that its claim to preeminence over Lebanon has come to be accepted by the international community, at least as long as Lebanese sovereignty is preserved in form. Israel's actions, on the other hand, seem to be subsumed under the general acquiescence toward Arab-Israeli violence the world has displayed since 1948.

## Israel/Tunisia (1985)

On October 1, 1985, Israeli aircraft bombed the headquarters of the PLO in Tunis. Israel claimed that it acted in response to the murders of three Israeli tourists in Cyprus by agents of the PLO on September 25, 1985. Apparently, civilian casualties were numerous.

Third-state reaction to this attack was negative. The United States criticized the raid, after first reacting positively. The United Kingdom, other European Community members, and Japan also reacted negatively. Arab states expressed outrage, and Egypt canceled scheduled territorial negotiations in protest. The Security Council adopted a resolution condemning what it characterized as Israel's act of aggression and expressing the opinion that Tunisia had a right to reparation, but it did not impose sanctions; the United States abstained in the voting.[278]

This was an act of reprisal in the context of the Arab-Israeli conflict, attracting a more serious negative reaction than was common, apparently because of the close relations between Tunisia and the United States. Even so, no sanctions beyond the rhetorical were imposed on Israel by third states, except for Egypt's suspension of negotiations, which proved to be temporary.

## Analysis

The conclusion of the First Indochina War left two states in Vietnam, each questioning the other's legitimacy. The Kashmir War did not resolve the issue of sovereignty over that territory. The ending of the first Arab-Israeli War was not accompanied by any political accommodation between the combatants. And the establishment of the Republic of Cyprus in 1960 left ethnic divisions on that island unaffected. In none of these cases were the parties subsequently able to bridge the divisions between them. Rather, in all instances, fighting resumed after intervals of between four and seventeen years. The second round in Vietnam came to involve Laos and Cambodia and lasted fourteen years. The second round between India and Pakistan in 1965 was followed by a third in 1971. The second round between Israel and Egypt in 1956 was followed by a third, also involving other Arab states, in 1967; while one might distinguish several different Arab-Israeli conflicts since that time, it would be more accurate to suggest that conflict has been essentially continuous, though at widely varying levels of intensity. The second round in Cyprus began in 1963 and was followed by the Greek-inspired coup and subsequent Turkish invasion and partition of 1974. In all four of these conflicts the second and later rounds of each can be seen as continuations of the first in each sequence, coming about because of the lack of resolution of the underlying questions between the combatants.

Third-state reaction to each of these conflicts has been divided. Each side has had partisans that have provided material and diplomatic support, making it difficult to argue that the actions of any of the combatants were seen by states generally as unlawful. Actions that have produced strong negative reactions when undertaken in other circumstances, particularly cross-border invasions, have received a more mixed reception in the context of these unresolved disputes.

This is not to say that third states have refrained from sanctioning behavior. In the 1956 Suez War, Israel's role in which was clearly a continuation of the earlier Arab-Israeli fighting, the United States threatened Israel with what Israel perceived as severe sanctions in order to obtain an Israeli withdrawal from the Sinai; even in that case, however, Israel was able to obtain guarantees for its interests. Similarly, the United States threatened sanctions against Turkey to deter it from invading Cyprus in 1964. And the sanctions actually employed against India and Pakistan in 1965 helped coerce those states into a cease-fire.

Nonetheless, third-state reactions to these episodes do not support the conclusion that the uses of force described in this chapter were seen as violations of law. The general reaction to the Second Indochina War was to urge negotiation; third-state reactions were not determined by their analysis of the issues of the juridical status of the Republic of Vietnam or the extent to which the right of self-defense permitted that state and the United States to use force against DRV forces in Cambodia. Turkey's actual uses of force in Cyprus encountered no sanctions. The sanctions employed against India and Pakistan in 1965 were aimed at starting negotiation, not at stigmatizing a wrongdoer; the rapid acceptance of Bangladesh as a state likewise suggests an international willingness to acquiesce in India's use of force against Pakistan in 1971.

Most notably, the events in the Middle East see the two most important states in the world arming the combatants rather than seeking solely to prevent their uses of force. Moreover, reactions to actual uses of force turned on an understanding of the interests of the combatants rather than on application of rules against resort to war. Thus, Resolution 242 in effect permitted Israel to hold Arab land hostage in return for peace talks. The international community likewise effectively acknowledged Israel's security interest in Lebanon, despite Israel's use of force against that state. But the interests of Jordan, Syria, and Egypt were also taken seriously, as indicated by the lack of third-party sanction against those states for their actions in 1967, 1973, and 1976.

How can these third-state reactions be reconciled with any view that sees interstate uses of force as subject to some sort of legal regulation? I suggest that one way to address this issue is to consider the analysis that concluded Chapter 4. It was suggested in that discussion that third states reacted weakly to postimperial wars because such wars were not seen as disturbing a preexisting stable status quo. Third-state reactions to the wars described in this chapter, I argue, can be explained in a similar way. In each of the cases described in this chapter force was used in a context of continuing international instability. The establishment of the Republic of Vietnam failed to address the interests of the DRV, interests considered highly legitimate in the early 1960s. The 1965 Kashmir War reflected the continued unsettled character of the controversy over Kashmir. Turkey's uses of force on Cyprus were reactions to continued threats to its coethnics on that island. And, of course, Israel, its Arab state neighbors, and the Palestinians all perceived themselves as being either at great risk from one another or else as the victims of a continuing wrong at one another's hands at the time of each of their conflicts. Unlike the uses of force described in Chapter 2, the uses of force recounted in this chapter did not breach a long-subsisting peace. Rather, they are better seen as particularly intense resorts to violence in contexts in which the status quo *was* violence.

In this context it would have made no sense for the international community to insist that the parties keep the peace when there was no peace to keep. To be sure, such a position could have been taken if third states had been prepared in these cases to bear the costs of compelling the parties to refrain from the use of force. Given the highly charged nature of each of these disputes, however, such coercion would have required serious military commitments in each of the four theaters of conflict discussed in this chapter. Clearly, third states not partisans of the combatants were unprepared to take this step, even assuming that it would have been possible in a Cold War context. Rather, third states have tried to move the parties to a situation in which stability could be created. This has involved focusing on the reasons why force has been used rather than solely on the fact of the use of force, with emphasis on movement toward stability. Thus, the flaccid international reaction to Turkey's invasion of Cyprus may reflect a belief that partition of that island was the only way to end the continuing conflict there and permit the beginnings of a stable situation. Reactions to the Second Indochina War reflected in part, to be sure, the strength of self-determination principles, but also concern at uses of force seen to widen the conflict, that is, uses of force perceived as retarding rather than increasing stability. In the subcontinent the thrust of international effort was toward moving the parties to reaching some agreement that could become a stable status quo. And in the Middle East, too, international reactions reflected both a willingness to tolerate uses of force by states facing a high degree of instability and continuing pressure on the combatants to find some arrangement with which they could live.

In sum, the international reaction to these continuation wars reinforces the conclusion that states are not prepared to demand of one another that they respect a status quo when there is none to respect. Equally, however, responses to these wars make clear that states see themselves as having an interest in preventing interstate uses of force; in these cases, however, that interest manifested itself in efforts to create conditions that would lead the combatants to stop fighting. That is, third states sought to create a status quo that could be respected. Absent such a respectable status quo, third states were unprepared to shoulder the burdens necessary to compel these warring states to end their fighting.

CHAPTER 6

# Civil Wars with International Elements

During the period covered by this study a number of states experienced civil strife that included some international element. In a few cases some third states regarded one of the combatants as an independent entity, even though most others regarded the conflict as purely internal to the state in question. In most of these wars, however, the international element took the form of significant third-state intervention to aid at least one of the internal combatants. Obviously, a state would undertake such intervention only to support a group with which it had good relations; in the conflicts discussed in this chapter, however, it would be inaccurate to characterize the internal factions receiving outside aid simply as puppets of the intervening states. But while these interventions differ from classic invasions as not being aimed at the de facto conquest of the state experiencing internal war, they raise legal questions, since these interventions necessarily have an impact on the domestic affairs of the state in which the intervention takes place. (This chapter does not address interventions by great powers maintaining their spheres of influence; these are discussed in Chapter 7. It also does not address interventions for the protection of the nationals of the intervening state; these are discussed in Chapter 9.)

## Greek Civil War (1946–1949)

In 1946 the Greek Communist Party (the KKE) put into effect its decision of December 1945 to resume its civil war against the Greek government. The three Communist states bordering Greece—Yugoslavia, Bulgaria, and Albania—provided base camps for the KKE forces and permitted them free passage over their borders with Greece. Yugoslavia also provided some food and transportation aid, and Bulgaria provided small quantities of material aid as well.[1] In late 1946 the three states agreed to increase their aid to the KKE in return for promises of territorial concessions after a KKE victory; Yugoslavia and Albania began to supply weapons, ammunition, and training as well as food.[2]

In December 1946 Greece complained of the activities of its three neighbors to the Security Council, but those states denied Greek accusations.[3] The United States proposed that the Council establish a commission from among its members to investigate the Greek charges; the Security Council agreed, the commission to consist of the five permanent members plus Brazil and Poland. It also agreed to Poland's suggestion that Greece, Yugoslavia, Bulgaria, and Albania be allowed to participate in the commission's work and that the commission have access to Greece and to border areas of its three neighbors.[4] Greece's neighbors and the KKE refused to cooperate with the commission.[5]

In the meantime, in March 1947 President Harry S. Truman proposed to the U.S. Congress that the United States provide aid, including military aid, to Greece. He argued that Greece was confronted with a violation of its rights under the United Nations Charter but also stressed the ideological danger to the United States from actions for which he held the Soviet Union ultimately responsible.[6] By May 1947 Congress had acted, and a military aid mission had been dispatched.[7] The American decision was criticized by the Soviet Union,[8] Poland,[9] Yugoslavia, Bulgaria, and Albania.[10] It was supported in the Security Council by Australia,[11] the United Kingdom, Belgium, Brazil, China, and Syria;[12] France[13] and Colombia[14] both expressed some reservations at the U.S. approach, but a Soviet proposal that the United Nations oversee American aid to Greece was voted down, drawing support only from Poland.[15]

Meanwhile, at the scene of the fighting, the KKE fell under increased Yugoslav influence. After unsuccessful efforts to capture territory that could serve as the capital of a provisional government, the KKE in mid-1947 was forced to submit to the guidance of a joint Balkan staff dominated by Yugoslavia. The aid it received was increased.[16]

In June the UN Commission released a report generally substantiating Greece's allegations that the KKE was being trained and supplied by Greece's neighbors.[17] Those three states, as well as Poland and the Soviet Union,[18] attacked the report. An American resolution based on that report and its recommendations received nine of eleven votes in the Security Council but was blocked by a Soviet veto.[19]

The United States subsequently prevailed on a "procedural"—and therefore nonvetoable—motion to refer the issue to the General Assembly.[20] The ensuing debate in October 1947 showed a division of opinion. The United States had developed a proposal to form a special committee on the Balkans to effect conciliation and supervise frontiers, seeking support by agreeing to omit charges against Yugoslavia, Albania, and Bulgaria if they cooperated with the committee.[21] This American proposal finally passed 32–1–12, with the Arab states, Scandinavia, and India abstaining.[22] A Soviet proposal blaming the United States, the United Kingdom, and Greece for border clashes and calling for the withdrawal of British troops from Greece and UN supervision of American aid failed 40–6–11, with India agreeing that the United States and United Kingdom were to blame for the clashes and with Poland and Egypt supporting the withdrawal of British troops, though not the supervision of American aid.[23]

Meanwhile, American aid began to arrive in Greece and affect the course of the war; by late 1947 the United States was effectively in command.[24] The KKE established a provisional government in December 1947,[25] but was recognized by no other government; the United States and the United Kingdom warned Yugoslavia, Bulgaria, and Albania that such recognition would be "a grave step."[26] The war was more strongly affected by two other developments. First, after American urging, the Greek government improved the training and command of its troops. Second, the KKE decided to support the Soviet Union when a split began to develop between Yugoslavia and the Soviets. In response, Yugoslavia began to reduce aid to the KKE and limit its movements. This development culminated in the July 10, 1949, announcement that Yugoslavia would close its border and cut off aid to the KKE. The KKE shifted operations to Albania and Bulgaria, but Albania—fearing invasion by Greece and doubting the reliability of the Soviet Union—announced in August

1949 that it would stop aiding the KKE, following this announcement up by seeking to disarm KKE troops and limit their movements. Finally, with most of its forces in Albania and Bulgaria, the KKE proclaimed a cease-fire on October 16, 1949. It had been defeated.[27]

The actions in question in this conflict include those of Albania, Bulgaria, and particularly Yugoslavia in providing extensive support to one side in the Greek civil war, at times exercising what amounted to command responsibility. But the United States and United Kingdom were also active, providing at least comparable aid to the established government. The motives of the states supporting the KKE were partly ideological and partly material: they hoped for territorial concessions. As they denied their actions, they offered little justification for them. The United States and the United Kingdom justified their actions as aid for a government threatened by aggression; they were moved by ideological opposition to the KKE.

Third-state reactions are difficult to summarize. First, it is clear that a majority of states were unprepared to agree that actions of the United States and United Kingdom in aiding the established government raised any questions under the UN Charter; even the Communist states did not take that position, since they criticized American and British activity in the context of characterizing the problem as one involving attacks by Greece on its neighbors. Beyond this point third-state reactions were striking in the relative prominence of the ideological element and corresponding lack of emphasis on legalities. To be sure, this was reflected in some obvious ways—for example, the way the Soviet bloc, on the one hand, and most Latin American states, on the other, chose sides. But some manifestations of this phenomenon were more surprising. Even several neutral states focused on the superpower element of the war as opposed to the narrow legal issues between the combatants, arguing that the defusing of this superpower element would contribute greatly to ending the conflict.

But an emphasis on ideology was not the only sense in which third states did not approach this matter primarily as a legal question. By stressing ending the fighting, as opposed to identifying a legally blameworthy party, several participants in the General Assembly debates effectively opted not to approach the issue as a legal matter. Thus, when the United States sought to gain support for its special committee resolution in the General Assembly, it did so by taking an approach that stressed simple resolution of the conflict, as opposed to one that would determine which party was legally at fault and deal with that party accordingly.

In the Greek civil war, then, behavior that amounted to heavy involvement by some states in an effort to overthrow a neighboring government was supported by some states because of ideology, opposed by others on the same grounds, and viewed by an uninvolved third group as presenting more of an ideological than a legal question. Furthermore, even many states whose focus was more on ending the conflict than on supporting one ideology or the other urged an approach that, as a practical matter, left little room for analyzing the problem primarily as a violation of rights under international law.

## Nicaragua/Costa Rica (1948)

On December 10, 1948, an armed group from Nicaragua invaded Costa Rica. The group was composed of Costa Ricans opposed to the government of that country and on good terms with the Somoza regime in Nicaragua. The Figueres government in Costa Rica, in turn, had been supportive of a group opposed to Somoza, called the Caribbean Legion. Apparently, the invading force was too small to cause much trouble. Costa Rica immediately invoked the Rio Treaty[28] and called upon the Organization of American States (OAS) for aid. The OAS quickly investigated and concluded that no Nicaraguan troops had been involved, though also concluding that Nicaragua had provided aid to the invaders. The OAS also took note of Costa Rica's aid to the Caribbean Legion. It established committees to ensure that each state ceased aiding the other's opponents and sponsored a pact of amity between the two states. The immediate crisis was thus defused.[29]

In this matter, then, one government aided the opponents of another to use force against it, presumably because of the enmity between the two governments. A regional organization was able to quickly calm the situation and remove the immediate irritants. Its focus was primarily on eliminating the causes of friction between the two states, and it imposed no sanctions, except to the extent that its overseeing of pacification measures may be considered a form of sanction.

## People's Republic of China/Tibet (1950)

By the end of the eighteenth century China had established its control over Tibet.[30] Although the British in India also sought to gain access to Tibet, the

United Kingdom acknowledged in treaties concluded as late as 1906 that Tibet was under the control of China; Russia took the same position as late as 1907.[31] The disorders accompanying the replacement of the Manchu dynasty by the Chinese Republic had an impact in Tibet, all Chinese being forced to leave during the period 1911–13.[32] Nonetheless, Great Britain continued to acknowledge Chinese suzerainty over Tibet after that period, and an official of the Republic of China was resident in Lhasa beginning in 1934.[33] Throughout the 1940s other states as well recognized China's status in Tibet, most notably the United States.[34]

By 1949, after the victory of the Communists in the Chinese civil war, the authorities in Lhasa sought aid against the new government of China from India, the United Kingdom, and the United States; all declined to receive Tibet's emissaries. The People's Republic of China (PRC), in the meantime, had demanded that representatives of Tibet appear in Beijing by September 6, 1950, the PRC taking the same position as other Chinese regimes, that Tibet was part of China. The Tibetans did not appear in Beijing by the deadline, and about one month later the Chinese Army was instructed to invade Tibet. The Chinese attacked Chamdo, a city in eastern Tibet, in mid-October and soon overcame Tibetan resistance. Tibet sought to raise the matter in the United Nations General Assembly, El Salvador speaking for it, but no state was willing to forthrightly support Tibet.[35] Both India and the United Kingdom deplored the violence but acknowledged the suzerainty of the PRC.[36] The United States deferred to India.[37] On November 24 the General Assembly voted unanimously to postpone debate on the issue, moved by Indian assurances that the problem could be settled peacefully.[38] On May 23 Tibet and the PRC entered into an agreement in which the PRC granted Tibet a measure of autonomy but in which Tibet both acknowledged the suzerainty of the PRC and agreed to the presence in Lhasa of Chinese troops and administrators.[39] On September 15, 1952, India took steps formally acknowledging that Tibet was a part of China.[40]

The Chinese entry into Tibet could be seen as cross-border invasion if Tibet were deemed to be a state. It appears, however, that third states had long acknowledged that Tibet was part of China, and the General Assembly's reaction to the matter suggests that this view was maintained at the time of the Chinese action. In essence, the rest of the world treated this matter as purely a matter of China's internal affairs rather than as a conflict between states. This is striking only in comparison to international reactions to the efforts by the Netherlands to recover control of Indonesia and of France to do the same thing in Indochina and to maintain itself in North Africa. The European presence in several of these areas was of long duration, comparable to the period of Chinese suzerainty of Tibet. Further, the recent history of the areas in question showed a considerably higher degree of control of European colonies by metropolitan powers than China had been able to maintain in Tibet. And while several states in the late 1940s had acknowledged Chinese authority over Tibet despite the weakness of actual Chinese control, during at least the first part of the same period the formal authority of European states in most of their colonies was similarly clearly established. Nonetheless, the PRC's effort to reestablish Chinese authority in Tibet was evaluated very differently from similar undertakings by European colonial powers, perhaps because the geographical and cultural link between China and Tibet was greater than that between the European states and their colonies.

## United States/Iran (1953)

In the first half of 1953 relations between the United States and Iran were under great strain. Muhammad Mossadeq, elected prime minister in 1951, had by May 1953 effectively stripped the shah of all power. He was embroiled in a controversy with the United Kingdom over British-owned oil interests,[41] and he had written to President Eisenhower seeking United States financial aid, his letter containing an implied threat to align with the Soviet Union if his demands were not met.[42] Mossadeq had permitted the Tudeh (Communist) party to function freely in Iran, and it had gained considerable strength.[43] In light of these developments the United States became concerned at the possibility of Communists taking power in Iran,[44] and decided to aid financially military officers seeking to overthrow Mossadeq.[45] The United Kingdom was also involved in this effort.[46] This group of officers moved against Mossadeq on August 16, 1953, one of its members seeking to deliver a decree from the shah removing Mossadeq from office. Troops loyal to Mossadeq interceded, however, and the effort failed.[47] Immediately thereafter Tudeh mobs became extremely active, threatening the government's control.[48] Mossadeq therefore asked the army to restore order;[49] it repressed the Tudeh but then turned on and overthrew Mossadeq.[50] This effort was aided by an anti-Tudeh mob composed in part of conservative groups.[51] By his reforms Mossadeq had alienated conservative elements that had earlier supported him, and this loss of support played a role in his overthrow.[52]

It may go too far to call this event a use of force by the United States and United Kingdom, but it is included since force was employed and those states had a role in procuring that use of force. Their action seems most easily classifiable as aiding one side in civil unrest. It does not seem to have evoked any considerable third-state reaction and thus says little about the attitudes toward this type of behavior of any states other than the two whose behavior is in question.

## Nicaragua/Costa Rica (1955)

On January 11, 1955, forces led by the son of a former president of Costa Rica invaded that country from Nicaraguan territory. President Somoza of Nicaragua was a friend of the former president and, as noted in the discussion of the 1948 dispute between these two states, an opponent of the Costa Rican government. Costa Rica sought the aid of the OAS, which concluded that unnamed foreign states were providing arms and air support to the invaders. Pursuant to an OAS call for assistance for Costa Rica the United States provided four fighter aircraft and a transport plane on January 17. Operations were resumed against the invaders on the following day, and they were quickly driven out. On January 20, 1955, Nicaragua and Costa Rica accepted an OAS proposal for a demilitarized zone along their common border.[53]

The OAS released a report on the incident on February 17, 1955, that blamed unnamed foreign powers for preparing, financing, arming, and transporting the invaders, as well as for providing air support and supportive radio broadcasts.[54] The OAS refused to label Nicaragua as an aggressor, though it implicitly placed most of the blame for the incident on that state.[55] Arguably, caution was necessary, given the support Somoza could have received from the other dictatorships that were then members of the OAS; in any case, the OAS avoided either condemnation or punitive action.[56] It did, however, obtain military aid from the United States, which also applied diplomatic pressure and thus contributed to Costa Rica's defense. Both the United States and the OAS were apparently seeking to rehabilitate reputations damaged by the previous year's overthrow of the Arbenz government.[57] In any case, third states focused first in this conflict on averting the immediate threat to Costa Rica, then on urging and assisting the parties to reach a peaceful settlement.[58]

In this case the OAS acted quickly and forcefully to provide military aid to a member state invaded from foreign territory. Nonetheless, it avoided either condemning or punishing the state known to be responsible for the invasion. Rather, as was true in many of the conflicts heretofore examined, the OAS relied more on negotiation between the parties than on third-party sanctions to address the dispute in question, though it did call for an armed response to the immediate crisis. It is also instructive to compare the reaction of the OAS to this exile invasion with its reaction to the similar event in Guatemala the previous year. In the former the extrahemispheric ideological element was absent, and the OAS responded vigorously.

## PRC/Republic of China (1958)

On August 23, 1958, the PRC commenced a heavy bombardment of Quemoy and Matsu, two Republic of China (ROC)–held islands in the Taiwan Straits, relatively close to the Chinese mainland.[59] Apparently, the PRC was at this time strongly of the view that the Communist states needed to be more willing to resort to limited war in their contentions with the non-Communist states; it objected to a focus on the need to avoid any action that could lead to a general war. More particularly, the Western states were at this period preoccupied with problems in the Middle East, leading the PRC to doubt that its action would be strongly opposed by the West. In any case, the PRC had reason to believe that it could not fail to gain all the offshore islands. It apparently believed that its bombardment would make supply of the islands impossible unless the United States was willing to bomb the Chinese mainland but that such bombing would necessarily pull the Soviet Union into the fighting on the PRC's side, which would in turn trigger pressure on the United States from its allies not to risk nuclear war over a minor matter.[60]

In fact, the United States *had* decided it would bomb the Chinese mainland if that step was necessary to defend the islands, viewing their defense as essential to that of Taiwan, and the defense of Taiwan as essential to the vital interests of the United States; however, it was also decided that hostilities would be limited to the extent possible.[61] On September 4 Secretary of State Dulles made clear in a speech that the United States would stand by its treaty commitments to defend Taiwan, that it would likewise defend the islands if necessary, that it thought the ROC's legal claim to the islands was strong, but that it was not necessary for the PRC to abandon its claim in order to resolve the crisis. Throughout, the United States stressed its treaty commitments to defend the ROC. In any event, American involvement was limited to providing convoy protection in international waters for ROC vessels carrying supplies from Taiwan to the islands. These resupply operations were effective. The Dulles speech may also have had some effect, since two days after it, on

September 6, the PRC signaled an intent to reduce tensions. The PRC eventually abandoned its efforts to isolate the islands.[62]

Neither the United States nor the PRC received much support from its allies. The PRC was presumably counting on strong Soviet support to force the United States to back down; however, Soviet statements on the crisis were extremely circumspect until after September 6, that is, until after the point at which it was clear that the PRC was willing to reduce tensions. Indeed, it is arguable that lack of strong Soviet support forced the PRC to take the course it did.[63] Similarly, American allies made clear to the United States their reluctance to risk war with the Soviet Union over Quemoy and Matsu.[64]

The use of force here was an unambiguous attack by the PRC on territory held by the ROC. It is also true, however, that this episode amounted to a continuation of the civil war between the PRC and ROC. It reflected the PRC's determination to reabsorb Taiwan and its dependencies and thereby destroy any argument that there was more than one entity that could be considered the government of China.[65] As far as the PRC was concerned, the ROC's possession of Quemoy and Matsu was a violation of China's legal rights, which the PRC sought to vindicate by force. From the point of view of the PRC this incident was not an *interstate* use of force, since it did not see the ROC as a state. The U.S. response was based primarily on its assessment of the effect of the loss of the islands on its strategic position vis-à-vis the Communist states, but also on its treaty commitments and its assessment of the legalities of the territorial claims.

This episode was an effort by a state to take territory as an element of what it regarded as an ongoing civil war. Most states were unprepared to react against the PRC. With the exception of the United States, states did not perceive the stakes as high enough to justify the risk of war—that is, high enough to require some sanctioning of China. And even the reaction of the United States, though heavily influenced by ideological factors, was relatively limited. While the Soviet Union's lack of support may have led the PRC to abandon its course of action, it seems strained to see weak support as the equivalent of a sanction. In summary, international reaction was focused more on preventing any broadening of the fighting than on sanctioning the party that was behaving aggressively.

## Laotian Civil War (1959–1975)

In the 1950s the United States sought to advance its containment policy in Southeast Asia by supporting those elements in Laos who favored alignment with the United States.[66] Since the 1954 Geneva Accords that country's politics had continued to reflect the differences in view that had developed during the First Indochina War; the Communist Pathet Lao, who operated through the Lao Patriotic Front (LPF), confronted both American-supported rightists and a significant neutralist element.[67] In 1957 these three groups combined to form a coalition government.[68] After an election in May 1958, in which the rightists were severely defeated, the United States–backed rightists increased their opposition to the LPF. This finally led to an effort by the Royal Laotian Army (RLA) to force two Pathet Lao battalions, scheduled to be integrated into the RLA, to go through with that union in the summer of 1959. When the Pathet Lao units refused, the RLA tried to force their surrender. One of the battalions escaped, however, and guerilla war began in July 1959.[69]

The Pathet Lao were assisted in this effort, contrary to the Geneva Accords, by troops of the Democratic Republic of Vietnam (DRV). The DRV had begun planning for an armed insurrection against the government of the Republic of Vietnam (ROV) that would require use of supply arteries through eastern Laos. Since the availability of those routes might be compromised if the government of Laos were unfriendly, the DRV had an incentive to aid the LPF.[70]

Laos sought aid from the Security Council as the fighting developed, arguing that it was the victim of DRV aggression. The Security Council, with only the Soviet Union objecting, appointed a subcommittee consisting of Argentina, Italy, Japan, and Tunisia to investigate the Laotian complaint, but the subcommittee's investigation was inconclusive.[71]

Perceiving no basis for overt intervention, the United States responded to this situation by greatly increasing its shipments of military equipment and by dispatching military personnel (in civilian clothes) trained in counterinsurgency, also in violation of the Geneva Accords.[72] A rigged election returned the rightists to power in April 1960, but this was followed by a neutralist coup in August of that year. Rightist military officers, supported by the United States, opposed the new government, which turned for military aid to the Soviet Union and resumed discussions with the Pathet Lao regarding a coalition.[73] Rightist forces captured the capital, expelled the neutralist government, and formed a government of their own, supported by Thailand, the United States, the United Kingdom, and France; the neutralist government was recognized by the Communist states and some nonaligned states.[74]

When President Kennedy took office in 1961, the rightist government's weakness forced him to consider whether to commit American troops to Laos.[75] Unwilling to dispatch an American force as large as his military advisors said would be required, and faced with renewed evidence of the weakness of the rightists in the success of a joint neutralist–Pathet Lao offensive in March 1961, President Kennedy supported dealing with the conflict through negotiation.[76] The Soviet Union and the United Kingdom, cochairs of the Geneva Conference, accordingly called for a cease-fire and a reconvening of that conference in April 1961; the cease-fire took effect, and the conference began the following month.[77] After a combination of American reassurance to Thailand and pressure on the rightist forces an agreement on the neutralization of Laos was reached in July 1962; the agreement required the withdrawal of all foreign troops from Laos and was signed by all fourteen states attending the conference.[78]

In 1963, however, fighting resumed, as neither the rightists nor the Pathet Lao had been willing to settle for the status quo. Both sides, furthermore, relied on outside aid; the DRV, dependent as it was on Laotian supply lines into the ROV, aided the Pathet Lao with troops, while the United States provided considerable military aid to the rightists. When the United States began using its air forces in Vietnam during the Second Indochina War, it also began bombing in Laos, attacking both the Ho Chi Minh Trail and Pathet Lao positions; the United States also organized various "irregular" units for the Laotian fighting. Despite all this activity, however, neither side made much headway in Laos; by 1973 the positions of the contending sides were little different than they had been ten years earlier. Also in 1973, shortly after the Paris Peace Accords on Vietnam, a peace agreement was reached in Laos as well, providing for a coalition government. By the end of 1975, however, the Communists had taken power.[79]

During the fighting in Laos the intervening powers' justifications varied. In the 1950s the United States sought to conceal its presence, its troops not wearing uniforms. It admitted its bombing in Laos as early as January 1965, apparently justifying it on the basis of Communist activities in that state; at least that justification was offered by the prime minister of Laos in 1969.[80] The DRV sought to conceal its activities within Laos,[81] but they were widely known.

Third-state reaction to all this was relatively muted after the failed effort in 1962 to neutralize Laos; presumably, the more intense fighting in Vietnam attracted more attention. In any case, aside from some negative reaction to an abortive ROV penetration of Laos in 1971 aimed at DRV supply routes,[82] there seemed to be little outside interest in non-Laotian activities in Laos after 1962.

This case, then, involved support of internal factions by outside states, which included active participation in combat. To the extent that they justified their actions, the outside states did so by reference to one another's activities. Their motives were ideological, with the DRV also seeking to protect its supply routes through Laos from interference. Third states reacted very little to the situation, apparently seeing it, understandably, as inseparable from the larger problem of the Second Indochina War.

## United Nations Operations in the Republic of the Congo (1960–1964)

The United Nations intervention in the civil strife in the Republic of the Congo (now Zaire) in the early 1960s is different from most of the uses of force discussed in this chapter in that it was from its inception a genuinely multilateral undertaking. The crisis that led to this unusual international action began as soon as the Congo formally attained its independence from Belgium on June 30, 1960. Violence between various groups erupted the next day, and within a few days a military mutiny had produced great disorder. As a consequence, the European population of the Congo found itself facing a potentially dangerous situation. Belgium had retained relatively large numbers of troops in the Congo and used them against the mutinous troops of the Congolese Army, ostensibly to protect the European population. This Belgian action was greatly resented by the government of the Congo, which called for assistance from the United Nations against what it labeled as Belgian aggression. To further complicate matters, the province of Katanga declared its secession from the rest of the Congo on July 11. On July 12 the Soviet Union demanded Belgian withdrawal from the Congo in terms implying a threat of intervention.[83]

It was against this background that, on July 14, the Security Council authorized Secretary-General Dag Hammarskjöld to assemble from troops offered by member states a force intended to maintain law and order.[84] Hammarskjöld's intention was to use this force solely to restore the peace, thereby eliminating the basis for Belgium's continued military presence in the Congo without having to address directly charges of Belgian aggression.[85] Made up principally of troops supplied by African states, units of the UN force began arriving in the Congo on July 15.[86]

United Nations forces remained in the Congo for nearly four years. The crisis did not end once a final withdrawal of Belgian military units had been achieved in September 1960,[87] but rather became focused on the Katangese secession, rightly seen as strongly supported by various European economic interests,[88] and on the continued infighting in the Congo's central government. The United Nations initially sought to avoid taking sides in the various intra-Congolese struggles,[89] but found itself drawn into opposing the Katangese secession because of the large number of foreigners involved in supporting the secessionist government in both administrative and military capacities.[90]

In the meantime, the United States had become heavily invested in supporting the operation.[91] The U.S. policy had originally been tightly focused on exclusion of anti-Western elements from the Congolese government.[92] The Kennedy administration broadened American objectives to include an effort to regain American influence among Third World states by acknowledging those states' opposition to continued European dominance of non-European areas; the United States also hoped to make more use of the United Nations as an instrument of diplomacy.[93] These objectives led to U.S. support of operations against Katanga, since the Congo's central government regarded the ending of the secession as crucial, to the point that its leaders spoke of seeking aid from the Soviet Union if necessary to gain this end.[94] Such a development could, in turn, force the United States to support Katanga, which would strengthen links between Third World nationalists and the Soviet Union; further, the United States feared that if the United Nations were to back down at this point the result could be serious damage to that organization.[95] In the end, multinational forces of the United Nations halted the Katanga secession in an operation beginning in December 1962.[96] Kantanga formally surrendered in January 1963, and the UN troops eventually completed their withdrawal from the Congo in June 1964.[97]

This operation was a multinational intervention in postcolonial civil strife within the Congo. Initially aimed against a foreign military presence, the UN force ended by supporting one side in an internal war, albeit a war in which the United Nations' opponent had considerable foreign support. The motives of the different parties varied. The Third World states were simply opposed to any vestiges of colonialism in Africa and perceived Katanga as a perpetuation of European control.[98] The United States, as noted, sought to avert the emergence of a pro-Soviet government in the Congo while aligning itself with the strong anticolonial views of the Third World. The Soviet Union had also associated itself with the anticolonialist side. And the United Nations itself, in the person of Hammarskjöld, sought to prevent the Congo from becoming an arena of great power rivalry.[99] Confused and overtaken by internal imperatives though it was, for purposes of this study the Congo operation can be seen as reflecting the view that European colonialism of non-European areas was intolerable and that force was justifiable as a device to eliminate such colonialism. Third World states obviously accepted this characterization, and all the other actors—the United States, the Soviet Union, and Dag Hammarskjöld—found themselves forced to accept it as well as a condition of achieving their own objectives.

## Yemeni Civil War (1962–1970)

On November 26, 1962, the government of Imam Mohammed of Yemen was overthrown in a military coup.[100] The United Arab Republic (UAR) was deeply involved in planning the coup, arguably because of its opposition to conservative Arab regimes and its desire to restore its prestige among Arab states, tarnished by political reverses.[101] In any case, UAR officials aided the plotters by putting into service armored vehicles used in the coup, supplying them with helicopters, and dispatching Egyptian troops to sustain the new government prior to the actual overthrow.[102]

In the weeks following the coup large numbers of UAR troops were sent into Yemen, without which the new Yemen Arab Republic would have been unable to maintain itself against the heavily armed and independent-minded tribesmen who made up much of Yemen's population; UAR troops even formed the bodyguard of the new president, as-Sallal.[103] The UAR justified its massive presence by claiming that its troops were present only at the request of the Republican regime to aid in resisting attacks from Saudi Arabia and Jordan; in fact, no such attacks took place.[104] By mid-October, meanwhile, it became clear that Imam Mohammed had survived the coup, and he and other members of the royal family began organizing a resistance to the Republic and its Egyptian supporters.[105] Moved by hostility to the UAR, Saudi Arabia began providing the Royalists with arms and money; Jordan also provided arms and training officers for the same reason.[106] In response, UAR aircraft bombed villages in Saudi Arabia, to little effect.[107] The United States sent military aid to the Saudis when it appeared that war might erupt between them and the UAR but also helped mediate an end to that aspect of the crisis.[108]

A stalemated civil war continued in Yemen for five years. During this period very large numbers of Egyptian troops were sent to Yemen, and the UAR essentially controlled Yemen's internal affairs; it was, however, unable to break the resistance of the Royalists.[109] The Royalists, in turn, received extensive financial support from Saudi Arabia, as well as aid from Jordan, Pakistan, Iran, the states of British-protected southern Arabia, and possibly from the United Kingdom itself, though the British denied providing assistance.[110]

In August 1967 the Saudis and Egyptians each agreed to end aid to the contending Yemeni factions; Egypt acted because President Nasser was reluctant to continue an unpopular war in the wake of his defeat in the Six-Day War with Israel, because of Saudi promises of financial aid if Egypt withdrew completely from Yemen, and because of the great costs of the war to Egypt.[111] The last Egyptian troops and administrators left Yemen by December 1967.[112] President as-Sallal of the Republican regime was overthrown in November 1967, and Saudi Arabia finally ended all aid to the Royalists in March 1968.[113] The new Republican regime was more moderate and expressed willingness to deal with supporters of the Royalists; Saudi Arabia induced the Imam to step aside, and the contending factions reached agreement in May 1970, following Saudi recognition of the Republic the preceding month.[114] This agreement ended the civil war.

Although this war could have been seen, prior to the Egyptian withdrawal, as an effort by Egypt to impose itself on Yemen, third states seemed willing to overlook the Republican regime's dependence on the UAR. The United States extended diplomatic recognition in 1962, despite Saudi objections and the Egyptian presence; so did many other governments, including American allies.[115] The United States also provided economic aid to the Republican regime.[116] The Soviet Union provided economic aid, as well as offers of military support, and the German Democratic Republic gave aid as well.[117] In December 1962 the General Assembly voted overwhelmingly to seat the Republican rather than the Royalist delegation, despite Saudi arguments to the contrary based on the degree of UAR control of the new regime.[118] The Arab League also accepted the credentials of a Republican delegation in March 1963 and in September of that year urged its members to aid and provide international support to the Republicans.[119] On the other hand, France and the United Kingdom did not recognize the Republican regime during the civil war, and conservative Arab states also maintained distant relations, thanks to Saudi Arabia's influence.[120]

The foregoing suggests a high degree of international acquiescence to the replacement of the Imamate, despite the circumstances of the coup. Beyond this point the international community had little effect on the war itself. While there were some international efforts to mediate the crisis—most notably a United Nations effort to monitor an ultimately unsuccessful disengagement agreement brokered by the United States—little was achieved[121] until after the Egyptian withdrawal and the fall of as-Sallal.

The Yemeni civil war was thus the product of an effort by the UAR to acquire an ideological ally and boost its prestige by establishing a satellite regime in Yemen. It sought to achieve this end by strongly supporting a coup by sympathetic Yemenis and then by propping up a highly dependent regime; it did not seek outright conquest. Some states effectively acquiesced in this plan by recognizing the Republican regime. Others opposed the UAR to the point of aiding the Yemeni Royalists, this opposition apparently reflecting more mistrust of President Nasser of the UAR than affirmative sympathy for the Imam. Most of the world seemed to pay little attention to the war; in any case, states generally did not see fit actively to oppose the war effort of the UAR.

## Cuba/Venezuela (1963, 1966, 1967)

In November 1963 an arms cache, subsequently proven by the OAS to be of Cuban origin, was discovered in Venezuela; the arms were intended to aid Venezuela's Communist Party overthrow the government of that state.[122] Cuba's motives, apparently, were straightforwardly ideological—it sought to help bring about the replacement of a non-Communist government with a Communist one.[123] The main international response to this action was that of the OAS which voted 15–4 (Venezuela not voting) in July 1964 to impose trade sanctions on Cuba because of its behavior and also called on OAS members to end diplomatic relations with Cuba; only Bolivia, Chile, Mexico, and Uruguay voted against the resolution. All of these except Mexico duly ended diplomatic relations with Cuba by September 1964; all fifteen states that had voted for the resolution had ended relations with Cuba prior to July 1964.[124]

Cuban interest in Venezuela did not end, however. Venezuelans trained by Cuba were landed in July 1966,[125] and a landing of Cuban officers in May 1967 was intercepted by Venezuela.[126] The OAS responded by condemning Cuban aggression and intervention, and by communicating its conclusions to the United Nations, urging members of the United Nations to impose economic sanctions on Cuba until it altered its policies.[127] The OAS communication was followed by a Soviet statement strongly supportive of Cuba.[128]

Cuba in this case sought to intervene in an internal conflict in Venezuela. The international response was limited. The OAS sanctions imposed in 1964 could not realistically have been thought likely to alter Cuba's behavior, and the actions taken in 1967 were even less likely to have an impact. States outside the Americas apparently did not react to these events. It would appear that Cuba's effort to subvert its neighbors was thought to require some sort of response but not considered serious enough to trigger a strong international reaction against it. Alternatively, given the reality of existing American sanctions against Cuba and the Soviet Union's support for that state, it may be that states found it hard to see what further steps could have been taken against Cuba that, given the ideological climate of the period, would not have risked another Cuban missile crisis. Certainly, it seems likely that the Soviet Union's support for Cuba influenced states' reactions to Cuban subversive activities.

## Omani Civil War (1965–1976)

On June 9, 1965, a rebellion began in the province of Dhofar against the Sultan of Oman, inspired by the repressiveness of the sultan's government and his refusal to permit any degree of economic or social development in his country. When South Yemen became independent as the People's Democratic Republic of Yemen (PDRY), that state began to offer extensive assistance to the rebellion, providing weapons, training, a base area, and extensive indoctrination in Marxism-Leninism. The Soviet Union and the PRC also provided arms to the rebels, whose movement was called the People's Front for the Liberation of the Arabian Gulf (PFLOAG). The interest of the PDRY, the Soviet Union, and the PRC was inspired by Oman's strategic position at the mouth of the Persian Gulf.[129] Presumably, the ideological opposition to conservative Arab rulers that had figured in the PDRY's own independence war also played a role in its decision to intervene in Oman.

In July 1970 the sultan was overthrown by his son, who himself became sultan. The new sultan introduced an ambitious program of development, fueled by oil revenues. He also devoted considerable sums to the fight against PFLOAG. He was assisted in this by the United Kingdom, which provided officers and noncommissioned officers for his forces, and by Iran, which sent combat units for about one year. Pakistan permitted the sultan to recruit within its territory, and Jordan sent both engineers and a special forces battalion.[130]

By 1974 PFLOAG—which had changed its name to the People's Front for the Liberation of Oman—was on the defensive. The PRC had ceased to provide it with supplies in 1972 at the urging of the Shah of Iran, in whose country the PRC had developed extensive economic interests, although the Soviet Union, Libya, and Cuba continued to provide arms and training.[131] By the end of 1975 the sultan's forces had managed to cut the crucial supply routes from the PDRY to the PFLO, despite the entry into Oman of PDRY regular troops in October 1975. The operations against the insurgents' supply lines had provoked artillery fire from the PDRY, to which Oman responded with air strikes, this cross-border combat beginning in October and ending on November 21, 1975. The sultan's forces captured the last insurgent-held village in December 1975, and the rebellion ended. This result was formalized on March 11, 1976, in a cease-fire agreement between Oman and the PDRY, the latter accepting a cease-fire in part because of Saudi diplomatic pressure.[132]

Aside from the outside participation described above, there was little third-state interest in this conflict. The General Assembly adopted a resolution calling upon the United Kingdom to permit the people of Oman to exercise their right to self-determination each year from 1965 through 1970, despite British arguments that Oman was already independent.[133] After the Security Council acted favorably on Oman's 1971 application for admission to the United Nations, the General Assembly duly voted to admit the country.[134] Other than this cajoling of the United Kingdom to grant independence to Oman, no UN organ addressed any question that could be deemed related to the civil war. Nor does there appear to have been any third-state reaction outside the UN context.

This conflict was a civil war with outside intervention on both sides. Each intervenor acted from admitted ideological motives. Third states took little interest; since Oman was in fact an independent state, and a member of the United Nations after 1971, it was difficult to fit this dispute within the self-determination context, which may explain the general indifference to the war. Neither side suffered any sanctions. Nor did Oman attack the PDRY, aside from responses to actual attacks from the PDRY, despite the fact that the latter's support for the insurgents included some limited commitment of PDRY troops.

## Chadian Civil Wars (1969–1972, 1975–1993)

In March 1969 President Tombalbaye of Chad sought additional aid from France to deal with an insurrection that had begun in 1966. It had been launched by the Arabicized Muslims of northern Chad in reaction to the oppression and anti-Muslim policies of Tombalbaye's non-Muslim government, which was drawn from the ethnic groups of the southern part of the country.

French troops regularly stationed in Chad had intervened in August 1968 to recapture from the rebels a fort in the northern sector of the country. When French combat troops withdrew from the country in November of that year, the rebellion, which was strongly supported by Libya, experienced a resurgence. In March 1969 Tombalbaye therefore asked the French to return. Accordingly, French troops were dispatched, France demanding as a condition that Chad accept a French mission intended to reform Chad's internal administration. By 1971 the situation had improved for Tombalbaye's government, and France elected to withdraw its troops. France took this step in order to improve its relations with Libya, the rebels' supporter. After the French withdrawal, however, the rebels' fortunes once again improved. France was not willing to see Tombalbaye defeated and demanded that Libya cease its aid to the rebels. Libya at this time was seeking to purchase jet aircraft from France and accordingly had an incentive to accede to French demands; a deal was therefore worked out. In 1972 Chad resumed diplomatic relations with Libya, while Libya reduced its support to the rebels, the main rebel headquarters shifting from Tripoli to Algiers. In 1973 Libya announced the annexation of the Aouzou Strip, adjacent to Libya in extreme northern Chad, an action to which Tombalbaye took no strong exception. France's withdrawal of all its combat troops was completed by September 1972.[135]

The motives of the two intervening states were strikingly similar in some respects. France apparently felt a degree of responsibility for maintaining stability in its former colony, but its motives were not entirely altruistic. It also sought to safeguard its access to Chad's mineral wealth. In addition, Chad's position relative to that of other states in France's African sphere of influence was quite important, and France sought to ensure that a state so located remained friendly. It was also concerned about a possible domino effect if similar rural risings spread throughout its area of interest; in this regard President de Gaulle's concern was shared by President Houphouet-Boigny of Côte d'Ivoire, who urged the intervention. France concerned itself as well with broader Western interests in Africa.[136]

Libya's initial intervention reflected some concern for aiding fellow Muslims facing oppression from a non-Muslim government but was also motivated by Libya's interest in keeping Chad weak and subject to heavy Libyan influence. This continuing interest had ideological, strategic, and economic aspects. Ideologically, Libya sought to unify the Arab and Islamic world behind a radical and Islamic social vision; Chad, with its significant Muslim, Arab, and Arabicized population, would be a natural component of such a unified entity. Strategically, Chad's location was more important to Libya than to France. Not only did Chad border on states that Libya wished to influence; it also bordered on Libya, and thus could have been a danger to Libya in unfriendly hands. Economically, Libya, like France, sought access to Chad's mineral wealth, in particular seeking to annex the mineral-rich Aouzou Strip.[137]

Third states seem to have reacted very little to either France's or Libya's interventions in this stage of Chad's civil war. France's actions may have evoked little response because the French return followed so closely on its departure in 1968 and because the French policy of supporting the incumbent government in Chad was little different from its policy elsewhere in Francophone Africa, and was supported by important states in that region. Neither intervenor faced any third-state sanctions, and both received some support from neighbors; Côte d'Ivoire, for example, supported France's actions, while Algeria aligned itself with Libya in permitting the Chadian rebels to headquarter in Algiers. Nor did either intervening state act against the other; indeed, the 1972 reduction in tensions came about because the intervenors were actively seeking to cultivate each other.

This episode, then, involved competing interventions in a civil war. One outside state sent troops to aid the incumbent government at its request; the other provided aid short of commitment of troops to the insurgents. This conflict attracted little third-state interest and no sanctions.

The Chadian civil war did not end with the events of 1972, however. Rather, it became considerably more complicated. In 1975 the Tombalbaye government of Chad was overthrown in a military coup. The new president, Malloum, was a southerner like Tombalbaye but considerably more anti-Libyan in his attitudes, opposed in particular to Libyan control of the Aouzou Strip. Despite its 1972 promises to the French, Libya had continued to provide assistance to the Front pour la Libération Nationale du Tchad (FROLINAT), the antigovernment group formed mostly from Muslims from northern Chad. In the summer of 1977 a FROLINAT offensive that included Libyan troops conquered much of northern Chad. Facing a battlefield defeat in March 1978, Malloum was forced to abandon efforts to take the matter to the Security Council and to accept the so-called Benghazi Accords, providing for a cease-fire but requiring the withdrawal of the remaining French troops in Chad and efforts at reconciliation between Malloum and FROLINAT. The accords further established Libya, Niger, and the Sudan as guarantors of their provisions, in effect recognizing a Libyan role in Chad's internal affairs.[138]

Libya had pushed FROLINAT into accepting the cease-fire, despite FROLINAT's favorable military position, apparently because of Libya's desire to maintain good relations with France. In any case, by April FROLINAT had broken the cease-fire and was advancing on Ndjamena, Chad's capital. Malloum was forced to call on France for aid, which was forthcoming in the form of both ground and air forces. Thanks to this French intervention in April and May 1978 the FROLINAT advance was halted.[139]

The summer of 1978 saw further developments of great significance for the Chadian civil war. First, in July, France and Libya effectively partitioned Chad at the 14th parallel, Libyan troops to remain north of that line and French to the south. Then, in August, under French pressure Malloum agreed to enter into a coalition government with Hissan Habré, commander of the Forces Armées du Nord (FAN), a group that had split from FROLINAT because of Habré's strong opposition to Libyan domination. The coalition failed, however, and Habré seized power in February 1979 in a bloody coup that saw the deaths of thousands of southern Chadians at the hands of FAN. Habré's coup was tacitly supported by France, which saw a northern-controlled government as the only way to end the civil war. In the postcoup confusion, however, the Libyan-supported insurgents seized their chance and took the capital. By this time the dominant group in the now-splintered insurgent camp was the Forces Armées Populaires (FAP) of Goukouni Oueddei, composed as was FAN primarily of non-Arab tribesmen from northern Chad. Also prominent in the Chadian maelstrom at this time were the Conseil Démocratique de la Révolution (CDR), an Arab group led by Asil Ahmat, and the Forces Armées Tchadiennes (FAT), composed of the southern Chadians who had formerly controlled the government.[140]

In 1979 a confused series of events led finally to the installation in Chad of a government friendly to Libya. After FAP's entry into Ndjamena, Nigeria organized a conference in its city of Kano to address the disorder in Chad. Attended by Libya, Cameroon, Sudan, and Niger as well as various Chadian factions, it led to the formation of a Gouvernement d'Union Nationale de Transition (GUNT) dominated by Goukouni and Habré and nominally including FAT but not CDR. The new government soon made clear that it was opposed to certain of Libya's designs on Chad, with even Goukouni—formerly allied with Libya—criticizing Libyan occupation of the Aouzou Strip. GUNT therefore provoked Libyan opposition. A second Kano conference led to pressure on GUNT to include pro-Libyan factions, but GUNT refused to respond. This in turn led to increased military and diplomatic action by Libya. A conference in Lagos in May 1979 led to demands by Libya, Niger, Nigeria, Cameroon, the Central African Empire, Sudan, OAU representatives, and the Chadian factions not represented in GUNT that GUNT broaden its base. These were reinforced by GUNT's exclusion from both the May 1979 summit of Francophone African states and the July 1979 OAU summit. Militarily, Libya provided arms and troops not only to its Arab, Muslim allies in the north but also to FAT, strongly opposed to the northern-dominated GUNT. France provided troops and aircraft to aid GUNT, but GUNT finally was forced to bow to pressure in August, adding FAT and various pro-Libyan groups.[141]

The reorganized GUNT collapsed in the spring of 1980, essentially over Habré's continued opposition to Libya. Fighting between FAN and the other factions began in March. In April Habré was formally expelled from the government and Goukouni—by this time president of GUNT—requested Libyan aid in dealing with FAN. In June 1980 Libya and GUNT signed a treaty of friendship, and large numbers of Libyan troops openly entered the fight against FAN in October. France had withdrawn its troops after Goukouni's request in May, and thus unaided FAN was unable to withstand the forces arrayed against it—all the other Chadian factions, as well as Libyan armor and aircraft. In December 1980 FAN lost control of Ndjamena.[142]

As will be discussed in more detail below, Libya had begun to encounter increasing third-state criticism for its intervention in Chad by late 1980. This criticism greatly increased in January 1981 when it was announced that Libya and Chad would be merged into one state. In fact, Goukouni had agreed to this idea only after being personally coerced, and other African states objected immediately. By October 1981 the Chadians' own objections to Libyan domination and diplomatic pressure from other African states led Goukouni to formally request Libya to withdraw its troops from Chad. Libya agreed to the extent of pulling all its forces back to the Aouzou Strip. Apparently, imminent military exercises in Egypt by American, Egyptian, Sudanese, and Omani forces contributed to Libya's decision to withdraw. Once Libyan troops withdrew, however, Goukouni was unable to resist Habré's forces, who were still in the field and were now allied with FAT since that group had become concerned at the extent of Libyan domination of GUNT. In June 1982 Habré's forces retook Ndjamena and he was recognized by the OAU as president of Chad; Goukouni and GUNT were forced to reestablish themselves in northern Chad under Libyan protection.[143]

Fighting resumed in the summer of 1983, as Libya was angered by the Habré government's refusal to enter into a treaty settling the border question and by its increasingly close relations with the United States. GUNT's forces were strongly supported by Congo, Algeria, Benin, and especially Libya, and Libya's involvement led the United States to provide Habré's troops with weapons and to pressure France to intervene militarily. France, pressured as well by its African allies but facing domestic dissatisfaction with its African policies, dispatched troops; it also sent aircraft that were used against the GUNT/Libyan forces to states bordering Chad. Zaire also sent troops to aid Habré. The advance of the anti-Habré forces was halted. In September 1984 France and Libya agreed to mutual troop withdrawals from Chad; France had complied by November, but Libya violated its agreement and maintained forces in Chad. Nonetheless, fighting died down for approximately two years.[144]

Over that period Habré was able to consolidate his hold on southern Chad and bring about a reconciliation with some of his opponents. Libya by this time had a number of permanent bases in Chad, as well as relatively large numbers of troops stationed there. GUNT saw its strength wane, becoming increasingly dependent on Libya. It attempted an offensive in early 1986, only to be repulsed by Habré. As the year progressed, factional fighting became a serious problem within GUNT, as various elements of that group fought each other and the Libyans. In the fall of 1986 Libya removed Goukouni as GUNT's leader, both angering his FAP forces and again raising questions among other African states as to Libya's intentions regarding Chad. FAP responded with attacks on Libyan troops. Habré seized his opportunity and began an offensive against the Libyans. Drawing increasing support from disillusioned GUNT factions and benefiting from a degree of French air support, Habré's Forces Armées Nationales Tchadiennes (FANT) made steady progress. By the fall of 1987 FANT had even driven Libya out of the Aouzou Strip and conducted a raid into Libyan territory, although a subsequent Libyan offensive recaptured at least some of the strip. During this period French ground troops had been present in Chad, although apparently they had not taken part in the fighting.[145]

In 1988 Libyan policy appeared to take a startling turn. Libya recognized the Habré government in May and agreed to diplomatic relations in October. In August 1989, with Algerian mediation, the two sides agreed to negotiate their differences over the Aouzou Strip and to take the question to the International Court of Justice (ICJ) if they could not resolve it. The matter finally was resolved by an ICJ decision in 1994 awarding the strip to Chad; both parties accepted the decision and obtained from the Security Council a promise of UN aid in carrying it out.[146]

The current state of relations between Libya and Chad is not entirely clear. In December 1990 Habré was overthrown in a military coup led by Idriss Deby; French troops in Chad remained neutral, ostensibly because the matter was a Chadian internal affair but apparently influenced by the poor human rights record of the Habré government. There is reason to think that an unsuccessful coup attempt by the new government's interior minister in October 1991 reflected renewed Libyan efforts to destabilize Chad, since this minister had earlier purported to conclude an agreement with Libya providing for broad-ranging cooperation between the two states that Chad quickly disavowed in light of outstanding Libya-Chad disputes. In December 1991 insurgents invaded Chad from Nigeria; the government claimed victory by January 3. French reinforcements had been sent on January 3 but were withdrawn four days later. The United States praised the French action and expressed concern at Libyan efforts to unseat Chad's government.[147]

The foregoing account mentions various actions taken by third states that had a concrete effect on the course of the Chadian civil war, but it will be helpful briefly to recall the actions of third states other than France, the United States, and Libya, as well as to mention certain actions taken that seemed to have had little effect. First, it will be recalled that in 1979 a number of Chad's neighbors exerted strong pressure on the first GUNT government to broaden its base. Nigeria in particular took an interest, four times serving as the venue for conferences dealing with Chad and dispatching troops in early 1979 in a vain attempt to help maintain order.[148] The Lagos Accords concluded later that year provided for an African peacekeeping force in Chad, but the force—eventually composed of troops from Congo and Nigeria—accomplished little.[149] After the Libyan-backed offensive by GUNT against FAN in the fall of 1980 the OAU's committee on Chad in November 1980 called for a cease-fire and for the withdrawal of "all foreign forces" from Chad but did not mention Libya.[150]

The beginnings of overt African concern at Libyan activities were manifested at another Lagos conference in December 1980. The Central African Republic, Cameroon, Niger, Sudan, Togo, Guinea, and Senegal all sought a declaration demanding a Libyan withdrawal; Nigeria, Benin, Congo, and Sierra Leone, however, held out for a resolution that did not name Libya, simply calling for the withdrawal of all foreign troops.[151] But by the end of 1980 the Central African Republic, Morocco, Senegal, Gambia, Gabon, Ghana, and Mauritania had all either broken diplomatic relations with Libya or expelled Libyan diplomats.[152] The proposed merger between Libya and Chad reinforced this trend, as Nigeria, Niger, Mali, and Upper Volta all broke relations with Libya, and the twelve-state OAU ad hoc committee on Chad issued a resolution calling for the withdrawal of all Libyan troops from Chad.[153] Gabon, Sierra Leone, Niger, and Guinea all condemned the merger, as did Benin and Congo. Concern at Libyan expansionism became widespread, and only Ethiopia defended Libya's action.[154] Continuing OAU pressure contributed to GUNT's decision to ask Libya to withdraw its troops in 1981.[155]

To ease Goukouni's concerns about the consequences of the Libyan withdrawal in late 1981, an OAU peacekeeping force was created to replace the Libyans, including troops from Zaire, Nigeria, Togo, Senegal, and Guinea. The United States and France had both urged the establishment of this force and had offered to provide it with financial assistance and military advice. Furthermore, the Security Council acknowledged the creation of the force and agreed on April 30, 1982, to provide it with financial, administrative, and logistic support. However, the force proved ineffectual when Habré renewed his offensive after the Libyans' departure and was withdrawn in June 1982 before UN assistance could begin.[156] After 1983 the OAU as an entity together with several of its members sought to mediate between Chadian factions and, after Habré's successes of 1987, between Chad and Libya.[157] None of these efforts bore fruit until the Algerian mediation of 1989, mentioned above. And while by 1988 most African states were opposed to Libya's policy in Chad as expansionist,[158] few were prepared to take steps against it, except as described above.

It should be noted, finally, that the Soviet Union consistently supplied Libya with arms and training throughout this period, though it is not clear whether Soviet personnel actually entered Chad to aid the Libyans. The Soviets apparently did not try to prevent Libya's use of Soviet-supplied weapons in Chad.[159]

The United Nations played almost no role in this crisis. As noted, the Security Council agreed to aid the OAU peacekeeping force in 1982. Also, in 1983 the Security Council by consensus called for a peaceful resolution of the dispute through the facilities of the OAU.[160] The debate on the 1983 resolution focused on the territorial dispute between the states and showed few states willing to press Libya on its continued claim to the Aouzou Strip, let alone on its continuing intervention in Chad.

The actual motives of France and Libya for intervening were described above, in connection with the first period of Chad's civil war. The justifications the two sides offered for their post-1975 actions differed. France essentially pointed to requests from whatever government was in power in Chad. Libya also relied on requests, albeit from the Chadian people, but also claimed to be contending against imperialism that was seeking to impose a regime in Chad and to be acting in self-defense, claiming that aid to the forces in Chad opposed to Libya was in fact directed against Libya. Libya also claimed to fear encirclement by hostile regimes and to be aiding fellow Muslims.[161] French justifications were more or less accurate, though they failed to capture the range of French motives. Libya's justifications were more misleading, given Libya's motives; in particular, its support of FAT against Habré and Goukouni amounted to aiding non-Muslims warring against Muslims, contrary to its claims.

As noted above, this conflict began as a civil war with foreign states aiding the opposing factions. It evolved into a more complicated conflict; one of the intervening states, Libya, became a primary combatant, with the goal of reducing the target state to a dependency. Third-state reaction, by and large, was weak. To be sure, Libya faced in France a rival for strategic influence in the affected region and in the United States a powerful ideological opponent; both of these states aided the internal opposition to Libya, providing military supplies and, occasionally, combat support. Otherwise, however, what might be called Libya's effort at a de facto subjugation of Chad met relatively little third-state opposition. In particular, other states in the region tended to focus on negotiated solutions to the conflict rather than on material opposition to Libya. It should be stressed, however, that regional opposition to Libya's plan to formally merge with Chad was very strong and ultimately a very important factor in the failure of that plan. It is also interesting that, despite evidence of Libya's occupation of areas of Chad even south of the Aouzou Strip, no UN organ made any serious effort to address the conflict, preferring to leave it to the OAU and its tradionally mediational approach.

## Syria/Jordan (1970)

In September 1970 the tense relations between Palestine guerilla organizations based in Jordan and the government of that country came to a head. After a series of actions by the guerillas clearly intended to undermine the government's authority, including an attempt to assassinate King Hussein and the seizure of the government of one Jordanian city, as well as airliner hijackings that brought the guerillas widespread condemnation, Hussein moved against them on September 16. The result was civil war.[162]

The Ba'ath regime in Syria, Jordan's neighbor, was a strong supporter of the Palestinians.[163] For this reason Syria dispatched a tank force into northern Jordan four days after the fighting erupted between the Jordanian government and the guerillas; it sought to conceal the fact of its intervention by disguising the force as a unit of the Palestine Liberation Army, although it was in fact Syrian.[164] By September 23 the Syrians had withdrawn.[165] In part this was because of the resistance put up by the Jordanian Army.[166] Israel's threat to intervene on behalf of Hussein also played a role,[167] that threat in turn having been made in part because of Israel's own desire to save Hussein and in part because of urgings from the United States, which promised support against Egypt and the Soviet Union if those states attacked Israel after an Israeli attack on Syria.[168] The United States also pressured the Soviet Union to urge Syria to withdraw, putting troops on the alert and stressing that it could not tolerate a change in the balance of power in the Middle East; the Soviets did in fact press the Syrians to back down.[169] They had originally acquiesced in the Syrian decision to attack, perhaps because they did not wish to jeopardize their relations with Syria and also because they stood to gain if King Hussein were overthrown.[170] Thus, in the face of American-inspired Soviet pressure, American-backed Israeli threats, and battlefield defeat at the hands of Jordan's Army, Syria withdrew its troops. King Hussein prevailed in the confrontation with the guerillas, finally expelling them completely in 1971.[171]

This Syrian attack was an intervention in a civil war. It was motivated by ideological affinity; no justifications were offered, since Syria denied that it was taking place. Third-state reaction was limited but powerful: Syria was threatened with severe military action if it did not withdraw. It should be noted, however, that the threat was grounded on concerns for the balance of power in the region; it was not phrased as a response to a violation of law.

## Tanzania/Uganda (1972)

After President Obote's government in Uganda was overthrown by Idi Amin in 1971 relations between Tanzania and Uganda deteriorated. In part this development reflected the good relationship between Obote and President Nyerere of Tanzania. It also was caused by Amin's claims to portions of Tanzanian territory and by Tanzania's fears of invasion from Uganda.[172] Incursions into Tanzania by Ugandan troops and a bombing incident by the Ugandan air force also affected Tanzania's attitude. Against this background Nyerere decided to support an invasion of Uganda by guerillas loyal to Obote by providing arms and Tanzanian bases for Obote's forces.[173]

The invasion took place on September 15, 1972, and was a fiasco. Ugandan troops defeated it quickly, and it appeared possible that Tanzania and Uganda would go to war, particularly after Ugandan air raids on Tanzanian territory.[174] The OAU and several individual African states sought to mediate, however, and an agreement proposed by President Barre of Somalia was finally accepted by both sides on October 7. Under the terms of this agreement each side would refrain from attacking the other and pull its troops back from the border. Tanzania agreed as well to pull Obote's guerillas back from the border and to cease supporting activities aimed at subverting Amin's goverment.[175]

Third-state reaction to this incident was mixed and limited. Some states condemned Tanzania, more or less harshly. These included Nigeria, Guinea, and Egypt; Libya went so far as to send troops to Amin's aid. The OAU was also critical. On the other hand, Sudan sought unsuccessfully to prevent the overflight of its territory by Libyan aircraft carrying troops and arms for Amin. And, as noted above, the OAU sought to mediate, as did Somalia.[176] The United Nations did not address the issue.

This conflict amounted to intervention by one state in internal fighting in another, the intervention consisting of provision of arms and base areas by the intervening state to the group rebelling against the government of the other state. The most significant third-state reaction was the provision of mediation services, which led to an agreement that halted the conflict. While support for the affected state was expressed, no sanctions were imposed on the intervenor.

## Mozambique Civil War (1975–1992)

In 1975 Rhodesia began to organize and fund an anti-FRELIMO organization in Mozambique, moved by the mutual hostility between itself and Mozambique, Mozambique's closure of its border with Rhodesia, and Mozambique's support for the Zimbabwe African National Liberation Army (ZANLA). Initially, the group was ineffectual. By 1977, however, it was operating a radio station and had begun to recruit among Mozambican émigrés in Lisbon and disaffected supporters of FRELIMO. The group, by now called the Resistencia Nacional Mozambicana, or RENAMO, began serious attacks in 1977. At this time RENAMO was purely a creature of Rhodesia, carrying out sabotage operations and attacking FRELIMO or ZANLA targets but operating at a rather modest level.[177]

During this period South Africa had provided both arms and propaganda aid to RENAMO. After the end of the Rhodesian war in 1980, and by previous arrangement with the Rhodesian military, South Africa took over operation of RENAMO. It sought to use RENAMO to destabilize Mozambique, forcing that state to cease its support for the African National Congress (ANC), which operated out of Mozambique. Initially, Mozambique's operations against RENAMO in 1980 appeared successful, and it refused to reduce its support to the ANC. But South Africa armed and trained new RENAMO units that it airlifted into Mozambique in late 1980. By late 1981 RENAMO, as well as South African special forces, were operating in wider areas of Mozambique and with increasing effectiveness.[178]

In 1983 the United States began to pressure South Africa to cease its destabilization of Mozambique, fearing that the military threat would drive Mozambique to seek greater aid from Communist states. South Africa in fact did agree to end its support for RENAMO in the Nkomati Accords of March 1984 in return for Mozambique's promise to end its aid to the ANC. South Africa also sought to broker peace talks between RENAMO and FRELIMO, but this effort was unsuccessful, the talks collapsing after an unexpected RENAMO walkout in October 1984, arguably inspired by that organization's internal divisions and its resulting inability to negotiate.[179]

After 1984 South Africa exercised much less control over RENAMO than it had earlier; it did not, however, end all its support in that year, despite its promises in the Nkomati Accords and despite American pressure.[180] By 1989, however, it appeared that the level of South African support for RENAMO had declined to a relatively low level, the earlier post–Nkomati South African aid arguably flowing from elements of the South African military acting in defiance of the country's political leadership. In any case, it was clear that RENAMO had for some time been more than a South African puppet; for example, in 1988 it attacked power pylons that formed part of the Cahora Bassa dam project despite South Africa's commitment to the success of that project.[181] Rather, although it lacked any political goal other than obtaining power for its leadership, and despite its brutal treatment of Mozambican peasants, RENAMO had been able to maintain itself by drawing on popular dislike for FRELIMO's economic plans and on its own sensitivity to Mozambicans' religious sensibilities, which FRELIMO tended to ignore.[182]

By June 1989 both FRELIMO and RENAMO realized that neither of them could defeat the other militarily, and they began the first cautious moves toward peace talks. In 1990 Mozambique decided to abandon its one-party political system, and on October 4, 1992, the two sides agreed to a peace treaty. That treaty provided for United Nations supervised elections, which the Security Council agreed to oversee in December 1992, though the holding of the elections called for in the peace plan was delayed by the slow arrival of UN peacekeeping troops.[183]

A number of third states reacted to this conflict. The United States and the United Kingdom consistently supported Mozambique with financial aid and through diplomacy, pressuring both South Africa and RENAMO.[184] Portugal sought to act as a mediator.[185] Zimbabwe contributed thousands of troops to aid Mozambique in the war against RENAMO, partly out of gratitude for Mozambican assistance during the Rhodesian War and partly because of its great dependence on communications routes running through Mozambique. Tanzania also assisted Mozambique, and Zambia conducted occasional cross-border raids on RENAMO, though it did not station troops in Mozambique.[186] Other states from time to time condemned South Africa's involvement with RENAMO but took no action directly bearing on the conflict. And, of course, the Security Council's decision to oversee the elections intended to end the conflict was an important contributor to stopping the fighting.

On the other side, Malawi was of assistance to RENAMO for years, partly because of ideological differences with then Marxist-Leninist Mozambique and partly because of territorial ambitions, though this support was reduced due to a combination of pressure from Zimbabwe and Zambia and resentment at the burdens the war next door imposed on Malawi. Kenya provided bases and training for RENAMO, while also being active in the FRELIMO-RENAMO mediation process.[187]

This conflict was essentially a foreign-inspired insurgency that went out of control. The states originally organizing the insurgency themselves faced internal fighting and acted as they did to counter the aid the target state gave to insurgents against their own authority. Other outside states aided the incumbent government against the foreign-organized insurgency. The aid received by the insurgents decreased over time, in part due to pressure—although not sanctions—from third states against the insurgents' chief supporter. Third states also sought to push forward diplomatic efforts to reconcile the combatants. The thrust of third-state activity was primarily diplomatic, with Zimbabwe also being heavily involved as a combatant against RENAMO, though not directly against South Africa. Except in one important respect, then, the conflict repeats the patterns seen in other postcolonial African insurgencies: no sanctions directed against the states supporting the insurgents, and a tendency for the fighting to end with the assistance of, rather than through sanctions imposed by, third states. The distinction between this and other insurgencies was that this one was itself an effort by states confronted by rebellions to sanction a state aiding those rebellions.

## First Angolan Civil War (1975)

At the time of the coup in Portugal and the subsequent cease-fire in the Angolan nationalist insurgency described in Chapter 3, three Angolan nationalist groups were contenders to take power in Angola: the Frente Nacional de Libertação de Angola (FNLA), the Movimiento Popular de Libertação de Angola (MPLA), and the União Nacional para a Independência Total de Angola (UNITA). The MPLA had received extensive military aid from the Soviet Union. The FNLA received arms from the United States, arms and training from the PRC, and arms, training, and the aid of regular forces from Zaire. UNITA had the highest degree of popular support and the weakest military base of the three.[188]

After some jockeying for position and pressure by the OAU, the three groups agreed on January 5, 1975, to cooperate peacefully. This was followed by an agreement between the three groups and the Portuguese on January 15, 1975, to establish a provisional government, with representation in the government and army for each group.[189] In March, however, the FNLA began to attack MPLA installations in Luanda, and fighting became heavy and widespread by July, after unsuccessful OAU efforts to urge cooperation.[190]

In the fighting that followed, each combatant relied heavily on outside support, at least for weapons. Seeking an opportunity to eliminate the "radical" MPLA, South Africa provided combat troops and leaders as well as training to the poorly armed, badly organized UNITA forces, which also received arms from the United States.[191] The PRC and Romania had provided aid for the FNLA but began to back off from that connection in the fall of 1975.[192] At the urging of other African states (Algeria, Congo, Guinea, Guinea-Bissau, and Mozambique), the MPLA sought aid from Cuba: first military advisors and in November combat troops.[193] Cuba acted because of ideological affinity with the MPLA, though its decision to dispatch troops was eased by South Africa's earlier choice to involve itself.[194] The MPLA also recruited troops of the former Katangese gendarmerie, who were hostile to Zaire's government,[195] which supported the FNLA.

An advance led by South African officers and including South African troops brought a combined UNITA/FNLA force to the city of Novo Redondo on the central coast of Angola by November 14. But by this point the MPLA had been bolstered by Cuban combat units. Thus reinforced, the MPLA's troops were able to defeat a poorly planned attack by the large but badly disciplined FNLA forces in what had been intended as a final push to take Luanda by November 11, 1975, the date set by the agreement of January 15 for independence. The MPLA then counterattacked, and the FNLA's forces were rendered militarily ineffective by January. The South Africans, whose advance had been stalled by extended supply lines and Cuban-stiffened MPLA resistance, also withdrew in January, forcing UNITA to withdraw to its areas of support in southern Angola. The MPLA had become the government of Angola and was formally acknowledged as such by winning OAU membership on February 11, 1976.[196]

Third states reacted to this civil war by ignoring it, by seeking to mediate, or by backing factions with which they were ideologically compatible. Portugal had military forces in Angola during this period but made no effort to intervene in the war.[197] The OAU made efforts to end the fighting; as noted above, however, various of its members were supporting different combatants, and nothing came of the OAU's intervention.[198] Other states, as noted, intervened with supplies of arms and, in some cases, with troops, on the side of whichever of the three internal combatants seemed most akin ideologicially or, in the case of Zaire's link to the FNLA, most subject to domination. Some states not otherwise intervening at least extended diplomatic recognition to the MPLA's government on November 11 while the issue was still in doubt.[199]

Subsequently, the Security Council considered the situation in Angola, adopting a resolution condemning South Africa's intervention.[200] The PRC did not vote, however, and France, Italy, the United States, the United Kingdom, and Japan all abstained; all six explained their actions as motivated by the resolution's failure to refer to intervention by states other than South Africa, the PRC specifying the Soviet Union's intervention in particular.[201]

This period of civil war in Angola was marked by extensive foreign intervention justified mainly by reference to the intervenors' own interests. This intervention went so far as to include action by regular armies of at least three states: Cuba, South Africa, and Zaire. It may be that this scramble was facilitated by one somewhat unusual feature of this civil war—none of the internal combatants could be said to be an incumbent government. Rather, the fighting itself determined which group would form a government. In this chaotic situation foreigners did not hesitate to use force with little regard for international boundaries. While some international organizations and third states ineffectually called for a peaceful settlement of the fighting, ideologically based intervention was the most important response to this conflict. None of the intervenors encountered any international sanction.

## Intervention in Zaire (1977)

In March 1977 troops of the Front Nationale de la Libération du Congo (FNLC) invaded Zaire's Shaba Province from Angola. The FNLC had been formed from troops of the Katangese gendarmerie and was strongly opposed to the government of President Mobutu of Zaire. It had fought for Portugal against the FNLA during Angola's independence war, seeing the FNLA as a creature of Mobutu. After Angola's independence it received training and bases from the new MPLA government, which had also opposed the FNLA.[202]

In April 1977, after a request for aid from Mobutu, Moroccan troops arrived in Zaire to assist that state in dealing with the invasion. France transported the Moroccans, who withdrew in three months, having repelled the FNLC.[203]

The motives of the states involved are not all clear. It is not certain why Angola permitted its territory to be used as a base to attack Zaire, though it is perhaps not irrelevant that Mobutu had aided the FNLA while the FNLC had been of considerable aid to the MPLA both before and after it took power.[204] France apparently acted out of concern at Soviet and Cuban activities in Africa and in line with its policy of aiding friendly African governments against subversion.[205] Morocco acted due to concerns about Communist subversion in Africa and about links between the groups invading Shaba and POLISARIO, the group fighting Morocco to obtain independence for the region known as the Western Sahara.[206]

Third-state reaction to this event was somewhat complex. The United States, wishing to help Zaire but believing that the invasion was neither serious nor involved the Soviet Union or Cuba, expressed support for Zaire, encouraged French involvement, and provided a small quantity of aid.[207] Thirteen Francophone African states expressed support for this operation, as did Egypt, Sudan, Uganda, and Iran.[208] The Saudis reportedly also supported Morocco's action.[209] The OAU implicitly supported Zaire's actions, in this case when it adopted a resolution in July 1977 expressing its full support for the inviolability of Zaire's borders. Belgium provided deliveries of arms.[210] Algeria, Nigeria, Angola, Cuba, and the Soviet Union all criticized the intervention, while the PRC supported it.[211] No United Nations organ addressed this use of force.

This was an ideologically motivated intervention in civil strife at the request of a government. Third states generally reacted favorably, and there was no strong opposition to the intervention nor any sanctioning of the intervening states.

## Libya, Algeria/Tunisia (1980)

On January 27, 1980, sixty Tunisian insurgents seized a town in the southwestern part of Tunisia. Tunisian forces, supported logistically by France, put down the revolt four days later. The insurgents had been aided by Algeria and in particular by Libya, which planned the operation and armed and trained the participants.[212]

Libya and Algeria never admitted participation in the plot, and their motives are not entirely clear. Arguably, Libya acted to punish Tunisia for its failure to agree with Libya's plans for the union of the two states, while Algeria sought to respond to Tunisia's support for Morocco's position on the Western Sahara question.[213]

Third-state reaction to this event was muted. Several Arab states raised questions about France's assistance to Tunisia, though none commented publicly on the insurgents' attack. Both the OAU and the Arab League dealt with the matter by adopting resolutions affirming the principles of noninterference in internal affairs and respect for national sovereignty, with no reference to France's action. The Arab League also established a commission that sought unsuccessfully to mediate the dispute between Libya and Tunisia.[214] No United Nations organ dealt with this event.

This episode involved an effort by two states to organize and support armed opposition to the government of a third. Third states in the affected region reacted by generally affirming the principle of nonintervention and by seeking to mediate between the parties. Some states, however, also expressed concern about the fact that a former colonial state aided the target government. No third state imposed sanctions on any of the parties.

## Liberian Civil War (1989–?)

In December 1989 a group calling itself the National Patriotic Front of Liberia (NPFL) began a revolt against the government of Liberian president Samuel Doe. A civil war soon began, pitting ethnic group against ethnic group and involving great brutality. By June 1990 NPFL troops had advanced to the capital, Monrovia. While they did not seek to take the city, fighting and extreme maltreatment of civilians continued. Although some Liberians hoped the United States would intervene to stop the fighting, it did not. Rather, it deployed ships off shore from Monrovia in June, and in August it sent ashore a force of marines in helicopters to evacuate American nationals. Otherwise, the United States did not get involved.

In mid-August the Economic Community of West African States (ECOWAS) elected to deploy a peacekeeping force in Liberia, citing the danger to nationals of member states then in Liberia and the refugee problem the war was creating for the region. The decision caused debate within ECOWAS, since a number of Francophone members supported the NPFL while Nigeria, which had ambitions for a wide regional role and was suspicious of the Libyan connections of the NPFL's leader, opposed that group. Nonetheless, troops from Nigeria, Ghana, Guinea, Gambia, and Sierra Leone were deployed. They took control of a small area of Monrovia by September.

After the killing of President Doe by a rebel group that had splintered from the NPFL—the Independent National Patriotic Front of Liberia (INPFL)—the situation deteriorated. The NPFL had in any case made clear its hostility to the ECOWAS intervention, and as the situation degenerated, the West African troops, allied with the remnants of Doe's army and the INPFL, attacked the NPFL, driving it from the vicinity of Monrovia.[215] After October 1990 the situation continued unsettled. The level of fighting decreased somewhat after a November 1990 cease-fire, but violence continued.

An Interim Government of National Unity (IGNU) was formed in August 1990 under ECOWAS auspices, and it eventually absorbed the INPFL. It was able to exercise control only in Monrovia, however. Further, after an incursion by an unidentified group into Sierra Leone caused casualties among both citizens of that state and Liberian refugees, a new Liberian organization called ULIMO was formed. ULIMO attributed the incursion to the NPFL and began fighting that group. IGNU and NPFL agreed to a peace plan in the autumn of 1991 calling for disarmament of all sides and new elections,[216] but the plan was never implemented.

In July 1993 United Nations-sponsored negotiations between NPFL, IGNU, ULIMO, and the remnants of Doe's army led to the establishment of a transitional government to be overseen by the United Nations, the OAU, and ECOWAS. The fighting did not end, however.[217] It was not until August 1995 that exhaustion finally led all the parties to the civil war to agree to a cease-fire and to arrangements for government of the country, thanks at least in part to mediation by Nigeria and ECOWAS under Ghana's chairmanship.[218] As of this writing that cease-fire has held, although fighting took place in January 1996 between ECOWAS troops and one of the militias, apparently arising from a dispute over division of profits from illicit diamond trading.[219]

Third-state reaction to this conflict was generally supportive of the ECOWAS intervention, though some states dissented from this view. On November 19, 1992, the Security Council adopted a resolution determining that the Liberian situation constituted a threat to the peace, imposing an arms embargo on Liberia under Chapter VII, commending the work of ECOWAS, and excepting that group from the arms embargo. It also provided for the dispatch of a UN representative.[220] In March 1993 it reaffirmed its support for ECOWAS, condemned attacks on it—a reference to NPFL—and called for support for the 1991 peace plan.[221] And, as noted above, the peace negotiations that led to the July 1993 agreement were under United Nations auspices. Further, the Security Council established a cease-fire monitoring operation after the 1993 agreement, which it kept in place despite doubts as to its effectiveness for the following two years,[222] and which was maintained after the 1995 agreement.[223]

Individual states also supported this approach. After the 1993 agreements Zimbabwe, Botswana, Egypt, and Zambia offered troops to the peacekeeping force to help allay the NPFL's continuing suspicion of it.[224] The United States supported ECOWAS.[225] As noted above, Nigeria and Ghana took active roles in brokering the 1995 agreement. On the other hand, some states continued to support the NPFL; this was alleged of Burkina Faso and Côte d'Ivoire in late 1992, and the United States withdrew its ambassador to Burkina Faso in November 1992 to protest Burkina Faso's action in this regard.[226]

This conflict was a civil war in which a regional organization intervened. The motives of that organization were mixed; the disruption in the region caused by the war was part of the motive, but apparently the ambitions of the largest intervening state were not irrelevant. Third states favored the intervention as the best way of restoring peace in the region and the Security Council supported the intervening group with resolutions invoking Chapter VII of the UN Charter. Most of the states of the region also backed the intervention, although this reaction was not unanimous. No serious sanctions were imposed on any of the state actors, although states undercutting the intervention apparently faced some diplomatic protests.

## Analysis

The conflicts described in this chapter differ in a number of respects. The PRC's invasion of Tibet and its exchanges of fire with the ROC in the Taiwan Straits were treated by third states not allied with one of the combatants as matters internal to China. The other conflicts all involved foreign interventions in civil strife. Some involved the dispatch of troops. In others, the intervenor limited itself to providing significant aid for one of the factions contending for power within the state in question. While some of the interventions were undertaken for ideological motives connected with the Cold War, others involved a desire to dominate the government of a neighboring state, or opposition to such a government. Those in the Congo and Liberia were multilateral undertakings aimed mainly at restoring order in a state that had fallen into chaos.

In one important respect, however, most of these interventions were alike. Almost none of the intervening states encountered sanctions from third states. To be sure, the OAS arranged military support for Costa Rica in response to Nicaragua's intervention in 1955 and imposed sanctions on Cuba in response to its actions in Venezuela. Further, the United States and Israel threatened Syria with a military response to its intervention in Jordan. Except in these cases, however, third-state reaction to these interventions was either nonexistent, divided, or focused on mediating between the intervening state and the target of its intervention. That last reaction was the case, for example, in the OAS's response to Nicaragua's 1948 intervention in Costa Rica; the U.S. response to the civil wars in Yemen and Mozambique; and the response of African states generally to Libya's actions in Chad and that of the Arab League to Libya's actions in Tunisia. A number of these interventions received indications of considerable international acquiescence—for example, the Egyptian intervention in Yemen and Libya's in Chad.

Certainly, it cannot be said that particular interventions in civil strife were generally opposed. This impression is reinforced when account is taken of some of the conflicts discussed in other chapters and how they could be considered interventions in civil strife. Both the Syrian and Israeli interventions in Lebanon, for example, fit this characterization, and each received considerable third-state support: the Arab League effectively paid Syria's expenses for several years, while third-state mediation helped Israel attain its goal of expelling the PLO from Beirut. Taking all these events together, then, it appears that interventions in civil strife are frequent and that there seems to be a high degree of international acceptance of such interventions. Applying the obey-or-be-sanctioned standard, it would appear that interventions of this type should not be considered unlawful.

This conclusion seems easy to reconcile with the patterns of behavior discussed in earlier chapters. Those chapters suggest that uses of force that do not challenge a preexisting stable status quo will not be treated as unlawful. Of course, in one sense that characterization seems most inappropriate as applied to these conflicts, since in all cases the interventions facilitated, if they did not cause, internal wars. However, in almost none of these cases did the intervenor propose to change the *international* status quo. Except in the case of Libya's intervention in Chad, the interventions discussed in this chapter were intended neither to subjugate the target state nor put a puppet regime in place. Rather, they sought to support compatible but not necessarily subservient regimes. The strong negative reaction to Libya's plan to absorb Chad underlines this point. Even states previously sympathetic to Libya's actions in the Chadian civil war objected to an action that would lead to Chad's disappearance. Once Libya abandoned this plan, the degree of opposition to its behavior declined.

A second point worth noting is the relative lack of legal objection to the sort of multilateral intervention carried out in the Congo and Liberia. Especially in light of the Security Council's enthusiastic support for the latter intervention, as well as the Council's effort to undergird the abortive peacekeeping effort in Chad, it would appear that such multilateral interventions may be considered affirmatively lawful.

One last point also seems significant. International reaction to these interventions does not appear to have turned on whether the intervening state could be said to have received an invitation from an incumbent government. To be sure, such invitations were present on a number of occasions, and intervening states were at pains to emphasize them when they existed, but Nicaragua's interventions in Costa Rica and Egypt's in Yemen were aimed at overthrowing existing governments, while the intervenors in Laos and Angola and Libya in Chad apparently paid little attention to the formal juridical status of the side they were supporting. Except for the OAS assistance provided to Costa Rica to deal with the 1955 intervention, however, it does not appear that the absence of such an invitation was a determining factor with regard to third-state reactions. For that matter, the existence of such an invitation did not shield the United States from criticism during its actions in Vietnam, discussed in Chapter 5. All of this suggests that the existence *vel non* of such an invitation is not determinative of third-state reactions to interventions in civil strife.

CHAPTER 7

# Maintenance of Spheres of Influence

On a number of occasions since World War II states seen as preeminent within certain spheres of influence have intervened forcibly in the internal affairs of smaller states subject to their domination. In a number of such cases third-state reaction to such uses of force has differed from that expressed in response to similar uses of force outside the sphere-of-influence context. Because of this difference in reaction it seems useful to collect for discussion conflicts involving forcible maintenance of spheres of influence. This chapter presents that discussion.

## United States/Guatemala (1954)

In the early 1950s the United States became convinced that the government of Guatemalan President Arbenz was controlled by Communists, who, it was taken for granted, were controlled by the Soviet Union.[1] To eliminate what was seen as a Communist threat, the United States began organizing a coup in 1953. The United States recruited a small force of Guatemalan exiles, picked one to be the leader, and established training camps in Honduras and Nicaragua with the cooperation of the governments of those states.[2] The decision to finally launch the coup was taken in May 1954 after Guatemala received a shipment of arms from Czechoslovakia; in fact, that shipment led to consideration of a blockade of Guatemala to intercept similar shipments, an idea abandoned apparently because of its illegality and because of objections from allied maritime states such as the United Kingdom.[3] The coup was launched on June 17, 1954, in the form of an invasion from Honduras by no more than 150 of the exiles.[4]

The American plan was based on deception. Rather than seeking to defeat the relatively large Guatemalan Army, the plotters broadcast over an American-run "Voice of Liberation" radio false reports of great success by the invading force and staged air raids on Guatemala City from bases in Nicaragua in planes flown by CIA employees. The combined effect of these false reports and air raids was to destroy the morale of the Arbenz government. On June 25 Arbenz ordered the army to distribute arms to local workers and peasants to face the totally fictional attack he thought was coming. The army refused, demanding instead that Arbenz either resign or come to terms with the invaders. Arbenz chose to resign on June 27 and a new government was formed.[5]

On June 20 Guatemala had sought to take this matter to the Security Council, claiming to be the victim of aggression launched from Honduras and Nicaragua. Those states denied complicity and argued that the Organization of American States was the more appropriate body to consider the issue. Brazil and Colombia proposed a resolution referring the question to the OAS that was supported by all members of the Security Council but the Soviet Union, which vetoed it. A second request from Guatemala for Security Council consideration of the matter was made on June 25. This time only four members of the Council voted to place the matter on the agenda; those opposing Security Council consideration—Brazil, Colombia, and the United States—noted that the OAS was addressing the matter and stressed the importance of letting the inter-American system function.[6] Apparently, the United States was able to obtain this result only by threatening Britain and France with loss of American support in matters important to those states; they abstained in the vote on the agenda.[7]

In fact, however, the OAS was not dealing with the matter. Arbenz had not agreed to receive a fact-finding mission from the Inter-American Peace

Committee until after the Security Council's second vote. The mission did not depart from New York until June 28, the day after Arbenz's resignation, and never reached Guatemala City; it was informed on July 2 by Honduras, Nicaragua, and the new junta in Guatemala that the problem had been resolved, so that there was no longer any need for it to find the facts.[8] In addition to the peace committee's action, the United States had requested the OAS Council to call a Meeting of Consultation of Foreign Ministers under the Rio Treaty on the day Arbenz agreed to the peace committee's visit. In making its request, the United States argued that the problem involved "international Communism,"[9] which had been declared in the Caracas Declaration of March 1954 to be a form of "aggression" within the meaning of the treaty.[10] In any case, there was confusion among the Latin American states. Although they were generally opposed to U.S. intervention in Latin America, they also were made anxious by the Czech arms shipment to Guatemala. Their deliberations in response to the U.S. request to the OAS Council reflected their hesitancy, and in the event, were halted after the provisional Guatemalan government was established.[11]

The United States concealed its part in the overthrow of Arbenz with considerable success.[12] Consequently, it offered no justification of its action, and there was at the time apparently no third-state reaction.

Despite the absence of third-party reaction to the coup itself, this incident offers some food for thought. Most obviously, the actions of the United States demonstrate that it thought itself justified in using force to overthrow a government in Latin America that it perceived to be a threat. It is also noteworthy, however, that it hesitated to impose an arms blockade against Guatemala in part because of legal advice and in part because other states made clear that they would stand on their rights in international law. Finally, the Latin states' difficulty in deciding how to react to the coup can be fairly labeled as a conflict of values, with their general aversion to actions like the invasion colliding with their perception of Communism as a threat to the hemisphere.

## Soviet Union/Hungary (1956)

In late October 1956 great popular discontent with the policies of the Hungarian Workers' (Communist) Party government of Hungary led to a series of massive demonstrations against that government. Fighting erupted, with the political police defending the government.[13] On October 24, 1956, the Central Committee of the Hungarian Workers' Party, with the approval of representatives of the Central Committee of the Communist Party of the Soviet Union, appointed Imre Nagy prime minister and János Kádár party leader, replacing unpopular hard-liners.[14] The fighting gradually died down, but the Nagy government moved to accommodate some popular demands, abolishing the one-party state and promising free elections.[15]

This posed a dilemma for the Soviet Union. Its troops stationed in Hungary had deployed on October 23 at the request of the hard-line government but had lacked orders from their superiors and had made little impact.[16] From the point of view of the Soviet Union the situation was becoming serious. It not only feared the loss of its position in Hungary but unrest in other Eastern European states as well.[17] Urged on by the government of the PRC, which feared "counterrevolution" in Hungary, the Soviet Union decided to intervene militarily in that state.[18] On October 30 representatives of the Soviet Central Committee met with Nagy, expressing no objection to a multiparty government and agreeing to a gradual withdrawal of Soviet troops from Hungary.[19] On the following night Soviet troops began to withdraw from Budapest; at the same time, however, other Soviet units were entering Hungary and seizing strategic points.[20] On November 4 the Soviet units—by this time encircling Budapest—attacked, crushing the Hungarian popular forces within a week; they justified their action by reference to a request from a government formed by Kádár,[21] who had left Budapest on November 1 and allied himself with the Soviet Union.[22] Thousands of Hungarians became casualties in the fighting, in which Soviet tactics were apparently quite brutal.[23]

Third-state reaction to these events was extremely negative but expressed almost entirely in the form of General Assembly resolutions and limited diplomatic actions. In November and December 1956 the General Assembly adopted a number of resolutions condemning the Soviet intervention in Hungary, calling for the withdrawal of Soviet troops, and also calling for free elections in Hungary and humanitarian assistance to the thousands of refugees who fled that state.[24] It also established a special committee of five states to investigate and report on the situation in Hungary.[25] All of these actions were taken by large majorities; typically, on the resolutions with a political content the Soviet Union and the Eastern European states were the only negative votes, while Finland, India, Yugoslavia, and several of the Arab states generally abstained.[26] In February 1957 the General Assembly also approved a report of its Credentials Committee recommending that no decision be taken on approving the credentials of the representatives of Hungary; however, this decision—though renewed in the next several sessions of the General Assembly—did not prevent Hungary from voting in the General Assembly either during the immediate aftermath of the Soviet invasion or in subsequent years.[27] The General Assembly also adopted resolutions harshly critical of the Soviet Union and the new Hungarian government in 1957[28] and again in 1958 after the execution of Nagy and certain of his colleagues.[29] But by the early 1960s General Assembly interest in the issue had begun to wane; and when Hungary finally announced in 1963 a general amnesty for persons involved in the 1956 events, the United States abandoned its campaign in the General Assembly against the Hungarian government and the credentials questions ceased to be raised.[30] Throughout this period of General Assembly activity the Assembly's actions appear to have had little effect on the situation in Hungary.

As noted above, outside the General Assembly third-state reaction to the invasion was limited. Concerned at the possibility of a world war and relying on the absence of any treaty obligation to aid Hungary, the United States made clear to the Soviet Union in late October that it would not interfere with developments.[31] Even diplomatic action on this matter was also muted. For example, the United States recalled its minister to Hungary in 1957 but did not break off diplomatic relations.[32]

This conflict involved a cross-border invasion by the Soviet Union of one of its satellites. Its justification was an invitation from the government of the satellite, but the government that had issued the invitation was of doubtful standing,[33] and in any case the decision to invade was taken before that government was formed. The actual motive of the Soviet Union was to maintain control of Hungary and prevent loss of control in other Eastern European states. Third-state reaction was, at bottom, acquiescent. To be sure, there were denunciations in the General Assembly but little action beyond that. Furthermore, the focus of negative actions was not the Soviet Union but the Hungarian puppet government, and even that government was not actually isolated: it was not prevented from voting in the United Nations or denied diplomatic representation. The language of the General Assembly resolutions adopted in response to the Soviet invasion indicates that the states of the world were greatly angered by the suppression of Hungary, but their actions indicate that they were prepared to live with and finally legitimate the results of the invasion.

## United States/Cuba (1961)

In March 1960 President Eisenhower approved a plan of covert action against the government of Fidel Castro, one element of the plan being the organization of a paramilitary force to invade Cuba.[34] The plan to take action against Castro was motivated by growing evidence of his Communist inclinations; it was conceded that the United States had no pretext for any sort of overt action.[35] Specifically, the plan called for recruiting a force of Cuban exiles to carry out an invasion that, it was believed, would spark a popular uprising against Castro; indeed, it was this uprising, rather than the invasion, that was expected to actually overthrow the Cuban government.[36]

In 1960 the CIA organized and began training and equipping the invasion force.[37] Upon being informed of the invasion plan after taking office in 1961, President Kennedy permitted it to go forward, again motivated by Castro's ideology.[38] He gave the final order for the invasion on April 14.[39] On the same day the 1,400 troops of the invading force, which had trained in Guatemala with the cooperation of the government of that state, set sail for Cuba from Nicaragua; they were seen off by Nicaraguan President Somoza.[40] The next day CIA-obtained aircraft flown by Cuban exiles bombed military airfields in Cuba, flying from bases in Nicaragua.[41] After the raid two of the planes proceeded to Florida; according to plan, the United States claimed that the crews were defectors from the Cuban air force.[42] Immediately attacked by Cuba in the United Nations and with its cover story unraveling, the United States canceled plans for further attacks on Cuban airfields to avoid having to tell further lies in the United Nations.[43] The invasion itself, which began on April 17, was a fiasco; it encountered unexpected Cuban troops, the chartered invasion fleet was repeatedly and successfully attacked by the Cuban air force, and the invading force was compelled to surrender by April 19, no sort of uprising having taken place anywhere in Cuba.[44]

The United States did not attempt to justify its role in the invasion, instead denying any connection with it.[45] Guatemala and Nicaragua took similar stances.[46] International reaction was surprisingly muted. In debates on the matter at the UN General Assembly only the Communist states directly attacked the United States and insisted on its entire responsibility for the affair, although several states made statements strongly implying a belief in American responsibility and urging an end to armed intervention in Cuba.[47] The assembly voted on two resolutions related to the crisis. One, proposed by Mexico, expressed concern about the situation in Cuba and insisted on the importance of the principle of nonintervention; this resolution received a majority in the assembly less than the required two-thirds and therefore failed to be adopted.[48] Most Western European states, Latin American states, and Francophone African states either voted against or abstained on the resolution, which was supported by the Communist states, the leading nonaligned states, and six Latin American states.[49] The second resolution, offered by seven Latin American states, originally called for the whole matter to be referred to the OAS; the operative paragraph of the resolution also failed to receive a two-thirds majority in the assembly, and the resolution as finally adopted called only for peaceful action to remove existing tension.[50] Outside the General Assembly a number of states made statements generally disapproving of outside intervention but not specifically condemning the United States.[51] For example, Indonesia criticized actions taken against Cuba but did not cancel a visit by President Sukarno to the United States planned for the week following the statement.[52]

This action, then, was an invasion of one state by a force composed of its own nationals but organized, financed, and completely controlled by another state. No attempt was made to justify it. It was motivated by a superpower's antagonism toward a state in its region that had adopted what was regarded as an alien ideology. Third-state reaction was muted, perhaps because the full extent of American involvement was not known at the time the matter attracted international attention.

## United States/Soviet Union, Cuba (1962)

On October 15, 1962, American intelligence analysts discovered from aerial reconnaisance photographs that the Soviet Union was installing in Cuba missiles designed to carry nuclear warheads and with a range adequate to reach broad sections of the United States and Latin America.[53] The following day the most important American national security officials, including President Kennedy, met to begin consideration of the appropriate American reaction to this information. There was considerable disagreement among the officials as to whether the missiles in Cuba significantly increased the ability of the Soviet Union to damage the United States in a nuclear exchange; despite this disagreement, however, all believed that the United States could not acquiesce in the Soviet action.[54] This consensus apparently reflected a conviction that the credibility of American defense commitments to smaller states and the firmness of American resolve would be put in doubt unless the United States eliminated the missiles from Cuba.[55] Domestic political considerations may also have played a role; in September President Kennedy had reacted to increasing criticism of what was perceived to be an arms buildup in Cuba by denying that this buildup amounted to an offensive threat and insisting that, if such a threat were to appear, the United States would "do whatever must be done to protect its own security and that of its allies."[56]

After considering a number of different responses to the situation, the group addressing the problem concluded that only two offered any prospect of resolving it satisfactorily. One was to impose a naval blockade to prevent the introduction of more missiles into Cuba than had already arrived. The other was to conduct an air strike on the missile bases.[57]

Those advising the president ultimately recommended the blockade for several reasons. There was considerable concern about the immorality of a surprise air attack by a large country on a smaller neighbor. There was concern, too, that the death and destruction that an air strike would necessarily cause would impel the Soviet Union to react strongly; the view of the American military that a massive strike, as opposed to a "surgical" attack, would be necessary to ensure removal of the missiles reinforced this concern. The blockade, or quarantine as it had come to be known, had the advantage of avoiding both of these problems while not foreclosing the option of resorting to more forceful action if the quarantine failed to produce the desired result. It was also argued that the quarantine could more easily be justified on legal grounds, especially if it received the support of the OAS and thus arguably could be considered action by a regional organization under Article 52 of the Charter of the United Nations.[58] On October 20, explaining that he preferred to start with limited action, President Kennedy decided to implement the blockade.[59]

On October 22 Kennedy delivered a televised speech explaining the situation. He characterized the Soviet action as "a deliberately provocative and unjustified change in the status quo which cannot be accepted by this country, if our courage and our commitments are ever to be trusted again by either friend or foe," announced the quarantine, and demanded the removal of the missiles from Cuba.[60] Despite the urgency of the matter, the speech had been delayed for one day, partly to ensure adequate time to seek support from the members of the OAS.[61] That organization met on October 23 to consider a resolution calling for the removal of missiles from Cuba and recommending, on the authority of the Rio Treaty, that members take all measures necessary, including the use of force, to achieve that end; the resolution also required reporting the matter to the Security Council.[62] The resolution was adopted by a vote of 19 votes to none, with Uruguay's ambassador abstaining, lacking instructions from his government.[63] Mexico, Brazil, and Bolivia abstained in the vote on the paragraph permitting the use of force but voted with the rest on the resolution as a whole.[64]

This matter was also discussed in the Security Council on October 23. The United States stressed that the Soviet action introduced a nuclear threat into an area previously free of it and that it struck at the territorial integrity of the Western Hemisphere. The United States also submitted a draft resolution calling for the removal of the missiles from Cuba under UN verification. Cuba and the Soviet Union accused the United States of perpetrating aggression against Cuba and described the quarantine as an act of war. The Soviet Union submitted a draft resolution condemning the actions of the United States and calling for an end to the quarantine. On the following day Ghana and the UAR introduced a draft resolution calling on Acting Secretary-General U Thant to confer with the parties and on the parties to refrain from aggravating the situation. The delegations of Chile, Venezuela, the United Kingdom, France, Ireland, and the ROC all supported the U.S. resolution. Romania supported the resolution of the Soviet Union. The UAR characterized the blockade as a violation of international law; Ghana agreed, declined to apportion blame, and called for negotiations. Also on that day U Thant informed the Security Council that he had requested that the Soviet Union suspend deliveries of arms to Cuba and that the United States suspend the quarantine. On October 25 the Security Council adjourned without voting on any of the resolutions.[65]

The United States Navy had deployed a naval task force to enforce the quarantine by October 24.[66] By October 25 it was clear that several Soviet vessels originally headed for Cuba had reversed course.[67] The only boarding during the quarantine—of a Soviet-chartered Lebanese flag vessel—took place on October 26 and was entirely peaceful.[68] There were a number of contacts between the United States and the Soviet Union during this period, the United States making clear its intention to resort to uses of force beyond the quarantine if there was no Soviet agreement to remove the missiles.[69] Finally, Chairman Nikita Khrushchev of the Communist Party of the Soviet Union agreed on October 28 to withdraw the missiles, the United States having undertaken not to invade Cuba and having explained its intention of removing from Turkey certain obsolete American nuclear-armed missiles, though insisting that this latter step not be publicly linked to the withdrawal of the Soviet missiles from Cuba.[70] Prime Minister Fidel Castro of Cuba strongly objected to this resolution of the matter and refused to cooperate with a plan for UN verification of the removal of the Soviet missiles; the Soviet missiles, as well as certain bombers that had also been stationed in Cuba, were removed anyway. The quarantine ended November 20, 1962.[71]

Third-state reactions to this crisis varied. As indicated above, the OAS voted to support the United States, and several states expressed support in the Security Council for the U.S. position. Further, Argentina, Colombia, Costa Rica, the Dominican Republic, Guatemala, Haiti, Honduras, and Panama all assisted in various ways with the quarantine operation.[72] Senegal and Guinea likewise assisted the United States by agreeing, on the basis of principles of nonalignment, to refuse to permit Russian aircraft carrying military equipment to land in their territory; absent landing rights in these states the Soviet Union would find it difficult to fly warheads in to Cuba for the missiles that were already in that state.[73] Australia, Canada, the Federal Republic of Germany, Italy, New Zealand, and Turkey all expressed support for the United States.[74]

On the other hand, several nonaligned states questioned the actions of the United States.[75] Cameroon, the Central African Republic, Chad, Congo (Brazzaville), Dahomey, Gabon, Ivory Coast, Madagascar, Mauritania, Niger, Senegal, and Upper Volta joined in an October 25 letter supporting U Thant's proposals.[76] And several important American states demonstrated by their abstentions in the OAS their disagreement with the American decision to use force in these circumstances.

This action involved the use of force in the form of a naval blockade aimed at coercing the Soviet Union to remove missiles it had stationed in Cuba. The United States never questioned the legality of the Soviet action; rather, it stressed as justification for its quarantine the upsetting of the status quo in the Western Hemisphere caused by the presence of the Soviet missiles. This seems to have been the actual motive of the United States in taking its action, mixed inextricably with concerns as to the importance of displaying American resolve. It is striking that the United States did not act or claim to act because of a conviction that the missiles in Cuba actually rendered it more vulnerable to Soviet attack. Rather, it took for granted the importance of its interest in preventing change in the balance of power in the Western Hemisphere. It is also striking that so many other American states agreed with this assessment. It is also noteworthy that the United States sought to fortify the legality of its action by seeking support from the OAS and structuring its quarantine to maximize the likelihood of gaining that support. At the same time, support for the United States, though significant, seems to have come mainly from the Western Hemisphere and from NATO; many states clearly questioned the actions the Americans took.

In this case, then, a superpower used force to prevent a fundamental change in the balance of power in a region of great importance to it. It was supported in this action by many states, including most of those in the region in question. Its actions incurred no sanctions.

## France/Gabon (1964)

The president of Gabon was taken prisoner in a military coup on the night of February 17, 1964. On February 18 French troops arrived in Gabon's capital and on the nineteenth put down the rising. The president returned to the capital on February 20.

France justified its action by reference to a 1961 mutual defense agreement between France and Gabon, allowing the latter to seek assistance from the former for internal as well as external defense. France also relied on the request for aid the vice president of Gabon claimed to have made on February 18.

Several Francophone African states—Madagascar, Central African Republic, Chad, Niger, Upper Volta, and Ivory Coast—expressed approval of France's actions. However, Mali, Algeria, and Ghana all criticized the French action as interference in Gabon's internal affairs. Beyond the criticism, France was apparently subjected to no sanction.[77]

This matter involved an outside state's intervention in a small civil war. It was justified both by treaty and by a request from the incumbent government, and was presumably motivated by France's desire to support a government friendly to it. There seems to have been little third-state reaction, most of that rhetorical, and much of the rhetoric favorable. This action, that is, was not generally treated as unlawful.

## Intervention in the Dominican Republic (1965)

In April 1965 a confused series of events in the Dominican Republic (DR) led to a unilateral American intervention in civil strife in that state, that intervention being almost immediately converted to a peacekeeping operation under OAS auspices. The incumbent DR government had taken power in a 1963 coup, ousting President Juan Bosch.[78] Several different groups, some supporting Bosch's return, were plotting efforts to overthrow the post-1963 government.[79] On April 24 an effort by the chief of staff of the army to arrest several officers thought to have links to pro-Bosch groups ended with the arrest of the chief of staff. The plotters then contacted a local civilian radio commentator linked to Bosch's political party, who announced that the incumbent regime had fallen.[80]

On April 25 the incumbent government's president was arrested, and the person then in the DR who had ranked highest in Bosch's administration was sworn in as provisional president. On the same day, however, groups within the military strongly opposed to Bosch's return began to act, attacking the presidential palace by air as negotiations regarding the formation of a new government were taking place. This use of violence, in turn, led civilians favoring Bosch's return to take to the streets of Santo Domingo in support of the coup. Over the next two days much of the civilian leadership of the coup abandoned the effort, fearing defeat and its consequences. The anti-Bosch military forces, however, were unable to take control of the heart of Santo Domingo, though they did form a junta. By April 27 the pro-Bosch forces controlled much of the city; these forces were not well disciplined, and the law and order situation in the city was bad. The junta had forces outside the city but was unable or unwilling to force an entry.[81]

As these events were unfolding, the attitude of the United States was evolving. The staff of the American embassy had initially assumed that the anti-Bosch forces would prevail, favoring that outcome due to misgivings about Bosch's ability to lead effectively and the belief that Bosch's return could easily lead to unrest in the country, and also because of increasing concern that the pro-Bosch forces included many Communists.[82] By April 27 there was growing doubt about the prospects of the junta, and by April 28 the American ambassador recommended landing American troops because of the failure of the efforts of the junta's forces and in light of perceived dangers to American citizens; he had earlier been informed by authorities connected with the junta of its inability to protect the lives of American citizens and had received a formal request from the head of the junta for American intervention to deal with what he labeled a Communist uprising.[83] (The evacuation of American citizens had begun on April 27 but was not completed by the twenty-eighth.[84])

At 6:00 P.M. on April 28 the American president, Johnson, accordingly ordered that Marines be landed from American naval vessels that had been stationed off Santo Domingo since the crisis had begun; about 500 were sent ashore.[85] In a press release President Johnson explained his decision as motivated solely by a desire to evacuate American citizens endangered by the fighting.[86] The next day, in the face of reports from the American embassy of the greatly decreasing effectiveness of the junta's forces, of numbers of suspected Communists involved with the pro-Bosch side, and of pro-Bosch atrocities that likely never occurred, President Johnson ordered more Marines to land and ordered an airborne division dispatched as well; within ten days American troops in the DR totaled nearly 23,000.[87]

The mission of these forces, according to their commander, was to prevent a Communist takeover of the DR.[88] In a speech on the night of April 30 President Johnson nonetheless continued to stress the evacuation of American citizens as the reason for the dispatch of American troops, though he referred as well to "signs that people trained outside the Dominican Republic are seeking to gain control," urging the OAS to deal with this aspect of the situation.[89] By the time of a second speech on May 2, however, Johnson was asserting that "Communist conspirators" had seized the pro-Bosch movement; he justified American actions by insisting that the United States could not tolerate the establishment of "another Communist government in the Western Hemisphere."[90]

While the United States was acting in the DR, it had also been taking diplomatic steps. The American ambassador to the OAS, Bunker, had informed that body on April 28 of the evacuations that had taken place the previous day and on the twenty-ninth of the landing of Marines the day before. Early in the morning of the thirtieth the OAS Council adopted a Chilean resolution calling for the convening of the OAS's highest organ, a Meeting of Consultation of Foreign Ministers, to deal with the situation in the DR; Uruguay's was the only negative vote, though the DR abstained. After that resolution passed, Bunker called on the council to adopt a resolution calling for a cease-fire in the DR and for the establishment of an "international zone of refuge" in the general area in which non-DR nationals had been assembling for evacuation. In his speech urging this course Bunker informed the council of the reinforcement of the American contingent in the DR but did not indicate either the size of the forces dispatched on April 29 or that the mission of these forces went beyond protecting American citizens. The council adopted the cease-fire/zone of refuge resolution, four states (Chile, Mexico, Venezuela, and Uruguay) abstaining. On May 1 the Meeting of Consultation authorized the dispatch to the DR of a special committee composed of representatives from Argentina, Brazil, Colombia, Guatemala, and Panama to "do everything possible" to reestablish peace and also to investigate the situation; only Chile's abstention prevented the vote from being unanimous.[91]

In the meantime, American troops had begun to arrive in the DR in strength. On April 30 Marines had secured the "zone of refuge," subsequently called the International Security Zone, or ISZ. On the same day, American airborne troops who had been landed at an airfield eighteen miles east of Santo Domingo advanced to the river that formed the city's eastern boundary and secured a bridge and a bridgehead on the west bank.[92] Initially, the United States government did not plan to use American troops to attack the pro-Bosch forces, although it was committed to the preservation of the junta, the only pro-American group in the country, as the foundation for an eventual government.[93] Instead of playing a combat role, the American troops were expected to relieve the junta's forces of the necessity for defending the ISZ and the bridgehead, allowing the junta to rest its troops and then use them against the rebels.[94]

By May 1, however, American commanders found the situation on the ground unsatisfactory. The Marines in the ISZ and the paratroopers at the bridgehead were separated, with no communications between the ISZ and the country's airfields and with the pro-Bosch forces in control of very important parts of Santo Domingo and free to organize and to fortify their positions.[95] The American ambassador was concerned about the strength of the pro-Bosch forces, and he urged that American troops be used to contain the rebels.[96] The United States government, however, refused to use the troops in an offensive manner; it stressed the necessity of cooperating with the OAS and of operating in as neutral a way as possible. Consequently, it authorized the troops to establish a cordon to link their positions but to use a route that would avoid the heart of the city and key pro-Bosch positions; it was thought that such a move could be justified by the need to create an overland route between the ISZ and the airports, which would facilitate the evacuations that were the stated rationale for the intervention.[97]

Accordingly, on May 2 the American commander secured the approval of the OAS special committee for the setting up of a corridor between the two American positions; in securing the committee's agreement he stressed the need for such a link to facilitate evacuations from the ISZ.[98] The corridor was established just after midnight on the night of May 2/May 3, with little opposition.[99] The effect of the maneuver was to cut off the pro-Bosch forces from the rest of the country and at the same time to permit the American troops to act relatively neutrally, since they were positioned between the two sides and thus could prevent either from defeating the other.[100]

On May 6, after several days of debate, the OAS Meeting of Consultation adopted a resolution originally proposed by the United States but including amendments proposed by other states that established an Inter-American Peace Force (IAPF) in the DR. The resolution provided that the IAPF would absorb the American forces then in the DR, that it would operate impartially to restore normal conditions in the DR, and that the Meeting of Consultation would determine the date of its withdrawal.[101] Chile, Ecuador, Mexico, Peru, and Uruguay voted against the resolution and Venezuela abstained;[102] it thus received the minimum number of votes required for passage.[103] The close vote presumably reflected a reluctance to legitimize the original American intervention; that the resolution passed, on the other hand, showed an awareness of the fact that creation of the force would enable the United States to reduce its presence and also was a function of the concern with Communism felt by some Latin states.[104] Eventually, six states other than the United States provided troops for this force: Brazil, Costa Rica, El Salvador, Honduras, Nicaragua, and Paraguay. The United States had hoped that Argentina, Colombia, and Venezuela would also supply troops, but they declined, apparently unwilling to associate themselves with the original intervention by the United States.[105]

After the Meeting of Consultation adopted the IAPF resolution the United States made no further unilateral moves with its forces. Once the IAPF had been formally established, the United States began to withdraw troops, American strength being reduced to 12,000 by June 6.[106] Indeed, after about the middle of May the United States took a more neutral position regarding internal DR politics and by the end of that month had abandoned unilateral political efforts to find a solution.[107] Rather, it left to an ad hoc committee established by a June 2 resolution of the Meeting of Consultation[108] the task of resolving the crisis—that committee, to be sure, including Ambassador Bunker as one of its three members.[109] The ad hoc committee eventually was able to craft an agreement providing for the establishment of a provisional government and for elections, which took place in June 1966; the last of the IAPF troops withdrew the following September.[110] During this period the IAPF was obliged to repel an attack from the pro-Bosch side on June 15[111] and also to provide support for the provisional government that took power in September 1965,[112] but otherwise played no role in Dominican internal affairs.

Third-state negative reaction to the original American intervention was largely rhetorical, albeit vehement. There was much criticism of the United States in the OAS, but that body never formally censured the United States and did not vote on resolutions submitted by Mexico and Chile calling for American withdrawal.[113] On the contrary, as noted above, the OAS ended by associating itself with the intervention and calling for the troops of other states to join those of the United States. In the Security Council the only outright support for the United States came from the United Kingdom, while a number of states stressed the importance of the principle of nonintervention and criticized both the United States and the OAS. Others limited themselves to arguing that the matter should be left to the OAS. However, when the Security Council voted on a Soviet resolution condemning the intervention and demanding an American withdrawal, six of eleven members voted "no" and four abstained regarding condemnation and six voted "no" and three abstained regarding withdrawal. The Security Council did adopt innocuous resolutions calling for the fighting to end, however.[114] There was also considerable criticism of the United States in the General Assembly,[115] but at no point did more than a few states actually endorse any measure that called for reversing the American action or that condemned the United States outright.

In this case the United States intervened in civil strife in an area that could be considered within its sphere of influence; this intervention was motivated in great part by the intervenor's concern that one of the sides in the internal fighting was dominated by an ideology the United States opposed, though concern for the American nationals also played a role. The United States justified its actions by reference to its main motive, though it put the greater weight on the lesser motive, that is, the concern for the lives of its nationals. Very quickly after the intervention, however, the United States began efforts to bring its operations under the umbrella of a regional organization, the OAS, and convinced most of the members of that body to endorse U.S. actions in what had been transformed into an effort to work out some compromise acceptable to all sides in the DR fighting. Thus, the third-state reaction with the most direct bearing on the conflict was the OAS decision to, in effect, reinforce the American contingent. The United States, that is, was able to gain regional support for its originally unilateral action, being reluctant to continue its intervention without such support. The United States was much criticized by other states, but efforts to sanction it enjoyed no success. It would appear, then, that the world acquiesced in the action of the United States—uncomfortably, to be sure.

## Soviet Union et al./Czechoslovakia (1967)

On January 6, 1968, Alexander Dubček replaced Antonin Novotny as the First Secretary of the Communist Party of Czechoslovakia. Over the next several months that party relaxed its hold on Czechoslovakia, permitting greater individual freedom and reviving the authority of the government against that of the party. On a number of matters policy did not change. Both party and state officials affirmed their loyalty to the Soviet Union and the Warsaw Pact on numerous occasions. The party did argue, however, in favor of its right to a "national way to socialism." Further, the more open public climate permitted persons not in government to advance more radical ideas—an independent foreign policy, for example, or a defense strategy focused on Czechoslovakia's needs.[116]

Despite the Czechs'/Slovaks' unequivocal affirmation of their ties to the Warsaw Pact, other members of that alliance, most especially the Soviet Union, became increasingly uneasy as 1968 advanced. The leaders of the Czechoslovak party met with the leaders of the other Pact parties twice during the period between January and August, apparently seeking to reassure those leaders; the leaders of the other parties apparently insisted that the Czechoslovak party reassert its leading role, resume control of mass media, close certain clubs, and end press attacks on the Soviet Union and other parties. This culminated in an August 17, 1968, letter from the Presidium of the Communist Party of the Soviet Union to the Presidium of the Czechoslovak party complaining of the latter's failure to meet what the Soviet party saw as its obligations.[117]

Three days later the armies of the Soviet Union, Bulgaria, the GDR, Hungary, and Poland invaded Czechoslovakia, quickly subduing the nonresisting country.[118] The Soviets claimed that they acted in part because of the imminence of the party congress at which the Czechoslovak party was planning to adopt a new statute institutionalizing its liberalized domestic institutions, as well as because of the failures mentioned in the August 17 letter. But beyond these motives there is reason to believe that the Soviet Union feared that internal changes in Czechoslovakia could lead ultimately to a weakening of the Warsaw Pact and to the position of the Communist party within Czechoslovakia and also that the ideas taking hold in Czechoslovakia could spill over into the other Eastern European states, or into the Soviet Union itself.[119] In any case, the Soviet Union defended its action—after first making and then abandoning a claim that the intervention had followed a Czechoslovak request for assistance—by enunciating the so-called Brezhnev doctrine. Under this view states of the "socialist commonwealth" had the right to intervene in any socialist state if developments in that state might damage socialism within it or threaten the fundamental interests of the other socialist states.[120]

The international reaction to the invasion was tepid. The United States quickly announced that it would take no action other than raising the matter in the United Nations, stressing its desire for arms control talks.[121] The United Kingdom took a similar position.[122] No other states imposed any sanctions.[123] Although numerous speeches were made in the General Assembly condemning the invasion,[124] no condemnatory resolution was considered.[125] In the Security Council a resolution condemning the invasion was defeated by the Soviet Union's veto, but in addition to the negative votes of the Soviet Union and

Hungary the resolution evoked abstentions from Algeria, Pakistan, and India. The Pakistani representative explained his vote by reference to his not having received instructions from his government. India affirmatively decided to abstain, however, agreeing on the importance of the withdrawal of foreign troops from Czechoslovakia but being unwilling to condemn the invasion. Algeria's abstention was motivated by the perceived double standard employed by Western states, contrasting their concern for Czechoslovakia with their reaction to events in the Middle East and Vietnam. A resolution expressing humanitarian concern for Czechoslovak leaders was not pressed to a vote.[126]

This action, then, was a cross-border invasion by a superpower to subjugate a state within its sphere of influence that the superpower feared was attempting to act in ways contrary to the superpower's interests. The invasion was justified in what amounted to sphere-of-influence terms—that is, on the ground that states within the ideologically defined sphere simply had no right to take even domestic actions that could threaten either their ideological purity or the interests of the sphere as a whole. Third states engaged in considerable rhetorical criticism of the action but refrained even from most symbolic sanctions, for example, a General Assembly condemnation. In essence, the world acquiesced in the invasion.

## France/Central African Empire (1979)

On September 20, 1979, French troops overthrew the government of the Central African Empire, replacing Emperor Bokassa I with David Dacko, who had been president of the state when it had been called the Central African Republic and who promptly upon his installation returned the country to its previous name. France retained its troops in the CAR for a time, after opposition to Dacko began to develop.[127]

France did not really justify its actions, equivocating about the central role it played in the coup.[128] It apparently had several motives for acting. France had extensive economic interests in the country and therefore valued good relations with it. However, Bokassa's government had come under severe criticism in 1979, after investigation confirmed the emperor's personal participation in a massacre of schoolchildren arrested after protest demonstrations. France had provided extensive economic support for Bokassa, whose human rights record had been bad even before the massacre and whose government was known to be extravagant. Aside from the embarrassment of association with such a government, France was concerned by growing domestic opposition to Bokassa from politicians not necessarily sympathetic to French economic interests and by Bokassa's efforts to cultivate Libya.[129]

Third-state reaction to France's action was muted but negative. Only Libya, Benin, and Chad publicly criticized the intervention,[130] and the matter was not the subject of action either by the OAU or by the United Nations. However, only Senegal and Zaire supported the action, and a number of West African presidents were at pains to make clear their ignorance of French plans to intervene. Apparently, France received considerable private criticism from African states with which it was allied.[131]

This incident amounted to the replacement by one state of the government of another, despite the absence of internal opposition to the replaced government. The intervening state's motives may have been partly humanitarian, in view of the terribly repressive character of Bokassa's government,[132] but they clearly were not entirely disinterested, given France's extensive economic interests in the target state and its reluctance to admit its role in the coup. Third-state reaction was not strong, however, and no sanctions were imposed on France, although the coup met with considerable disapproval.

## United States, Argentina, Honduras/Nicaragua (1981–1988)

After the Sandinistas defeated the Somoza regime in the Nicaraguan civil war, some of their opponents, without outside aid, began in August 1979 to plan an effort to overthrow the new government.[133] In 1980 the government of Honduras, apparently because of ideological opposition to the Sandinistas, began to funnel arms and equipment to the anti-Sandinista rebels; it was also prepared to offer them a base in Honduras.[134] By May 1981 Argentina had begun to provide financial aid to the rebels and, in the next few months, to provide training and advisors as well; apparently, Argentina acted partly because of ideological opposition to the Sandinistas, who had provided a base for leftist opponents of the Argentine government, and partly in the belief that their action could improve Argentina's relations with the United States.[135]

In the meantime, relations between the United States and the Nicaraguan government had deteriorated. The Carter administration had suspended aid to Nicaragua on January 19, 1981—its last day in office—after President Jimmy Carter had become convinced that the Sandinistas were supplying military aid to the leftist insurgents in El Salvador. Carter was correct in this conclusion. In November 1980 Nicaragua had reversed its earlier policy of evading requests for aid from the Salvadoran rebels after it had become clear that the Salvadorans planned to proceed with an offensive in January 1981 and the Nicaraguans confronted the possibility that their refusal to provide aid could lead to the defeat of that offensive. In April 1981 the new Reagan administration terminated aid to Nicaragua, acknowledging that Nicaragua had ended arms supplies to the Salvadorans but arguing—apparently with little evidence—that Nicaragua was continuing other supply efforts and was also "accumulating" arms for the Salvadorans.[136]

Earlier, on March 9, President Ronald Reagan had signed a "presidential finding" authorizing covert operations by the CIA to interdict arms shipments to Marxist rebels in Central America. On this authority, in August 1981 the CIA made contact with the Nicaraguan rebel groups already forming with Honduran and Argentine assistance and began to organize a political superstructure for these rebels. In November 1981 President Reagan authorized CIA funding and direction of a Nicaraguan rebel force for the purpose of interfering with the "Cuban infrastructure in Nicaragua" that was arming and training the Salvadoran guerillas.[137]

The Reagan administration's concerns went beyond El Salvador, however. First, there was concern about the general security threat the Sandinistas posed to other Central American states in light of the size of their armed forces and of their receipt of relatively heavy arms from the Soviet Union. Also, the initial CIA contacts with the Nicaraguan rebels had addressed a broader goal: overthrowing the Sandinistas, or at least pressuring them to democratize. The November decision, then, was not addressed simply to changing Nicaragua's behavior toward other states; it also sought to prevent acts that it was not clear Nicaragua was contemplating and to alter Nicaragua's domestic policy, if not its government. Shortly after the November decision the United States began to supplant Argentina as the rebels' chief patron, trainer, and advisor.[138]

In March 1982 the rebels—or contras, as they came to be called—made their first serious attack: CIA-trained contras destroyed two bridges in Nicaragua. Nicaragua responded by declaring a state of emergency and implementing a domestic crackdown. In the next month Eden Pastora, one of the heroes of the war against Somoza, held a news conference in Costa Rica harshly criticizing the Sandinistas for their close ties to Cuba. In June 1982 he announced the formation of ARDE, an anti-Sandinista guerilla organization distinct from the group that the CIA was training, the FDN. ARDE began operations in April 1983 and was apparently more independent of the CIA than was the FDN, but received CIA money, though its objective was clearly the overthrow of the Sandinistas, not simply interdiction of arms.[139] Also in 1982 members of Nicaragua's Indian community, reacting to the Sandinistas' harsh policies, began to receive aid from the CIA, having earlier been aided by the FDN.[140]

Events over the next several years made clear that American policy was moved to a great extent, at least, by the desire to overthrow the Sandinistas. In the summer of 1983 President Reagan approved a new policy toward Nicaragua, focusing on "destabilizing" that state's government. The intent of this policy was not made entirely clear, given the apparently chaotic internal workings of the Reagan administration; some officials understood it as calling for the overthrow of the Sandinistas, while others saw it as seeking only a modification of their behavior.[141] In October 1983 a group of speedboats organized by the CIA attacked Nicaraguan petroleum storage facilities located close to the sea. Apparently quite concerned at the implications of the successful American invasion of Grenada in October 1983, the Sandinistas in November and December ordered the high command of the Salvadoran rebels out of Nicaragua and refused to continue to supply them. The United States, however, did not seize this opportunity to seek a diplomatic solution to its dispute with Nicaragua, in part because of the lack of clarity of American goals and in part due to lack of central direction of competing policymakers.

In December 1983 President Reagan authorized the CIA to lay mines in Nicaraguan waters. The intent of the operation was to deter foreign shipping from entering Nicaraguan ports; the mines used were intended to cause damage but not to sink ships, although after they were laid in January and February 1984 they did sink two Nicaraguan fishing boats in addition to damaging merchant vessels flagged by several states.[142] When Congress reacted to the revelation of the mining by cutting off military aid to the contras, the administration sought replacement funds from Saudi Arabia and Brunei, establishing the operation subsequently exposed in the Iran-contra affair.[143] In late 1986, moved in part by a Nicaraguan incursion into Honduras to attack contra camps the previous March, Congress restored military aid to the contras.[144] Shortly thereafter, however, the facts of the Iran-contra operation became public, undercutting the administration's credibility with respect to, among other things, its policy toward Nicaragua.

The resulting pressure forced the administration to at least appear to seek a peaceful solution to the Central American situation, and House Speaker Jim Wright was enlisted in this effort. Wright's work in the summer of 1987 coincided with a diplomatic initiative undertaken by President Sánchez Arias of Costa Rica. That initiative produced an agreement among the Central American presidents on a peace plan in August 1987; the circumstances precluded American opposition to the plan. Also, the importance of supporting the Arias plan was a central argument in the rejection by the House of Representatives in February 1988 of an administration request for further military aid for the contras. American aid to the contras ended on February 29, 1988. Fifteen days later Nicaraguan forces began another incursion into Honduras against contra camps. On March 16 the United States dispatched troops to Honduras. On the twenty-first, however, Nicaraguan and contra leaders agreed to a cease-fire, effectively ending the war.[145]

After initially denying any link to the contras,[146] the United States sought to justify its actions as collective self-defense with El Salvador in response to Nicaragua's supply of arms to the Salvadoran rebels.[147] As noted above, however, its motives went beyond the interdiction of arms. In contrast, Argentina was apparently never called upon to justify its aid to the contras, while Honduras sought to deny the existence of contra camps in its territory.[148]

Third states responded to this series of events primarily by seeking to end the fighting rather than by seeking to impose sanctions on any of the combatants. Clearly, the most significant reaction was the Contadora peace process, which came to involve Colombia, Mexico, Panama, Venezuela, Argentina, Brazil, Peru, Uruguay, Canada, and the five Central American states. The secretaries-general of both the United Nations and the OAS also became involved. Although the Contadora process itself did not succeed, President Arias built upon the ideas developed during Contadora in devising his plan.[149] It should be stressed as well that the United Nations and the OAS played important roles in the eventual formal end of the fighting by providing both observers for the 1990 Nicaraguan elections and peacekeeping forces to oversee the limitation of the activities and ultimate demobilization of the contras.[150]

While these ultimately successful efforts to settle the dispute were the most important third-state reactions to this conflict, third states also reacted by criticizing the United States. Security Council debates in 1983 and 1984 showed that few states endorsed U.S. support for the contras.[151] Further, the mining of Nicaragua's harbors provoked an effort to impose sanctions on the United States. A resolution submitted by Nicaragua condemning the mining and calling upon the United States to end that operation was defeated in the Security Council only by the veto of the United States; the United Kingdom abstained on the vote, while all other members of the Council, including states friendly to the United States such as Egypt, France, and the Netherlands, voted in favor of the resolution. Further, a number of states not members of the Security Council—to be sure, mostly leftist states—also were critical of the U.S. action.[152] (The mining led France to offer to sweep the mines laid by the United States.[153]) Subsequently, the United States abandoned the mining, though domestic as well as third-state reaction apparently played a role in this decision.

In 1985 the United States vetoed a provision in an otherwise unanimously accepted Security Council resolution that would have criticized its economic embargo of Nicaragua; the General Assembly adopted a resolution condemning the embargo by a vote of 91–6–49. Further, the tenor of debate continued to be critical of the United States.[154] In 1986 the United States twice vetoed Security Council resolutions that would have called upon it to obey the ICJ's judgment in *Nicaragua v. United States*;[155] no other state voted against these resolutions, and the tenor of debate was, once again, critical of the United States. The General Assembly also called on the United States to adhere to the court's judgment by a 94–3–47 vote, and again by a similar margin adopted a resolution condemning the embargo.[156] In 1987 there was yet another General Assembly call for compliance with the court's judgment and condemnation of the embargo.[157] With all of this, however, no sanctions were imposed upon the United States beyond the criticism implied by predictably ineffective votes against it in the Security Council and the General Assembly. It should also be noted that neither Honduras nor Nicaragua encountered any significant criticism or sanction from third states, despite the former's role as a sanctuary for the contras and the latter's violations of Honduran territory in its anticontra operations. It should also be noted that, in light of the aid given the contras by Saudi Arabia and Brunei, it cannot be said that the United States had *no* third-state support for its actions.

This episode involved the support by several states of an insurgency against the government of another, the support being crucial to the existence of the insurgency. The intervening states justified their actions by reference to their target's external acts but were widely known to be at least as concerned about its domestic policies. While third states objected strongly to certain aspects of the intervention, especially the planting of maritime mines that damaged third-state vessels, no sanctions beyond the rhetorical were imposed. Rather, the most important third-state impact was the ultimate mediation of the dispute.

Several aspects of this conflict require particular comment. First, the most important intervening state was a great power acting within its sphere of influence. Second, that state felt constrained to at least avoid the appearance of interfering with the third-state mediation process described above, and indeed to acquiesce in it, this attitude reflecting in part domestic political imperatives. Finally, target-state incursions into the state harboring the insurgents triggered no sanctions or criticism from third states.

## Indian Intervention in Sri Lanka (1983–1990)

Relations between the Sinhalese and Tamil communities on Sri Lanka had become very bad by the early 1980s, as the minority Tamils sought to resist repression by the Sinhalese majority. By 1983 there was considerable disorder in Sri Lanka because of fighting between Tamil militants, seeking to partition the island and establish a separate Tamil state, and Sri Lankan government forces. India took an interest in Sri Lankan affairs for two reasons. First, India sought to dominate south Asia and objected to efforts by the government of Sri Lanka to form closer relationships with the United States and the ASEAN states. Prime Minister Indira Gandhi of India warned Sri Lanka against extraregional involvement in 1983. Beyond this fact, there was a large and politically significant Tamil population in the southern Indian state of Tamil Nadu; India's central government was reluctant to offend this group, which was in turn intensely supportive of Sri Lankan Tamils.[158]

Against this background India sought to pressure Sri Lanka into reaching an agreement with the Tamils, though it did not support Tamil independence. In 1983 India began arming and training Tamil militants, among them a rabidly proindependence group called the Liberation Tigers of Tamil Eelam (LTTE), and permitted the state government of Tamil Nadu to do the same thing. After Prime Minister Gandhi was assassinated in 1984 her son Rajiv took office and sought unsuccessfully to mediate the Sri Lankan controversy. By early 1987 the Sri Lankan government had opted to use force against the militants.[159]

A Sri Lankan offensive against Tamil militants in May 1987 resulted in heavy civilian casualties. India objected, but Sri Lanka persisted. On June 3, 1987, an unarmed Indian food convoy bound for Tamil areas of Sri Lanka was turned back by the Sri Lankan Navy. The next day, without obtaining Sri Lanka's consent, India dispatched aircraft to drop relief supplies over Tamil areas of Sri Lanka; these aircraft were escorted by Indian warplanes. Immediately after this Indian action the Sri Lankan military curtailed its activities.[160]

By the end of the following month India and Sri Lanka had negotiated a far-reaching agreement under which Sri Lanka consented to a cease-fire in its civil war and to the return to barracks of its troops. The agreement further provided for the surrender of arms by Tamil militants, with India undertaking to close Tamil bases in India to prevent arms supplies from reaching the militants. India undertook to provide military assistance to the Sri Lankan government to carry out the agreement, if requested. The agreement also provided for elections in the mainly Tamil areas of Sri Lanka and required Sri Lanka to coordinate with India important elements of Sri Lankan foreign and defense policies. On July 30, 1987, the day after the agreement became effective, Sri Lanka requested Indian military assistance.[161]

India soon found itself in a quagmire. The Tamil militants, most especially the LTTE, had not been consulted as the July agreement was being negotiated. They refused to surrender their arms as the agreement required, and by the fall India decided that it had no alternative to undertaking military operations against the LTTE in order to disarm that group. Those operations inflicted casualties on the militants but failed to crush them, while destroying relations between India and the LTTE. Over the next two years India unsuccessfully waged a war against LTTE fighters, whose hold on the Tamil population was never really challenged. The situation was further complicated on June 1, 1989, when President Ranasinghe Premadasa of Sri Lanka asked India to withdraw its troops. Prime Minister Gandhi was reluctant to do so, arguing that the 1987 agreement entitled India to remain in Sri Lanka until all of its provisions were carried out. In fact, India was concerned not only about avoiding chaos in Sri Lanka but also by the loss of prestige the government would suffer if it simply deferred to Sri Lanka's demand, 1989 being an election year. However, India also had good reasons to favor withdrawal, since the war was clearly stalemated. An agreement was finally reached in September 1989; the last Indian troops left Sri Lanka in March 1990.[162]

As noted above, India's motives for intervening reflected both the demands of domestic politics and a desire to assert regional preeminence. It was relatively frank about its motives, its former high commissioner in Sri Lanka offering in March 1989 three justifications for India's policy. First, as a multiethnic state itself, India had an interest in avoiding the disintegration of a neighboring multiethnic state along ethnic lines. Second, Sri Lanka's efforts to attract external assistance to deal with its security problem raised security problems for India. Finally, it was necessary to take account of the Indian Tamils' interest in the issue.[163]

Third-state reaction to India's actions was muted. Sri Lanka was unable to attract support from any of the permanent members of the Security Council at the time of India's June 1987 intervention, and therefore did not take the matter to the United Nations. The European Community at the same time called for a peaceful settlement.[164] Several of the other states of south Asia objected to the initial intervention, but these same states either welcomed or reacted neutrally to the agreement of July 1987. The United States praised the agreement and acquiesced in India's claim to oversee Sri Lanka's security policy.[165] When India expressed reluctance to bow to Sri Lanka's 1989 withdrawal demand, it received some foreign criticism,[166] but no real pressure. Apparently, third states were unprepared to criticize India's effort to end a bloody ethnic conflict in a smaller neighbor with which its relations were close.

This episode was an intervention by one state in a civil war in another. It was undertaken by invitation, but an invitation issued only after the intervening state had made clear its determination to take a hand in the conflict and after the rest of the world had shown no interest in blocking that intervention. The intervention ended when its failure had become clear and when the invitation was withdrawn, albeit after a delay adequate to protect the prestige of the intervening state. Third states throughout the episode simply deferred to the intervening state, perhaps in recognition of the fact that it is clearly the dominant state in the region.

## United States/Grenada (1983)

On March 13, 1979, a bloodless coup by the New Jewel Movement (NJM) overthrew the corrupt and repressive government of Grenada, which had been dominated by its prime minister, Sir Eric Gairy.[167] The leftist orientation of the new government was reflected in both its foreign and domestic policies, and its relations with the United States began to deteriorate after the coup. This deterioration continued after the Reagan administration took office in the United States in 1981. The chief points of contention between the two states involved Grenada's foreign policy. More specifically, its armed forces were relatively large and received arms from Cuba, the Soviet Union, and the DPRK; in light of the military weakness of Grenada's neighbors, the size of Grenada's armed forces was seen as troubling. Even more significant in American eyes was Grenada's construction of an airport with a runway long enough to accommodate large jet aircraft. It appears that Grenada's principal motive for constructing the airport was to improve its tourist industry by making itself directly accessible to transcontinental jets. The runway was large enough to accommodate large military transport aircraft, however, and some members of Grenada's government intended to make it available to the governments of Cuba and the Soviet Union for military purposes. This use of the airport was intended to be, at most, a secondary function, but the United States saw the airport's construction as an exclusively military undertaking and reacted negatively.[168]

The prime minister of the NJM government of Grenada was Maurice Bishop, an extremely popular figure. The NJM, however, included a number of persons whose doctrinaire Marxism-Leninism reflected an attitude quite different from that of the Grenadan population. Bishop came to perceive the costs to Grenada of maintaining a hostile attitude toward the United States and with difficulty persuaded the leadership of the party to moderate its public statements. This led to a relaxation in the American attitude toward Grenada and to an invitation to Bishop to visit the United States in May 1983. Over the opposition of some NJM leaders the invitation was accepted. Similarly, by late 1982 Grenada's relations with other English-speaking Caribbean states had begun to improve, as Grenada's neighbors began to conclude that they could work with Bishop's government and as that government, in turn, sought to meet those states' concerns by such steps as releasing political prisoners.[169]

This relaxation in Grenada's external relations, however, was accompanied by an increase in tension within the NJM. A number of party members had become convinced that the policy direction Bishop favored was insufficiently Marxist-Leninist and sought by various means to curtail his powers, supported in this policy by the leaders of the Grenadan military. This infighting culminated in Bishop's house arrest on October 13, 1983. As Bishop continued to be immensely popular, the reaction to these events in Grenada was quite negative. After one demonstration was repressed with deadly force, another on October 19 freed Bishop from his house arrest. The party leadership responded by ordering the military to execute Bishop and his chief supporters; those orders were carried out after the military broke up a crowd supportive of Bishop in an episode in which soldiers and many civilians were killed. Later on October 19 the government was declared replaced by a revolutionary military council.[170] The new government immediately took steps to reassure foreign residents of their safety, stating that the airport would reopen on the twenty-fourth and that all foreigners wishing to leave would be permitted to do so.[171]

The United States had begun to consider an intervention to evacuate its nationals, including particularly a number of medical students, in the early days of the Grenadan crisis. By October 20 the United States was seriously contemplating such an operation, placing no trust in the assurances of the new

Grenadan government regarding the safety of foreigners. Further, some in the American government argued for an intervention against the Grenadan regime, but no decision was taken along that line.

On October 21, however, a meeting of the Organization of Eastern Caribbean States (OECS), minus Grenada but with the attendance of Jamaica and Barbados, determined to impose economic and political sanctions on the new Grenadan government and to request the United States to join with the group to intervene militarily against that government. (The OECS included Antigua, Dominica, Grenada, Montserrat, St. Kitts-Nevis, St. Lucia, and St. Vincent.) Apparently, this idea had originated on October 20 with the prime minister of St. Lucia. The request to the United States was conveyed by a telegram received on October 22. The United States ultimately decided to intervene on that day, moved in large part by fear of a situation reminiscent of the Iranian hostage crisis and its accompanying image of impotence and in part by fear of the spread of Communism in the Caribbean (the latter despite Cuba's cold reaction to the ouster and murder of Bishop). This decision was reinforced the next day, when word was received of the bombing of the U.S. Marine barracks in Beirut, an event that apparently reinforced President Reagan's conviction that the United States was confronted by worldwide challenges from Communists and terrorists before which it could not be seen to quail.

President Reagan gave final orders for the Grenada invasion on October 24. Grenada was invaded the following day by a force composed almost entirely of American troops, although a police contingent from the Caribbean states that had requested the intervention was landed on October 28, after all resistance was eliminated and the revolutionary government overthrown. American combat troops were withdrawn from Grenada by December 15. A year later Grenada held elections for a new government, and the last American noncombat troops left the island in June 1985. The intervention, it should be noted, was very popular among the Grenadan people.[172]

The intervening states proffered a number of legal justifications for their action. Ultimately, the U.S. position relied on (1) an invitation from the governor-general of Grenada, Sir Paul Scoon; (2) an invitation from the OECS, acting under the authority of the treaty establishing that organization; and (3) the need to protect U.S. citizens. Earlier statements on the intervention by President Reagan had relied on the danger to Americans on Grenada, and also on the danger to Grenadans themselves from the new government. The justifications for intervention given by the Caribbean states largely tracked those of the United States, though the Caribbean states did not claim to be protecting their nationals and made what amounted to an anticipatory self-defense argument, focusing on the great strength of the Grenadan military relative to that of Grenada's neighbors.[173]

It should be noted that only the argument based on protecting the Grenadans from the new government seems reasonably firm on the facts, at least given the Grenadans' enthusiasm for the intervention. As for the other justifications, it is not clear whether Sir Paul issued his invitation prior to the invasion or that his position in the Grenadan government would authorize him to take such a step in any case. The OECS treaty does not appear to authorize intervention by the organization in the internal affairs of one of the member states and, if it did, may conflict with other international instruments, such as the United Nations Charter. It is not clear either that foreigners on Grenada were in danger or that evacuating foreigners required the overthrow of the revolutionary government. As to the self-defense argument, there is some doubt as to Grenada's actual capacity to attack its neighbors, and in any case there had been, at the time of the intervention, no indication that the Grenadan revolutionary authorities intended to carry out such attacks.[174]

As indicated above, while the actual motives of the United States for the invasion reflected some concern for American lives, particularly in light of the situation in the Middle East, opposition to Communism and the perceived need to avoid the appearance of weakness also played a role. The other intervening states apparently acted because of their hostility to leftist governments generally, their fears of the consequences of the removal of moderating forces in the Grenadan government, and their revulsion at the brutality of the coup.[175]

The immediate third-state reaction to the intervention was negative. A Security Council resolution that would have deplored the invasion as a violation of international law and called for the immediate withdrawal of foreign troops was defeated only by an October 28 veto by the United States. Three Security Council members (Togo, the United Kingdom, Zaire) abstained, while all others voted in favor, including France and the Netherlands. Almost all speakers in the debates, which included a number of states not members of the Council, were critical of the intervention, almost all labeling it illegal and some calling it aggression. The General Assembly adopted a resolution deploring the intervention as a violation of international law; the vote was 108–9–27, with France, Ireland, Italy, Spain, and the Nordic states voting for the resolution and only the United States, the other intervening states, El Salvador, and Israel voting against. Again, American allies made clear their belief that the invasion was illegal.[176] However, no sanctions other than these statements of disapproval in the United Nations were imposed on any of the intervening states by third governments, and the United Nations recognized the credentials of the new Grenadan government in 1984.[177]

This episode was a multinational intervention in the internal affairs of a state to replace a regime that had recently taken power violently. Concern for nationals of the intervening states and for the future intentions of the new government apparently played a role in the decision to intervene, but that decision ultimately turned on ideological objections to the new government. Third states harshly criticized the intervention but otherwise imposed no sanctions and subsequently recognized the government that came to power after the intervention. It should be noted that the intervening states included both a superpower, within whose sphere of influence the intervention took place, and the near neighbors of the target state.

## United States/Panama (1989)

By 1989 relations between the United States and the government of Panama, dominated by General Manuel Noriega, had become very bad. Noriega had been indicted in the United States for drug trafficking in 1988, and the United States had imposed an embargo on Panama to induce Noriega to relinquish power. Noriega had nullified an election held in May 1989 that apparently had been won by a political opponent. While a number of states objected to this action, none other than the United States was prepared to act against Noriega's regime. In October a number of Panamanian military officers staged an unsuccessful coup against Noriega, having been encouraged by the United States.

Relations continued to deteriorate after that time, the United States on November 30 forbidding Panamanian-flagged vessels to dock at American ports. On December 15, 1989, the Panamanian National Assembly declared Panama to be in a state of war with the United States. The next day one American marine stationed in Panama was killed at a Panamanian military roadblock; an American naval officer was beaten the same day. On December 17 the United States decided to invade Panama. The invasion was carried out on December 20 by a relatively large force. Guillermo Endara, the actual winner of the May 1989 elections, was sworn in as president of Panama on an American military base in the Canal Zone shortly before the invasion. Resistance was quickly overcome. By February 20, 1990, U.S. troop strength in

Panama had been reduced to preinvasion levels, and a government under President Endara had been installed.[178]

The United States offered five justifications for its invasion. It claimed it acted in self-defense, given the Panamanian declaration of war and the attacks on American military personnel on December 16. It also claimed that it acted to protect the lives of the 35,000 Americans in Panama. It further argued that its invasion helped defend democracy in Panama. Additionally, it justified the invasion as directed against drug trafficking. Finally, the United States asserted that the invasion was necessary to protect the regime of the Panama Canal treaties.[179]

All of these justifications are problematic. It is by no means clear that the United States faced any kind of military threat from Panama, despite the December proclamation of a state of war; there is little evidence indicating a threat to American troops in Panama, much less to the territory of the United States. Likewise, it is by no means clear that American lives were in jeopardy in Panama. The argument under the canal treaties is flawed for two reasons. First, it is not clear that there was a threat to the canal at the time of the invasion. Second, it is doubtful that those treaties authorize the United States to interfere in the internal affairs of Panama as an element of defending the canal, at least when that interference extends to overthrowing Panama's government.[180] The other two justifications are more plausible factually—it may be assumed that permitting an elected government to take power advances democracy and arresting an individual indicted for drug trafficking contributes to some extent to repressing drug trafficking—but whether states generally see such motives as permissible bases for the use of force is less clear.

If the justifications for the invasion are debatable, neither are the motives for it entirely clear, though it is plain that President George Bush and his administration greatly disliked Noriega, given their efforts before the invasion to remove him.

Third-state reaction to the invasion, in any case, was negative but limited. A Security Council resolution critical of the United States was vetoed not only by that state but also by France and the United Kingdom, who objected to the resolution as implying support for an illegitimate government. Canada also voted against the resolution, and Finland abstained.[181] The General Assembly adopted a resolution "strongly deploring" the invasion and labeling it a "flagrant violation of international law," but the margin for passage was 75–20–39, with the Western European states, joined by Canada, Australia, New Zealand, and Japan, voting solidly against the resolution. Further, the assembly permitted a diplomat representing the new government of Panama to vote on the resolution, implying recognition of that government.[182] The OAS adopted a resolution "regretting" the invasion, with only the United States voting "no."[183] No state imposed sanctions on the United States by reason of the invasion.

This episode involved the invasion by a great power of a small state within its sphere of influence in order to replace the dictator of the state with the victor in elections held before the invasion. Although it attracted considerable criticism, it drew no sanctions and was supported by an important group of states that apparently were influenced by the brutal character of the dictator's government.

## Analysis

The conflicts described in this chapter share several elements. In all but one of these cases a relatively powerful state used force to adjust to its liking the internal politics of a state within what was conceded to be its sphere of influence, an area in which it claimed preeminence. The one exception was the Cuban missile crisis, in which the United States saw the immediate threat to its interest as coming from the presence of Soviet missiles in Cuba rather than from the character of the Cuban government. In all cases the acting state made explicit its claim to a special relationship with the region. Further, in none of these cases did third states impose sanctions on the acting states. To be sure, in cases involving the United States and the Soviet Union there were numerous critical comments and occasional critical General Assembly resolutions, but negative reactions stopped at the rhetorical level. On the other hand, in several of these cases the acting state received either active assistance from third states, as the United States did in the Cuban missile crisis, the Dominican intervention, and Grenada, or a degree of diplomatic support, as was given the United States regarding Panama. In others, third states fairly quickly made their acquiescence clear, as the United States did in response to the Soviet Union's invasion of Czechoslovakia and to the Indian intervention in Sri Lanka, and as the General Assembly did in seating governments of Grenada and Panama installed by American interventions. Certainly it cannot be said that there was a general negative reaction beyond the rhetorical level in any of these cases.

The impression that the international community will tolerate the intervention by dominant states into the internal affairs of smaller states within their spheres of influence is reinforced when conflicts discussed in earlier chapters are considered. Presumably one of the reasons that states generally acquiesced in the French and Libyan interventions in Chad was that both were seen as having interests in the area; indeed each acknowledged the other's interest by their various de facto agreements to effectively partition that country. Similarly, international acquiescence in Syria's domination of Lebanon apparently reflects acceptance of Syria's claims of interests in that state.

It might be asked why states have generally acquiesced in these uses of force. To be sure, many of them involve interventions in civil strife, and the preceding chapter demonstrates that states generally seem willing to tolerate such interventions as long as they do not purport to alter the formal international status quo. Further, the American intervention in the Dominican Republic was soon converted into a multilateral intervention, and, as noted in Chapter 6, such interventions enjoy a higher degree of international acceptance than do purely unilateral actions. And while a number of these interventions clearly did not follow invitations by incumbent governments, that factor is not crucial, as Chapter 6 points out.

But in a number of cases described in this chapter no civil strife provoked the interventions in question. The Cuban quarantine involved a flagrant interference with the freedom of the seas under circumstances that even the acting states did not claim involved an exercise of self-defense. Many states supported that action, however, and no sanctions were imposed. The invasions of Czechoslovakia and Panama took place at a time when the incumbent governments in those states had been in power for some time and faced no organized opposition. Although the governments of Hungary and Grenada were very newly established when those two states were invaded, both apparently were in control in their states at the times of the invasions. Even in those cases, however, the international community acquiesced in the uses of force: the invaders were not sanctioned, and the newly installed governments were recognized. Such reactions are in stark contrast to the international reactions to the invasions of Afghanistan and of Kampuchea.

It is suggested, however, that these reactions are less puzzling if one considers the context in which force was used in each of these cases. All involved states acknowledged to be preeminent in a particular region taking steps to enforce their preeminence. These uses of force, that is, did not threaten the status quo in these areas; they reinforced it. They merely underlined what the world had already accepted concerning each of these regions: that the dominant power in the area would prevent developments it perceived as threatening to its interests. This circumstance distinguishes the uses of force in this chapter from the invasions of Afghanistan, Kampuchea, and all the others described in Chapter 2. In those conflicts the status quo was challenged in a direct and sweeping way; the conflicts described in this chapter, however, were aimed at turning back developments perceived as challenges to the status quo. Third states frequently criticized these attempts to preserve the status quo through warfare but were not prepared to go beyond rhetorical disapproval in their reactions.

CHAPTER 8

# Neocolonial Wars

Chapter 3 detailed the increasing acceptance in the international community of the idea that uses of force in aid of national self-determination are lawful. That chapter also indicated the uncertain legality of efforts by colonial powers to resist such uses of force. In all the cases discussed in that chapter, however, the colonial powers were European and the colonies were located at some distance from the home territory of the colonial power. This chapter discusses two conflicts in which non-European powers sought to acquire territory immediately adjacent to their own. Since the territories in question were not recognized as states at the start of these conflicts, these uses of force do not fit the definition of the classic invasion as used in Chapter 2. Third-state reaction to these uses of force reinforces conclusions strongly suggested by the discussions in earlier chapters of this work.

# Western Sahara (1973–1991)

Beginning in 1973 fighting began over the future of the area known as the Western Sahara. In that year the Popular Front for the Liberation of Sakiet el-Hamra and Rio de Oro (POLISARIO) began operations against the Spanish colonial authorities in the area then known as Spanish Sahara. Based in Mauritania, their objective was independence for the area.[1]

By 1976, however, POLISARIO's enemy had changed. Determined to avoid being caught up in a colonial war, Spain had decided to support self-determination for the region. Morocco and Mauritania, however, each claimed that the area in question was a part of its national territory, which Spain had colonized and which should revert upon Spain's departure. Morocco's claim was based both on that state's assertion that it was the successor to the Berber Empire and thus entitled to rule all the lands that had formed part of that empire, and on the long-acknowledged religious authority of the Sultan of Morocco in Western Sahara, a significant fact in light of the very close link between religious and secular authority in Islamic law. This claim was strongly supported by all segments of the Moroccan political spectrum.[2] Mauritania's claim, in contrast, was based on the strong ethnic affinity between the inhabitants of the Western Sahara, the Sahrawis, and elements of the Mauritanian population.[3]

In the fall of 1974 these two states, with Algeria's blessing, had agreed to partition the area, Mauritania abandoning its separate claim due to its fear of POLISARIO, which included members of the Mauritanian opposition. Mauritania also realized that it could not defeat Morocco, and furthermore was concerned by the Soviet presence in Angola and hoped that cooperation with Morocco would lead to closer ties between itself and the western states with which Morocco maintained good relations.[4] Later that year Morocco convinced the General Assembly to seek an advisory opinion from the International Court of Justice regarding the status of the Western Sahara.[5]

Several significant events took place in 1975. First, Spain, disheartened by the difficulties it was facing in Western Sahara, announced in May that it would surrender sovereignty over that region as soon as possible.[6] Second, it had become clear by August that Algeria had reneged on its support for a Moroccan/Mauritanian partition of the area, supporting instead self-determination. While the precise motive for Algeria's change of position is not clear, several factors make it comprehensible. As a matter of ideology, Algeria presumably was more comfortable supporting the concept of self-determination. Moreover, Algeria and Morocco differed sharply in ideology, making socialist, "progressive" Algeria less likely to support the interests of its conservative, pro-Western neighbor. Again, Morocco and Algeria were regional rivals, reinforcing Algeria's reluctance to strengthen Morocco. Finally, Algeria could reasonably expect that a self-determination vote would lead to the independence of the Western Sahara, producing a weak state Algeria could dominate easily. In any event, if the reason for Algeria's change of position was not clear, the effect of it was: without Algerian support POLISARIO could not have carried on its war against Morocco.[7]

The third development in 1975 was the rendition of the ICJ's advisory opinion. That opinion acknowledged ties between both Mauritania and Morocco, on the one hand, and the Western Sahara, on the other, but also stated that those ties were not such as to affect application to the Sahrawis of the principle of self-determination.[8] Despite this result, Morocco read the opinion as vindicating its position.

The fourth significant event was the conclusion between Spain, Morocco, and Mauritania of the Tripartite Agreement of November 11, 1975, whereby Spain agreed to yield administrative control, but not sovereignty, over Western Sahara to the other two states before March 1976; the agreement further required respecting the views of the local assembly of notables (the Jemaa) concerning the ultimate fate of the area.[9]

The final development affecting this issue was the adoption by the General Assembly on December 10, 1975, of two resolutions on Western Sahara that appear to conflict. Resolution 3458A strongly endorsed the application of the principle of self-determination to the Western Sahara. Resolution 3458B also reaffirmed the right of self-determination but also "takes note" of the Tripartite Agreement, more or less legitimizing it.[10]

On February 26, 1976, a majority of the Jemaa accepted partition of Western Sahara between Morocco and Mauritania, though surrounding circumstances make clear that a majority of this body had also endorsed POLISARIO. The next day POLISARIO proclaimed the existence of the Saharan Democratic Arab Republic (SDAR).[11]

Even prior to this time, however, POLISARIO had begun to resist the Moroccan/Mauritanian occupation of the Western Sahara. In this it received strong support from Algeria, which did not employ its own troops in this connection except for two incidents in 1976.[12]

The ensuing war was unusual. During the period 1976–79 POLISARIO clearly had the initiative. Its military operations were so effective that Mauritania, whose population was in any case divided on supporting the war, abandoned its claim to any portion of Western Sahara in August 1979, secretly recognizing POLISARIO. Morocco immediately claimed the area earlier allotted to Mauritania, but it too was suffering defeat after defeat. Then, in 1980, Morocco made important changes in its approach to the war. It reorganized its command structure, made better use of its air force in a ground support role, and altered its strategy. Rather than attempting to defend the entire area it claimed, Morocco constructed a wall of sand, protected by a deep ditch, enclosing an area beginning in southern Morocco, reaching to the Atlantic, and including the northwestern portion of the Western Sahara. (This part of the Western Sahara included several important settlements and mineral deposits.) The wall so seriously inhibited POLISARIO's operations, which depended on a high degree of mobility, that Morocco was able to secure the area within the wall.[13]

Subsequent military developments favored Morocco. It progressively extended the wall, by 1988 leaving outside it only a very small portion of the Western Sahara, in the southeast. POLISARIO was unable to operate within the area protected by the wall, its military operations being limited to attacks on the wall itself. In essence, Morocco greatly limited, if it did not end, POLISARIO's ability to interfere with Moroccan control of almost all of Western Sahara.[14] In August 1988 Morocco and POLISARIO accepted in principle a peace plan proposed by UN Secretary-General Perez de Cuellar, calling for a cease-fire and a United Nations–supervised referendum on the political future of the area. The cease-fire did not take effect immediately but finally went into force in September 1991. In any case, POLISARIO's ability to continue military operations seemed doubtful since Algeria agreed with Morocco in February 1992 to end military support for POLISARIO.[15] The Security Council voted to provide the administrative support needed to carry out the referendum, but, at this writing, disagreements on its terms have not been resolved and the United Nations is considering the withdrawal of its assistance if agreement is not reached.[16]

Third-state reaction to this conflict was divided. As indicated, Algeria strongly supported POLISARIO until the early 1990s. POLISARIO also received considerable diplomatic support. For example, the SDAR was admitted to the OAU in 1982. In November 1983 the General Assembly reaffirmed the Sahrawis' right to self-determination and called for negotiations between Morocco and POLISARIO.[17] The General Assembly took essentially the same position in December 1989.[18] At least seventy states extended diplomatic recognition to the SDAR.[19]

On the other hand, Morocco received considerable aid from states who professed neutrality. France was Morocco's leading arms supplier, providing among other things the aircraft that played a large role in Morocco's taking the military initiative against POLISARIO.[20] The United States also provided arms to Morocco, while calling for a referendum.[21] Early in the conflict Libya supported POLISARIO,[22] but by 1988 it was urging the reintegration of Western Sahara with Morocco.[23] Until it collapsed, the Soviet Union also attempted to maintain its neutrality, permitting Algeria to transfer Soviet arms to POLISARIO but otherwise seeking to avoid worsening its relations with Morocco, with whom it had important economic links.[24] Saudi Arabia and other conservative Arabian monarchies were not neutral, providing Morocco with extensive financial support.[25] And other international actors took steps indicating their de facto recognition of Moroccan control of the Western Sahara; for example, the European Community entered into a fishing agreement with Morocco covering the waters off the Western Sahara coast.[26] In short, a number of significant third states reacted to Morocco's effort to absorb the Western Sahara either by taking actions that facilitated it or by avoiding the appearance of opposing it.

This conflict was unusual. From the point of view of POLISARIO it was a struggle for self-determination. But Morocco was not simply trying to retain a long-held colonial possession; it was seeking to acquire territory not under its control in this century, in the face of opposition by a national liberation group that had some degree of international standing. Given the international reaction to the other national liberation wars examined in this work, one would expect Morocco to have been treated as a pariah by third states. This did not happen. It would appear that the crucial difference between this case and the others studied was that this is not a matter of *European* colonization. Rather, a third-world state was seeking to assert its authority over a neighboring region with which it admittedly had some relationship. In these circumstances the world reaction was hesitant. Morocco obviously did not receive universal support. However, it received too much support to permit the conclusion that its effort was generally condemned.

## Indonesia/East Timor (1975–1983)

Shortly after the military coup in Portugal of April 1974 political groupings began to appear in the Portuguese colony of East Timor (the western portion of the island of Timor was part of Indonesia). One, the Frente Revolucionaria de Timor Leste Independente (FRETELIN), called for independence and tended to attract the support of more radical elements of the population. Another, the União Democratica Timorense (UDT), was more conservative in its outlook, favoring continued links with Portugal and attracting the wealthier elements of the community. Relations between these two groups deteriorated over time. In the summer of 1975 violent clashes between the two groups began. Finally, on August 11, 1975, the UDT staged a coup in Dili, the capital of East Timor, claiming that its objective was to get rid of the Communists. The Portuguese authorities did not act, having neither instructions from their government nor military forces sufficiently disciplined to carry out orders. FRETELIN fought back, however, and defeated the UDT in the ensuing civil war. By the end of the first week of September FRETELIN was in control of East Timor, the Portugese authorities having abandoned their posts on August 27.[27]

As these events were unfolding in East Timor, Indonesian policy was evolving. Initially, Indonesia took the position that it had no claim to the territory of East Timor. However, as FRETELIN adherents began to sound more radical, Indonesian leaders expressed concern on a number of occasions about the security risk that left-wing elements in East Timor would pose for Indonesia. Once FRETELIN had won the civil war, Indonesia initiated the use of force, having earlier obtained requests by defeated UDT members for the union of East Timor and Indonesia. Indonesian forces raided Timorese territory beginning in September 1975. On October 16 a force of 1,000–2,000 Indonesian troops invaded East Timor, moving very slowly and opposed by FRETELIN forces. By the middle of November, however, the Indonesian advance was moving more rapidly.

Apparently in the belief that a declaration of independence would increase their international support, the FRETELIN government declared East Timor to be independent on November 28. It was immediately recognized only by those states of Africa that had formerly been Portuguese colonies. At the same time, the UDT and like-minded groups declared East Timor to be part of Indonesia. On December 7, 1975, Indonesian sea- and airborne troops attacked Dili; by the end of January 1976 Indonesian forces in East Timor totaled more than 20,000. FRETELIN forces apparently put up considerable resistance into 1977; after that time, however, they began to grow weaker. By 1983 their effectiveness was quite limited, although they had not been completely eliminated. Indonesia, in the meantime, had incorporated East Timor as its twenty-seventh province on July 17, 1976, after a request for this step from a popular representative assembly whose representative character was doubtful.[28]

Throughout its military operations in 1975 Indonesia insisted that its troops were not involved;[29] somewhat inconsistently it also justified its attack on Dili as flowing from a request from pro-Indonesian groups in East Timor.[30] Indonesia subsequently sought to justify its absorption of East Timor, despite its earlier disclaimers, on the basis of the request of the popular representative assembly by claiming that it formed part of a precolonial Indonesian empire and by stressing the ethnic links between the peoples of East Timor and various Indonesian groups. In fact, Indonesia apparently acted out of concerns about the establishment of a radical regime on its border.[31]

Third-state reaction to the subjugation of East Timor was split. Immediately after the attack on Dili the General Assembly on December 12, 1975, adopted a resolution strongly deploring Indonesia's action and calling upon it to withdraw and respect the rights of East Timor to self-determination. Ten states voted against the resolution, however, including India, Japan, Saudi Arabia, and all the ASEAN states except Singapore. Forty-three states abstained. Ten days later the Security Council unanimously adopted a resolution deploring the intervention and calling upon Indonesia to withdraw.[32] On April 22, 1976, the Security Council adopted another resolution calling upon Indonesia to withdraw, with the United States and Japan abstaining this time. The General Assembly adopted a resolution on December 1, 1976, similar to that adopted the previous year, with the addition of a paragraph rejecting Indonesia's claim that it had integrated East Timor; this time, however, twenty states voted against the resolution, including the United States and several Muslim states, in addition to most of those who had voted against the 1975 resolution. Moreover, since only sixty-eight states voted for the resolution while forty-nine abstained, those states refusing to support the resolution outnumbered those supporting it.[33] In 1978 the Security Council did not address the matter. Also in 1978 the General Assembly adopted a resolution that reaffirmed East Timor's right to self-determination but did not mention Indonesia by name. The vote was 59–31–44, with those against the resolution including Australia and most Muslim states.[34] By 1987 only the Committee on Colonial Countries addressed the matter; the General Assembly did not.[35]

Events among the Nonaligned Movement followed a pattern similar to those in the United Nations. The Nonaligned Movement summits in 1976 and 1979 affirmed East Timor's right to self-determination. By 1983, however, fewer than half of the states at the summit favored a similar statement, and no such statement was included in the conference's declaration.[36]

Aside from the significance of states' votes in the United Nations, acts by several states outside that body indicated their acquiescence in Indonesia's conquest. Seven states—India, Iran, Malaysia, New Zealand, Nigeria, Saudi

Arabia, and Thailand—accepted invitations to be present at the ceremony in 1976 that Indonesia argued served to satisfy its self-determination obligations,[37] thereby helping to legitimize that event. The United States had advance knowledge of Indonesia's invasion plans but did not seek to halt them. Indeed, there is some evidence that the attack on Dili was postponed at the request of American officials so as not to coincide with a visit by President Ford to Indonesia.[38] By July 19, 1977, the United States made explicit its acceptance of the annexation of East Timor, the legal advisor to the State Department stating that he did not view American policy in this case as "setting a legal precedent" and arguing that "decisions whether . . . to treat an entity as part of another entity are most often taken as political decisions."[39] On January 20, 1978, Australia formally recognized the integration of East Timor into Indonesia.[40] On December 11, 1989, Australia entered into an agreement with Indonesia providing for joint oil exploration in the sea between East Timor and Australia.[41] In 1985 the United Kingdom indicated that it regarded the issue of East Timor as one between Indonesia, Portugal, and the United Nations, not involving Britain, suggesting acquiescence in the existing situation.[42] Even the PRC and Vietnam, who provided considerable diplomatic support to East Timor, refused to provide material assistance to FRETELIN's resistance to Indonesia.[43] Subsequently, both states sought to improve their relations with Indonesia.[44]

This issue is not entirely closed as of this writing. Portugal continues to negotiate with Indonesia on the question of self-determination for East Timor and unsuccessfully brought suit against Australia in the International Court of Justice, challenging Australia's agreement with Indonesia regarding oil exploration in the Timor Sea, the court holding itself without jurisdiction to consider Portugal's claim absent the participation of Indonesia in the litigation.[45]

This conflict involved the conquest by one state of an area formerly a colony of a second state, the conquest taking place during a period when the status of the target area was unclear. The conquering state had no previous claim to the territory, though there were ethnic and geographic links between it and the target area. It justified its actions by reference to (1) spurious claims that its actions had been taken at the request of the people of the area, (2) precolonial territorial boundaries, and (3) supposed ethnic affinity. Despite the weakness of the conquering state's claims, a significant number of important states, including all the states in its immediate area, refused to criticize its actions. International organizations came to deal with the matter on a pro forma basis only. Essentially, the states of the world with few exceptions accepted Indonesia's action. In considering this result it should be noted that

Indonesia was not a European state and that the basis for its claim that self-determination criteria were satisfied in this case was little different from that supporting its similar claim regarding West Irian.[46]

## Analysis

In both the cases discussed in this chapter the area conquered was not a generally recognized state at the time these conflicts began, though both target areas had very active independence movements. Both Morocco and Indonesia were criticized for their actions, but both also enjoyed a fair degree of third-state support. General reaction to these attempts at conquest was acquiescent. The United Nations is organizing a referendum on the future of the Western Sahara, implying that it sees Morocco's claim as not wholly illegitimate. Similarly, a number of important states have recognized Indonesia's absorption of East Timor, and the question of that region's right to self-determination has all but ceased to be considered in international fora.

These two conflicts appear to reflect a tolerance for wars aimed at gaining territory, provided that the territory is not claimed by an existing state and the expansion does not involve distant colonization by a European power. The international support for Indonesia's claim to West Irian, despite Indonesian opposition to self-determination for that area, reinforces the impression that states are prepared to tolerate such neocolonialism.

In particular, it should be noted that neither of these conflicts involved an attack on a generally recognized state. Neither, that is, challenged the foundations of the international status quo by seeking to formally eliminate a full member of the international community.

CHAPTER 9

# LIMITED USES OF FORCE

The uses of force described in this chapter were undertaken for a wide variety of reasons. They share two characteristics, however. All involved the regular armed forces of the state initiating the use of force. And all had limited objectives; their purposes, that is, were something less than subjugating the target state, acquiring a large portion of its territory, or replacing its government.

## Soviet Union/Iran (1946)

At the end of World War II Soviet troops were stationed in Iranian Azerbaijan, as permitted by a 1942 treaty.[1] Under the terms of the treaty the Soviets were obliged to withdraw by March 2, 1946. They refused to do so when that date arrived, however. They justified their refusal by their desire to protect "democratic forces" in Azerbaijan, referring to an autonomous local government that had been established in a revolt the previous November.[2] The Soviets had interfered with efforts by Iranian government forces to suppress that revolt and had continued to protect the Azerbaijanis.[3] Their motives, apparently, were less disinterested than they suggested; they sought both access to oil fields in the area and the control they could exert over a nominally autonomous Azerbaijan.[4]

The Security Council had refused to act on the matter prior to March 2, preferring to defer to negotiations between the parties concerned.[5] When the Soviets declined to withdraw on March 2, stating that they intended to remain until the situation had been "clarified,"[6] both the United States and the United Kingdom protested.[7] Over the next few weeks the Soviets reinforced their units and began to advance.[8] Iran appealed to the Security Council in mid-March,[9] with U.S. support in the face of some intimidation from the Soviets.[10] The key vote in the Security Council came on March 28, on a Soviet motion to postpone debate; the motion failed 9–2. The other four permanent members, as well as Australia, Brazil, Egypt, Mexico, and the Netherlands all opposed the motion; only Poland supported the Soviet Union, which proceeded to walk out.[11] But the Security Council voted to table the issue April 4, 1946, after the Soviet Union and Iran jointly reported an agreement resolving the issue and providing for Soviet withdrawal by May 6.[12] In return for the Soviet withdrawal Iran agreed to provide the Soviet Union with an oil concession and to guarantee the autonomy of Azerbaijan.[13] Following the pact, the Iranian government felt pressure both to enter into an agreement directly with the Azerbaijani government and to name three Communists to its cabinet.[14] The Soviets accordingly withdrew on May 9.[15] However, the Iranian central government subsequently brought down the Azerbaijani provincial government in December 1946, and on October 22, 1947, the Iranian Majlis (parliament) refused to ratify the oil agreement of May 1946 with the Soviet Union.[16] The three Communists had been dropped from the Iranian cabinet in October 1946, after a tribal revolt.[17]

Here, the Soviet Union sought to retain in Iran troops whose original entry was not challenged but whose continued presence violated a treaty commitment. The situation was made more serious by the employment of those troops to aid a group defying the authority of the Iranian government. The Soviet Union offered a disinterested justification—defense of democratic forces—but was widely believed to be motivated by a desire for economic gain and political control. Third states opposed the Soviet position, and the Soviets gave way.

This summary obscures several interesting aspects of this matter, however.

First, the Soviets' rationale for their presence—support for "democratic forces"—is a case in which a use of force was justified by reference to values not found in the UN Charter. Further, although the Soviets were unable to block the Security Council's action, the Council appeared focused exclusively on the presence of the Soviet troops. Once the troops left, the fact that the Soviet Union had gained important political and material concessions through their use was not addressed by the Security Council. Rather, Iran's success at escaping from its arrangement with the Soviets apparently depended on its ties to the ideological opponents of the Soviet Union. Most of the world, that is, seemed uninterested in depriving the Soviet Union of the gains it had made through its use of force.

## United Kingdom/Albania (1946)

On October 22, 1946, two Royal Navy warships proceeding through the Corfu Channel in Albanian territorial waters struck mines and were severely damaged. On November 13, 1946, a group of British warships returned to the area in order to sweep for mines. The British ships entered Albanian territorial waters to carry out this mission. The British in fact discovered mines, twenty-two of which were seized.

The British subsequently claimed that the second entry into Albanian waters, although not amounting to innocent passage, was nonetheless lawful as undertaken to obtain evidence for an international judicial proceeding.

There was no third-state reaction to the British action on November 13, so it is difficult to evaluate its validity as a matter of customary international law. It should be noted, however, that in an International Court of Justice case subsequently brought by the United Kingdom against Albania to recover damages for the harm done its warships, the court held that the British action in sweeping the mines on November 13 was unlawful. However, in its finding of facts on the British claim in respect of the October 22 mining the court relied on the evidence that the Royal Navy had obtained on November 13.[18] The court's treatment of this case is therefore ambiguous, since its refusal to exclude the "illegally" seized evidence arguably amounted to acquiescence in the seizure.[19] Lacking any evidence of state practice other than that of the United Kingdom, however, it is in any case difficult to evaluate this incident.

## United Kingdom/Yemen (1949)

As early as 1926 the Imam of Yemen claimed that the states of southern Arabia, which were under British protection, rightfully formed part of Yemeni territory.[20] In 1934 Britain and Yemen agreed to stabilize the frontiers between the areas each ruled, but neither side renounced any territorial claims.[21] This agreement led to some years of peace between Yemen and the protected states,[22] but there was trouble between the two in 1949.

In March 1949 Yemeni troops prevented the construction of a customs house in one of the states of the United Kingdom's South Arabian Protectorate and subsequently built a fort believed by the British to be in protectorate territory. After several warnings the Royal Air Force destroyed the fort. This incident took place against a background of border disputes in this region.[23] Apparently, third states took no interest.

The British action could be seen either as self-defense or as a reprisal for the destruction of the customs house, depending on where the border was. Similarly, the Yemenis were either invaders or protecting their own territory. In any case, no other state seems to have expressed an opinion on the matter.

## Saudi Arabia/Muscat and Oman (1952, 1955)

The Buraimi Oasis on the Arabian peninsula came under the shared control of the states of Abu Dhabi and Muscat and Oman in 1869. In 1914, by which time these states were protectorates of the United Kingdom, the United Kingdom and the Ottoman Empire agreed that the boundary between the empire and the territories of the two protectorates was far to the west of the oasis. In 1935, however, the Kingdom of Saudi Arabia, successor in this region to the Ottoman Empire, claimed a boundary further east than that earlier accepted by the Ottomans. In 1949 Saudi Arabia made a claim still further east, which included the Buraimi Oasis. Negotiations over the next three years were inconclusive.[24]

In 1952 Saudi Arabia sent an official with forty troops to the oasis, in violation of a standstill agreement with Muscat and Oman. Muscat and Oman and the British resident in the Trucial States each responded by sending large contingents of troops to the area, the Saudis countering with reinforcements. The United States then asked the United Kingdom to request the Sultan of Muscat and Oman not to attack. The United Kingdom made the request, and the sultan complied. The parties agreed on October 26, 1952, to maintain the then-existing status quo and resume negotiations.[25]

It was decided in the negotiations that followed to settle the dispute by arbitration, but the British member of the arbitration panel quit in September 1955, alleging Saudi duplicity.[26] Then, on October 26, 1955, the sultan seized the oasis from the very small Saudi contingent then occupying it; the two sides together suffered seven casualties.[27] The United Kingdom subsequently proclaimed a boundary close to that which it had offered as a counter to the first Saudi proposal of 1935. Saudi Arabia brought the matter to the attention of the United Nations Security Council, alleging aggression by the United Kingdom.[28] The United Kingdom responded by arguing that the forces of Abu Dhabi and Muscat had simply reoccupied their own territory after Saudi repudiation of arbitration and stressed its obligations to its Arab allies.[29] The Saudis seem to have dropped the matter, which apparently was resolved much later.[30]

This matter was a border dispute, exacerbated by a succession of states and, presumably, by the nature of the terrain involved. Each side could claim self-defense, since each claimed the territory in question. It should be noted that a significant period of fruitless negotiation preceded both uses of force. It also appears that outside powers other than the United Kingdom took no interest beyond that shown by the 1952 American request that force not be used—another situation in which the third state's main interest seems to have been in avoiding violence rather than in identifying and sanctioning a rule breaker. It is noteworthy that the United Kingdom clearly felt free to resort to force upon the failure of arbitration to reverse the original Saudi action even without any new basis for action. It is also interesting that the British did not seek any sort of UN aid or approval before acting.

## Thailand/Cambodia (1953–1962)

Very shortly after France's withdrawal from Cambodia in late 1953,[31] Thai police occupied a rocky promontory claimed by Cambodia on which were located the ruins of the Khmer temple of Preah Vihear.[32] The parties negotiated to no effect until 1958. In that year Thailand reacted angrily to a visit to Beijing by Cambodia's Prince Sihanouk and to Cambodia's recognition of the PRC, perceiving an attempt to intimidate them. In November diplomatic relations were broken, and troops began massing on the borders; mediation by a special representative of the UN secretary-general led to a resumption of diplomatic relations in February 1959, but tension soon increased again. Later in that year, after evoking no response from Thailand to suggestions for solving the problem, Cambodia brought the matter to the International Court of Justice, taking advantage of the fact that Thailand had submitted to the compulsory jurisdiction of the court. Relations continued to deteriorate over the next few years, diplomatic relations again being broken and troops again being placed on alert. The ICJ rendered its judgment in the Preah Vihear case on June 15, 1962, awarding the temple to Cambodia and requiring Thailand to remove its troops. Thailand was outraged, but—apparently moved by representations from the United States and Australia—finally complied with the court's decision, though justifying its compliance by the argument that war with Cambodia would only serve to aid the Communists.[33]

This matter was a territorial dispute that Thailand sought to resolve by coup de main, yielding finally to judicial resolution of the controversy after encouragement by powerful outside states and, at least ostensibly, more because of strategic considerations than because of respect for law. Third states clearly played a role in dissuading Thailand from defying the ICJ. Thailand's use of force, then, was reversed when an international judicial decision was supported by influential states. It should also be noted that the matter arose in the immediate aftermath of the end of Cambodia's colonial status, against a precolonial background of Thai-Cambodian hostility.

## United Kingdom/Yemen (1957)

The 1949 border incidents between Yemen and the United Kingdom were followed by more border fighting between those combatants in 1954. The immediate cause was a Yemeni desire to block the formation by the United Kingdom of a federation among its southern Arabian protectorates. Partly this desire reflected Yemen's claim to the area, but it also was a product of the realities of Yemen's domestic politics. The Imam of Yemen was an adherent of the Zeidi sect of Islam, and his rule depended on the Yemeni Zeidis' domination of the Shafei adherents who made up the majority of Yemen's population. The federation the British planned would be a Shafei state, and the Imam feared that a stable Shafei state on his southern frontier would be a threat to him.[34]

Initially, the Yemeni government armed dissidents in southern Arabia, who in turn carried out several raids in 1954.[35] At about the same time Yemen laid claim to the territory of the protectorates in the United Nations.[36] The fighting died out in 1955 when it appeared that the planned federation would not be formed. It resumed in January 1957 after the Yemeni foreign minister's leadership of an unsuccessful coup attempt led to his replacement by a successor who had been educated in Egypt and who sought to associate Yemen with Egypt and its nonalignment policy, in contrast to his predecessor's efforts to improve relations with the West. The new approach produced considerable arms aid for Yemen from the Soviet Union and the PRC, the first shipments arriving in October 1956. Yemen immediately sought to use the arms against the protectorates, employing both its regular army and dissident tribesmen. Finally, in March 1957 the United Kingdom responded with air strikes against one tribe that could not be contained by other methods.[37]

Throughout this period Yemen justified its actions by its claim to southern Arabia. The British saw themselves as acting in self-defense in repelling assaults on the protected states.[38] To the extent that third states reacted, Yemen was supported by Egypt, which was greatly opposed to the British presence in the Arab world, and by Saudi Arabia, which also objected to the British presence, in particular because of the Buraimi Oasis dispute.[39] Further, as noted above, Yemen received arms aid from the Communist great powers. Third-state reaction was otherwise limited; no UN organ addressed this matter. It should also be noted that this conflict occurred against a background of increasing opposition to the European presence in the Arab world as reflected in the support given the Algerian Revolution, discussed in Chapter 3, and in reaction to the Suez crisis.[40] This conflict was thus a territorial dispute, complicated by elements of opposition to European domination of non-European areas.

## Egypt/Sudan (1958)

In February 1958 both Egypt and the Sudan were preparing for elections. On February 1 Egypt complained about Sudan's including among its electoral constituencies certain areas that were part of Egyptian territory. The Sudan responded that the areas in question were in fact Sudanese. (The dispute turned on the proper interpretation of administrative arrangements established by the British during their administration of the Sudan.) Egypt sent troops into the area, and Sudan referred the matter to the Security Council on February 20, 1958. In the Security Council Egypt denied any intention of resolving this territorial dispute through the use of force. The members of the Security Council expressed the hope that the parties would settle the matter between themselves. Egypt withdrew its troops from the disputed areas before February 25, and the parties agreed to hold the matter in abeyance until after the two states' elections had been held.[41]

This was a border dispute in which one party, apparently, at least considered threatening the use of force to defend its territory but ended by choosing not to do so. Since each side insisted on its peaceful intentions, there was no occasion for the international community to react even to a threat. Not surprisingly, the Security Council contented itself with urging the parties to act on their professed desire for peace.

## Nicaragua/Honduras (1958)

In February 1958 Honduras created a new province in an area awarded to Honduras in a 1906 arbitration but still claimed by Nicaragua. On April 18, 1958, fifty Nicaraguan troops crossed the river that formed the international border in the area and occupied a town. A Honduran battalion with air support attacked the Nicaraguans on May 1, killing thirty-five. Both states took the matter to the OAS on May 1. That body quickly promised an investigation and called for a cease-fire, which both sides accepted. The OAS further arranged for troop withdrawals and the establishment of a buffer zone, and urged the parties to take the matter to the International Court of Justice, which they did. The court rendered judgment in 1961, and the OAS oversaw the enforcement of that judgment. At no point did the OAS label either side an aggressor or itself address the controversy underlying the fighting.[42]

In this case Nicaragua resorted to the use of force to make a boundary claim. It should be noted that Honduras, the victim of the use of force, was able to defend itself without assistance, so the question of aiding the defense of the victim of an attack never arose. In any case, the OAS concentrated on neutral measures aimed at stopping the shooting and providing a means for ultimate judicial resolution of the problem. Instead of focusing solely on the use of force and applying a sanction, it took steps to see that the fighting stopped *and* that a judicial body settled the controversy that had given rise to the use of force. The organization, that is, addressed itself to halting current fighting and bringing the parties to the point where they would have nothing in the future to fight about rather than treating the use of force itself as a wrong requiring redress.

## Afghanistan/Pakistan (1961)

At the time of the partition of British India in 1947 Afghanistan had challenged its border with Pakistan, known as the Durand Line, claiming the border between the two states should rest instead on the Indus River. Somewhat contradictorily, it strongly supported the idea that the Pakhtun (Pathan) people should be able to create an independent state, Pakhtunistan. Since Pakhtun tribes lived on either side of the Durand Line the creation of such a state would also serve to remove Pakistan from that boundary;[43] to the extent that Afghanistan could dominate the new state Pakhtunistan's creation would serve the same Afghan end as a change in the border.

In September 1960 Afghanistan's push for an independent Pakhtunistan led it to bribe the ruler of one of the small states within Pakistan to attack one of his feudatories. In May 1961, after Pakistan had accused Afghanistan of fomenting trouble between the two rulers, fighting broke out between the two states. They broke diplomatic relations in July, reestablishing relations only after mediation by the Shah of Iran in May 1963.[44]

Outside reaction was limited. The Soviet Union supported the creation of Pakhtunistan even after the initial tribal fighting.[45] One may speculate that this stand was at least partly motivated by hostility to Pakistan, which had aligned itself with the United States in the Cold War. The United States, in contrast, sought to remain neutral, not wishing to drive Afghanistan closer to the Soviet Union.[46] In line with this approach the United States offered its good offices to help resolve the dispute but did not go so far as formally proposing itself as a mediator, and offered no suggestions regarding the basic dispute.[47]

This small conflict was a border dispute left over from the period of British colonial rule on the Indian subcontinent. Afghanistan was seeking to alter its border by the use of force and also by manipulating the doctrine of self-determination. Outside attitudes, to the extent that they existed, seemed determined primarily by ideology—the Soviet Union opposed an ally of the United States, while the United States tried to avoid either offending its ally or alienating the other party to the dispute. The only effective outside intervention was the shah's, and that took the form of mediation rather than identifying a wrongdoer and sanctioning that party.

## PRC/India (1962)

The brief war between India and the PRC in 1962 had its roots in a long-standing border dispute between the two states. India claimed that the so-called McMahon Line marked the eastern portion of its frontier with China. The PRC responded that, while the British had claimed that border when India was a British colony, no Chinese government had ever accepted that claim and that the authority of the British Indian government had not been exercised so far north. The two states also differed as to the location of their western border in the area called Ladakh. The issue was even more confused concerning this region than was true for the eastern part of the boundary, neither state having an irrefutable basis for its claim.[48]

The two states assumed quite different attitudes toward dealing with this problem. India took the position that her claims were indisputable and refused to consider negotiations aimed at establishing mutually agreeable boundaries.[49] The PRC, in contrast, argued that disputes existed and that negotiations were the best way to address the problem, pointing to the success of such negotiations in resolving similar problems between the PRC and others of its neighbors.[50]

The disagreement led to border clashes in both the vicinity of the McMahon Line and in Ladakh in 1959.[51] The resentment these clashes triggered in India hardened attitudes in that state,[52] and eventually led to a change in policy. Specifically, in 1961 India elected to begin establishing small border posts in the disputed regions. In Ladakh, which was very important to the PRC as a means of access to Tibet and which the PRC had begun to develop accordingly, this operation would take the form of establishing Indian posts in places that would cut off existing Chinese posts. In the McMahon Line vicinity there were no Chinese posts on what India considered its side of the border, but the new policy required Indian troops to establish posts directly on that border, remote though it was.[53] Chinese protests of this policy and threats to respond with force if it was not changed produced no change in Indian behavior.[54]

As part of the new policy, India established a post in the McMahon Line vicinity on the south bank of a watercourse called the Namka Chu on June 4, 1962; this step was taken despite a 1959 agreement with the PRC to preserve the status quo in that area, which the PRC had observed.[55] This post was actually north of the McMahon Line; India, however, argued that the line had been intended to follow the highest crests of the mountains in the region, that in the area in question the line as drawn did not follow those crests, that the line was thus, in effect, in the wrong place, and that India could in essence unilaterally alter the placement of the McMahon Line.[56] On September 8 PRC troops moved into positions across the Namka Chu from the Indian post, dominating it. The commander of the post reported, incorrectly, that his position was surrounded. On September 9 the Indian government decided to expel the PRC force because it was on the Indian side of the line of the highest mountain crests, albeit on the Chinese side of the McMahon Line as actually drawn.[57]

On October 3 the PRC responded to an Indian suggestion, made the previous August, for negotiations on mutual troop withdrawals from the disputed area in Ladakh by calling for discussions on all border issues. India responded on October 6 by withdrawing its suggestion, refusing to enter into any talks with the PRC unless the Chinese troops on the Namka Chu withdrew to the Chinese side of the highest crest line.[58] India was convinced that the Chinese would not react forcibly to any move it might make, even if India expelled the Chinese troops on the Namka Chu; Indian thinking apparently was influenced by the assumption that India's reputation as a state wedded to nonviolence would inhibit any Chinese response to India's actions.[59]

In the meantime both sides had reinforced their troops on the Namka Chu, with the Chinese clearly in greater strength. On October 9 Indian troops in the area began moves preliminary to an attack on the Chinese. The Chinese responded on October 10 with troop movements that made clear the impossibility of any successful Indian offensive action.[60] The Indian government reacted to these developments on October 11, deciding to abandon attack plans for the moment but to leave the troops in place; the next day, however, Prime Minister Nehru responded to a press question by stating that the Chinese would be forced to withdraw, though he did not specify a time frame.[61] His remarks were widely interpreted as presaging an Indian attack, and in fact the Indian troops on Namka Chu were subsequently reinforced and were disposed in positions more suitable for offense than defense.[62]

In the end, however, it was the Chinese who finally attacked on the Namka Chu. They moved on October 20, routing the Indians.[63] They did not stop there, however; they attacked along the length of the McMahon Line and also attacked the Indian posts in Ladakh. By November 20 the Indians had been driven in disorder across the lines the PRC asserted were the historic borders both in the east and the west.[64] Two days later the PRC, though in a commanding position, announced a unilateral cease-fire; it further announced that by December 1 it would begin to withdraw its troops twenty kilometers north of the McMahon Line in the east and a similar distance behind the border the PRC claimed in the west and insisted that Indian troops approach those same lines no closer than twenty kilometers.[65] The PRC proceeded to effect the cease-fire and withdrawal as announced.[66] This cease-fire ended the fighting between the two states. The underlying border dispute, however, has not been resolved as of this writing, although negotiations on the subject have taken place in recent years.[67]

The two sides' justifications for their actions were diametrically opposed. The PRC claimed, falsely, that it had been attacked in force by Indian troops both on the Namka Chu and in Ladakh and that its actions were taken entirely in response to these imaginary Indian attacks.[68] On October 24, however, in a statement released in Beijing, the PRC proposed high-level negotiations on the border dispute and a cease-fire under which each side would withdraw twenty kilometers from the "line of actual control."[69] That term was not defined in the statement and conceivably referred to the areas controlled as of October 24 when the statement was issued; however, throughout its dealings with India on border questions, the PRC had used that term to refer to the positions each side had occupied when the dispute had first come to a head in 1959. If that was in fact the PRC's meaning, India would have had to withdraw its advanced posts in Ladakh, almost all of which the Chinese had captured anyway, and could not have maintained positions north of the McMahon Line, such as that on the Namka Chu.[70] In response India denounced the PRC's actions as aggression and accused the PRC of occupying substantial Indian territory and then using that territory as a bargaining chip; India's counterproposal to the PRC's suggestion demanded Chinese withdrawal to pre-September 8 positions, with any talks to focus only on "easing tension," not on the underlying border dispute.[71]

Third-state reactions to the fighting differed. Both the United States and the United Kingdom agreed with India's position on the location of the border—an issue on which the United States had not previously committed itself—and provided aid, including weapons.[72] The Federal Republic of Germany, Yugoslavia, Turkey, Canada, New Zealand, Rhodesia, Italy, France, and Australia all provided aid to India, and the United Arab Republic provided diplomatic support.[73] Ethiopia and Cyprus also sided with India,[74] as did several Latin American and European states and several important Asian countries.[75] But most Arab and African states were noncommittal; Ghana went so far as to criticize the United Kingdom for offering arms aid to India, and other states' comments took the form of calls for restraint and offers of mediation.[76] The

Soviet Union, to India's dismay, took the PRC's side in the dispute, perhaps influenced by a desire to avoid alienating an important Communist state in the midst of the Cuban missile crisis.[77]

This case, then, involved, in the first instance, a use of force by India in sending troops into areas whose sovereignty was disputed. Further, India had made clear its intention to open hostilities on the Namka Chu at some point, and the dispositions of the Indian troops in that area could have led the PRC commanders to believe that such action was imminent. The PRC's response, however, went beyond dealing with the problem on the Namka Chu, since it involved not only eliminating that threat but also expelling Indian troops from the disputed areas in the west and driving the Indian army out of the entire area north of the border claimed by the PRC in the east. The two states' justifications turned essentially on competing claims to the territory, each focusing on the illegitimacy of the other's presence. Third-state reaction was divided. Many states reacted to what was perceived as Chinese aggression by condemning the PRC and providing aid to India. Several others, however, took a more nonjudgmental approach, focusing on stopping the fighting rather than on evaluating the legality of the two sides' resort to force. In other words, at least some states were simply unprepared to see the use of force itself as requiring some sort of negative reaction. No state imposed sanctions on either combatant.

## Morocco/Algeria (1963)

The border between Morocco and Algeria had not been definitively delimited during the period of France's control of the latter. Upon Algeria's attaining independence, the uncertainty continued. The issue assumed particular importance with respect to the vicinity of Tindauf because of significant iron ore deposits in that region, and it was exacerbated by ideological differences between socialist Algeria and the Moroccan monarchy. On October 1, 1963, the underlying dispute and accompanying bad feeling finally led to the seizure by Moroccan forces of two oases controlling the route to Tindauf. Algerian troops counterattacked on October 8, recapturing the oases, but a subsequent Moroccan assault on October 14 retook them. Fighting continued for two more weeks, during which Morocco held the oases and expanded its area of control but was unable to prevent retaliatory seizures of Moroccan territory by Algeria.

Several states sought to mediate, but mediation efforts foundered over the terms of a cease-fire, Algeria urging withdrawals to positions held prior to October 1, before the initial Moroccan capture of the oases, while Morocco insisted that withdrawals should be to positions held before October 8, when the oases were in Moroccan hands. Finally, after mediation in Bamako by the emperor of Ethiopia and the president of Mali, the two states agreed to a cease-fire calling for a withdrawal to positions held prior to October 1, the establishment of a demilitarized zone in the affected area, and the creation of an arbitration commission to examine both the fighting and the border question. Over time, relations between the two states improved; on June 15, 1972, they finally signed an agreement establishing a border following the de facto frontier as of the time of Algeria's independence. This arrangement put the ore deposits in Algeria, but the agreement also called for exploring the idea of joint Algerian-Moroccan exploitation of the deposits.[78]

This matter was not taken to the United Nations, but there were extensive regional efforts to stop the fighting. The OAU adopted a resolution on October 19, 1963, deploring the hostilities and calling for a pullback of forces to positions occupied prior to the start of the conflict. The resolution blamed neither state, but Morocco rejected it at the time as calling for Morocco to abandon the territory it had occupied and that it claimed. Most states in the region took neutral positions, although Syria, Iraq, and the UAR all expressed strong pro-Algerian positions and the UAR admitted sending troops to Algeria, albeit with orders to remain within that state's borders (of course, since the argument was over where those borders were, that instruction did not limit the freedom of the Egyptian contingent as much as it might have done). Apparently, this stand reflected the ideological affinity between Algeria and the other three states. During the fighting Algeria also received a shipment of tanks from the Soviet Union, along with Cuban technicians to service them, but Algeria insisted that the shipment was the product of an agreement reached long before the fighting started and had no relation to it. Morocco nonetheless severed diplomatic relations with Cuba.[79]

This conflict was a border dispute arising from uncertainties left over from a period of colonialism and heightened by ideologicial differences. Most states who reacted focused on halting the fighting rather than on identifying the aggressor. Efforts by third states were directed at seeking agreement between the parties to the conflict. The few states who chose sides apparently did so on the basis of ideology, not by examining either the question of the use of force or the merits of the border question. The ultimate resolution of the matter involved no sanction for the use of force, focusing instead on the underlying dispute.

## United States and Belgium in Congo (1964)

In September 1964 rebels against the government of the Republic of the Congo proclaimed the existence of the Provisional Revolutionary Government under the presidency of Christopher Gbenye in Stanleyville. The Congo government, at that time led by Moise Tshombe, was receiving from the United States aid in training its troops and considerable quantities of military equipment. Its army included significant numbers of white mercenaries from South Africa, Rhodesia, and Portuguese territories.[80] The Gbenye forces received aid from the UAR, Algeria, Ghana, the Sudan, and Kenya.[81]

On September 26 Gbenye announced that foreigners then in Stanleyville would not be permitted to leave; in effect, he was holding them hostage. The number of persons so held approximated 1,300, including about 600 Belgians and about 400 Indians and Pakistanis, with most of the remainder being other Europeans or Americans. Over the next several months American and Belgian authorities negotiated unsuccessfully to free the hostages; efforts directed at the United Nations, the OAU, the International Red Cross, and individual African heads of state all proved fruitless.

Finally, on November 21 Tshombe officially requested Belgian and American aid in freeing the hostages. The following day Belgian officers met with the leader of the mercenaries in the employ of the Republic of the Congo to coordinate plans for an attack on Stanleyville.[82] Such coordination made sense, it should be noted, because troops of the republic's army spearheaded by mercenaries had, since early November, been advancing against the rebels in Stanleyville.[83] On November 23 American President Johnson ordered that the rescue operation proceed, and on the following day American planes, flying from Ascension Island, a British possession, dropped 600 Belgian paratroops on Stanleyville. The Belgians succeeded in taking the city, in conjunction with an attack by mercenary-led Congolese forces. A total of 1,800 foreigners and 300 Congolese were flown out by the American-Belgian forces before the operation ended on November 28.[84] The Congolese forces, in the meantime, killed hundreds of Gbenye's rebels; the paratroop drop also contributed to the eventual success of the republic's troops in the rebelling areas.[85]

Third-state reaction to this Belgian-American operation was sharply divided. On December 18 the OAU condemned it by twenty votes to none, with ten states abstaining.[86] The Security Council also discussed the operation at the request of Afghanistan, Algeria, Cambodia, Indonesia, the Sudan, the UAR, Yugoslavia, and fifteen sub-Saharan African states, who had characterized it as an intervention in African affairs and a flagrant violation of the UN Charter; the Security Council at the same time considered a complaint from the Tshombe government accusing Algeria, the Sudan, Ghana, the UAR, the PRC, and the Soviet Union of intervening in the Congo's affairs. The twenty-two states attacked the operation as an intervention aimed against the Gbenye forces and supporting the Tshombe government, whose legitimacy they denied. They insisted that the concern expressed for the lives of the foreign hostages in Stanleyville was but a pretext for the operation and dismissed the request from the Tshombe government, questioning that government's legality and stressing the extent of domestic opposition to it. The Soviet Union and Czechoslovakia echoed the claims of the twenty-two states, the Soviet Union insisting that the true objective of the operation was an attack on Gbenye's forces.[87]

The United States, the United Kingdom, and Belgium all insisted on the purely humanitarian character of the operation. They were supported in this position by France, Brazil, the ROC, Bolivia, and Norway, who also stressed the request of the Congolese government. Nigeria relied solely on this latter point in rejecting the characterization of the operation as intervention. Ivory Coast and the Central African Republic also acknowledged the legitimacy of the Congo's government, though "deploring" the airdrop on Stanleyville. Morocco acknowledged the humanitarian character of the operation but nonetheless emphasized the inadmissibility of interventions in states' domestic affairs.[88] The Security Council subsequently adopted a resolution requesting an end to interventions in the Congo, calling for a cease-fire, and also calling for an end to the use of mercenaries. The resolution was adopted by ten votes to none, France abstaining.[89] It should be noted that in the debate only two states took positions suggesting that they considered unlawful a state's intervention in a second state to protect the intervenor's nationals; most who opposed the airdrop dismissed the asserted humanitarian motive as a pretext for a political intervention rather than rejecting it as irrelevant.[90] It should also be noted that, aside from the criticism voiced in this debate, the United States and Belgium were not sanctioned in any way for their participation.

It is easy enough to describe the actions of the United States and Belgium; they captured a town in cooperation with the Congolese military, rescued over 2,000 people, and left. In the meantime the Congolese military proceeded to do considerable damage to rebel forces. It is not easy to be certain of the intervening states' motives. While one may doubt that there would have been any intervention had the hostages not been present, one may also doubt that the intervenors—who were already aiding the Tshombe government—were disturbed that their intervention assisted that government's forces against its opponents. In any case, third-state reaction split according to the view the reacting state took of the intervenors' motives. Negative reactions insisted that the intervention was procolonial and condemned it on that ground. Positive reactions rejected that characterization, stressing instead both the permission obtained from the territorial sovereign and the humanitarian character of the intervenors' actions. That is, there seems to have been general agreement that a truly humanitarian intervention would have been defensible and that a procolonial intervention could not be justified; the disagreement was over how to characterize this action. In any case, no sanction was imposed and significant numbers of states defended the intervention.

## PRC/Soviet Union (1969)

In March 1969 troops of the Soviet Union and the PRC twice engaged in combat that cost at least dozens of fatalities; the occasion for these clashes was a dispute about sovereignty over an island in the Ussuri River, which formed the boundary between the two states according to treaties dating from the nineteenth century.[91] Later in the summer there was further bloody border fighting between the two states, both along the Amur River and on the border between the Soviet Union and Sinkiang.[92] After attempts at mediation by the DRV, whose war effort depended on support from both combatants, the Soviet prime minister met with his Chinese counterpart in Beijing in September following the funeral of Ho Chi Minh. This meeting served to reduce tensions, and the two sides began negotiations on outstanding territorial questions the following October.[93] Those talks have yet to fully resolve the border dispute between the parties.

The motives behind this dispute were complex. Since the early 1960s the PRC had taken the position that the treaties establishing its border with the

Soviet Union were unequal and should be renegotiated.[94] The PRC also argued that, even under those treaties, the islands in dispute in the Ussuri were within its territory.[95] The Soviet Union rejected this position, insisting that the treaties were not unequal and that they clearly established its sovereignty over all the disputed territories.[96] With respect to particular incidents, each claimed that its troops had been at all times within its own territory and each claimed that the other had fired first,[97] except that the Soviets admitted firing first in one of the later incidents, insisting that they were responding to an incursion by Chinese troops.[98]

It seems clear that these clashes involved more than a border dispute. Rather, there is reason to believe that the parties' actions reflected their competition in the Communist world and may have represented efforts by each of them to improve its standing in that competition.[99]

Except for the Warsaw Pact satellites of the Soviet Union, third states generally reacted to this matter by asserting their neutrality, as did the United States, Romania, and Yugoslavia.[100] The United Nations did not address this matter, and the DRV's intervention was about the only effort to mediate.

This dispute involved serious border fighting unrelated to a recently terminated colonial situation. It evoked little interest among third parties; the calls for negotiation and efforts at mediation so common in the other disputes discussed in this work were much less apparent in this case. There were also no third-party moves to sanction either of the combatants. One is forced to conclude that with respect to this matter the rest of the world decided that direct moves and/or sanctions by outsiders to end the fighting were inadvisable.

## El Salvador/Honduras (1969)

In 1969 relations between El Salvador and Honduras deteriorated for a number of reasons. Both were members of the Central American Common Market, but that arrangement had worked out badly for Honduras while El Salvador had benefited from it. Further, on April 30 Honduras elected to seize land farmed by many thousands of squatters from overpopulated El Salvador for distribution to landless Hondurans and to require the Salvadorans to return home. As the first refugees returned to El Salvador, tensions were further inflamed by reports in both states that supporters of each of their World Cup teams had been seriously maltreated in the other's capital. After unsuccessful efforts to obtain guarantees of better treatment for Salvadorans in Honduras, and in a climate of popular belligerence, El Salvador invaded Honduras on July 14.[101]

After advancing for five days, El Salvador's forces halted; that state accepted an OAS cease-fire on July 18, having encountered supply problems and pressure from the United States.[102] Despite its acceptance of the cease-fire, however, El Salvador's troops continued to advance in places, refused to permit OAS observers to enter certain areas, and refused to withdraw as urged by an OAS Council Resolution of July 18. Accordingly, an OAS Meeting of Consultation of Foreign Ministers was called on July 26, which by July 29 was preparing to invoke the Rio Treaty to impose on El Salvador serious economic sanctions—an embargo on the purchase of Salvadoran coffee. Faced with this threat, El Salvador withdrew its troops in August. Relations between the two states continued to be bad for some time, however.[103]

The justifications and motives for El Salvador's invasion were closely related. El Salvador complained of the maltreatment of its nationals and invaded in a burst of nationalistic fervor. It claimed it acted in self-defense, in light of the persecution it asserted its nationals were suffering in Honduras.[104] In addition to this nationalistic justification, the invasion took place against a background of economic rivalry; further, the government of El Salvador was facing various internal problems and may have welcomed a diversion.[105]

Apparently, only states in the Americas reacted to this invasion, but they did so with dispatch and forcefulness. Not only did the OAS supply observers to facilitate the maintenance of the cease-fire in line with that organization's traditional mediatory approach, but it also threatened serious sanctions to coerce El Salvador into ending its occupation of Honduran territory. That threat of sanctions apparently was effective, contributing greatly to El Salvador's decision to withdraw.

This conflict was a cross-border invasion, motivated by what amounted to mutual bad feeling between two states, aggravated by the invader's concern for its nationals and by economic differences. Third states reacted sharply, coercing the invader into withdrawing its troops. Thus, while the circumstances in which El Salvador used force were not among those treated as legitimate by the states of the world, third-state reaction reinforced, rather than eroded, that illegitimacy. It should be stressed that in this case third states reacted to the use of force itself rather than finessing the issues a use of force presented as part of an effort to address the political questions underlying a particular dispute.

# Yemen Arab Republic/People's Democratic Republic of Yemen (1972)

In February 1972 a powerful sheikh resident in the Yemen Arab Republic (YAR) was lured across the border into the YAR's southern neighbor, the People's Democratic Republic of Yemen (PDRY), and there murdered, apparently in revenge for his role in aiding Saudi Arabia to arm refugees from the PDRY. Relations between the YAR and the PDRY rapidly deteriorated over the rest of the year, the situation being aggravated by the ideological rivalry between the Saudi-oriented YAR and the Marxist-Leninist PDRY. In September border fighting began between the armed forces of the two states, each accusing the other of invading. The fighting continued into October, finally ending October 13 after an Arab League mediation group persuaded the combatants to cease fire. On October 28 they agreed to end sabotage campaigns against one another, to permit repatriation of refugees wishing to return home, and to close military training camps for one another's refugees. On November 28, after talks in which Libya participated, the two states agreed to merge.[106]

The third-state reaction to this episode was as noted; the Arab League mediated and obtained both a cease-fire and an agreement eliminating some of the causes of tension between the two states. The matter was not taken to the United Nations. No third state imposed sanctions.

This conflict amounted to border skirmishing brought on by bad blood between neighbors. Each combatant claimed to be the victim of the other's aggression; the facts were not clear. The rest of the world did not focus on clarifying the facts but rather generally ignored the matter, except for other Arab states who concentrated on stopping the shooting and relieving some of the tension between the two Yemens. As in a number of other conflicts hitherto examined, outside reaction was directed toward ending hostilities and addressing the underlying problem rather than toward identifying an aggressor and sanctioning the aggression.

# Israel/Iraq, Lebanon (1973)

On August 10, 1973, Israeli military aircraft entered Lebanese airspace to intercept an Iraqi civilian aircraft flying from Beirut to Baghdad; the Israelis forced the Iraqi plane to land in Israel. After the passengers were interrogated, the aircraft, crew, and passengers were released. Israel justified its action by asserting that it had information that George Habash, the leader of the Popular Front for the Liberation of Palestine, would be aboard the plane and that it had hoped to capture Habash.[107]

Third-state reaction was negative, though limited. The Security Council unanimously adopted a resolution condemning the interception, both the American and British delegates criticizing Israel's action as a clear violation of international law. The International Civil Aviation Organization likewise condemned Israel for the interception. Neither body imposed sanctions on Israel, however; nor were sanctions imposed by any third state acting individually.[108]

This was an effort by a state to forcibly exercise jurisidiction within the territory of a second state against an aircraft licensed by a third state. The acting state sought to justify its action by explaining that the purpose of the exercise was to arrest a terrorist. Third states expressed strong disapproval of the action and of the justification but imposed no sanctions beyond the rhetorical.

## PRC/Republic of Vietnam (1974)

On January 11, 1974, the PRC repeated a claim it had previously made to sovereignty over the Spratly and Paracel islands, small archipelagoes in the South China Sea. The ROV also claimed the islands and rejected the Chinese statement on January 12. Both states had troops in the Paracels, and clashes between them took place on about January 16, followed by a naval engagement on January 19. The Vietnamese were defeated in all engagements and forced to retreat, leaving prisoners behind.[109]

The ROV took the matter to the Security Council through a communication asserting that the islands were Vietnam's and that the PRC had thus attacked Vietnamese territory. The PRC responded by claiming that the islands were its territory and that the Vietnamese had started the fighting.[110]

Third states reacted with indifference. The United States stressed its noninvolvement, while deploring the use of force and expressing doubt that the incident demonstrated the PRC's intent to dominate the region. The DRV called for settling the problems through negotiations. The Security Council refused to take up the matter; the United States, the United Kingdom, Australia, Costa Rica, and possibly Austria favored hearing the Vietnamese complaint, but the PRC, the Soviet Union, Byelorussia, Iraq, and Indonesia all opposed the idea, while Kenya, Mauritania, Peru, and Cameroon indicated that they would abstain on a vote, and France did not take a public position. In these circumstances the ROV withdrew its request for Security Council action.[111]

This conflict amounted to a border clash in an area where sovereignty was clearly in dispute. Each side claimed self-defense. Third states took no action. One can speculate that this absence of third-state response reflected both the murkiness of the territorial claims and a reluctance on the part of the ROV's main ally, the United States, to jeopardize its evolving relationship with the PRC by involving itself in the matter.

## Burkina Faso/Mali (1974–1986)

Disputes over the location of their postcolonial borders led to fighting between Burkina Faso (then called Upper Volta) and its neighbor Mali beginning November 25, 1974. The fighting continued until December 26, with each side accusing the other of invasion. The mediation of Senegal and Togo led to a cease-fire and the establishment of a mediation commission composed of those states plus Guinea and Niger. After further fighting the following June, halted through the efforts of the mediation commission, the two combatants for several years sought to resolve their border problem. Finally, in 1983 they elected to take the matter to the International Court of Justice. However, in December 1985 conflicts over a census by Burkina Faso led to renewed fighting beginning December 25, involving air raids by both sides and an airborne landing by Mali. The parties to the Non-Aggression and Defence Aid Agreement (Ivory Coast, Mauritania, Senegal, Niger, Togo, and the two combatants) worked out a truce on December 31. A December 1986 ICJ judgment settled the border dispute.[112]

These outbreaks represent another example of former colonies turning to force to resolve questions regarding the placement of borders inherited from colonial powers. As in other such cases the response of third states was limited. Here, it was the combatants' neighbors who reacted, specifically by mediating. Third-state reaction did not take the form of seeking to sanction a party judged guilty of unlawfully using force but rather was manifested in an effort to stop the fighting.

## Lao People's Democratic Republic/Thailand (1975–1988)

Over the period 1975–88 Laos and Thailand engaged in numerous border clashes, each accusing the other of incursions into its territory, with the situation exacerbated by disputes concerning the location of the border and by the differing ideologies of the two governments. (Thailand during this period was frequently under the control of rightist military governments while Laos was a Marxist-Leninist state.) Particularly serious fighting took place in the period April to October 1984, involving disputed sovereignty over three border villages. There was also border fighting in 1985 and 1986, and a quite bloody encounter over disputed territory that began in December 1987 and was ended by a February 1988 cease-fire. After that time the two states established a joint border commission, and relations improved between them.[113]

There seems to have been relatively little third-state reaction to these episodes of fighting. During the 1984 period of tension Vietnam expressed support for Laos in the United Nations, while Kampuchea blamed the problem on Laos.[114] During the same period, however, the Security Council met on the matter but took no action at all, no state addressing the dispute other than the two parties to it.[115]

This lengthy but episodic and mainly low-level conflict was an ideologically charged border dispute. Each side justified its actions by claiming the other was intruding into its territory, much of the territory in question being, in fact, disputed. Third states took little interest in the conflict, and none imposed sanctions on either combatant or even, apparently, sought to encourage negotiation. The parties finally came to an understanding by themselves.

## United States/Kampuchea (1975)

On May 12, 1975, Kampuchean forces seized an American-flag merchant vessel, the *Mayaguez*, as it was passing in an international shipping lane 6.5 miles from an island claimed by Kampuchea, which was in turn about 60 miles from the Kampuchean mainland. Those forces also seized the crew, composed of American nationals. The United States delivered two notes of protest to the Kampuchean government on that day, evoking no response. On the following day the vessel was ordered to anchor close to an island about 34 miles from the port of Kompong Som. On May 14 the crew was removed and put aboard a fishing boat for transfer to the mainland. American aircraft attacked this fishing boat, desisting when it was realized that the *Mayaguez* crew might be aboard, and also attacked several Kampuchean naval vessels, some of the latter being sunk or damaged. The vessel carrying the American crew reached the mainland.

Several things happened on May 15. In a radio broadcast Kampuchea explained the reasons for its seizure of the ship and announced its intention to release the ship and crew. American ground forces landed on the island near which the *Mayaguez* was anchored, seeking to rescue any crew members that might be held there, but encountered heavy Kampuchean fire and suffered relatively heavy casualties. An American naval vessel in the meantime recovered the *Mayaguez* without incident, and American aircraft carried out heavy attacks against the Kampuchean mainland. Later that evening a second American naval vessel intercepted the Kampuchean vessel that was returning the crew of the *Mayaguez* to their ship and took them aboard without firing.[116]

The United States asserted that the *Mayaguez* was in international waters or, if in Kampuchean territorial waters, engaged in innocent passage; it justified its use of force as an act of self-defense under Article 51 of the United Nations Charter because it was necessary to protect the lives and property of American citizens.[117] There is some evidence that, while American government officials were in fact concerned for the crew of the *Mayaguez*, the United States was also moved to act by a desire to restore what it perceived to be its damaged international standing.[118] Kampuchea justified its seizure of the vessel by stressing the ship's presence in Kampuchean territorial waters and asserting, somewhat contradictorily, that the vessel must necessarily have entered Kampuchean waters to conduct espionage and provoke incidents in view of the unlikelihood that a well-equipped American vessel could get lost and also that the seizure had been for the purpose of determining the reason for the presence of the *Mayaguez* in Kampuchean waters.[119]

There was relatively little third-state reaction to this incident. The American troops engaged in the operation had moved from a base in Thailand, and the Thai government vigorously protested what it considered an infringement of its sovereignty.[120] The government of the FRG expressed approval at the vigorous American reaction.[121] The government of India withheld comment.[122] Israel expressed relief and satisfaction at the rescue.[123] Japan declared that it believed the American action was justified.[124] The PRC and DRV criticized the seizure, however, while the Soviet Union withheld official comment.[125] No third state imposed sanctions on either combatant.

This incident involved a raid by a state into the territory of a second state to rescue nationals seized by the second state under circumstances of doubtful international legality. While the motives of the raiding state were not unmixed, since considerations of international prestige were involved, the humanitarian motive was apparently uppermost. Third states were generally either supportive of the action or unprepared to criticize it, let alone treat it as a violation of law.

## Israel/Uganda (1976)

On June 27, 1976, in a joint operation by the Baader-Meinhof Gang of German terrorists and the Popular Front for the Liberation of Palestine, an Air France jet flying from Tel Aviv was hijacked to Entebbe airport in Uganda. Receiving the cooperation of the Ugandan government, the terrorists proceeded to release their non-Jewish hostages and to demand the release of terrorists imprisoned in a number of states as the price for the release of the Jewish hostages. Many of the hostages were Israeli nationals, and Israel determined to rescue them. Accordingly, Israeli troops landed at Entebbe in cargo aircraft on the night of July 3, rescued the hostages, and departed. They killed a number of Ugandan troops who were assisting the terrorists to guard the hostages and destroyed a number of Ugandan fighter aircraft that could have attacked the Israeli planes, but otherwise did no damage to Ugandans or Ugandan territory. The Israeli force refueled its aircraft in Kenya and then returned to Israel.[126]

Israel defended its action as necessary to rescue its nationals. Uganda denied its complicity with the terrorists and labeled Israel's action as aggression. Third-state reaction to this operation was divided. European states and the United States were uniformly supportive of Israel, the United States asserting in the United Nations that states had the right under international law to rescue their nationals under circumstances such as those obtaining in this case. On the other hand, African, Arab, and Communist states condemned Israel's action as aggression. Two resolutions were offered to the Security Council, one condemning hijacking and the other condemning Israel. The first attracted six votes and nine abstentions and therefore failed of adoption, while the second was not put to a vote.[127] The Organization of African Unity unanimously condemned the Israeli raid, though there is reason to doubt that all states voting for the condemnatory resolution in fact objected to Israel's action; Kenya, for example, voted for the resolution, but Kenyan newspapers allied to the government expressed approval of the rescue.[128] No sanctions were imposed on any state by any other state as a result of this operation, although the United States provided Kenya with combat aircraft and dispatched a naval task force as moral support when Kenya expressed fears of a retaliatory attack from Uganda.[129]

This episode was a raid by one state into the territory of another solely to rescue nationals of the raiding state whose lives had been put in danger with the connivance of the second state. Third states disagreed over the propriety of the raid, but some expressed strong support for the rescue, and certainly it could not be said that it was generally condemned.

## Interventions in Zaire (1978)

In May 1978 a force from the Front Nationale de la Libération du Congo (FNLC), the group that had invaded Zaire's Shaba province the previous year, again invaded Shaba. This time the invaders targeted European civilians. As he had done in 1977, President Mobutu of Zaire called for outside aid. The United States, having been stung by Zairean criticism of its weak reaction to the 1977 invasion and claiming to believe in Cuban involvement in this second attack, which was in any case a more serious threat to Mobutu's government,[130] provided logistic support for a second intervention, this time involving Belgian and French troops. The former landed on May 20 and confined their activities to rescuing Europeans in need of aid. The latter had landed on the nineteenth and not only worked to protect their citizens but also undertook operations aimed at aiding the Zairean government and restoring order in Shaba, which was of considerable economic importance to France. The Belgians withdrew on May 22, the French not until May 25. On June 4 the United States began flying Moroccan troops to Zaire to replace the European contingents. Six days later Angola promised to disarm the FNLC, and on May 26 the United States reported an Angolan undertaking to try to prevent new invasions.[131] In addition to Morocco, the states of Senegal, Ivory Coast, Togo, and Gabon agreed to provide forces to protect Zaire after the European troops' departure.[132] Egypt and Sudan also sent contingents.[133]

As indicated, the intervening states were moved by a variety of interests. The United States wished to improve its relations with Zaire and dispel the impression that it was unwilling to react to Communist actions in Africa; this latter goal apparently contributed to an overly hasty assertion of Cuban involvement, since in June 1978 the United States announced that it no longer believed that Cuba had been involved in the invasion.[134] France and Belgium wished to protect both their economic interests in Shaba and their nationals.[135] Egypt and Sudan acted out of concern for Communist activities.[136] Morocco's motives presumably were the same in 1978 as in 1977, that is, suspicion of links between the FNLC and POLISARIO and fear of Communist activity in Africa.

This intervention evoked some negative reactions from third states. Tanzania strongly objected to foreign intervention to protect "corrupt" African regimes. Nigeria also criticized what it called "gunboat diplomacy and neocolonialism." The OAU repeated its support for Zairean territorial integrity but condemned the "invitation of foreign forces to intervene in African conflicts."[137] Still, as mentioned, a number of states cooperated with the intervenors, sending troops themselves.

This episode involved intervention in civil strife by outside powers acting at the request of an incumbent government. It was also an effort by the intervenors to protect their nationals. Third-state reaction was divided, as the intervention involved direct support by France for Mobutu's government. There was, however, no strong, united opposition to the intervention, much less the imposition of sanctions. It is worth noting that the negative reactions to the second Shaba intervention were more restrained and less widespread than such reactions to the similar interventions in Zaire in 1964. Indeed, neither the 1977 nor the 1978 actions were addressed by any UN organ, in contrast to the very strong negative reaction to the 1964 intervention expressed by several states in the Security Council.

## Egypt/Libya (1977)

After the Yom Kippur War of 1973 relations between Libya and Egypt deteriorated over the next several years for a number of reasons. Egyptian President Sadat's dismissive treatment of Colonel Qaddafi immediately before and after the war caused serious harm both to Qaddafi's international standing and to the domestic stability of his government. Libya's stability was further weakened by Egypt's decision to withdraw its troops from Libya in 1974, contributing to a domestic perception of Libya's leaders as isolated and ineffective in their region and possibly helping to explain attempts to stage coups and assassinate Colonel Qaddafi during this period.[138]

Libya responded to this situation by seeking shelter in ideology, stressing its revolutionary purity and Egypt's corruption, as evidenced by Egypt's dealings with the United States and its cease-fire with Israel. Libya also sought to undermine Sadat's legitimacy by undermining his government, alternating subversion with efforts at conciliation to forestall intervention.[139] Libya's subversive activities, including terrorism, led to a massing of troops on the border between the two states in 1976. A year later, in July 1977, a terrorist group assassinated a former Egyptian cabinet minister, and Egypt claimed that it had evidence of a much more widespread plot involving planning for a coup, all supported by Libya.[140]

Relations between the two states were also harmed by Libya's close ties to the Soviet Union. The Soviets maintained a radar installation in Libya capable of monitoring aircraft activity within Egypt's borders and had in general assumed the role of Libya's protector. When it began to appear in the spring of 1977 that Egypt was planning to attack Libya, the Soviet Union made statements warning that the "results" of such an attack would be "difficult to anticipate." Instead of deterring Egypt, however, the Soviet warning incensed Egypt's leadership.[141]

It was against this background that Egypt attacked Libya in late July 1977. Fighting broke out on July 19, artillery exchanges being followed by aerial attacks, with each side accusing the other of invading with ground troops. Egypt destroyed the offending Soviet radar installations. Both sides ceased fire on July 24, after mediation by Kuwait, Algeria, the Arab League as an entity, and the PLO in the person of Yasser Arafat, who apparently was especially effective. The two sides each withdrew forces from the border on September 10, after agreeing to high-level meetings and to an end to their mutual propaganda attacks. Relations apparently began to improve later in the fall of 1977.[142]

Third-state reaction to this event was limited. The Soviet Union denounced Egypt as a warmonger,[143] and of course the Arab states sought to mediate, but there seems to have been little reaction otherwise. In particular, the matter was not discussed in any organ of the United Nations.

This brief conflict involved border fighting only. Neither side admitted attacking the other, so neither proffered a justification other than self-defense. Egypt as the stronger power was apparently the initiator, however, moved partly by anger at Libyan subversion efforts and partly by a desire to assert its primacy in the region. Third states, including the Soviet Union, stayed out of the conflict except to serve as mediators. Apparently, the states of the world were not prepared to react to limited fighting not seen to directly threaten either combatant.

## Egypt/Cyprus (1978)

In February 1978 two Palestinian gunmen murdered the Egyptian president of the Afro-Asian People's Solidarity Conference in the Greek Cypriot portion of Cyprus, then hijacked an airplane in an effort to escape. They were not permitted to land anywhere, however, and were forced to return to Cyprus. In the midst of negotiations between the hijackers and Cypriot officials, Egypt surreptitiously flew seventy-five commandos to Cyprus, without the permission of Cypriot authorities. The commandos sought to raid the hijacked aircraft but were fired upon by the Cypriot national guard and suffered heavy casualties and the loss of their aircraft. On February 19 Cyprus denounced the violation of its sovereignty but later expressed hope that its relations with Egypt would improve. Its subsequent sentence of the Palestinians to life imprisonment was seen as an effort to improve relations with Egypt. Egypt's only justification for its actions was its claim that Cyprus was on the verge of permitting the gunmen to go free.[144]

There was apparently no third-state reaction to this incident.

This action amounted to an effort by Egypt to use force within the territory of another state to arrest particular persons without the consent of the territorial sovereign. Although this would appear to be a serious breach of the sovereign rights of Cyprus, third states were not moved to speak or act against Egypt's behavior, perhaps because Cyprus dealt with the problem with relative ease. In any case, Egypt suffered no sanctions for its behavior.

## PRC/SRV (1979)

By the autumn of 1978 relations between the PRC and the SRV had become very bad. There were a number of reasons for this. Historically, China had sought to dominate a number of areas of Asia, including Vietnam, while Vietnam had sought both to avoid Chinese control and itself dominate the

Indochinese region. Aside from this underlying rivalry, a number of more concrete issues had damaged relations between the two states. The PRC saw Vietnam as ungrateful for the aid it had received from China during the First and Second Indochina Wars, while Vietnam resented what it saw as China's betrayals at the 1954 Geneva Conference and during 1972 as the PRC sought to improve relations with the United States despite the continuing war in Vietnam. The two states differed in their attitude toward the Soviet Union: China was at odds with the Soviet Union, while Vietnam eagerly accepted reconstruction aid and further cultivated Soviet backing in preparation for Vietnam's contemplated attack on Kampuchea. Kampuchea itself was a third area of disagreement between the two, the SRV seeking to dominate that state while the PRC sought to aid it to maintain itself as a check on Vietnam.

Against this background territorial disputes between China and Vietnam exacerbated the situation. The two disagreed concerning the location of the land border between them, concerning the boundary between their respective territorial seas in the Gulf of Tonkin, and concerning sovereignty over the Paracel and Spratley islands. By 1978 these border disputes had led to relatively frequent clashes between troops of the two states at their land border. Finally, Vietnam's harsh treatment of the overseas Chinese resident both in the former South Vietnam and along the Vietnamese-Chinese border strained relations, both because of the PRC's resentment at the imposition of hardships on people to whom it felt a link and because Vietnam forced into China tens of thousands of people for whom China was obliged to provide.[145]

The situation further deteriorated as the autumn of 1978 wore on. During that period China began to consider using force against Vietnam as it learned of that state's decision to overthrow the Khmer Rouge government of Kampuchea, as the scale of border fighting increased, and in particular after Vietnam concluded a friendship treaty with the Soviet Union.[146] For its part, Vietnam appears to have increased the scale of the fighting on the border in an effort to strengthen its case for a treaty with the Soviet Union, which it viewed as a prerequisite for the attack it had decided to make on Kampuchea.[147]

Over the period November 11 to December 11, 1978, the PRC elected not to send troops directly to the aid of Kampuchea after it was invaded by Vietnam in December. Such a move was seen as hegemonic, and thus a violation of the PRC's principles, as well as likely to produce a negative world reaction. Also, the PRC feared an experience like that suffered by the United States in Vietnam. As an alternative, Deng Xiaoping, the dominant figure in both China's Communist party and its government, pushed for an attack on Vietnam at the common border. This attack, Deng argued, was less likely than other options to attract international condemnation as it would be seen as a sanction for Vietnam's attack on Kampuchea. It was also less risky for a variety of reasons. By December 25 China had tentatively decided to attack Vietnam. On that date it warned Vietnam that it would counterattack if the Vietnamese activity along the common border continued.[148]

During a visit to the United States in late January and early February Deng informed President Carter of his intention to attack Vietnam. He publicly stated that China would act against the SRV because of that state's attack on Kampuchea. While Carter pointed out to Deng possible drawbacks of that policy, the United States did not, during the visit, either criticize Deng's plans or actively seek to dissuade him from carrying them out. After Deng's return to China, the final decision to attack was made by February 12, one factor in that decision being the absence of strong American opposition. The PRC was planning to teach Vietnam a lesson.[149]

The PRC attacked Vietnam along their common border on February 17, 1979. As early as February 19 the PRC declared that it had no intention of taking Hanoi and that the war would be limited in time and space. The Chinese troops met heavy resistance, however, and suffered severe casualties, even though Vietnam was holding its first-line troops in reserve for an attack on the Chinese if they reached the plains around Hanoi. The PRC took the town of Lang Son on March 3, then announced on March 5 its intention to withdraw from Vietnam. On March 7 the SRV countered that the withdrawing troops would not be attacked. The withdrawal was complete on March 16. The two sides together lost over 100,000 troops killed and wounded.[150]

After the withdrawal relations between the two states continued to be tense for some time. Through 1987 border fighting—taking the form of artillery shelling and troop incursions—was not uncommon. In particular, the PRC often launched such efforts in response to Vietnamese offensives in Cambodia. The most serious incident involved an attack in 1987 by the PRC in division strength. Thereafter, however, relations between the two states began to improve as the political differences between them lessened and as the SRV's ability to rely on the Soviet Union disappeared. In September 1991 the two states normalized relations.[151]

International reaction to this situation was focused on the 1979 war rather than on the subsequent border fighting. That reaction was surprisingly calm. The United States declared its neutrality and called for the withdrawal of Chinese troops from Vietnam and Vietnamese troops from Kampuchea; it also stressed, however, that Vietnam had attacked first and that normalization of U.S. relations with China would not be affected by the attack, thereafter permitting a scheduled trip to China by the secretary of the treasury to proceed. The Soviet Union made a number of belligerent public statements in support of Vietnam, reinforced its naval forces off the coast of Vietnam, and commenced an airlift of military supplies to Vietnam; however, its diplomats also privately stated that the Soviet Union would not intervene militarily as long as the fighting remained limited.[152] Mongolia, Afghanistan, Angola, Mozambique, Czechoslovakia, Hungary, Bulgaria, Cuba, and Laos all denounced the invasion, while Romania and Yugoslavia called for a cease-fire and withdrawals of Vietnamese troops from Kampuchea and Chinese troops from Vietnam. France and the United Kingdom took positions similar to those of the latter two states, the British indicating that their relations with China were friendly. India recognized the Vietnamese-installed regime in Kampuchea to show its displeasure at the Chinese invasion. Neither the ROK nor the DPRK took sides. Thailand, Singapore, Malaysia, and Indonesia all publicly called for a Chinese withdrawal while privately indicating that they did not object to the Chinese invasion in light of their strong opposition to the Vietnamese invasion of Kampuchea.[153] The Security Council adopted no resolution on the conflict, being blocked by Chinese and Soviet vetoes. Most other Security Council members sought to remain neutral.[154]

The 1979 conflict was a cross-border invasion perhaps best described as a punitive expedition, as indeed China characterized it.[155] In its public statements preceding the attack, China justified its action by reference both to Vietnam's activities along the two states' common border and to Vietnam's invasion of Kampuchea. Its actual motives apparently tracked its justifications closely, although the PRC's assumption of its entitlement to oversee the behavior of its smaller neighbors may also have played a role.

Third-state reaction was at worst neutral, no state imposing sanctions on China and only a few states providing any aid to Vietnam. Even Vietnam's most important ally, the Soviet Union, was unwilling to intervene militarily. Several other states made clear, in various ways, that they saw the PRC's action as a sanction against Vietnam for its invasion of Kampuchea and that it was therefore tolerable. Most significantly, the United States was at pains to indicate no serious disapproval of China's use of force even as it called for the withdrawal of China's troops. In short, several third states seemed to see Vietnam's actions against Kampuchea as rightly laying it open to sanction, and even Vietnam's supporters were unwilling to act strongly against China so long as the fighting was confined to the two states' border regions. Third-state reaction therefore fell somewhere between acquiescence in and positive approval of China's attack. After 1979, when border fighting between the two states became commonplace, there was apparently very little reaction to it by third states.

## PDRY/YAR (1979)

In late February 1979 troops of the PDRY and a dissident North Yemeni group called the National Democratic Front (NDF) invaded the YAR. Relations between the two states had been deteriorating for some years prior to this incident, which presumably accounted for the use of force. The fighting finally ended on March 16, after both sides accepted an Arab League–mediated cease-fire that called on each side to withdraw its troops to its own side of the border. Although PDRY units, which the PDRY insisted were solely NDF troops, had penetrated fairly deeply into the YAR, they did in fact withdraw. On March 30 the combatants once again agreed to unify, though the unification was postponed.[156]

The PDRY's justification for its action was self-defense, it having falsely claimed to have been attacked first. Its motivation in acting was the bad relations between the two states, which were at least partly a reflection of their ideological differences, as pronounced in 1979 as they had been in 1972.[157]

The United States and Saudi Arabia both reacted sharply to the invasion; each provided shipments of weapons to the YAR, and the Saudis put their troops on alert. In addition, the United States sent an aircraft carrier task group to the area. The Republic of China also sent pilots to the YAR, who were to be paid by the Saudis. Apparently, this intense reaction was provoked by the close relations between the PDRY and Cuba and the Soviet Union, both of which had advisors in the PDRY.[158] Aside from these actions and those of the Arab League, third states apparently paid little attention to this conflict.

This was a border war that conceivably could have become more serious. Most third states ignored the conflict, although two provided military aid to the state that had been attacked, and the Arab League managed to convince the parties to settle their dispute peacefully. Aside from the American and Saudi actions, nothing was done by third states that could be considered imposition of sanctions; the more important third-state reaction was the mediation that ended the fighting.

## United States/Iran (1980)

On November 4, 1979, an Iranian mob seized the United States embassy in Teheran and its staff, together with a number of American private citizens present in the embassy.[159] It quickly became clear that the Iranian government was supporting the seizure, and the United States undertook a diplomatic campaign to secure the release of the Americans held hostage. A few weeks after the seizure female and African-American hostages were released, but otherwise the American effort failed.[160]

Given this situation, in April 1980 the United States undertook a raid into Iran to rescue the hostages. The complicated plan for the raid did not call for any offensive action within Iran other than at the embassy but did assume that Iranian guards at the embassy would be targets of attack and did provide for air support from gunships ordered both to prevent Iranian aircraft based in Teheran from taking off and to protect the raiding party from any mobs that might form to interfere with the rescue. Had the plan succeeded, Iranian casualties could have been numerous. However, mechanical failures forced the mission to be aborted on April 24.[161]

The United States had several reasons for undertaking the raid. One important motive was humanitarian, the simple desire to free the hostages. This was the justification President Carter gave following the raid's failure. Also important, however, were domestic and international political considerations. Domestically, Carter's administration faced great pressure to act, it being an election year. Further, there was fear that failure to act would promote an image of American weakness among other states; Egypt, for example, had stressed the necessity of American action.[162]

Third-state reaction to the raid was divided but on the whole was critical. The United Kingdom had acquiesced in the use of its refueling facility on the island of Diego Garcia in connection with the raid. Egypt and Oman had also permitted their territory to be used for refueling of aircraft, though they were not informed of the planes' mission. After the failure of the raid only Canada, the United Kingdom, Egypt, and Israel expressed support. Most Arab states condemned the raid. Japan and Italy criticized the use of force, and other European states privately objected, in particular because the European Community had agreed to impose economic sanctions—albeit weak ones—shortly before the raid in hopes of forestalling American military action. The PRC took no public position. The Soviet Union condemned the raid, arguing that its humanitarian justification was a pretext only. No UN organ addressed the raid.[163] Similarly, no third state imposed sanctions on the United States because of the raid.

This episode was a cross-border incursion to rescue nationals held hostage under the authority of a foreign state. It was justified as a humanitarian operation and was undertaken for humanitarian reasons, but also to maintain national prestige. It was supported by some states but criticized by others, though none suggested that sanctions were appropriate or imposed them.

## Peru/Ecuador (1981)

In the early 1940s Peru and Ecuador engaged in hostilities over the location of their boundary, particularly in the area of the headwaters of the Amazon. In 1942 the two states entered into the Rio Protocol after the mediation of the United States, Argentina, Brazil, and Chile. That agreement established their boundary and was guaranteed by the four mediating states. Subsequent mapping, however, revealed that the Rio Protocol boundary was based on false geographic assumptions, and Ecuador denounced that agreement in 1960. This development apparently did not disturb relations between the two states until January 1981. In that month Ecuador claimed that a Peruvian helicopter had violated its border, while Peru claimed that the helicopter had been fired upon by Ecuador. On January 28 ground fighting broke out over three border posts Ecuador had recently established in what Peru considered its territory. After mediation by the four guarantor powers a cease-fire came into effect on February 2. Further fighting took place on February 20, but on February 26 the guarantors announced an agreement on a mutual troop pullback and more talks, which in turn led to a firm agreement on March 5.[164]

Aside from the actions of the guarantor powers, third states apparently took little interest in this conflict. No UN organ addressed the issue. The OAS Permanent Council did meet on the problem in late January and called for a Meeting of Foreign Ministers, but Peru rejected the action and insisted that only the guarantor states under the Ecuador-rejected Rio Protocol had the authority to act. When the Meeting of Foreign Ministers convened on February 2, only seven states were represented, and six of those were the guarantor powers and the parties to the dispute. The meeting contented itself with congratulating the contending sides on their cease-fire agreement and in essence calling for that agreement to be observed. In addition, the four guarantors stressed their responsibilities as guarantors. The OAS did not further address the problem.[165]

No solution to this dispute has been reached as of this writing. Indeed, tensions rose between the two countries in 1984 after another border clash and again in 1991 as they exchanged charges of border violations. The 1991 episode led to another mutual troop withdrawal after the intercession of Argentina, Bolivia, and Chile, Ecuador having rejected the involvement of the Rio Pact guarantors. By 1992 the two states were discussing arbitration of the dispute.[166]

This episode was a border dispute that degenerated into violence as each side insisted that the other had violated its territory. Third states acted to mediate rather than to identify and sanction a wrongdoer. It is noteworthy that the intervention was not by an international organization but by a group of guarantors to whose authority the relevant regional organization deferred.

## Cameroon/Nigeria (1981)

In May 1981 troops from Cameroon fired on Nigerian troops aboard a boat on a river in the vicinity of the two states' common border. The border was in dispute in the area in which the clash occurred. The combatants disagreed as to whether the site of the incident was in Nigeria or Cameroon. Although the OAU did not put the matter on the agenda of its 1981 Heads of State/Government Meeting, the OAU's secretary-general and the foreign minister of Kenya, whose president was at that time president of the OAU, visited the area in July. Côte d'Ivoire, Niger, and Togo also sought to mediate. On July 20 the president of Nigeria announced that Cameroon had apologized and offered compensation. On January 13, 1982, both presidents expressed regret that the incident had taken place.[167]

This was a border clash in which one state apparently admitted wrongly firing on troops of another. Third states and the OAU sought to mediate, but it appears that the states involved ultimately resolved the matter between themselves.

## Israel/Iraq (1981)

By the fall of 1980 Israel considered itself to be facing a serious situation regarding a nuclear reactor Iraq was constructing with the assistance of other states, most notably France. Iraq had insisted that the reactor would be used for research only and pointed to its adherence to the Nuclear Nonproliferation Treaty and its subjection to inspections by the International Atomic Energy Agency (IAEA) to reinforce its argument that it could not use the reactor to develop a weapon. Israel, however, was concerned by several aspects of Iraq's undertaking. First, Iraq's uranium purchases were more consistent with a weapons' production program than with scientific research. Second, existing control regimes were weak; IAEA inspections were relatively easy to circumvent, and the Nonproliferation Treaty was subject to denunciation. Third, Iraqi official sources had repeatedly stressed Iraq's intention to acquire nuclear weapons for use against Israel.[168]

Israel had made repeated diplomatic approaches to various Western states, seeking to persuade those states to prevent Iraq from proceeding with its plans. These diplomatic efforts were unsuccessful. In particular, Israel had postponed action against Iraq until after the May 1981 election in France in the hope that the Socialist Party would win the election; the Socialists in their campaign had criticized France's policy of providing Iraq with nuclear technology. Once victorious, however, the Socialists indicated that they intended to fulfill existing contracts with Iraq to supply nuclear materials.[169]

One final concern for Israel was the date upon which the reactor would become active. The reactor was being constructed near Baghdad; an attack launched on it after it became active could spread radioactivity throughout the Baghdad area. Israel apparently had reliable information that the reactor would become active no later than September 1981, and possibly earlier.[170]

In these circumstances Israel finally decided to carry out an air attack to destroy the reactor on June 4, 1981. The attack took place three days later and succeeded in its objective. The Israelis attacked no other targets. One French technician was killed in the attack, which was timed so as to minimize casualties.[171] After the attack Israel decided to pay compensation for the death of the French national, though it did not acknowledge a legal obligation to do so.[172]

Third-state reaction to the attack was overwhelmingly negative. The Security Council unanimously adopted a resolution condemning Israel and expressing the opinion that Iraq was entitled to reparation from Israel, though the United States supported the resolution only after it had been stripped of provisions providing for sanctions and only on the ground that Israel had failed to exhaust peaceful alternatives to its raid. A very large number of states strongly criticized Israel, and the General Assembly adopted a resolution labeling the Israeli action as aggression and calling for an arms embargo against Israel by a vote of 109–2–34, Israel and the United States voting against and western and northern European states and some Latin American states abstaining. The United States suspended the sale of four jet aircraft to Israel. The IAEA voted to suspend provision of assistance to Israel and subsequently, in its 1982 general conference, refused to accept the credentials of the Israeli delegation.[173]

Some of the states critical of this action took the position that Israel's attack was simply one more instance of what they characterized as that country's persistent acts of aggression against Arab states. Other states objected to the raid as unnecessary in light of their view that Iraq was not developing a nuclear capability and that existing safeguards against such an eventuality were adequate. Others were concerned that Israel's action undermined the conditions necessary to achieve a peaceful settlement in the Middle East. Israel's argument that it had acted in self-defense in light of the Iraqi nuclear threat received no support.[174] It should be noted, however, that France's subsequent offer to Iraq to help rebuild the reactor was conditioned upon Iraq's acceptance of safeguards upon the use of the reactor stricter than those originally proposed and that the conditions led to an Iraqi rejection of the French offer.[175]

This event was a cross-border air raid by one state against another to eliminate a nuclear reactor that the attacker considered to be a threat to its security. The attacking state did not claim that it had been attacked or was about to be attacked. Nor did it assert that its target had any specific plans to attack it in the future, nor that it had the ability to attack. It did not even assert that its target was about to acquire the ability to attack. Rather, Israel asserted that Iraq was about to acquire the means to create the ability to attack and that the imminence of this development permitted a defensive response, given the established fact of Iraq's great hostility toward Israel. While this chain of argument is somewhat attenuated, Israel also stressed that attacking when it did permitted it to minimize Iraqi casualties. Third states were apparently more concerned by the remoteness of the threat than by Israel's stress on holding down casualties, since almost all states condemned the attack. Nonetheless, aside from the IAEA action, no sanctions were imposed by reason of this attack.

## United States/Libya (1981)

In August 1981 elements of the United States Navy entered the Gulf of Sidra to carry out maneuvers. The gulf was claimed by Libya as part of its territorial waters, but the claim was doubtful under international law and challenged by the United States. The ostensible purpose of the operation was to conduct training and to register dissent to Libya's territorial claim. Additionally, however, the United States hoped for an occasion to use force against Libya in light of that state's support of terrorism. That opportunity presented itself on August 19, 1981, when two Libyan aircraft opened fire on two American aircraft flying over the gulf thirty miles from the Libyan coast. The Libyan pilots missed; the American pilots returned fire and did not miss, shooting down both Libyan planes.[176]

Third-state reaction to this incident was limited. The United States was criticized by Arab states and by the Soviet Union, and condemned for aggression by the Arab League. Otherwise, states did not publicly react negatively to the engagement, although the wisdom of the naval maneuvers was questioned. Both Libya and the United States reported the incident to the Security Council, but neither requested further action and no UN organ acted in the matter. Except for rhetorical criticism, no third state imposed sanctions upon either of the parties to the encounter, although it could be that those disapproving of Libya's action regarded the outcome of the dogfight as sanction enough.[177]

This incident could be seen as a border dispute, with one state claiming as territorial waters an area another state regarded as part of the high seas; the claimant asserted that its use of force was aimed at protecting its territory and therefore defensive, while the challenging state saw the claimant's use of force as unlawful and as triggering its own right of self-defense. Third states sanctioned neither party, which under the circumstances suggests that at least the action of the United States was not seen as unlawful and that possibly Libya's action was likewise not seen as raising legal questions.

The foregoing analysis is misleading, however, in that it omits an important element of the U.S. reason for seeking the confrontation: its conviction that Libya was deeply involved in international terrorism. Although it was widely known that this American belief was part of the reason the United States sought this confrontation, this knowledge did not lead otherwise sympathetic states to reject American self-defense arguments. On the other hand, the United States was not at this time willing to rely on Libya's terrorist connections as basis enough for a use of force against Libya; rather, the United States preferred to provoke a Libyan move to justify any American action.

## Chad/Nigeria (1983)

In April and May 1983 troops of Chad and Nigeria were involved in border clashes over islands in Lake Chad. Nigeria claimed French troops also took part in the fighting on behalf of Chad. The presidents of the two combatants agreed to a cease-fire in July, ending the episode. Apparently, there was no reaction by third states.[178]

This was a violent border dispute in which each side claimed to be defending its territory and in which third states took no interest.

## United States/Egypt (1985)

On October 7, 1985, the Italian cruise ship *Achille Lauro* was hijacked by four Palestinian terrorists off the coast of Egypt. Under the hijackers' orders the vessel sailed to the Syrian coast but was refused entry into that state. It then returned to Egypt, where after negotiations the hijackers surrendered on October 9. Unknown to Egyptian authorities during the negotiations, on October 8 the hijackers had murdered an American citizen traveling as a passenger aboard the ship. Even after this information became public on the ninth, however, Egypt persisted with its plan to permit the hijackers to leave Egypt, to be tried by the PLO. This agreement violated Egypt's obligations under the 1979 Convention on the Taking of Hostages, under which Egypt was obliged either to try the hijackers or extradite them to a state falling within one of the categories specified in the convention. On October 10 the hijackers and a senior PLO official left Egypt aboard an Egyptian plane. They intended to travel to Tunis but were denied landing permission by both Tunisia and Greece and attempted to return to Egypt. Before they could do so, however, American naval aircraft intercepted the Egyptian plane over the Mediterranean and forced it to land at a NATO base in Italian territory, where the hijackers were taken into custody.[179]

The United States apparently acted both in response to domestic anger at the murder of an American citizen and in line with its strong opposition to terrorism.[180] It offered no real legal justification for its action, essentially asserting that the fact that terrorists were aboard the Egyptian aircraft was basis enough for intercepting it.[181] Third-state reaction was generally positive or muted. Egypt, Iran, and Iraq all condemned the American action, but Sudan and Kuwait were restrained in their reactions and other Arab states declined to comment. Western governments were generally positive in their comments, the United Kingdom, Italy, Canada, and Australia all either praising the interception or labeling it not unlawful. Even Communist states were restrained in their reactions, the Soviet Union condemning terrorism in very harsh terms and criticizing the United States only for its granting of asylum in

1970 to two Lithuanian hijackers. Further, a number of states distanced themselves from the PLO in the immediate aftermath of the interception, despite its agents having been the actual victims in that episode, assuming there were any. And no state sought to raise the matter in any UN organ.[182]

This incident involved forcible interference by one state with an aircraft of another over international waters. It was carried out because the aircraft was seeking to carry to safety four terrorists guilty of the murder of a citizen of the intercepting state. Third states generally did not criticize the interception, and some praised it; further, in various ways they expressed disapproval of the organization of which the terrorists in question were members. A consistent theme in their reactions was the absolute unacceptability of terrorism. No effort was made to impose sanctions on the intercepting state. Apparently, third states were unprepared to label as illegal a bloodless interception of an aircraft undertaken in order to apprehend terrorists.

## Israel/Libya (1986)

On February 4, 1986, Israeli jets intercepted a Libyan aircraft over the Mediterranean, forcing it to land in Israel. Israel acted in the belief that the Libyan plane was carrying certain Palestinian guerillas. It developed that the Israelis were mistaken in their belief; no Palestinians were aboard. Once the Israelis discovered this to be the case, the Libyan aircraft was allowed to proceed to Syria, its original destination.[183]

Third-state reaction to this episode was mixed. A number of Arab, Communist, and Third World states expressed outrage when the matter was brought before the Security Council on February 4. However, a resolution that would have condemned the interception was vetoed by the United States; Australia, Denmark, France, and the United Kingdom abstained in the vote on the resolution. The United States explained its veto by complaining that the resolution assumed that all interceptions of civilian aircraft were unlawful, whereas the United States believed that such interceptions were justifiable if the intercepting state had strong evidence that terrorists were aboard the intercepted aircraft. The United Kingdom and France likewise faulted the draft for its failure to address the problem of terrorism as part of the context in which Israel had acted.[184]

This episode amounted to a state's forcible exercise of jurisdiction over a foreign-registered aircraft over the high seas. It was justified as being an effort to arrest terrorists. While many third states objected strongly, none imposed sanctions. Moreover, one significant state accepted the justification in principle, and two others clearly gave it weight.

## United States/Libya (1986)

After the aerial encounter between Libya and the United States in 1981 relations between the two states did not improve. Rather, relations declined as the United States became convinced of Libya's deep involvement with terrorist groups and particular terrorist incidents, and as Libya adopted policies toward its neighbors of subversion and intervention. Thus, over this period Libya apparently made plans several times to murder American officials, including President Reagan; continually intervened in Chad; sought to subvert the Sudan; carried out terrorist acts in the United Kingdom; attempted to infiltrate terrorists accredited as reporters to the Los Angeles Olympics; planted mines in the Red Sea; made plans to seize the Grand Mosque in Mecca during the Hajj; and became the primary patron of the Abu Nidal terrorist group, which carried out attacks against civilian targets in Western Europe, most notably at the Rome and Vienna airports in December 1985. Throughout the period, moreover, Libya stressed its emnity toward the United States and its belief in the desirability of harming Americans and American interests.[185]

During this period the United States had some success in influencing Libya's behavior through the use of force. Thus, as noted in Chapter 6, American maneuvers in Egypt in November 1981 contributed to the Libyan decision in that year to pull back its troops in Chad. Similarly, part of the reason for the 1983 French intervention in Chad was American urging; this intervention, in turn, contributed to the limited success of GUNT/Libyan operations against the Habré government. But while such actions affected Libya's tactics at particular times and places, as the decade wore on the United States did not perceive any change in Libya's readiness to resort unhesitatingly to violence in circumstances the United States regarded as illegitimate.

It was against this background that the United States determined to make yet another foray into the Gulf of Sidra in March 1986. A large naval force was ordered into the gulf, ostensibly to carry out routine maneuvers and to assert the American claim that the gulf was part of the high seas, not Libyan territory. This latter goal was particularly significant in light of Libya's proclamation of a "line of death" in the gulf, drawn at a considerable distance from the Libyan coast. In fact, American officials hoped to provoke a Libyan reaction that would in turn justify an American use of force.

American aircraft began operating on the Libyan side of the line of death on the night of March 22. On the afternoon of March 24 three ships also crossed the line. Libya responded on March 24 by firing surface-to-air missiles at American aircraft operating across the line. That night, when radars controlling Libyan missiles were activated—indicating an intention to fire again at American aircraft—American planes responded by firing missiles at the radar installations. Prior to activating its radar, Libya had dispatched a missile-armed patrol boat into the gulf in the direction of the American fleet. The United States responded by destroying the patrol boat in an air attack. Over the next several hours American aircraft attacked other similar Libyan vessels venturing into the gulf, some being sunk or damaged. There were no encounters between the two sides after noon on March 25, and the American ships withdrew across the line of death on March 27.[186]

Third states reacted in various ways. The United Kingdom and Israel strongly supported the United States. The Netherlands was sharply critical of Libya. France, the FRG, and Spain acknowledged the American argument that its forces had acted only in self-defense but also called for restraint. Canada called for a peaceful resolution of the dispute, and Greece deplored the violence. The Arab League condemned the American action but refused to impose either diplomatic or economic sanctions. The Soviet Union, which had been warned by the United States of its intention to cross the line of death, had given little support to Libya during the confrontation and had reportedly regarded Libya's actions as a "quixotic venture"; it condemned the American action after the event, however.[187] The Security Council debated the episode for several sessions. Most of the speakers represented Communist states or their allies, and the tenor of the debate was harshly critical of what were described as American provocations against Libya. Malta, the United Kingdom, and France, however, rejected Libya's territorial claims, and the Security Council did not act on a Soviet/Bulgarian resolution condemning the United States.[188]

Libya responded to this event by planning various terrorist actions. In particular, Libyan agents, possibly in collaboration with Syria, planted a bomb in a nightclub in Berlin frequented by American military personnel on April 4, 1986. Three persons, including 2 Americans, were killed and 229, including 79 Americans, were injured. The United States was at pains to gather evidence demonstrating the Libyan connection to the bombing; the United Kingdom, the FRG, and Italy all subsequently acknowledged the strength of the American demonstration of Libyan complicity. The United States also learned of Libyan plans for further Libyan attacks on American diplomats and private individuals. However, when the United States sought to convince its European allies to impose strong nonmilitary sanctions on Libya in light of its connection to terrorism, they refused. Apparently, the Europeans feared that their nationals in Libya could become hostages if they acted, were reluctant to give up the economic benefits of trade with Libya, expressed doubt about the effectiveness of sanctions, and—in the case of the United Kingdom and the FRG—wished to avoid setting a precedent for sanctions against South Africa.[189]

It was against this background that the United States decided to launch an air strike against Libya. In part the motive was reprisal for the Berlin bombing. The United States also felt, however, that an attack might deter the ongoing plots it had detected and thus would constitute anticipatory self-defense as well as reprisal. Further, it was felt that an attack would increase the costs to terrorists and possibly deter not only Libya but other states supporting terrorism. American credibility was also seen to be at stake; indeed, it was feared that inaction would be perceived by Libya as acquiescence.[190]

American allies, however, offered little support for the plan. To be sure, the United Kingdom agreed that aircraft based in its territory could be used in the raid. Considerations of alliance solidarity, gratitude for American support during the Falklands War, and the United Kingdom's own troubles at Libya's hands all played a role in this decision but so did the American argument that the raid was intended as a defensive measure as well as retaliation. But no other Western state offered any aid. France and Spain denied overflight rights; Italy, Greece, and Spain refused to permit aircraft based in their territories to be used in the attack, and the FRG refused sanctions. A meeting of European Community foreign ministers called to head off American action did not consider economic sanctions; rejected the idea of closing Libyan diplomatic posts; agreed to name Libya as a terrorist state only over the objections of France, the FRG, and Italy; and could agree only on restrictions on Libyan diplomats.[191]

The raid took place on April 15, 1986. All the targets were military, including military airfields and training facilities for terrorists and the Libyan military. Apparently, considerable damage was done. Libya subsequently claimed that thirty-seven civilians were killed in the raid; Libyan military casualties were uncertain. The United States lost one plane and its crew.[192]

Third-state reaction to the raid was mixed. Great Britain, Israel, Canada, and Australia supported the raid, as did Chad and several small Caribbean states. The Soviet Union was highly critical, however, and canceled a planning meeting for the scheduled Reagan-Gorbachev summit; that summit itself, however, was held in October. Further, the Soviet Union took steps indicating displeasure with the Libyan government. The PRC reacted mildly. Most Latin American governments were either silent or temperate in their criticisms, censuring terrorism as well. Several non-Arab Muslim states reacted negatively, but Indonesia rebuffed pressure to cancel a visit from President Reagan planned for May. Most Arab states were sharply critical but took no action against the United States, except for Sudan's recalling its ambassador. In particular, Libya failed in its efforts to convene an Arab summit to condemn the United States shortly after the attack, with only Syria and South Yemen agreeing with Libya that the agenda should be limited to dealing with the attack. Moreover, Tunisia did not comment on the attack, and Egypt, Iraq, and Jordan were lukewarm in their criticisms. There is, indeed, some evidence that some Arab governments were pleased that the United States had acted, and in fact Libya felt that it received little support from other Arab states. The OAU and the Nonaligned Movement both adopted resolutions condemning the attack, but OPEC refused to consider an oil embargo against the United States. Western European states criticized but did not condemn the attack, and coupled their criticisms with condemnations of terrorism; apparently, their criticisms were based in part on their belief that the raid heightened the risk that they would face Libyan reprisals.[193]

The Security Council's debate on the matter was overwhelmingly critical of the United States, most of the speakers being Communist, nonaligned, or Arab states. A resolution condemning the U.S. action and also condemning terrorism was defeated by a vote of 9–5 (United States, United Kingdom, France, Australia, Denmark) –1 (Venezuela). France and the United Kingdom both stressed Libyan responsibility for terrorist acts and the imbalance of a resolution that failed to mention Libya. Australia took the same position. Denmark and Venezuela also criticized the imbalance of the resolution, though both expressed objection to the American use of force. The General Assembly later adopted a resolution condemning the American raid by a vote of 79–28–33, with 18 absent; that is, as many states did not vote for the resolution as did. The abstentions included Egypt, Greece, and Turkey—all of whom had criticized the raid—and Mexico. The absentees included Bahrain, Oman, and Tunisia.[194]

Clearly, these two incidents are distinguishable. The first was essentially a repeat of the 1981 United States versus Libya confrontation. Though a number of states were concerned about the use of force, a considerable number acknowledged American rights of self-defense under the circumstances. This was true despite widespread knowledge of the mixed American motives for the naval maneuvers. The second American use of force, however, attracted little support. Apparently, it was seen as an armed reprisal and therefore objectionable. In particular, few states seemed willing to endorse unreservedly the American self-defense argument. However, Libya likewise attracted relatively little support and most of that was rhetorical. States normally considered allies by Libya refused to take concrete actions to sanction the United States. Even the General Assembly vote against the United States was, under the circumstances, quite close.

These observations suggest that American actions in the first case were seen as defensible. More specifically, the fact that the United States was known to have sought a confrontation and to have engaged in activity likely to provoke Libya was seen by a number of states as not vitiating the American right to self-defense, particularly when the "provocative" action consisted of refusing to honor a territorial claim most states regarded as indefensible. The ambivalent reaction to the second American use of force seems to reflect a strong reaction against armed reprisals, coupled with a perhaps uneasy understanding of the difficulties Libya created for other states. The American self-defense argument, apparently, was either seen as specious or else rejected due to the indirectness of the connection between the targets of the American raid and the particular attacks it wished to forestall. But neither were states truly outraged by Libya's situation, and in any event the criticism of the United States did not extend to the imposition of sanctions. It would appear, in short, that states were simultaneously unwilling to endorse the American response to Libya's behavior and unwilling to manifest their disapproval of the actions of the United States except rhetorically.

## Analysis

The almost three dozen conflicts discussed in this chapter fall into a number of different categories. To simplify analysis each category will be discussed separately, with a short summary to follow.

### *Border Fighting*

Fifteen of the conflicts discussed in this chapter arose out of disagreements between neighboring states concerning the location of the border between them. These differed from cases such as the early disputes between Somalia and its neighbors, where Somalia was challenging the legitimacy of borders whose location was not in dispute. Rather, in these conflicts the states' disagreement turned on the proper location of the border.

In none of these cases did third states impose sanctions, although India received considerable support after the PRC's attack in 1962, apparently reflecting the assumption that the PRC was engaging in unprovoked aggression against a peaceful India. Even in that case, however, the Soviet Union expressed support for the PRC. Also, in the Cambodia-Thai and Honduras-Nicaragua disputes third states pressured the parties to abide by the ICJ's judgments. Generally, however, third states reacted to these conflicts by seeking to halt the fighting and mediate between the combatants, to the extent that they took any interest. In several cases they did not react at all.

These reactions suggest that third states do not see a use of force triggered by a border dispute as unlawful. They also indicate, however, that third states often do not simply ignore these problems but see the proper response as helping the parties resolve the underlying problem rather than identifying and sanctioning a wrongdoer.

### *Localized Wars*

El Salvador's 1969 attack on Honduras was relatively localized but did not reflect a territorial dispute; rather, it was motivated by mutual bad feelings. Similarly, the fighting between the two Yemens in 1972 and 1979 and Egypt's 1977 attack on Libya were all limited in space and motivated by bad blood between the combatants. Third states stopped the fighting between El Salvador and Honduras by threatening El Salvador, the attacker, with sanctions. In the other three cases the combatants were at least temporarily reconciled through Arab League mediation, with no third state imposing sanctions.

As with border disputes, third states reacted to these localized wars by seeking to encourage the parties to solve their problems peacefully. Except in the El Salvador–Honduras case, that was all third states did. The OAS states, however, were prepared to see the use of force by El Salvador as separable from the underlying dispute, such that they were willing to invoke sanctions to deal with that aspect of the problem alone.

### *Rescue of Nationals*

On a number of occasions during the period covered by this work, states used force to rescue certain of their nationals facing physical danger in another state. Belgium did so in 1964 and in 1978 in Zaire, with American assistance and joined by France in the latter case; Israel did the same in Uganda in 1976; the United States did likewise in Cambodia in 1975, attempted the same thing in Iran in 1980, and, as noted in Chapter 6, carried out such an operation in Liberia in 1990. The ECOWAS intervention in Liberia was likewise in part justified by the desire to protect nationals of the intervening states. Also, the American actions in the Dominican Republic in 1965 and Grenada in 1983 were justified on similar grounds, with limited plausibility.

While each of these operations was criticized, the criticism tended to reflect doubt that the intervening states' aims were as limited as they claimed rather than rejection of the right to rescue nationals. Further, each operation received significant third-state diplomatic support, and sanctions were imposed in none.

## *Retaliation*

Several of the uses of force described in this chapter can best be understood as retaliation for actions by the target state perceived as unacceptable by the retaliating state. This is true of the United Kingdom's attacks on Yemen in 1949 and 1957, as well as the raid it carried out during the course of the South Yemen War in 1964. The American attack on Libya in 1986 was also a response to an act seen as illegitimate, as, arguably, were the earlier American operations in the Gulf of Sidra in 1981 and 1986.

Further, a number of conflicts described in earlier chapters seem to have retaliatory aspects. Thus, Israel attacked guerilla bases in neighboring Arab states very frequently beginning in the early 1950s, extending its operation to Tunisia in 1985. It also attacked the Beirut airport in 1968 in response to what it perceived as Lebanon's failure to control guerillas operating from its territory.

These actions have frequently been analyzed as reprisals, but, except for the United Kingdom's actions against Yemen, this seems misleading. The actors in the other cases claimed to be acting in self-defense, not in reprisal. More specifically, each attacking state asserted that it had reason to believe that it was to be the target of future actions by the groups against whom retaliatory action had been taken and that the purpose of the attack was to deter these future attacks. Its purpose was not, that is to say, mere punishment but rather was oriented toward preventing expected future behavior by the target of the attacks. Indeed, it seems likely that even the United Kingdom's actions against Yemen were taken with an eye toward influencing Yemen's future behavior.

Third-state reaction to these attacks has varied. Israel's actions have drawn much criticism but no significant sanctions. The same is true of the United Kingdom's attacks on Yemen. And the actions of the United States, particularly those against Libya in 1986, received a fair degree of international support and much less criticism than could reasonably have been expected.

It must be stressed that in all these cases the groups/states subjected to retaliation were believed (1) to have a regular policy of carrying out or supporting uses of force against the retaliating state, (2) to have perpetrated or aided in the perpetration of uses of force prior to the one that triggered the retaliatory response in question, and (3) to intend to carry out similar uses of force in the future. The retaliating states, therefore, could reasonably consider themselves as the targets of a campaign of violence initiated or supported by the states against which retaliatory action was taken.

In such circumstances arguments that retaliatory acts should be seen as a type of self-defense take on some plausibility. It is not absurd to label as defensive efforts to convince a group or state planning future uses of force to cancel its plans. One form such efforts might take is responding forcibly to a given use of force to convey the message that future uses of force will draw a similar response; the objective, presumably, is to deter the future attacks and thus eliminate the occasion for future forcible responses. In such circumstances forcible responses intended to convey a deterrent message certainly have a defensive element.

Perhaps because of sympathy for an argument similar to the foregoing, states generally have not imposed sanctions by reason of retaliatory acts. Of course, in 1964 Israel, the United States, and the United Kingdom received considerable criticism for their actions, but the criticism did not extend to a determination to impose sanctions. Rather, third states seem frequently to acquiesce in such behavior. Further, the United Kingdom at least was sufficiently impressed by this concept of retaliatory self-defense to permit the United States to use British-based aircraft in the 1986 attack on Libya for such a purpose.

At the same time it is important to contrast third-state reactions to these uses of force with reactions to similar activities that evoked rather different responses. For example, South Africa compared its attacks on supposed ANC bases on its neighbors' territory with the second American attack on Libya in 1986; the United States indignantly rejected the comparison and imposed minor diplomatic sanctions. More generally, third states worked assiduously to end South Africa's activities in this regard, albeit not imposing sanctions for this purpose. Further, most other states contending against national liberation movements based in neighboring states were circumspect about attacking such bases, encountering a weakening of their international positions when they did so, for example, Portugal after its attack on Guinea, France after its assault on the FLN's base in Tunisia.

It would appear, then, that approval of retaliatory uses of force depends very much on the general character of the use of force that triggered the retaliation. That is, if the pattern of violence that retaliation is intended to interrupt is generally perceived as legitimate, then retaliation is likely to cause difficulty for the retaliating state. It is only when third states perceive as legitimate the interests the retaliating state seeks to insulate from violence that retaliation will encounter a degree of acceptance. The end, that is, can taint the means.

## *War as a Sanction*

China justified its 1979 attack on Vietnam in part as a sanction for Vietnam's invasion of Kampuchea. Several states expressed approval of China's action at the time, the United States—though forewarned—failed to protest, and the Soviet Union reacted lukewarmly. While relations between China and Vietnam were not good generally and were complicated by conflicting border claims, it appears that China's ability to characterize its action as a reaction to Vietnam's harshly criticized invasion served to mute criticism of China's own action.

This type of use of force is distinguishable from a retaliatory use of force, since in this case the PRC purported to be inflicting a sanction for a wrong done to a third state rather than for one done to itself. Nonetheless, the two types of uses of force are related, since each purports to be a response to an illegitimate act. Presumably, third states' reluctance to impose sanctions in the two types of cases reflects this similarity, third states apparently being unwilling to dismiss as illegitimate unilateral forcible responses to uses of force themselves generally deemed unacceptable.

## *Use of Force to Extend State Jurisdiction*

States used force to, in effect, extend their criminal jurisdiction on four occasions during the period covered by this study. Israel forced down an Iraqi plane believed to be carrying Palestinian guerillas in 1973 and did the same thing to a Libyan aircraft in 1986. The United States took a similar action toward an Egyptian aircraft in 1985. And in 1978 Egypt dispatched commandos to Cyprus to seize the murderers of a highly placed Egyptian. Israel's 1973 action triggered a Security Council condemnation, but none of the other three actions produced generally negative responses. Third states took little interest in the Cyprus episode, while the other two took place during a period of increasing concern over terrorism and, apparently, of correspondingly increased willingness by some states to accept extraordinary measures if directed against terrorism.

It is instructive to compare international responses to Israel's actions in 1973 with reactions to American actions in 1985 and Israel's actions in 1986. To be sure, Israel incurred no serious sanctions in 1973, but it suffered a degree of inconvenience, received considerable rhetorical criticism, and was defended by no other state. Its 1986 action, however, was vigorously defended by the United States, and other states were willing to acknowledge that Israel's concerns were entitled to consideration.

This change in reaction presumably reflects changes in perception between 1973 and 1986. In that period terrorism was thought to have become more common and tolerance for its use declined greatly. This change in state attitudes toward terrorism apparently led to changes in attitudes toward responses to terrorism. Once most states came to agree more or less on terrorism's unacceptability, they were less willing to dismiss out of hand forcible responses to unacceptable acts. That is, as with retaliatory uses of force and war as a sanction, states' uses of force to obtain jurisdiction over persons seen as a type of international outlaw was treated as a tolerable response to acts whose illegitimacy was generally acknowledged.

## *Collection of Evidence*

The United Kingdom's sweeping of mines within Albania's territorial waters is the only instance since World War II of a state's using force within another state's territory to gather evidence for a judicial proceeding. There was no third-state reaction, and the ICJ, though labeling the minesweeping as unlawful, admitted the evidence.

## *Summary*

None of the uses of force described in this chapter raised any serious threat to the international status quo. The pattern of state reactions to uses of force described in earlier chapters of this work would suggest that third states would be unlikely to impose serious sanctions on nonstatus quo threatening uses of force, and that is in fact what happened with almost all the conflicts this chapter addresses.

Two other points should also be made, however. First, in many cases in which third states did not seek to sanction a use of force, they nonetheless responded to it as a matter of international concern. This concern took the form of seeking to mediate between the combatants rather than of attempting to identify and act against a wrongdoer.

Second, a number of the uses of force discussed in this chapter were cases in which the states using force targeted a state that had not only used force illegitimately in the past but was likely to do so in the future. In most such episodes, attacks on such a target evoked a degree of acquiescence and even approval. The use of force to break a pattern of illegality by the target state, that is, appears to have a degree of affirmative acceptance in the international community.

# CHAPTER 10

# Self-Defense

The last category of use of force to be examined in this work is self-defense. Since all the conflicts in which self-defense was important have been discussed in other chapters, this chapter will confine itself to analysis. Perhaps surprisingly, self-defense presents certain analytic problems.

States have frequently asserted self-defense as a justification for the use of force, often in circumstances in which the claim was palpably false. The fact that states see self-defense as a plausible excuse for the use of force certainly suggests that actual defensive uses of force should be seen as lawful. This conclusion is reinforced by the fact that, since World War II, third states have often acquiesced in uses of force that clearly had defensive elements. Difficulties are presented, however, for two reasons. First, in some of the cases in which third states acquiesced in defensive uses of force, factors unrelated to the defensive character of the force apparently contributed to these third-state reactions. Second, on a number of occasions different third states reacted very differently to what appeared to be defensive uses of force; that is, the defensive character of the use of force was not adequate to overcome some states' objections to it.

Consider first cases in which extraneous factors apparently contributed to third-state reactions. The United States labeled as defensive its responses to Libya's forcible reactions to the American forays into the Gulf of Sidra in 1981 and 1986, and a number of states accepted that characterization. However, since the United States provoked both incidents, it may be wondered whether Libya's bad reputation had something to do with third-state reaction. Similarly, Tanzania justified its invasion of Uganda as a reaction to Uganda's earlier invasion of Tanzania. Tanzania received much third-state support, and the government it installed in Uganda after it ousted the Amin regime was immediately recognized, so it appears that the invasion was not perceived as unlawful by third states. At the same time, it is unclear how much the brutal character of the Amin regime contributed to this reaction, given Tanzania's arguably disproportionate response to the threat it faced.

Conversely, in several cases in which self-defense could plausibly have been invoked, the international reaction was mixed. The PRC's attack on India in 1962 could reasonably have been characterized as defensive, given India's forceful encroachments on disputed territory, its apparently attack-oriented troop dispositions, and its belligerent statements. Nonetheless, the PRC's attack produced significant aid for India and much criticism of the PRC, though no sanctions were imposed on that state. This result may well reflect the obscurity of the facts of this matter at the time, as well as third states' predispositions to accept India's version of events and reject the PRC's, particularly in light of the latter's false claim of being the victim of an actual attack. The scope of China's attack, which exceeded that required by purely defensive objectives, may also have contributed to this reaction.

Similarly, the mixed reaction to Israel's behavior at the start of the Six-Day War is hard to reconcile with the lawfulness of defensive force. Clearly, Israel had excellent reason to fear an attack at the time it commenced hostilities; further, its behavior may fairly be characterized as limited to that necessary to protect itself. Nonetheless, it was criticized widely. While Israel also received much support and was not sanctioned, so that it cannot be said to have been treated as a lawbreaker, neither was it generally treated as justified in its action, nor were its adversaries treated as lawbreakers. This latter circumstance may well reflect states' general reluctance to apply strict standards to continuation wars, but the lack of sympathy for Israel is more puzzling. It may simply reflect general hostility to that state.

In both of the foregoing cases the state with a plausible self-defense claim initiated the subsequent conflict. Even in some striking cases in which the state using force defensively did not begin hostilities, third-state reaction has been lukewarm. Many states had considerable misgivings about the United Kingdom's use of force to expel Argentina from the Falkland Islands. As noted in detail in Chapter 2 third states reacted with indifference to Iran's plight after that state was attacked by Iraq. Indeed, though the effort to expel Iraq from Kuwait received a very high degree of international support, some states opposed even that defensive use of force.

Of course, some uses of force with defensive elements also had aspects that could reasonably have counseled third states to caution. India characterized its 1971 war with Pakistan as having been started by Pakistan, but since India planned to launch the war in any case, the minor Pakistani air strikes against India that began the conflict seem like a detail. India argued with more plausibility that it was justified in attacking Pakistan because of the considerable burden on India created by Bengali refugees from the Pakistan Army and the necessity of installing in Dhaka a government that would induce the refugees to return home. This argument did not evoke widespread support. To be sure, no sanctions were imposed on India for its invasion, unless the mere presence of the American task group in the Bay of Bengal should be considered a sanction. Also, the new state of Bangladesh was quickly recognized by many states, suggesting acquiescence in the process whereby that state came into being. Nonetheless, there were misgivings about India's actions. It may be speculated that at least two reasons account for this. First, India had not been a victim of any serious armed attack, nor did it claim that Pakistan was contemplating one. Its use of force was directed against a threat that, though very significant, was not itself a use of force. Second, given the long-standing hostility between India and Pakistan, there may well have been some feeling that India's motives for its action included a desire to cripple its rival.

Again, Israel characterized its 1981 destruction of Iraq's nuclear reactor as defensive but was nonetheless harshly criticized for its action, the criticism including a Security Council condemnation. To be sure, the Security Council did not impose sanctions on Israel, and no individual state did, either, except for the U.S. cosmetic delay in delivering certain aircraft. Indeed, the most significant negative state reaction connected with this incident was France's decision to toughen the terms of its nuclear dealings with Iraq. Still, Israel's action can hardly be said to have received general approval. In this case, it may be that the remoteness of the threat against which Israel was acting influenced third-state reactions.

Finally, neither the ROV's resistance to the DRV nor the SRV's attack on Kampuchea were generally treated as justified acts of self-defense, although both the ROV and the SRV clearly had been subjected to uses of force by the DRV and Kampuchea, respectively. The unwillingess of many third states to support the ROV presumably reflects the fact that the Second Indochina War raised confusing issues of colonialism, the propriety of interventions in civil strife, and the breach of the 1954 Geneva Accords. As for Vietnam's invasion of Kampuchea, the attacker's objectives were accurately seen as going far beyond self-defense, and this perception doubtless explains third-state reactions to Vietnam's behavior.

Self-defense is thus a curious category of the use of force. Statements by governments all assume that defensive uses of force are lawful, but states often disagree concerning the proper application of the concept of self-defense in concrete cases. The facts seem to support a few generalizations. It seems clear that uses of force seen as motivated by nondefensive objectives will not be treated as defensive, even if the state using force can accurately describe itself as the victim of uses of force at the hands of its adversary. Also, states seem reluctant to legitimize as defensive uses of force aimed against something other than an imminent military threat. And if a particular use of force is an episode in a general pattern of hostilities, third states seem disinclined to separate that use of force from its context, even if it is arguably defensive when taken in isolation.

Having said all this, however, it remains true that international support for clearly defensive uses of force has been rather weaker than might reasonably have been expected. Self-defense is too frequently invoked by states to be dismissed as a basis for the use of force, but the practice of states indicates that even clearly defensive uses of force are unlikely to receive universal support from third states.

# CHAPTER 11

# CONCLUSIONS

The preceding chapters catalog the cases in which states used force internationally in the period between 1945 and 1991. This chapter seeks to do three things. First, it will characterize generally the state practice described in the earlier chapters. Second, it will analyze other writers' formulations of the rules of international law regarding the use of force in light of the state practice described in this book. Finally, it will offer some thoughts about the development of this area of international law.

## State Practice Regarding the Use of Force

The preceding chapters make possible a number of generalizations about state practice regarding the use of force. Most obviously, states used force so frequently in the period 1945 through 1991 (over 110 times) that it seems impossible to say that, in practice, states do not use force against one another.

Beyond this point, it appears that one can divide uses of force into three broad categories: those that are likely to receive affirmative approval from third states; those that are either very uncommon, are likely to encounter significant third-state sanctions, or both; and those that are likely to evoke either the acquiescence of third states or else a divided reaction, with some third states providing support even as others take actions that could be considered as sanctions.

## *Approved Uses of Force*

Uses of force most likely to receive affirmative approval are those aimed at dislodging a European power from a colonial territory and those involving multilateral intervention in civil strife. The former proposition is demonstrated by the state practice recounted in Chapter 3, while international reaction to the UN operations in the Congo and to ECOWAS operations in Liberia, as described in Chapter 6, and to the OAS's multilateralization of the U.S. intervention in the Dominican Republic discussed in Chapter 7 support the second. As Chapter 10 shows, it seems impossible to question the lawfulness of the use of force in self-defense, given the degree of support that concept has in state rhetoric; as that chapter also shows, however, state practice demonstrates considerable uncertainty over the application of this concept. Finally, Chapter 9 suggests that at least some actions directed against terrorism, including attacks on bases and efforts to extend state jurisdiction in order to effect arrests, are likely to command a rather broad range of support.

## *Uncommon/Disapproved Uses of Force*

The use of force most likely to evoke third-state sanctions is the classic invasion as described in Chapter 2. Even this type of use of force received a degree of acquiescence when carried out in opposition to European colonialism, but outside that context it can be said that such invasions are unusual and are almost always severely sanctioned when they take place. The only exception to this proposition is Iraq's invasion of Iran, and, as suggested in Chapter 2, the international nonreaction to that event is likely explained by the great anxiety Iran was creating at the time. Also as noted in Chapter 2, this pattern of behavior means that a rule of international law forbidding classic invasions would satisfy the obey-or-be-sanctioned standard explained in Chapter 1; states generally obey this rule, outside the self-determination context, and are sanctioned when they do not.

It should also be noted that there are very few examples of states that are experiencing insurgencies attacking the structures of states that provide bases for the insurgents; the former may attack insurgent bases in the latter but seldom use force against the latter state's military or its civilian population except as a by-product of attacks on the insurgents. There have been only five cases contradicting a rule forbidding such attacks: France's attack on Egypt at Suez, Portugal's cooperation in the attack on Guinea, South Africa's attacks on Angola because of Angola's support for SWAPO, the American mining operations against Nicaragua because of the latter's support for the Salvadoran rebels, and the establishment and support of RENAMO by Rhodesia and South Africa. France was forced by third-state pressure to abandon the Suez operation, Portugal did not repeat its unsuccessful effort against Guinea, domestic and international pressure led the United States to desist from itself directly attacking Nicaragua (as opposed to intervening in its civil war), and international pressure—if not sanctions—led South Africa to cease supporting RENAMO. Only South Africa's efforts against Angola seemed to acquire a measure of acquiescence. In other words, few states have engaged in this behavior, and most of those few either stopped fairly quickly or were persuaded by other states to stop eventually.

These observations support an argument that a rule forbidding attacks on the state structures of states assisting insurgencies in other states would also satisfy the obey-or-be-sanctioned standard. While there are few examples of sanctions for violations of the rule, there are also few examples of violations. This conclusion may be accepted tentatively, but one qualification is in order. As Chapter 6 shows, there appears to be no practice of refraining from intervention in civil strife in other states. If a state was supporting civil strife in a second state, and that state was, in turn, to intervene in civil strife in the first state, it is not clear that state practice would support the conclusion that the second state's intervention in the first state was more questionable than the first state's original intervention in the second.

## *Common Uses of Force Not Triggering Sanctions*

Finally, there remains the category of uses of force that, though not affirmatively approved, do not evoke general sanctions from third states. These would include postcolonial wars, wars continuing unresolved national liberation or postcolonial wars, outside intervention in civil strife, maintenance of preeminence by dominant states within a region, neocolonial wars, and all the limited uses of force described in Chapter 9. It should be made explicit that, since these types of use of force are common and rarely evoke sanctions from third states, a rule characterizing them as illegal does not satisfy the obey-or-be-sanctioned standard of Chapter 1.

It should also be observed that all the uses of force within this category share the characteristic that they do not threaten a formal, peaceful international status quo. In the case of postcolonial wars there is no status quo. In the case of continuation wars the status quo is one of conflict rather than peace. Intervention in civil strife does not threaten the formal status quo, since neither the existence nor the independence of the target state is necessarily threatened by the intervention. Likewise, neocolonial wars do not threaten the formal status quo, since the victim entities in such wars have no formal international standing. Maintenance of spheres of influence and the use of force in self-defense reinforce the status quo; they do not threaten it. And by definition the uses of force described in Chapter 9 are limited and thus not directed against the status quo.

It is important to stress, however, that, while the conflicts in this category may not be treated as illegal by third states, neither does the practice of states suggest that the international community regards such uses of force with indifference. Rather, states—acting either through regional organizations or, if they are large enough, unilaterally—frequently involve themselves in conflicts affecting their interests by seeking to help the combatants make peace. Almost every conflict discussed in this book—including wars in which the use of force was generally approved, wars in which the state using force was ultimately sanctioned, as well as wars in this third category—saw an effort at mediation or settlement by some state, or by a group of states, or by an international organization. If states are not prepared to treat states using force as lawbreakers except in extreme circumstances, neither are they generally indifferent to other states' uses of force. But their interest is most often shown by seeking a way to persuade combatants to make peace rather than by identifying and sanctioning a wrongdoing state.

Furthermore, there are few examples of such mediation efforts being rejected out of hand. To be sure, mediations failed frequently. States or organizations attempting mediation, however, were seldom treated as somehow interfering in matters that did not concern them. Indeed, on a few occasions combatants disinclined to end particular hostilities nonetheless felt constrained to treat mediation seriously as, for example, the United States felt forced to do when confronted with the Arias Central American peace initiative in the late 1980s, and as seems to have happened in the Angola/Namibia fighting.

These observations suggest the need to consider the legal significance of these offers of mediation in the context of uses of force. Could it be argued that this third-state interest in ending conflicts could support arguments that the obey-or-be-sanctioned standard defines too narrowly the uses of force that could be fairly characterized as illegal?

Such an argument, it would appear, would be difficult to sustain. In the first place, while an effort to mediate conflicts certainly suggests that states generally believe the use of force to be undesirable, such beliefs do not necessarily demonstrate a further conclusion that the use of force is illegal. More fundamentally, offers to mediate controversies in which force has been used would seem, in important respects, to be *inconsistent* with the view that the use of force was itself illegal.

This conclusion would seem to follow from an examination of the efforts at mediation described in this work. Since mediation, by definition, seeks to bring the parties to an agreement, it must address both parties' problems with reaching agreement. Such an approach seems inconsistent with treating the state using force as a lawbreaker, since it requires putting that state on a level of equality with its victim if agreement is to be achieved.

More basically, to say that a use of force is illegal would appear to mean that the use of force itself is intolerable, regardless of the circumstances that gave rise to it. Specifically, such an assertion must mean that desisting from the use of force is seen as obligatory, not optional; that the state using force would have no basis for claiming any advantages deriving from its use of force; and that the use of force itself must give rise to a claim for reparation by the victim state.

A mediatory approach, however, is inconsistent with all of these consequences of a label of illegality. Since it depends upon persuasion, that approach necessarily is inconsistent with demands that the state using force desist. Also, a mediator must necessarily take the parties as it finds them, including acknowledging whatever bargaining advantages that a state using force has acquired through its behavior. Finally, since mediations can succeed only by obtaining the parties' agreement, mediation necessarily requires a focus on the dispute underlying the use of force if the agreement of the state using force is to be obtained. But such a focus would appear to be inconsistent with treating the use of force as a distinct problem, requiring reparation whatever the settlement of the underlying dispute. In short, while the very frequent efforts to settle controversies that have led to the use of force certainly show that states generally regard the use of force as undesirable, they necessarily are so solicitous of the interests of the putatively wrongdoing state that they would not seem to show the flat rejection of the use of force that would seem to be logically necessary if the use of force in question is regarded as illegal.

Collecting the observations offered under the three preceding headings, one may say that uses of force posing a significant threat to the international status quo—such as a classic invasion—are likely to be rare and to evoke sanctions when they occur. A rule labeling such uses of force unlawful would therefore satisfy the obey-or-be-sanctioned standard. While state practice suggests that an exception to this rule should be made for those cases in which the threatened status quo involves European colonialism, the disappearance of formally colonial arrangements makes such an exception no longer relevant. State practice also indicates that a rule prohibiting uses of force that do not threaten the formal status quo could not satisfy the obey-or-be-sanctioned standard and that such uses of force thus could not be said to violate customary international law.

## *Other Observations Regarding the Use of Force by States*

The foregoing generalizations spell out the general practice of states regarding the use of force. Certain other observations are also in order, however.

First, aside from the general practice of states, state practice in the Americas suggests that the states of that region hold themselves to a standard more restrictive than the general standard. Leaving aside uses of force by the United States in order to maintain its sphere of influence, American states used force against one another on only six occasions during the period covered by this study.[1] Further, the other states in the region acted quickly in five of the cases to bring the fighting to an end. Action took different forms in different situations. The OAS threatened El Salvador with serious economic sanctions when it was tardy in agreeing to withdraw its troops from Honduras after its invasion of that state in 1969. When Costa Rica was attacked by Nicaraguan-supported rebels in 1955, the OAS provided Costa Rica with military assistance. OAS mediation helped end the 1948 conflict involving those same two states, and OAS pressure led Honduras and Nicaragua to accept a judicial resolution of the border dispute that led to hostilities between them in 1958. Finally, mediation by other states in the region helped end the fighting, if not the dispute, between Peru and Ecuador in the 1980s and 1991.

A second aspect of state practice regarding the use of force relevant to this discussion is the continuing acknowledgment by states of the authority of the UN Security Council. This calls for comment because it is somewhat surprising that the Security Council remains an authoritative body. It would not have been startling if during the period of its paralysis during the Cold War, states had treated the Council with less and less seriousness, perhaps becoming completely indifferent to it. That did not happen. Rather than ceasing to care what took place in the Security Council, states—especially the permanent members—continued to care very much. Permanent members took the Security Council seriously enough to veto resolutions they disliked instead of simply ignoring those they found troubling. The rare resolutions adopted pursuant to Chapter VII of the UN Charter continued to carry weight in international relations. When the Cold War finally ground to a halt, and states invoked the full panoply of the Security Council's power to deal with Iraq's invasion of Kuwait, states did not argue that the Security Council's authority had ceased to exist during the period of its weakness even while some of them were questioning the wisdom of its method of dealing with Iraq. In short, in the Security Council the states of the world continue to possess a body treated as having the legal authority to deal with uses of force in whatever way it thinks best.

This preceding observation suggests another: there is reason to doubt that states' unwillingness to act more vigorously to limit uses of force during the period 1945–91 can be ascribed primarily to the ideological division that characterized the Cold War. To be sure, ideology induced states to use force in some circumstances in which they otherwise would not have done and also to support, or at least not to sanction, uses of force by other states because of ideological affinity with those other states. However, it also appears that ideologically motivated uses of force were of types more or less generally tolerated anyway, such as interventions in civil wars and acts by great powers to maintain their spheres of influence. Nor did Cold War ideology *greatly* skew third-state reactions to uses of force. It had an impact, of course, but less than might have been expected. If the Soviet Union supported the DPRK's attack on the ROK, it also pushed the DPRK to make peace. The USSR and the PRC did not let the Second Indochina War prevent them from improving relations with the United States. The United States acknowledged legal restraints on its ability to act against perceived ideological threats even within the Americas when it avoided overt action against Guatemala in 1954 and Cuba in 1961. And it opposed Somalia's attack on Ethiopia despite the character of Ethiopia's government. But if it is difficult to ascribe attitudes toward the use of force since 1945 primarily to Cold War ideology, those attitudes may well survive the end of the Cold War. The passing of that period, that is, will not of itself lead to a sea change in states' attitudes toward regulating the interstate use of force.

## State Practice and Formulations of the International Law of Force

The preceding discussion describes the practice of states regarding the use of force. The next stage of the argument will test purported rules of customary international law against this pattern of state practice.

### *The UN Charter Standard*

The most obvious rule to test first against this standard is that of the UN Charter. According to Oscar Schachter, that rule permits a state to use force unilaterally only when it is (1) engaging in self-defense, (2) aiding a second state's self-defense, (3) responding to a request for aid from one of the contenders in civil strife in a state *after* a previous intervention by another state to aid another contender, or (4) rescuing its nationals in a foreign country who are in imminent danger and are not receiving adequate protection from the territorial sovereign.[2]

Measured against the obey-or-be-sanctioned standard, this purported rule fares poorly. To be sure, all the circumstances in which Professor Schacter argues that the use of force is lawful have been treated as lawful in state practice, though the boundaries of the self-defense concept are unclear. However, as the preceding chapters indicate, there have been many instances since World War II in which states have used force without encountering international sanctions in circumstances unlawful under Professor Schachter's formulation. Further, in some of those instances the international community may be said to have actively approved the use of force, for example, when force was used against European colonialism. It thus appears that state practice simply does not support the proposition that the rules of the UN Charter can be said to be a rule of customary international law. Indeed, this is hardly a novel observation; Professor Reisman has argued for some time that the Charter standard cannot be said to state the law when measured against the practice of states.[3] Professor Arend has taken a similar position.[4]

This conclusion is reinforced by considering several instances in which the United Nations has taken formal action that has had the effect of weakening the status of the Charter rule as customary law. The Security Council's adoption of Resolution 242 permitted Israel to retain territory acquired by force as a bargaining chip to force Arab states to address the political disagreements underlying the Arab-Israeli wars. While Israel acquired the territory through a defensive use of force, the permission to retain territory so acquired for political purposes seems contrary to the absolutes of Article 2(4). Likewise, Security Council efforts to accommodate Israel's interests in southern Lebanon seem to be inconsistent with respecting the territorial integrity of Lebanon, however sensible they may be in light of the realities on the ground.

Several resolutions adopted by the Security Council during the Iran-Iraq War also cast doubt on the customary law status of the Charter's rule. These resolutions were grounded on the assumption that certain states were entitled to be treated as "neutral" with respect to the Iran-Iraq conflict. As explained in the discussion of that conflict in Chapter 2, however, if the Charter's rules are rules of customary law as well as treaty rules, they leave no room for neutrality. The Security Council's acceptance of the possibility of neutrality necessarily implies that body's belief that states are free *not* to take sides in a war, which in turn is consistent with law only if not taking sides does not mean acquiescence in lawbreaking. If the Charter's rules are rules of customary law, however, not taking sides *is* acquiescence in lawbreaking, since at least one of the combatants must be in violation of the charter (at least in the Iran-Iraq War). Therefore, the Security Council's resolutions on the Iran-Iraq War are inconsistent with the proposition that the charter rules are rules of customary law.

Finally, UN mediators have played a role in pressuring Bosnia-Herzegovina to accept its defeat at the hands of the Bosnian Serbs, despite the support given the Bosnian Serbs by Serbia, arguably in violation of Article 2(4). This action reinforces the impression that even UN organs are not prepared to treat Article 2(4) as binding in all situations.

It may be argued, however, that these doubts about the customary law status of the Charter's rules ignore the fact that a number of uses of force during this period were condemned by the Security Council. To be sure, in most of those cases the condemnation was not accompanied by any sort of concrete sanction, but—it might be asserted—the very act of condemnation amounts to imposing a sanction upon the condemned conduct.

The difficulty with this argument is that it uses the term "sanction" in a way that distorts its meaning in this context. As explained in Chapter 1, behavior may count as a sanction as that term is used here if it can have the effect of reversing the conduct of the acting state and of leading that state to make good any harm it has done. If states other than the actor react to the conduct with behavior clearly not capable of reversing the conduct, they in effect indicate that they are willing to live with the conduct in question. That, in turn, suggests that those states do not regard the conduct as unlawful, since labeling behavior "unlawful" in a customary system is simply another way of saying that the participants in the system have concluded that they *cannot* live with the behavior and will take steps to see that it does not occur.

Thus it appears that for an action to count as a "sanction" for purposes of customary international law, the action must be reasonably capable of reversing the conduct to be sanctioned. Security Council condemnations could meet this definition if the obloquy of being sanctioned was enough to induce a state to reverse its behavior and make reparation for any damage it had caused. States have never, however, reacted to Security Council condemnations in this way. Condemnations might have also served the function of sanctions if states not reversing their behavior in response to condemnations were subsequently subjected to sanctions. In such circumstances states might alter their behavior after being condemned to avoid the inevitable consequences of failure to do so. In fact, however, states not altering their behavior in response to condemnations are very frequently not sanctioned subsequently. Condemnations standing alone, then, cannot reasonably be expected to affect state behavior and therefore are not "sanctions."

Further, member-states of the Security Council are aware that their condemnation of state behavior is not likely to alter that behavior—that is, they cannot expect their condemnations to have the effect of sanctions. This suggests that condemnations are not likely even to be intended as sanctions. Security Council practice offers some support to this conclusion; as noted several times in the preceding chapters, states sometimes vote for resolutions condemning behavior only on the condition that those resolutions neither contain nor threaten sanctions. If Security Council condemnations are not sanctions, then, they cannot count as the "sanction" aspect of the obey-or-be-sanctioned standard for purposes of evaluating the customary law status of the charter's rule.

In sum, it seems clear that, measured against state practice, putative rules regulating interstate uses of force derived from the United Nations Charter cannot be said to represent customary international law.

## *Other Possible Formulations*

Other scholars have suggested different possible rules of customary international law addressing the lawfulness of the use of force but departing from the rule of the UN Charter. Professor Reisman has argued that intervention in a state's internal affairs to replace an undemocratic government with a democratic regime is not unlawful, giving as examples the American interventions in Panama and Grenada and the Tanzanian intervention in Uganda.[5] Professor Tesón has similarly argued that humanitarian interventions to replace regimes guilty of serious human rights violations are lawful, citing the Grenadan and Ugandan examples and also mentioning France's overthrow of Emperor Bokassa in the Central African Empire and India's aid to Bangladesh in 1971.[6] While it is certainly true that none of the intervening states in these cases was subjected to serious sanctions by third states, there are nonetheless several difficulties with these positions.

First, the absence of sanctions in each of these cases can be explained without citing the principles to which these scholars refer. The interventions by the United States and France were the acts of great powers acting within their spheres of influence. Those by Tanzania and India reflected defensive motives, at least in part.

Second, while all the examples of prodemocratic or prohuman rights invasions fall within one of the categories of not-unlawful uses of force described earlier in this chapter, there is one outstanding example of an invasion that certainly served humanitarian ends that nonetheless attracted a strong, negative international reaction—that of Kampuchea by Vietnam. The brutality of the government of Democratic Kampuchea was considered irrelevant by many states when they chose to sanction Vietnam for its invasion.

Third, these arguments assume that international law especially disfavors regimes that are undemocratic or destructive of human rights. This assumption seems inconsistent, however, with the fact of widespread acceptance of particular uses of force that had negative effects for democracy or human rights, or both—for example, the responses to Morocco's activities in the Western Sahara and, in particular, the responses to Indonesia's activities in East Timor.

Of course, uses of force otherwise not unlawful will not somehow become unlawful because they support democracy and human rights. It is not unlawful for states to support insurgents who fight for those principles, or for great powers to intervene within their spheres of influence in support of them. But it is not clear that the cases relied upon by Professors Reisman and Tesón are best explained by reference to the principles they cite.

## Final Thoughts

As of mid-1994 we find that the practice of states has produced a legal regime regarding the use of force containing several elements. First, state behavior is consistent with the proposition that international law forbids the most serious and rarest uses of force—those in which a state seeks to subjugate another established state or conquer a portion of such a state's territory. Second, states generally do not treat as unlawful a broad range of other uses of force, though the states of the Americas appear to adhere to a standard higher than that generally followed. Third, states' preferred reaction to almost all uses of force is negotiation aimed at persuading combatants to stop fighting; the alternative—coercing the combatant perceived to be a lawbreaker—is reserved for the most serious uses of force, with the coercion threshold being lower in the Americas than elsewhere. Even in cases serious enough to call for coercion, states prefer to deal with the problem through negotiation. Finally, the Security Council's authority remains potent, providing a mechanism for addressing unacceptable uses of force.

While it is tempting to suggest some grand scheme for controlling interstate uses of force consistent with the foregoing, none will be forthcoming here; this work seeks only to demonstrate what limits on their behavior states have been willing to accept, not to devise means for further restraining international violence. However, there is one last matter that seems worth addressing. It might well occur to persons seeking to control interstate war to try to attain that end by attempting to strengthen the capacity of the international legal system to compel states to refrain from interstate violence. The reality of the Security Council's continued authority and the relative harmony of views between the permanent members since 1990 might suggest that the Security Council could be a vehicle for a more legalized approach to this problem—an approach, that is, reflecting a collective international willingness to enforce rules against the use of force. It seems worthwhile to explain why that approach seems problematic.

The basic difficulty with expanding reliance on law-based methods of dealing with international armed conflict is that such a step is possible only if the attitudes toward legalized dispute settlement that sustain domestic legal systems can be transferred to the international setting. It seems doubtful that such a transfer is possible, however, given the fundamental differences between the conflicts domestic legal systems must resolve and those that would be presented by cases involving international uses of force. This point can be better understood if one reflects on the assumptions that underlie legal resolution of disputes in domestic legal systems and considers whether those same assumptions could be made as to legal resolution of questions of interstate violence.

Suppose that in some domestic legal system P sues D, alleging that D inflicted a severe beating on P. One can assume several things about the ensuing litigation. First, the focus will be on the facts of the case: Did D beat P? Unless D claims self-defense, D's motive will not be relevant. Nor will the personal relationships of P and D with the individuals involved in resolving the dispute weigh very heavily; it is a fair assumption, for example, that the judge will not be influenced in charging the jury by any concern regarding the effect of the verdict on the judge's dealings with the parties. Second, it can be assumed that if D is held liable, force is available if D declines to pay the judgment; the sheriff can execute the judgment against D's property if necessary.

These assumptions rest on others still more basic. We can expect the legal system to focus solely on the correct application of the legal rule because, at bottom, society is indifferent to the outcome of any particular dispute, provided all parties are treated fairly and no bad precedents are set. We can expect the legal system to enforce the judgment, if need be, because members of society generally can identify with a plaintiff facing a recalcitrant defendant and are willing to tax themselves to pay the relatively small costs of maintaining the machinery needed for executing a judgment.

But assumptions regarding a focus on the facts of a particular dispute and of the availability of force to execute a judgment are more problematic in the international setting. First, to insist on ignoring a state's motive for its action is to make a negotiated solution difficult, since any such solution is easier to obtain if it addresses the parties' reasons for their actions. As noted above, however, states greatly prefer to deal with problems involving the use of force through negotiation. Indeed, it seems most unlikely that states would agree to institutionalize an approach toward dealing with uses of force that focused solely on the fact that force had been used without reference to the basis of the dispute between the parties; that conclusion is strongly suggested by states' great stress on negotiations to deal even with uses of force that seem clearly unjustifiable, such as Argentina's seizure of the Falklands or Iraq's subjugation of Kuwait.

Second, it is difficult for states to consider the legalities of a dispute without taking into account their relations with the parties to the dispute. The international community numbers fewer than two hundred members, many of whom must deal with one another over a wide range of issues; unlike the situation between court personnel and litigants, states must assume that their attitudes toward ostensibly legal matters will affect their other dealings with the disputants. Obviously, the more crucial the matter for the disputant, the more pressure third states will encounter to lend support without regard to legalities. Needless to say, disputes that have led to the use of force tend to be very crucial for the states involved in them; such disputes are therefore particularly difficult for third states to approach solely on the basis of the legalities at issue.

Third, if most members of society can be indifferent to the outcome of a lawsuit provided no bad precedent is set, this cannot be said of the situation of third states as they contemplate the outcome of an international dispute. If the application of a legal rule generally supported by some state not involved in a particular dispute would result in a blow to the interests of an important ally of the uninvolved state, that uninvolved state has an interest in the matter beyond the mere application of the correct rule—quite possibly, interest enough to make it hesitate to support that rule. Again, matters involving the use of force are especially likely to be serious enough to raise this problem.

Finally, and perhaps most obviously, the enforcement of legal rules raises much different questions internationally than it does domestically. As stated above, relative to the resources of a given state, the costs of enforcing a particular domestic judgment are likely to be trivial. If it is necessary to enforce a rule of international law regulating the use of force, however, the costs for the enforcing states could be very high indeed—they can amount to immense sums of money and many lives lost. If those states are themselves not parties to the original dispute, but are acting primarily to uphold the rights of another state, yet another problem is presented. The citizens of the enforcing states may well not identify with the state whose rights are being upheld to the point of being willing to bear the costs of enforcement. Sacrifices that might seem reasonable to a population defending itself may seem excessive if expended for the benefit of some foreign state.

Greater reliance on legal mechanisms to deal with issues raised by interstate uses of force would, in short, be costly. Such an approach would make negotiated resolutions of international disputes harder, force states to put at risk their relations with the parties to the disputes, require them to ignore their own interests in the well-being of their allies, and require their populations to accept the deaths and expenditures that would be necessary to enforce the rules.

This is not to say that it would be impossible to design a system that respects states' preferences for negotiated solutions to disputes involving the use of force but keeps coercive power in reserve. On the contrary, the experience of the OAS described above demonstrates a number of successes in using that technique. In each of the cases involved, however, the OAS had available techniques of coercion that were significant in relation to the particular context in which they were used but nonetheless fairly cheap for the coercing states: five aircraft, or a threat of a coffee embargo. Further, the stakes for the state being coerced were not crucial; that is, yielding to coercion in these contexts did not pose great risks to the states coerced. One must be cautious, therefore, in assuming that the methods of conflict resolution used by the OAS could be employed in situations in which coercion would be costly or the state targeted for coercion would be most unwilling to back down, or both. And of course it is possible that whatever factors account for the general rarity of the use of force within the Americas also help explain the success of the OAS's techniques—and these factors may not be replicable elsewhere.

In sum, then, it seems doubtful that either states or their citizens would consider it desirable to move toward a fundamentally more legalized approach toward dealing with the problem of interstate uses of force. Law is, after all, only the reflection of the political will of the community it governs. The practice of states demonstrates a great reluctance on the part of the world community to consider as legal matters questions involving the use of force. As long as this attitude persists, the contributions law can make toward controlling international violence will necessarily be modest.

# NOTES

## Chapter 1

1. See, e.g., *Treaty on Pacific Settlement of International Disputes*, 1 TIAS 230, 32 Stat. 1779, T.S. No. 392 (1899).

2. *Covenant of the League of Nations, Hudson International Legislation*, vol. 1 (1931), at 1.

3. *Treaty Providing for the Renunciation of War as an Instrument of National Policy*, 46 Stat. 2343, T.S. No. 796 (1928; entered into force for the United States July 24, 1929).

4. *Charter of the United Nations*, 59 Stat. 1031, T.S. No. 993 (1945) (hereafter *Charter of the United Nations*).

5. *Statute of the International Court of Justice*, 59 Stat. 1055, T.S. No. 993 (1945), Artlcle 38 (hereafter *ICJ Statute*).

6. See, e.g., Ian Brownlie, *Principles of Public International Law*, 3d ed. (Oxford: Clarendon Press, 1979), at 4–12; Georg Schwarzenberger and E. D. Brown, *A Manual of International Law*, 6th ed. (Milton, U.K.: Professional Books, 1976), at 26–27.

7. 1986 *International Court of Justice Reports* 14 (hereafter *ICJ Reports*).

8. Id. at 97–110, ¶¶s 183–209.

9. Id. at 98–101, ¶¶s 187–90.

10. See, e.g., Yoram Dinstein, *War, Aggression, and Self-Defence* (Cambridge: Grotius Publications, Ltd., 1988), at 83–97.

11. 1986 *ICJ Reports* at 98, ¶ 186.

12. Oscar Schachter, Remarks, American Society of International Law, Washington, D.C., 1990, *Proceedings of the 81st Annual Meeting* (hereafter *81st ASIL Proceedings*), at 159.

13. Louis Henkin, "International Law: Politics, Values, and Functions," *Recueil des Cours*, vol. 216 (Dordrecht: Martinus Nijhoff Publishers, 1990), at 9, 146.

14. Id. at 149.

15. Article 59, *ICJ Statute*.

16. See, e.g., Fred L. Morrison, *81st ASIL Proceedings*, at 260; Yoram Dinstein, *81st ASIL Proceedings*, at 266; Daniel B. Magraw, Jr., *81st ASIL Proceedings*, at 270; Anthony D'Amato, "Trashing Customary International Law," *American Journal of International Law*, vol. 81 (January 1987), at 101; Thomas M. Franck, "Some Observations on the ICJ's Procedural and Substantive Innovations," *American Journal of International Law*, vol. 81 (January 1987), at 116.

17. H.L.A. Hart, *The Concept of Law* (New York: Oxford University Press, 1961), at 84.

18. Myres S. McDougal, "Law and Minimum World Public Order: Armed Conflict in Larger Context," *UCLA Pacific Basin Law Journal*, vol. 3 (1984), at 21, 23–24.

19. W. Michael Reisman, "International Lawmaking: A Process of Communication" (the Harold D. Lasswell Memorial Lecture), American Society of International Law, Washington, D.C., 1983, in *Proceedings of the 75th Anniversary Convocation,* at 101, 111.

20. Id. at 111.

21. Max Weber, *Law in Economy and Society,* ed. Max Rheinstein and trans. Edward Shils and Max Rheinstein (Cambridge: Harvard University Press, 1954), at 13–15.

22. The observations in this paragraph were suggested by the discussion in Thomas M. Franck, *The Power of Legitimacy Among Nations* (New York: Oxford University Press, 1990), at 29–30.

23. *Charter of the United Nations,* Chapter VII.

24. This example was suggested to me by a reading of chap. 4, "Use of Force Against Nuclear Installations," in Anthony A. D'Amato, *International Law: Process and Prospect* (Dobbs Ferry, N.Y.: Transnational Publishers, Inc., 1987), at 75.

25. *Charter of the United Nations,* Article 17.

26. This conclusion is supported by the rule relied upon in the *Case of the S.S. Lotus,* Permanent Court of International Justice Reports, Ser. A, No. 10 (1927), at 18, that restrictions on the independence of states are not to be presumed, i.e., if it is not clear that a rule of law exists forbidding certain conduct, then the conduct cannot be said to be unlawful.

27. Roger Fisher, "Bringing Law to Bear on Governments," *Harvard Law Review,* vol. 74 (1961), at 1130, 1131–34.

28. Id. at 1132–33.

29. General Assembly Resolution 3314(XXIX), U.N. GAOR, 29th Sess., Supp. No. 31, at 42, U.N. Doc. A/29/31 (December 14, 1974).

30. Article 59, *ICJ Statute.*

31. *Charter of the United Nations,* Articles 10–14, 17.

32. Stephen M. Schwebel, "The Effect of Resolutions of the U.N. General Assembly on Customary International Law," *Proceedings of the American Society of International Law* (Washington, D.C., 1979), at 301, 302.

33. Hart, at 86–88, 102.

34. Id. at 132–37.

35. For a discussion of the possibility of deriving rules of customary law from treaties, see Anthony A. D'Amato, *The Concept of Custom in International Law* (Ithaca: Cornell University Press, 1977), at 103–66.

36. Article 38, *ICJ Statute.*

37. D'Amato, *Concept of Custom in International Law,* at 103–66.

38. For a discussion of the effect of divergent practice on both rules of customary law and treaties, see Arthur M. Weisburd, "Customary International Law: The Problem of Treaties," *Vanderbilt Journal of Transnational Law,* vol. 21 (1988), at 11–22, and sources therein cited.

39. See Thomas M. Franck, "Who Killed Article 2(4)? or: Changing Norms Governing the Use of Force by States," *American Journal of International Law,* vol. 64 (1970), at 809; W. Michael Reisman, "Article 2(4): The Use of Force in Contemporary International Law," American Society of International Law, Washington, D.C., 1986, in *Proceedings of the 78th Annual Meeting,* at 75.

40. For a similar argument asserting that acceptance of violations of basic principles of international law can lead to dangerous erosion of those principles, see Thomas M. Franck, "Dulce et Decorum Est: The Strategic Role of Principles in the Falklands War," *American Journal of International Law,* vol. 77 (1983), at 109.

41. Richard M. Goodman, "The Invasion of Czechoslovakia: 1968," *The International Lawyer,* vol. 4 (October 1969), at 42, 73–75.

42. This view is another that contradicts the rule in the *Case of the S.S. Lotus.*

43. Hart, at 18–25; Reisman, "International Lawmaking," at 109–10.

44. See, e.g., for a description of the confusion among the Soviets on this occasion, *Los Angeles Times*, November 11, 1990, §M, p. 2.

## Chapter 2

1. Arguably, the Korean War would also meet that definition. The fact that each of the two Koreas claimed to be the government of the whole peninsula and regarded the other Korea as illegitimate, however, makes the applicability of the third element of the definition uncertain. It should be noted that Israel's involvement in the Suez War does not satisfy the fifth element of the definition of a classic invasion, since it reflects in part issues left unresolved after the first Arab-Israeli War. The Suez War is nonetheless included in this chapter because neither the United Kingdom nor France had a history of armed conflict with Egypt.
2. Hugh Thomas, *Suez* (New York: Harper & Row, 1967), at 17, 21–25.
3. Id. at 26.
4. Id. at 47–52.
5. Id. at 47.
6. Id. at 32–38.
7. Id. at 65–84, 101–2, 105–6.
8. Id. at 95–96, 101.
9. *1954 Yearbook of the United Nations* (New York: Columbia University Press, 1955), at 62–64.
10. Ze'ev Schiff, *A History of the Israeli Army* (New York: Macmillan, 1985), at 68–85.
11. See, e.g., *1955 Yearbook of the United Nations* (New York: Columbia University Press, 1956), at 31–35.
12. Schiff, at 88–89.
13. Id.; Thomas, at 84.
14. Thomas, at 85, 96–97.
15. Id. at 88, 108–9.
16. Id. at 113–15.
17. Id. at 123.
18. Id. at 123–25.
19. Id. at 125, 128.
20. *1956 Yearbook of the United Nations* (New York: Columbia University Press, 1957), at 25–27.
21. Thomas, at 129.
22. *1956 UN Yearbook*, at 28.
23. Id. at 29.
24. Thomas, at 137.
25. Id. at 141–44.
26. *Keesing's Contemporary Archives*, vol. 10 (November 17–24, 1956), at 15203.
27. Thomas, at 142–47.
28. Id. at 147–48.
29. Id. at 424–31.
30. Donald Neff, *Warriors at Suez* (New York: Simon and Schuster, 1981), at 415.
31. *1956 UN Yearbook*, at 33–34, 38.
32. Neff, at 416.
33. Michael Brecher, *Decisions in Israel's Foreign Policy* (New Haven: Yale University Press, 1975), at 289–91.
34. Neff, at 416–17.
35. Brecher, at 291.

36. Id. at 291–302, 314–15.

37. Id. at 309–11.

38. *Keesing's Contemporary Archives*, vol. 10 (November 3–10, 1956), at 15185.

39. Neff, at 434.

40. *Keesing's Contemporary Archives*, vol. 10 (November 17–24, 1956), at 15211.

41. Id.

42. Neff, at 424.

43. *Asian Recorder*, vol. 2 (November 24–30, 1956), at 1152–55.

44. Neff, at 422.

45. Thomas, at 145; Brecher, at 282–83.

46. Australia and New Zealand expressed support in the General Assembly for the action by Britain and France on the basis of its being a police action designed to end the fighting. *Keesing's Contemporary Archives*, vol. 10 (November 17–24, 1956), at 15208–9.

47. See remarks of Netherlands delegate at November 3, 1956, emergency session of the General Assembly, id. at 15201.

48. *Keesing's Contemporary Archives*, vol. 12 (December 3–10, 1960), at 17796; vol. 13 (May 27–June 3, 1961), at 18121.

49. *Keesing's Contemporary Archives*, vol. 12 (December 3–10, 1960), at 17796.

50. *Keesing's Contemporary Archives*, vol. 13 (June 30–July 7, 1962), at 18845.

51. Id.

52. Id. at 18846.

53. *General Assembly Official Records*, 16th Session, Annexes (XVI) 88 and 22(a) at 26, Doc. A/L.368, November 24, 1961.

54. *General Assembly Official Records*, 16th Session, Plenary Meetings, meeting 1066, November 27, 1961, at 873.

55. Id.

56. Id.

57. *Keesing's Contemporary Archives*, vol. 13 (June 30–July 7, 1962), at 18846–49.

58. *Keesing's Contemporary Archives*, vol. 13 (August 25–September 1, 1962), at 18939.

59. Id. at 18941.

60. P. D. Gaitonde, *The Liberation of Goa* (New York: St. Martin's Press, 1987), at 1–2.

61. Id. at 58–70.

62. Id. at 133, 154.

63. Id. at 154–56.

64. Quincy Wright, "The Goa Incident," *American Journal of International Law*, vol. 56 (July 1962), at 617, 629 n. 36.

65. Id.

66. *Keesing's Contemporary Archives*, vol. 13 (March 10–17, 1962), at 18635, 18638.

67. Id. at 18635–36, 18638.

68. Gaitonde, at 157–59.

69. Id. at 160.

70. Id. at 161–68.

71. Wright, at 620–21.

72. Id. at 622.

73. Id. at 629–31; *Keesing's Contemporary Archives*, vol. 13 (March 17–24, 1962), at 18659–61.

74. *Keesing's Contemporary Archives*, vol. 13 (March 17–24, 1962), at 18661.

75. Gaitonde, at 175.

76. Wright, at 627, n. 32; Sarto Esteves, *Politics and Political Leadership in Goa* (New Delhi, Bangalore: Sterling Publishers Private, Ltd., 1986), at 57–60.

77. Robert F. Gorman, *Political Conflict on the Horn of Africa* (New York: Praeger, 1981), at 35–36.

78. *Keesing's Contemporary Archives*, vol. 14 (August 29–September 5, 1964), at 20254.
79. Gorman, at 27–37.
80. Id. at 38, 39–40.
81. Id. at 41–45.
82. Id. at 56.
83. Id. at 61–65.
84. Id. at 54–55, 61–71.
85. Id. at 116–23.
86. Id. at 116.
87. Id. at 123.
88. Id. at 183.
89. Id. at 130–32, 138.
90. Id. at 123.
91. *Keesing's Contemporary Archives*, vol. 24 (May 26, 1978), at 28989–95.
92. Id. at 28993.
93. Gorman, at 133.
94. Id. at 133–34.
95. Id. at 135–36.
96. Id.
97. Id. at 136.
98. Id. at 116–17.
99. Id. at 138.
100. Id. at 183–85.
101. Id. at 210–12.
102. *Keesing's Contemporary Archives*, vol. 27 (September 4, 1981), at 31057; id., vol. 28 (September 10, 1982), at 31689–91.
103. Id., vol. 30 (October 1984), at 33138–39; *Keesing's Record of World Events*, vol. 34 (July 1988), at 36006–7.
104. *Keesing's Record of World Events*, vol. 34 (May 1988), at 35872; (July 1988), at 36006–7.
105. Gorman, at 130–34.
106. Tony Avirgan and Martha Honey, *War in Uganda* (Westport, Conn.: Lawrence Hill & Company, 1982), at 33–35.
107. Id. at 32–38, 48–52.
108. *Keesing's Contemporary Archives*, vol. 25 (June 22, 1979), at 29669–70.
109. Avirgan and Honey, at 53–142; *Keesing's Contemporary Archives*, vol. 25 (June 22, 1979), at 29672.
110. Avirgan and Honey, at 197–236.
111. Id. at 77–79.
112. Id. at 84–86.
113. Id. at 74–77.
114. *Keesing's Contemporary Archives*, vol. 25 (June 22, 1979), at 29669–72; (September 21, 1979), at 29838–41.
115. *Keesing's Contemporary Archives*, vol. 25 (June 22, 1979), at 29673–74; (September 21, 1979), at 29840–41; Avirgan and Honey, at 89–90; *1979 Yearbook of the United Nations* (New York: United Nations Department of Public Information, 1982), at 262–63.
116. Fernando R. Tesón, *Humanitarian Intervention: An Inquiry into Law and Morality* (Dobbs Ferry, N.Y.: Transnational Publishers, Inc., 1988), at 159–75.
117. Gary Klintworth, *Vietnam's Intervention in Cambodia in International Law* (Canberra: Australian Government Publishing Service, 1989), at 7.
118. Id.

119. Steven J. Hood, *Dragons Entangled* (Armonk, N.Y: M. E. Sharpe, Inc., 1992), at 59, 64–65, 74–75.
120. Klintworth, at 7.
121. Leszek Buszynski, "The Soviet Union and Vietnamese Withdrawal from Cambodia," in Gary Klintworth, ed., *Vietnam's Withdrawal from Cambodia: Regional Issues and Realignments* (Canberra: Australian National University, 1990), at 32, 39–40.
122. *Keesing's Record of World Events*, vol. 35 (September 1989), at 36881–82.
123. Hood, at 69, 104–7; *Keesing's Record of World Events*, vol. 37 (October 1991), at 38511–12.
124. Michael Leifer, "Cambodia in Regional and Global Politics," in Gary Klintworth, ed., *Vietnam's Withdrawal from Cambodia: Regional Issues and Realignments* (Canberra: Australian National University, 1990), at 4, 10–11.
125. Klintworth, at 10–11, 17–23.
126. Hood, at 43–50; Pao-Min Chang, *The Sino-Vietnamese Territorial Dispute* (New York: Praeger, 1986), at 44–47; King C. Chen, *China's War with Vietnam, 1979* (Stanford: Hoover Institution Press, 1987) at 32–36.
127. Buszynski, at 32–35.
128. *1979 UN Yearbook*, at 273–75.
129. Chen, at 91–92.
130. Id.
131. Klintworth, at 8–10; Hood, at 67–69.
132. Buszynski, at 40–47.
133. Leifer, at 4–5, 10–11, 13–15.
134. Mark Urban, *War in Afghanistan* (New York: St. Martin's Press, 1990), at 7–25.
135. Id. at 25–47, 279–83.
136. Id. at 47–246; Arthur S. Banks, ed., *Political Handbook of the World: 1992* (Binghamton, N.Y.: CSA Publications, 1992), at 4–6.
137. Banks, at 4–6.
138. Urban, at 52–57, 162–65, 210–20.
139. Amin Saikal, "The Regional Politics of the Afghan Crisis," in Amin Saikal and William Maley, *The Soviet Withdrawal from Afghanistan* (Cambridge: Cambridge University Press, 1989), at 52, 57–58.
140. *Keesing's Contemporary Archives*, vol. 26 (May 9, 1980), at 30229–42.
141. Id. (August 1, 1980), at 30385.
142. *Keesing's Contemporary Archives*, vol. 27 (May 22, 1981), at 30881.
143. Id. (June 12, 1981), at 30914.
144. *1980 Yearbook of the United Nations* (New York: United Nations Department of Public Information, 1983), at 296–307; *1981 Yearbook of the United Nations* (New York: United Nations Department of Public Information, 1985), at 232–38; *1982 Yearbook of the United Nations* (New York: United Nations Department of Public Information, 1986), at 350–51, 354; *1983 Yearbook of the United Nations* (New York: United Nations Department of Public Information, 1987), at 233–34; *1984 Yearbook of the United Nations* (New York: United Nations Department of Public Information, 1988), at 226–28; *1985 Yearbook of the United Nations* (Dordrecht: Martinus Nijhoff Publishers, 1989), at 237–38; *1986 Yearbook of the United Nations* (Dordrecht: Martinus Nijhoff Publishers, 1990), at 215–17; *1987 Yearbook of the United Nations* (Dordrecht: Martinus Nijhoff Publishers, 1992), at 214–15.
145. Urban, at 299–304.
146. Stephen C. Pelletiere, *The Iran-Iraq War* (New York: Praeger, 1992), at 7–10; Phebe Marr, "The Iran-Iraq War: The View from Iraq," in Christopher C. Joyner, ed., *The Persian Gulf War* (Westport, Conn.: Greenwood Press, 1990), at 59, 61–62.
147. Pelletiere, at 29–34; Marr, at 60–63.

148. Pelletiere, at 33–34; Marr, at 63–65.

149. Marc Weller, "The Use of Force and Collective Security," in Ige F. Dekker and Harry H. G. Post, eds., *The Gulf War of 1980–1988* (Dordrecht: Martinus Nijhoff Publishers, 1992), at 71–72; Ige F. Dekker, "Criminal Responsibility and the Gulf War of 1980–1988: The Crime of Aggression" in id. at 249, 255–56; *Further Report of the Secretary-General on the Implementation of Security Council Resolution 598 (1987)*, U.N. Doc. S/23273, December 9, 1991.

150. Pelletiere, at 35–148; Eric Hooglund, "Strategic and Political Objectives in the Gulf War: Iran's View," in Christopher C. Joyner, ed., *The Persian Gulf War* (Westport, Conn.: Greenwood Press, 1990), at 39, 39–54; Boleslaw A. Boczek, "The Law of Maritime Warfare and Neutrality in the Gulf War," in id. at 173, 181; Francis V. Russo, Jr., "Neutrality at Sea in Transition: State Practice in the Gulf War as Emerging International Customary Law," *Ocean Development and International Law*, vol. 19, no. 5 (1988), at 381, 392–93.

151. Pelletiere, at 49–59.

152. *1980 UN Yearbook*, at 312–19.

153. R. K. Ramazani, "Who Started the Iran-Iraq War? A Commentary," *Virginia Journal of International Law*, vol. 33 (Fall 1992), at 69, 84–85.

154. *1982 UN Yearbook*, at 362–63.

155. *1983 UN Yearbook*, at 239–40; *1986 UN Yearbook*, at 220–22, 226–29.

156. *1984 UN Yearbook*, at 234–36.

157. *1987 UN Yearbook*, at 223–25.

158. Pelletiere, at 71–72, 82–84; Edgar O'Ballance, *The Gulf War* (London: Brassey's Defence Publishers, 1988), at 51–53, 72–74, 97, 102–3.

159. Joseph H. Kechichian, "The Gulf Cooperation Council and the Gulf War," in Christopher C. Joyner, ed., *The Persian Gulf War* (Westport, Conn.: Greenwood Press, 1990), at 91, 104; Pelletiere, at 82–84; O'Ballance, at 152–53, 188–89.

160. Boczek, "Law of Maritime Warfare," at 174–75, 186; David D. Caron, "Choice and Duty in Foreign Affairs," in Christopher C. Joyner, ed., *The Persian Gulf War* (Westport, Conn.: Greenwood Press, 1990), at 153, 161; A. Gioia and N. Ronzitti, "The Law of Neutrality: Third States', Commercial Rights and Duties," in Ige F. Dekker and Harry H. G. Post, eds., *The Gulf War of 1980–1988* (Dordrecht: Martinus Nijhoff Publishers, 1992), at 221, 237–40.

161. Caron, at 164–65.

162. Louis Henkin, "Commentary" (January 26, 1988), in "Conference Report: The Persian/Arabian Gulf Tanker War—International Law or International Chaos," *Ocean Development and International Law*, vol. 19, no. 4 (1988), at 299, 308–10; Mark W. Janis, "Neutrality," in Horace B. Robertson, ed., *International Law Studies, 1991: The Law of Naval Operations* (Newport: Naval War College Press, 1991), at 148, 149.

163. See, e.g., Boleslaw A. Boczek, "Law of Warfare at Sea and Neutrality: Lessons from the Gulf War," *Ocean Development and International Law*, vol. 20, no. 3 (1989), at 239, 240–41; Michael Bothe, "Neutrality at Sea," in Ige F. Dekker and Harry H. G. Post, eds., *The Gulf War of 1980–1988* (Dordrecht: Martinus Nijhoff Publishers, 1992), at 204; Richard Grunawalt, "The Rights of Neutrals and Belligerents" (January 26, 1988), in "Conference Report: The Persian Gulf War—International Law or International Chaos," *Ocean Development and International Law*, vol. 19, no. 4 (1988), at 299, 302–5; "Air Attacks on Neutral Shipping in the Persian Gulf: The Legality of the Iraqi Exclusion Zone and Iranian Reprisals," *Boston College International and Comparative Law Review*, vol. 8 (Summer 1985), at 517, 521–23.

164. Martin Middlebrook, *Operation Corporate* (London: Viking, 1985), at 22–25; Alfred P. Rubin, "Historical and Legal Background of the Falkland/Malvinas Dispute," in Alberto R. Coll and Anthony C. Arend, eds., *The Falklands War* (Boston: George Allen & Unwin, 1985), at 9–20; Alberto R. Coll, "Philosophical and Legal Dimensions of the Use of Force in the Falklands War," in Alberto R. Coll and Anthony C. Arend, eds., *The Falklands War* (Boston: George Allen & Unwin, 1985), at 34, 40–41.

165. Middlebrook, at 15–16.
166. Coll, at 39–43.
167. David C. Gompert, "American Diplomacy and the Haig Mission: An Insider's Perspective," in Alberto R. Coll and Anthony C. Arend, eds., *The Falklands War* (Boston: George Allen & Unwin, 1985), at 106, 108–9.
168. Douglas Kinney, *National Interest/National Honor* (New York: Praeger, 1989), at 230–36.
169. Middlebrook, at 64–68.
170. Kinney, at 104, 112–13, 114.
171. Middlebrook, at 103–385.
172. Inis L. Claude, Jr., "UN Efforts at Settlement of the Falkland Islands Crisis," in Alberto R. Coll and Anthony C. Arend, eds., *The Falklands War* (Boston: George Allen & Unwin, 1985), at 118, 123.
173. *1982 UN Yearbook*, at 1321, 1347.
174. Id. at 1321, 1335–36, 1347.
175. Id. at 1329–32.
176. Kinney, at 147–48, 151–59, 181–85, 195–215, 234–35.
177. Id. at 147; Middlebrook, at 91.
178. Claude, at 127–28.
179. Id. at 125–26.
180. Srilal Perrera, "The OAS and the Inter-American System: History, Law, and Diplomacy," in Alberto R. Coll and Anthony C. Arend, eds., *The Falklands War* (Boston: George Allen & Unwin, 1985), at 132, 146.
181. Id. at 146–51.
182. Lawrence Freedman and Efraim Karsh, *The Gulf Conflict, 1990–1991* (Princeton: Princeton University Press, 1993), at 28–62.
183. Id. at 42–45, 67–69, 99.
184. Id. at 61–63.
185. John Pimlott, "The Gulf Crisis and World Politics," in John Pimlott and Stephen Badsey, eds., *The Gulf War Assessed* (London: Arms and Armour, 1992), at 35, 39–40.
186. Freedman and Karsh, at 72–81; Security Council Resolution 660, August 2, 1990.
187. Security Council Resolution 661, August 6, 1993.
188. Freedman and Karsh, at 84–99.
189. Id. at 108–9.
190. Id. at 109–26, 143–51; Security Council Resolution 665, August 25, 1990.
191. Freedman and Karsh, at 163–215, 227–33; Security Council Resolution 678, November 29, 1990.
192. Freedman and Karsh, at 246–75, 299–300, 374–85, 394–406.
193. Id. at 345–61.

## Chapter 3

1. Stephen H. Longrigg, *Syria and Lebanon Under French Mandate* (New York: Oxford University Press, 1958), at 340.
2. Id. at 345–55.
3. Ellen J. Hammer, *The Struggle for Indochina, 1940–1955* (Stanford: Stanford University Press, 1966), at 104–20.
4. Id. at 153–79.
5. Id. at 183–87.
6. Id. at 207.
7. Id. at 199.

8. Id. at 189–91.
9. *New York Times*, April 6, 1947, page 45, column 3.
10. *New York Times*, February 19, 1947, page 20, column 5.
11. Hammer, at 201.
12. Id. at 202.
13. Id. at 213.
14. Id. at 247–50.
15. Id. at 250–51.
16. Id. at 266–70.
17. Id. at 271.
18. Id. at 313–14.
19. Id. at 267.
20. *New York Times*, May 4, 1954, page 4, column 3.
21. Hammer, at 311–12.
22. Id. at 304–7.
23. Id. at 249–50.
24. Id. at 252.
25. Id. at 327–29.
26. Id. at 327.
27. *New York Times*, May 4, 1954, page 4, column 3.
28. Id.
29. *The Times*, April 9, 1954, page 8b.
30. *New York Times*, May 5, 1954, page 1, column 7.
31. Hammer, at 335–37.
32. Id. at 337.
33. Id. at 321.
34. Id. at 332–34.
35. *Le Figaro*, May 27, 1954, page 3, column 5.
36. Anthony J. S. Reid, *The Indonesian National Revolution 1945–1950* (Hawthorn, Victoria: Longman, 1974), at 25–39.
37. Id. at 42–45.
38. Id. at 45–54, 104–8.
39. Id. at 104–12.
40. Id. at 110–12.
41. *Security Council Official Records*, meetings 172 and 173, August 1, 1947.
42. Id., meeting 18, February 13, 1946.
43. *New York Times*, November 19, 1946, page 15, column 2.
44. Id., April 1, 1947, page 16, column 8, and April 18, 1947, page 17, column 6.
45. *Security Council Official Records*, meeting 171, July 31, 1947; and meeting 173, August 1, 1947.
46. *New York Times*, July 22, 1947, page 3, column 1; July 25, 1947, page 3, columns 1 and 2; July 31, 1947, page 1, columns 1 and 2, and page 3, columns 1, 2, 5, 6, and 8; *Le Monde*, July 27 and 28, 1947, page 2a; July 29, 1947, page 8e.
47. *Security Council Official Records*, meeting 173, August 1, 1947.
48. Id., meeting 194, August 25, 1947.
49. Reid, at 112–14.
50. Id. at 149–51.
51. *New York Times*, December 23, 1948, page 1, columns 1 and 2.
52. Id., April 1, 1949, page 14, column 1; Reid, at 158.
53. The states involved were Afghanistan, Egypt, Syria, Lebanon, Iraq, Iran, Saudi Arabia, Yemen, Ethiopia, Turkey, Palestine [sic], Burma, Ceylon, the Philippines, Siam, Nepal, China, Australia, New Zealand, and India. *New York Times*, January 23, 1949, page 1, columns 6 and 7.

54. *Le Monde*, December 24, 1948, page 8d; December 25, 1948, page 2a.
55. Id., December 22, 1948, page 12d.
56. *Security Council Official Records*, meeting 391 of December 23, 1948; meeting 397 of January 7, 1949; and meeting 400 of January 14, 1949.
57. Id., meeting 392 of December 24, 1948, and meeting 406 of January 28, 1949.
58. Id., meeting 391, December 23, 1948.
59. Id., meeting 421 of March 23, 1949.
60. Reid, at 160–62.
61. *Security Council Official Records*, meeting 455 of December 12, 1949, and meeting 456 of December 13, 1949.
62. Dwight L. Ling, *Tunisia: From Protectorate to Republic* (Bloomington: Indiana University Press, 1967), at 31–35.
63. Id. at 51–56.
64. Id. at 104–30.
65. Id. at 133–56.
66. Id. at 164–72.
67. Id. at 182–83.
68. *1952 Yearbook of the United Nations* (New York: Columbia University Press, 1953), at 267.
69. *Security Council Official Records*, meeting 574 of April 4, 1952, and meeting 575 of April 10, 1952.
70. Ling, at 159–60.
71. *1952 UN Yearbook*, at 270–78.
72. Ling, at 162–63.
73. Rom Landau, *Moroccan Drama: 1900–1955* (San Francisco: American Academy of Asian Studies, 1956), at 255–57.
74. Id. at 149–60, 250–55.
75. Id. at 258–316.
76. Id. at 317–83.
77. Mark I. Cohen and Laura Hahn, *Morocco: Old Land, New Nation* (New York: Praeger, 1966), at 75–86.
78. *1952 UN Yearbook*, at 278–84.
79. Id. at 284–85.
80. *1953 Yearbook of the United Nations* (New York: Columbia University Press, 1954), at 198–203.
81. Id. at 203–8.
82. Landau, at 355.
83. *1954 Yearbook of the United Nations* (New York: Columbia University Press, 1955), at 86; *1955 Yearbook of the United Nations* (New York: Columbia University Press, 1956), at 64–65.
84. Landau, at 336–39.
85. Id. at 339.
86. Id. at 359–60.
87. Cohen and Hahn, at 68–69.
88. Id. at 56–57.
89. Id. at 72.
90. *New York Times*, August 29, 1955, page 8, column 2.
91. Alistair Horne, *A Savage War of Peace* (New York: Penguin Books, 1987), at 88–91.
92. Id. at 98.
93. Id. at 94–95.
94. Id. at 531.
95. Id. at 343–44, 506, 514–15.

96. Arnold Fraleigh, "The Algerian Revolution as a Case Study in International Law," in Richard A. Falk, ed., *The International Law of Civil War* (Baltimore: The Johns Hopkins University Press, 1971), at 208, 214.
97. Id. at 208.
98. Horne, at 130.
99. Id. at 261, 405, 406.
100. Fraleigh, at 213–14.
101. Id. at 225–29.
102. *1956 Yearbook of the United Nations* (New York: Columbia University Press, 1957), at 115–16.
103. Fraleigh, at 224–25.
104. *Keesing's Contemporary Archives*, vol. 12 (January 23–30, 1960), at 17222; vol. 13 (March 18–25, 1961), at 17992.
105. John H. E. Fried, "United States Military Intervention in Cambodia in Light of International Law," in Richard A. Falk, ed., *The Vietnam War and International Law* (Princeton: Princeton University Press, 1972), vol. 3, at 118.
106. Id. at 118–19.
107. See Horne, at 249–50.
108. Fried, at 119–21.
109. Id. at 120–21.
110. Horne, at 247.
111. Id. at 247, 465.
112. *Keesing's Contemporary Archives*, vol. 12 (January 23–30, 1960), at 17221–22; vol. 13 (March 18–25, 1961), at 17992.
113. Nancy Crawshaw, *The Cyprus Revolt* (London: George Allen & Unwin, 1978), at 22.
114. Id. at 20.
115. *Peace Treaty Between the Allied Powers and Turkey*, Lausanne, July 24, 1923, Article 20, in Fred L. Israel, ed., *Major Peace Treaties of Modern History, 1648–1967* (New York: Chelsea House Publishers, 1967), at 2310.
116. Crawshaw, at 22–24.
117. Id. at 43.
118. Id. at 57–74.
119. Id. at 62–63.
120. Id. at 76–77.
121. Id. at 90–114.
122. Id. at 20, 51, 107, 113.
123. Id. at 174, 344–45.
124. Id. at 115–21, 152–56.
125. Id. at 288–94.
126. Id. at 285–88.
127. Id. at 288–94.
128. Id. at 258–59.
129. Id. at 338–45.
130. Id.
131. Id. at 217–29, 266–73, and 328–29.
132. *The Times*, December 28, 1956, page 5a; February 12, 1957, page 6e; March 21, 1957, page 10e; March 27, 1957, page 8d; January 28, 1958, page 6c; June 5, 1958, page 9c.
133. John A. Marcum, *The Angolan Revolution* (Cambridge, Mass.: The MIT Press, 1969), vol. 1, at 126–30.
134. Id. at 49–100, 130–58.

135. Id. at 228–43; John A. Marcum, *The Angolan Revolution* (Cambridge, Mass.: The MIT Press, 1978), vol. 2, at 218.
136. Marcum, *Angolan Revolution,* vol. 1, at 13–48, 181–200.
137. Marcum, *Angolan Revolution,* vol. 2, at 212–14.
138. Id. at 160–67.
139. Id. at 217–18.
140. Id. at 218–21.
141. Id. at 241.
142. Id. at 241–43.
143. Id. at 255.
144. Id. at 246.
145. Marcum, *Angolan Revolution,* vol. 1, at 181–200.
146. Id. at 255–63.
147. Douglas G. Anglin and Timothy M. Shaw, *Zambia's Foreign Policy: Studies in Diplomacy and Dependence* (Boulder, Colo: Westview Press, 1979), at 314–15.
148. Marcum, *Angolan Revolution,* vol. 2, at 227–37.
149. *1962 Yearbook of the United Nations* (New York: Columbia University Press, 1964), at 92–93, 653–54.
150. *1973 Yearbook of the United Nations* (New York: United Nations Office of Public Information, 1976), at 753–54, 975.
151. *1969 Yearbook of the United Nations* (New York: United Nations Office of Public Information, 1972), at 135–37.
152. Neil Bruce, *Portugal: The Last Empire* (New York: John Wiley & Sons, 1975), at 87.
153. Id. at 87–88.
154. Id. at 89–90.
155. Id. at 84–96.
156. Id. at 132.
157. *1969 UN Yearbook,* at 137–43; *1970 Yearbook of the United Nations* (New York: United Nations Office of Public Information, 1972), at 187–91; *1971 Yearbook of the United Nations* (New York: United Nations Office of Public Information, 1974), at 116–21.
158. *Sekou Toure* (London: Panaf Books, 1978), at 148–52, 168; *1970 UN Yearbook,* at 187–91.
159. *1973 UN Yearbook,* at 146–47.
160. Julian Paget, *Last Post: Aden 1964–1967* (London: Faber and Faber, 1969), at 26–37.
161. Id. at 45–99, 109–253; *1966 Yearbook of the United Nations* (New York: United Nations Office of Public Information, 1968), at 190–93.
162. *1964 Yearbook of the United Nations* (New York: Columbia University Press, 1966), at 182–86.
163. *1966 UN Yearbook,* at 561–69.
164. Paget, at 189–96.
165. *The Times,* January 4, 1967, page 8c.
166. Thomas H. Henriksen, *Revolution and Counterrevolution* (Westport, Conn.: Greenwood Press, 1983), at 13, 25.
167. Id. at 30.
168. Id. at 27–58.
169. Id. at 184–98.
170. Id. at 198–203.
171. Id. at 172–82.
172. Robert S. Jaster, *Adelphi Papers 253: The 1988 Peace Accords and the Future of South-Western Africa* (London: Brassey's Defence Publishers, 1990), at 5.
173. Id.; *1966 UN Yearbook,* at 595–96.

174. *1966 UN Yearbook,* at 596–602, 605–6.
175. *1970 UN Yearbook,* at 752–54.
176. Jaster, at 6–7.
177. Id. at 7.
178. Id. at 9–10.
179. Id. at 10–11.
180. Id. at 12–13, 14.
181. Chester A. Crocker, *High Noon in Southern Africa* (New York: W. W. Norton & Company, 1992), at 38–43.
182. Jaster, at 14–15.
183. Id. at 15.
184. Id. at 15–16.
185. Id. at 17–22.
186. Crocker, at 49.
187. Id. at 371–72; Jaster, at 22–23, 28–32.
188. Crocker, at 37–38, 85.
189. Id. at 38–43.
190. Id. at 36–40, 63–70.
191. Id. at 415–21, 506–11; Jaster, at 28–29.
192. Crocker, at 441–42.
193. Id. at 443–45.
194. Id. at 421–23, 432–33; Jaster, at 36–39.
195. Jaster, at 45–46.
196. Crocker, at 486–89.
197. See, e.g., "Fate of Angola Hangs in the Balance," Agence France Presse, June 4, 1994, available in LEXIS, Nexis Library, Curnws file.
198. Jeffrey Davidow, *Dealing with International Crises: Lessons from Zimbabwe* (Muscatine, Iowa: The Stanley Foundation, 1983), at 3 and 21, n. 1.
199. Id.
200. David Martin and Phyllis Johnson, *The Struggle for Zimbabwe* (Boston: Faber and Faber, 1981), at 65–72.
201. Id. at 2, 9–10.
202. Id. at 9.
203. Id. at 1–2, 9, 12–34, 73–91.
204. Harry R. Strack, *Sanctions: The Case of Rhodesia* (Syracuse: Syracuse University Press, 1978), at 16–21.
205. See, e.g., *1966 UN Yearbook,* at 114–16; *1967 Yearbook of the United Nations* (New York: United Nations Office of Public Information, 1969), at 117–19.
206. Strack, at 85–87; Jeffrey Davidow, *A Peace in Southern Africa: The Lancaster House Conference on Rhodesia, 1979* (Boulder, Colo.: Westview Press, 1984), at 42–43.
207. Davidow, *Peace in Southern Africa,* at 81; Strack, at 63–65, 70–74, 114–41, 146–52.
208. Strack, at 21.
209. Davidow, *Peace in Southern Africa,* at 45.
210. Martin and Johnson, at 10, 12–34, 73–84.
211. Strack, at 173–74, 237–38.
212. See, e.g., Martin and Johnson, at 215–22.
213. Davidow, *Peace in Southern Africa,* at 20–22.
214. Id. at 26–32.
215. Davidow, *Dealing with International Crises,* at 10–11.
216. Davidow, *Peace in Southern Africa,* at 23, 42–43, 100–101.

217. Davidow, *Dealing with International Crises*, at 9.
218. Davidow, *Peace in Southern Africa*, at 44–45.
219. Id. at 89–90, 100–101.
220. Id. at 101.
221. *Keesing's Contemporary Archives*, vol. 32 (January 1986), at 34087–89.
222. Id.; *1985 Yearbook of the United Nations* (Dordrecht: Martinus Nijhoff Publishers, 1989), at 189–92.
223. Edward Kwakwa, "South Africa's May 1986 Military Incursions into Neighboring African States," in *Yale Journal of International Law*, vol. 12 (Summer 1987), at 421, 425–26.
224. Id. at 429–32; *1986 Yearbook of the United Nations* (Dordrecht: Martinus Nijhoff Publishers, 1990), at 166–67.

## Chapter 4

1. Lord Birdwood, *Two Nations and Kashmir* (London: R. Hale, 1956), at 39–51.
2. Id. at 53–56.
3. Id. at 57–60.
4. *United Nations Document S/1196, Security Council Official Records, Supplement for January 1949*, at 45.
5. See, generally, *Security Council Official Records*, meetings 226–46 of January 1–February 15, 1948; meetings 284–86 of April 17–21, 1948; and meeting 382 of November 25, 1948.
6. Id., meeting 230 of January 20, 1948.
7. Id., meeting 286 of April 21, 1948.
8. *United Nations Document S/1100, Security Council Official Records, Supplement for November 1948*, at 18.
9. *United Nations Document S/1430, Special Supplement No. 7, 1949*, at 38–39.
10. *United Nations Document S/1100*, at 31–33.
11. *United Nations Document S/1430*, at 36–60.
12. Birdwood, at 153–55.
13. David and Jon Kimche, *A Clash of Destinies* (New York: Praeger, 1960), at 27.
14. Id. at 55.
15. Id. at 33.
16. Id. at 38–41, 48.
17. Id. at 48–56, 60.
18. Id. at 57, 79–80.
19. Id. at 73–78, 85–91.
20. Id. at 92–93.
21. Id. at 105–8, 149–58.
22. John F. Murphy, *The United Nations and the Control of International Violence* (Totowa, N.J.: Allanheld, Osmun, 1982), at 26.
23. Kimche and Kimche, at 197; *Security Council Official Records*, meeting 306 of May 27, 1948; meetings 307 and 308 of May 28, 1948; meeting 310 of May 29, 1948.
24. Kimche and Kimche, at 221–22.
25. Id. at 230; *Security Council Official Records*, meeting 338, July 15, 1948.
26. Kimche and Kimche, at 244–51.
27. Id. at 255–56.
28. *Security Council Official Records*, meeting 377, November 4, 1948.
29. Kimche and Kimche, at 251.
30. Id. at 257–63; *Security Council Official Records*, meeting 381 of November 16, 1948.
31. Kimche and Kimche, at 266–71.

32. Compare map at id., p. 33, with map at id., p. 264.
33. Id. at 274.
34. *Security Council Official Records*, meeting 296 of May 19, 1948; meeting 298 of May 20, 1948; and meeting 302 of May 22, 1948.
35. Id., meeting 374 of October 28, 1948.
36. See, e.g., id., meeting 296 of May 19, 1948, and meeting 306 of May 27, 1948.
37. Murphy, at 27–28.
38. *New York Times*, August 20, 1948, page 5, column 4.
39. Murphy, at 27.
40. Peter Lowe, *The Origins of the Korean War* (New York: Longman, 1986), at 19–20.
41. Id. at 24.
42. Id. at 25–36.
43. Id. at 36–37.
44. Id. at 43–48.
45. Id. at 48–49.
46. Id. at 49–51.
47. Id. at 49–53.
48. Id. at 59.
49. Id. at 67–68.
50. Id. at 39–40.
51. Id. at 57–61.
52. Id. at 59–61.
53. Id. at 119–20; Alexander L. George and Richard Smoke, *Deterrence in American Foreign Policy: Theory and Practice* (New York: Columbia University Press, 1974), at 159–61.
54. Lowe, at 154–56.
55. Id. at 54, 163, 165, 167.
56. George and Smoke, at 157, 175.
57. Lowe, at 156.
58. Id.
59. Id. at 155.
60. Id. at 160–70; George and Smoke, at 148.
61. *Security Council Official Records*, meeting 473 of June 25, 1950; meeting 474 of June 27, 1950; and meeting 476 of July 7, 1950.
62. Id.
63. The states contributing combat units were Australia, Belgium, Canada, Colombia, Ethiopia, France, Greece, Luxembourg, Netherlands, New Zealand, the Philippines, Thailand, Turkey, the Union of South Africa, the United States, and the United Kingdom. Those contributing medical units were Denmark, Italy, India, Norway, and Sweden. Lowe, at 217.
64. *The Times*, July 31, 1950, page 3c.
65. Id., July 3, 1950, page 5d.
66. Id., July 1, 1950, page 4b.
67. *New York Times*, July 4, 1950, page 4, column 3.
68. Lowe, at 182–83.
69. Id. at 176–77.
70. George and Smoke, at 192–98.
71. Id. at 186.
72. Id.
73. Edwin P. Hoyt, *The Day the Chinese Attacked* (New York: McGraw-Hill, 1990), at 77–81.
74. George and Smoke, at 213–14.
75. Lowe, at 209.

76. Richard Whelan, *Drawing the Line* (Boston: Little, Brown and Company, 1990), at 348–69.
77. George and Smoke, at 159–62.
78. *Keesing's Contemporary Archives*, vol. 14 (July 11–18, 1964), at 20176–77; (August 29–September 5, 1964), at 20254; *Facts on File*, vol. 21 (January 19–25, 1961), at 28; (April 6–12, 1961), at 132; *1964 Yearbook of the United Nations* (New York: Columbia University Press, 1966), at 121.
79. Alan J. Day, ed., *Border and Territorial Disputes*, 2d ed. (Detroit: Gale Research Company, 1987), at 144–50.
80. J.A.C. Mackie, *Konfrontasi* (New York: Oxford University Press, 1974), at 210.
81. Id. at 41–45.
82. Id. at 122–28, 153–57, 179–94, 329–33.
83. Id. at 175–77.
84. Id. at 181.
85. Id. at 117–21, 210–11.
86. Id. at 210–17, 258–64.
87. Id. at 264, 309–18.
88. Id. at 217–21, 317–18.
89. Id. at 318–22.
90. Id. at 32, 210–15, 216–17, 263–64.
91. *The Times*, January 31, 1964, page 9c; March 18, 1964, page 10c; April 17, 1964, page 13c; July 29, 1964, page 9b; September 5, 1964, page 8a; September 22, 1964, page 9a; October 30, 1964, page 10b.
92. *1964 UN Yearbook*, at 135–39.
93. Mackie, at 267–68.
94. Id. at 193.
95. *The Times*, December 19, 1963, page 8f.
96. Id., December 23, 1963, page 5b; April 15, 1964, page 10f.
97. Id., October 30, 1964, page 10g.
98. *Keesing's Contemporary Archives*, vol. 15 (February 13–20, 1965), at 20579.
99. *Asian Recorder*, vol. 11 (August 20–26, 1965), at 6621–22.
100. *New York Times*, August 2, 1964, page 4, column 2.
101. *The Times*, May 7, 1964, page 11b.
102. Id., February 14, 1964, page 10f.
103. *New York Times*, February 7, 1964, section IV, page 3, column 6.
104. *The Times*, January 1, 1964, page 10d.
105. Mackie, at 212–14, 261–62.
106. Id. at 225–35.
107. Hélène Carrère d'Encausse, *The End of the Soviet Empire: The Triumph of the Nations* (New York: Basic Books, 1993), at 47–72; *Keesing's Record of World Events*, vol. 38 (February 1992), at 38774; (March 1992), at 38828; (October 1992), at 39156; *The Times*, July 27, 1993, page 12; *The Guardian*, April 7, 1993, page 10; *New York Times*, March 14, 1992, page 1, column 1; August 2, 1993, page 4, column 6 (National Edition); May 23, 1994, section A, page 6, column 1 (Late Edition); June 2, 1994, section A, page 1, column 5 (Late Edition); *Houston Chronicle*, April 24, 1994, §A, page 21; *Los Angeles Times*, May 17, 1994, part A, page 1; Security Council Resolution 822, April 30, 1993, S/RES/822 (1993); Security Council Resolution 853, July 29, 1993, S/RES/853 (1993); Security Council Resolution 874, October 14, 1993, S/RES/874 (1993).
108. *The Independent*, July 29, 1994, page 16.
109. *Los Angeles Times*, October 14, 1995, part A, page 2; *Financial Times*, February 29, 1996, page 2.
110. *Keesing's Record of World Events*, vol. 37 (June 1991), at 38274–75; (August 1991), at

38373–76; (September 1991), at 38420–22; (October 1991), at 38512–13; (December 1991), at 38684–85; vol. 38 (January 1992), at 38703–4.

111. Id.; *Financial Times*, September 30, 1991, page 3.

112. Security Council Resolution 713, September 25, 1991; Security Council Resolution 724, December 15, 1991; Security Council Resolution 743, February 21, 1992.

113. *Keesing's Record of World Events*, vol. 37 (November 1991), at 38559–60; (December 1991), at 38684.

114. *Keesing's Record of World Events*, vol. 38 (March 1992), at 38832–33; (April 1992), at 38848–49; (May 1992), at 38918–19; (December 1992), at 39240; *New York Times*, July 31, 1993, page 1, column 8.

115. *New York Times*, August 7, 1995, page A6; September 19, 1995, page A1.

116. Security Council Resolution 757, May 30, 1992; Security Council Resolution 761, June 29, 1992; Security Council Resolution 769, August 7, 1992; Security Council Resolution 770, August 13, 1992; Security Council Resolution 771, August 13, 1992; Security Council Resolution 781, October 9, 1992; Security Council Resolution 787, November 16, 1992; Security Council Resolution 816, March 31, 1993; Security Council Resolution 819, April 16, 1993; Security Council Resolution 820, April 17, 1993; Security Council Resolution 827, May 25, 1993.

117. *New York Times*, February 21, 1994, section A, page 1, column 6; April 27, 1994, section A, page 1, column 6.

118. Id., September 15, 1995, page A1.

119. Id., June 9, 1994, page 1 (National Edition).

120. *The Guardian*, July 6, 1994, page 12.

121. Security Council Resolution 942, September 23, 1994.

122. *New York Times*, September 27, 1995, page A1.

123. Id., October 12, 1995, page A1.

124. Id., November 22, 1995, page A1.

125. Security Council Resolution 1022, November 11, 1995.

126. U.N. Doc. SC/6183, February 27, 1996.

127. *Keesing's Record of World Events*, vol. 38 (December 1992), at 39240.

128. Statute of the International Tribunal for the Prosecution of Persons Responsible for Serious Violations of International Humanitarian Law Committed in the Territory of the Former Yugoslavia Since 1991, Annex, *Report of the Secretary-General Pursuant to Paragraph 2 of Security Council Resolution 808 (1993)*, U.N. Doc. S/25704 (1993).

## Chapter 5

1. William S. Turley, *The Second Indochina War: A Short Political and Military History* (Boulder, Colo.: Westview Press, 1986), at 5–7.

2. R. B. Smith, *An International History of the Vietnam War*, vol. 1, *Revolution Versus Containment, 1955–1961* (New York: St. Martin's Press, 1983), at 31–33.

3. Turley, at 21.

4. Smith, *International History of the Vietnam War*, vol. 1, at 33.

5. Id. at 62–67.

6. Turley, at 24.

7. Id. at 27.

8. Id. at 27–28.

9. Smith, *International History of the Vietnam War*, vol. 1, at 227–31.

10. Turley, at 30.

11. Id. at 41–44.

12. Id. at 22–23, 30–31; Smith, *International History of the Vietnam War*, vol. 1, at 231.

13. See, e.g., Richard A. Falk, "International Law and the United States Role in the Vietnam War," in Richard A. Falk, ed., *The Vietnam War and International Law* (Princeton: Princeton University Press, 1968), vol. 1, at 363, 379 (discussion assuming NLF and DRV were independent entities).

14. Turley, at 38; R. B. Smith, *An International History of the Vietnam War*, vol. 2, *The Kennedy Strategy* (New York: St. Martin's Press, 1985), at 26.

15. Turley, at 15–18.

16. Id. at 36–38.

17. Id. at 38–39; Smith, *International History of the Vietnam War*, vol. 2, at 25–27.

18. Smith, *International History of the Vietnam War*, vol. 2, at 27.

19. Id. at 27–28, 347.

20. Id. at 74–75.

21. Turley, at 45–48.

22. Id. at 48–54, 72, 207.

23. It should be noted that there is some doubt that the second attack occurred, though it was the report of this second attack that provoked the American retaliatory strikes. Smith, *International History of the Vietnam War*, vol. 2, at 278–83.

24. Id. at 346–47.

25. Turley, at 69–70.

26. Peter A. Poole, *Eight Presidents and Indochina* (Huntington, N.Y.: R. E. Krieger, 1978), at 128–30.

27. Id.; Paul M. Kattenburg, *The Vietnam Trauma in American Foreign Policy* (New Brunswick, N.J.: Transaction Books, 1980), at 122–23.

28. Kattenburg, at 127, 197, 201–5.

29. Id. at 134–36; Turley, at 72–73; R. B. Smith, *An International History of the Vietnam War*, vol. 3, *The Making of a Limited War, 1965–1966* (New York: St. Martin's Press, 1991), at 100–103, 110, 142–69, 173–81.

30. Turley, at 81–82.

31. Id. at 100.

32. Id. at 106–8.

33. Id. at 81, 108–12.

34. Id. at 110.

35. Poole, at 192–94.

36. Id. at 198.

37. Turley, at 208.

38. Id.

39. Id. at 120–21; Smith, *International History of the Vietnam War*, vol. 3, at 105.

40. Turley, at 209.

41. Id. at 126–27, 130, 140–45.

42. Id. at 145–51.

43. Id. at 158–84.

44. "The Legality of United States Participation in the Defense of Viet-Nam," *Department of State Bulletin*, vol. 54 (March 28, 1966), at 474–78 (hereafter "Legality").

45. Smith, *International History of the Vietnam War*, vol. 3, at 59.

46. "Legality," at 477.

47. Glen St. J. Barclay, *A Very Small Insurance Policy* (St. Lucia: University of Queensland Press, 1988), at 165.

48. Id.

49. Kattenburg, at 216–20.

50. M. S. Rajan and T. Israel, "The United Nations and the Conflict in Vietnam," in Richard A.

Falk, ed., *The Vietnam War and International Law,* vol. 4, *The Concluding Phase* (Princeton: Princeton University Press, 1976), at 114, 131.

51. Id. at 134–35.
52. Smith, *International History of the Vietnam War,* vol. 3, at 264.
53. Rajan and Israel, at 124–27.
54. Id.
55. Kattenburg, at 252–55.
56. Turley, at 93, 138–39, 163–64; Smith, *International History of the Vietnam War,* vol. 3, at 138–39, 239, 285–86, 302–3.
57. Turley, at 141–42.
58. Id. at 253–54.
59. Thomas Ehrlich, *Cyprus: 1958–1967* (New York: Oxford University Press, 1974), at 39, 45.
60. Id. at 37–38.
61. Id. at 45–46.
62. Id. at 57–60.
63. *1964 Yearbook of the United Nations* (New York: Columbia University Press, 1966), at 154–56.
64. Id. at 155.
65. Id.
66. Ehrlich, at 64.
67. Richard A. Patrick, *Political Geography and the Cyprus Conflict, 1963–1971* (Waterloo, Ontario: Department of Geography, Faculty of Environmental Studies, University of Waterloo, 1976), at 67.
68. Ehrlich, at 82–85.
69. *The Times,* June 15, 1964, page 10d.
70. Ehrlich, at 64.
71. Patrick, at 67.
72. Ehrlich, at 90.
73. Patrick, at 68.
74. Ehrlich, at 62–63, 85–86.
75. *1964 UN Yearbook,* at 158.
76. Id. at 158–59.
77. Id.
78. Ehrlich, at 91–94, 96–97, 101–2.
79. Patrick, at 134–36.
80. Ehrlich, at 97–98.
81. Id. at 98.
82. Patrick, at 142.
83. Id. at 143; Ehrlich, at 112–13.
84. Id. at 112, 113.
85. *1967 Yearbook of the United Nations* (New York: United Nations Office of Public Information, 1969), at 280–82.
86. Ehrlich, at 106, 112–16.
87. *1964 UN Yearbook,* at 163–64.
88. Egypt: *The Times,* September 1, 1964, page 11a; DRV: *New York Times,* September 16, 1964, page 39, column 3; Soviet Union: *New York Times,* September 16, 1964, page 39, column 4; German Democratic Republic: *New York Times,* September 17, 1964, page 7, column 1.
89. *The Times,* September 11, 1964, page 10a.
90. France: *The Times,* August 15, 1964, page 5d; Israel: id., August 11, 1964, page 5b.
91. Sumit Ganguly, *The Origins of War in South Asia* (Boulder, Colo.: Westview Press, 1986), at 67–74.

92. Id. at 26, 45, 60–61, 76.
93. Id. at 75, 79–80.
94. Id. at 76–79.
95. Russell Brines, *The Indo-Pakistani Conflict* (London: Pall Mall Press, 1968), at 287–90.
96. Id.
97. Id. at 294–95.
98. Ganguly, at 87.
99. Id. at 57, 88; Brines, at 304–6.
100. Ganguly, at 88.
101. Brines, at 307–9.
102. Id. at 318–19.
103. Id. at 360, 366.
104. Id. at 319–21.
105. Id. at 325–28.
106. Id. at 334–46; Ganguly, at 58–59.
107. Brines, at 346.
108. Ganguly, at 91–92.
109. Brines, at 356–57.
110. Id.
111. Id. at 362–65.
112. Id. at 352.
113. *New York Times*, September 9, 1965, page 1, column 6.
114. Brines, at 362, 371–73, 375–78.
115. *1965 Yearbook of the United Nations* (New York: Columbia University Press, 1967), at 173.
116. Id. at 173–74.
117. Id. at 174.
118. Brines, at 366–67.
119. *1965 UN Yearbook*, at 166–67.
120. Brines, at 370–71, 373–74.
121. Id. at 374–75.
122. Id. at 313.
123. Michael Brecher and Benjamin Geist, *Decisions in Crisis* (Berkeley and Los Angeles: University of California Press, 1980), at 42–43.
124. Chaim Herzog, *The Arab-Israeli Wars* (New York: Vintage Books, 1984), at 147–48.
125. Id. at 148–49; Brecher and Geist, at 44–46.
126. Brecher and Geist, at 45–47; Herzog, at 148–49.
127. Brecher and Geist, at 47–50, 104–70.
128. Id. at 104–70.
129. Id. at 166–68.
130. *1967 UN Yearbook*, at 175, 195–96.
131. Herzog, at 151–66.
132. Id. at 169–83.
133. Brecher and Geist, at 273–77, 326.
134. *1967 UN Yearbook*, at 174–79.
135. Brecher and Geist, at 279–84, 326, 337.
136. Id. at 283–85.
137. See, e.g., id. at 110–11.
138. *1967 UN Yearbook*, at 188.
139. Brecher and Geist, at 279.
140. Id. at 284–85.

141. *1967 UN Yearbook*, at 188, 191–209, 220–21.
142. Id. at 221.
143. Id. at 257–58.
144. Herzog, at 195–223; Ze'ev Schiff, *A History of the Israeli Army* (New York: Macmillan, 1985), at 178–89.
145. Herzog, at 195–223; Frederic C. Hof, *Galilee Divided* (Boulder, Colo.: Westview Press, 1985), at 71–72.
146. *1968 Yearbook of the United Nations* (New York: United Nations Office of Public Information, 1971), at 191–237; *1969 Yearbook of the United Nations* (New York: United Nations Office of Public Information, 1972), at 185–208; *1970 Yearbook of the United Nations* (New York: United Nations Office of Public Information, 1972), at 223–44.
147. *The Times*, March 26, 1970, page 6a.
148. Id., September 26, 1969, page 6f; February 3, 1970, page 1b; March 23, 1970, page 6e.
149. Herzog, at 219.
150. Hof, at 71–75.
151. Id. at 74–75.
152. See, e.g., *1973 Yearbook of the United Nations* (New York: United Nations Office of Public Information, 1976), at 178.
153. Hof, at 74.
154. Id. at 75–76.
155. *1974 Yearbook of the United Nations* (New York: United Nations Office of Public Information, 1977), at 207.
156. Hof, at 73, 75.
157. *1974 UN Yearbook*, at 206–7.
158. *1970 UN Yearbook*, at 227–40, 243–44; *1972 Yearbook of the United Nations* (New York: United Nations Office of Public Information, 1975), at 157–71, 172–73; *1973 UN Yearbook*, at 173–92; *1974 UN Yearbook*, at 206–11; *1975 Yearbook of the United Nations* (New York: United Nations Office of Public Information, 1978), at 223–30.
159. William Shawcross, *Sideshow* (New York: Simon and Schuster, 1979), at 64.
160. Id. at 21, 28, 68–70, 93–94.
161. Id. at 19–22.
162. Ben Kiernan, *How Pol Pot Came to Power* (London: Verson, 1985), at 301–2.
163. Id. at 304–5.
164. Id. at 305; Shawcross, at 162.
165. Shawcross, at 130–46, 149, 398.
166. Id. at 399.
167. Id. at 209–19, 280–99, 350–53.
168. Kiernan, at 307; Tran Dinh Tho, *The Cambodian Incursion* (Washington, D.C.: U.S. Army Center of Military History, 1978), 163–64.
169. Kiernan, at 321; Shawcross, at 200–202.
170. Kiernan, at 357–62; Shawcross, at 248.
171. Shawcross, at 202–3, 270–71, 313–16, 344–65.
172. *The Times*, May 2, 1970, page 1, column 3.
173. Id., May 9, 1970, page 5, column 5.
174. *New York Times*, May 6, 1970, page 9, column 1.
175. Id., May 2, 1970, page 8, column 5.
176. Id., columns 2 and 5; id., May 5, 1970, page 3, column 4, and page 5, column 8.
177. Id., May 2, 1970, page 8, column 2.
178. Richard Sisson and Leo E. Rose, *War and Secession* (Berkeley and Los Angeles: University of California Press, 1990), at 21–34; Robert Jackson, *South Asian Crisis* (New York: Praeger, 1975), at 15–26.

179. Sisson and Rose, at 54–90.
180. Id. at 90–133.
181. International Commission of Jurists, *The Events in East Pakistan* (Geneva: International Commission of Jurists, 1972), at 24–45.
182. Sisson and Rose, at 146–60; Jackson, at 34–45, 75.
183. Sisson and Rose, at 177–87.
184. Id. at 166–76, 187.
185. Id. at 210.
186. Id. at 182–83, 210–13.
187. Id. at 213–15, 230–34.
188. *1971 Yearbook of the United Nations* (New York: United Nations Office of Public Information, 1974), at 146–47, 154.
189. Sisson and Rose, at 194–95.
190. *Security Council Official Records*, meeting 1606, December 4, 1971.
191. Sisson and Rose, at 200–202, 240–44.
192. Id. at 153.
193. Id. at 219–20.
194. Id. at 261, 262–64; Jackson, at 125.
195. Sisson and Rose, at 261–62; Marvin Kalb and Bernard Kalb, *Kissinger* (Boston: Little, Brown and Company, 1974), at 258–63.
196. Sisson and Rose, at 251–53.
197. *1971 UN Yearbook*, at 150–51.
198. *Asian Recorder*, vol. 18 (May 13–19, 1972), at 10762; (December 2–8, 1972), at 11113.
199. Herzog, at 227–306.
200. *1973 UN Yearbook*, at 213.
201. Id. at 192–93.
202. Herzog, at 314.
203. Mohamed Heikal, *The Road to Ramadan* (New York: Quadrangle/New York Times Book Company, 1975), at 247.
204. Herzog, at 307–11.
205. Heikal, at 23–24.
206. Herzog, at 322.
207. Kalb and Kalb, at 485.
208. *1973 UN Yearbook*, at 196–97.
209. Kalb and Kalb, at 485; Heikal, at 245–49.
210. Kalb and Kalb, at 488–96.
211. Id. at 484; Heikal, at 273–74.
212. Schiff, at 220.
213. *The Times*, October 24, 1973, page 8d.
214. Id., October 22, 1973, page 11a.
215. *1973 UN Yearbook*, at 197.
216. Herzog, at 322–23.
217. Christopher Hitchens, *Cyprus* (New York: Quartet Books, 1984), at 64–71; Michael Attalides, *Cyprus* (New York: St. Martin's Press, 1979), at 130–34.
218. Hitchens, at 71–72; Attalides, at 134–35.
219. Hitchens, at 77–85; Attalides, at 164.
220. Hitchens, at 93, 96–97; Attalides, at 164.
221. *1974 UN Yearbook*, at 291.
222. Attalides, at 164.
223. Id. at 164–65; Hitchens, at 104–5.

224. Hitchens, at 107, 111–12.
225. *1974 UN Yearbook*, at 263.
226. Hitchens, at 94; Attalides, at 170–71.
227. *1974 UN Yearbook*, at 266.
228. Id. at 277, 278–79.
229. Attalides, at 176, 186–87.
230. Hitchens, at 84–85.
231. Attalides, at 176–77.
232. Hitchens, at 92–93.
233. *The Times*, August 15, 1974, page 4a.
234. Attalides, at 177–79.
235. Hitchens, at 107; *New York Times*, September 27, 1978, page 8.
236. *1974 UN Yearbook*, at 288–90, 295–96.
237. Naomi Joy Weinberger, *Syrian Intervention in Lebanon* (New York: Oxford University Press, 1986), at 82–135.
238. Id. at 147–51.
239. Id. at 14–18, 51–81; Trevor N. Dupuy and Paul Martell, *Flawed Victory* (Fairfax, Va.: Hero Books, 1986), at 33; Yossi Olmert, "Syria in Lebanon," in Ariel E. Levite, Bruce W. Jentleson, and Larry Berman, eds., *Foreign Military Intervention* (New York: Columbia University Press, 1992), at 95, 100.
240. Weinberger, at 161–75.
241. Id. at 178–84.
242. Id. at 185–211.
243. Id. at 211–28.
244. Id. at 228–30.
245. Olmert, at 103–21; *Keesing's Record of World Events*, vol. 35 (September 1989), at 36903–4; (October 1989), at 36986; vol. 36 (October 1990), at 37792; vol. 37 (May 1991), at 38214; *New York Times*, September 2, 1991, page 3, column 3; *Orlando Sentinel Tribune*, September 2, 1991, page A10.
246. Weinberger, at 256–65; Olmert, at 103; Jean Pierre Isselé, "The Arab Deterrent Force in Lebanon, 1976–1983," in Antonio Cassese, ed., *The Current Legal Regulation of the Use of Force* (Dordrecht: Martinus Nijhoff Publishers, 1986), at 179, 198–200.
247. Olmert, at 102; Shai Feldman, "Israel's Involvement in Lebanon: 1975–1985," in Ariel E. Levite, Bruce W. Jentleson, and Larry Berman, eds., *Foreign Military Intervention* (New York: Columbia University Press, 1992), at 134.
248. Weinberger, at 309–13.
249. Olmert, at 119–21.
250. Dupuy and Martell, at 207–8.
251. Feldman, at 134; Hof, at 79–81.
252. Feldman, at 135; Hof, at 81–83.
253. Feldman, at 137–38; Hof, at 87–93.
254. Dupuy and Martell, at 49.
255. *Keesing's Contemporary Archives*, vol. 25 (June 8, 1979), at 29649.
256. *1978 Yearbook of the United Nations* (New York: United Nations Office of Public Information, 1981), at 297–302, 312.
257. Dupuy and Martell, at 56–57; *1979 Yearbook of the United Nations* (New York: United Nations Department of Public Information, 1982), at 321–38; *1980 Yearbook of the United Nations* (New York: United Nations Department of Public Information, 1983), at 347–58.
258. Dupuy and Martell, at 62–63; Feldman, at 138–41; Hof, at 97–100.
259. Feldman, at 139–41; Dupuy and Martell, at 57–65.

260. *1981 Yearbook of the United Nations* (New York: United Nations Department of Public Information, 1985), at 283–93.

261. Dupuy and Martell, at 79–81; Feldman, at 141–43; Hof, at 98–102.

262. Hof, at 101–2; Feldman, at 143–44; Dupuy and Martell, at 81–83, 91.

263. Feldman, at 142–45.

264. Id., at 143–45; Dupuy and Martell, at 95–97; Ze'ev Schiff and Ehud Ya'ari, *Israel's Lebanon War* (New York: Simon and Schuster, 1984), at 153–56.

265. Dupuy and Martell, at 98–163.

266. Id. at 176–95; Feldman, at 150.

267. Dupuy and Martell, at 196–212; Feldman, at 150–57.

268. See, e.g., *New York Times*, August 2, 1993, page 1, column 5 (National Edition).

269. *1982 Yearbook of the United Nations* (New York: United Nations Department of Public Information, 1986), at 449, 452, 454–57, 475; *Keesing's Contemporary Archives*, vol. 29 (January 1983), at 31918; *New York Times*, September 17, 1982, page 1.

270. *1982 UN Yearbook*, at 436, 440, 454–56.

271. Schiff and Ya'ari, at 154–58; Olmert, at 108–9.

272. Olmert, at 111.

273. Id. at 109–10; Schiff and Ya'ari, at 219–20.

274. *1984 Yearbook of the United Nations* (New York: United Nations Department of Public Information, 1988), at 284–86.

275. Schiff and Ya'ari, at 210; Feldman, at 148.

276. *1982 UN Yearbook*, at 433–87; *1983 Yearbook of the United Nations* (New York: United Nations Department of Public Information, 1987), at 290–94; *1984 UN Yearbook*, at 282–98; *1985 Yearbook of the United Nations* (Dordrecht: Martinus Nijhoff Publishers, 1989), at 295–305.

277. Compare *1986 Yearbook of the United Nations* (Dordrecht: Martinus Nijhoff Publishers, 1990), at 286–88, 295, 298–99, 302–3; *1987 Yearbook of the United Nations* (Dordrecht: Martinus Nijhoff Publishers, 1992), at 279–80, 282–83; *1991 Yearbook of the United Nations* (Dordrecht: Martinus Nijhoff Publishers, 1992), at 236–42.

278. *Keesing's Contemporary Archives*, vol. 31 (December 1985), at 34076–77; *1985 Yearbook of the United Nations* (Dordrecht: Martinus Nijhoff Publishers, 1990), at 285–91.

## Chapter 6

1. Edgar O'Ballance, *The Greek Civil War, 1944–1949* (New York: Praeger, 1966), at 121–25.
2. Id. at 131.
3. *Security Council Official Records*, meeting 84, December 16, 1946.
4. *Security Council Official Records*, meeting 85, December 18, 1946.
5. O'Ballance, *Greek Civil War*, at 136.
6. *The Times*, March 13, 1947, page 4a.
7. O'Ballance, *Greek Civil War*, at 137.
8. *Security Council Official Records*, meeting 126, April 7, 1947.
9. *Security Council Official Records*, meeting 127, April 10, 1947.
10. Id.; *Security Council Official Records*, meeting 129 of April 14, 1947, and meeting 130 of April 18, 1947.
11. *Security Council Official Records*, meeting 126, April 7, 1947.
12. *Security Council Official Records*, meeting 131, April 18, 1947.
13. *Security Council Official Records*, meeting 130, April 18, 1947.
14. *Security Council Official Records*, meeting 131, April 18, 1947.
15. Id.
16. O'Ballance, *Greek Civil War*, at 143–50.

17. *Security Council Official Records*, meeting 147, June 27, 1947.
18. *Security Council Official Records*, meeting 148 of June 27, 1947; meeting 150 of July 1, 1947; and meeting 159 of July 17, 1947.
19. *Security Council Official Records*, meeting 170, July 29, 1947.
20. *Security Council Official Records*, meeting 202, September 15, 1947.
21. *New York Times*, October 5, 1947, page 1, column 1; *1947–1948 Yearbook of the United Nations* (Lake Success, N.Y.: United Nations Department of Public Information, 1949), at 65–73.
22. *The Times*, October 11, 1947, page 3f.
23. Id., October 14, 1947, page 3b.
24. O'Ballance, *Greek Civil War*, at 153–56.
25. Id. at 163.
26. *New York Times*, January 8, 1948, page 16, column 2.
27. O'Ballance, *Greek Civil War*, at 173–202.
28. *Inter-American Treaty of Reciprocal Assistance*, 62 Stat. 1681 (1947).
29. Charles D. Ameringer, *Don Pepe* (Albuquerque: University of New Mexico Press, 1978), at 76–84.
30. A. Tom Grunfeld, *The Making of Modern Tibet* (London: Zed Books, Ltd., 1987), at 37–45.
31. Id. at 57.
32. Id. at 61.
33. Id. at 67–72.
34. Id. at 84–88.
35. Id. at 94, 105.
36. *Keesing's Contemporary Archives*, vol. 8 (November 25–December 2, 1950), at 11101–4.
37. Grunfeld, at 94.
38. *Keesing's Contemporary Archives*, vol. 8 (January 27–February 3, 1951), at 11240.
39. Id. (July 21–28, 1951), at 11610.
40. Grunfeld, at 113.
41. Ervand Abrahamian, *Iran: Between Two Revolutions* (Princeton: Princeton University Press, 1982), at 267–73.
42. Richard Cottam, *Nationalism in Iran* (Pittsburgh: University of Pittsburgh Press, 1979), at 223–24.
43. Abrahamian, at 319–21.
44. Cottam, at 230.
45. Abrahamian, at 279.
46. Sepehr Zabih, *The Mossadegh Era* (Chicago: Lake View Press, 1982), at 139–43.
47. Abrahamian, at 279.
48. Cottam, at 225–26.
49. Abrahamian, at 280.
50. Id.
51. Cottam, at 51, 226.
52. Abrahamian, at 274–78.
53. *Keesing's Contemporary Archives*, vol. 10 (February 12–19, 1955), at 14048.
54. Id. at 14142.
55. Mary Jeanne Reid Martz, *The Central American Soccer War: Historical Patterns and Internal Dynamics of OAS Settlement Procedures* (Athens: Ohio University Center for International Studies, 1978), at 34.
56. Id. at 34–35.
57. Id. at 35.
58. Id. at 35–36.
59. Dwight D. Eisenhower, *Waging Peace, 1956–1961* (Garden City, N.Y.: Doubleday & Company, 1965), at 297.

60. Donald S. Zagoria, *The Sino-Soviet Conflict, 1956–1961* (New York: Atheneum, 1969), at 201–7; *Keesing's Contemporary Archives*, vol. 11 (September 13–20, 1958), at 16391.

61. Eisenhower, at 294–95.

62. Id. at 297–304.

63. Zagoria, at 210–17.

64. Eisenhower, at 300, 302.

65. Zagoria, at 17, 175–76.

66. R. B. Smith, *An International History of the Vietnam War*, vol. 1, *Revolution Versus Containment, 1955–1961* (New York: St. Martin's Press, 1983), at 77.

67. Martin Stuart-Fox, *Laos* (Boulder, Colo.: Lynne Rienner Publishers, 1986), at 20–23.

68. Id. at 23.

69. Id. at 23–24.

70. Id. at 24–25.

71. *1959 Yearbook of the United Nations* (New York: Columbia University Press, 1960), at 62–66.

72. Id. at 25; Smith, *International History of the Vietnam War*, vol. 1, at 185–86.

73. Stuart-Fox, at 26–27.

74. Id. at 27.

75. Smith, *International History of the Vietnam War*, vol. 1, at 211–12, 245–46.

76. Id. at 245, 250–51.

77. Id. at 251.

78. R. B. Smith, *An International History of the Vietnam War*, vol. 2, *The Kennedy Strategy* (New York: St. Martin's Press, 1985), at 60–61, 64–65; Stuart-Fox, at 27–28; the states attending the conference were Burma, Cambodia, Canada, the DRV, France, India, Laos, the PRC, Poland, the ROV, the Soviet Union, Thailand, the United Kingdom, and the United States, *Keesing's Contemporary Archives*, vol. 13 (January 27–February 3, 1962), at 18654.

79. Stuart-Fox, at 29–35.

80. *Keesing's Contemporary Archives*, vol. 15 (December 3–10, 1966), at 21746; vol. 17 (July 18–25, 1970), at 24090–91.

81. Stuart-Fox, at 172.

82. *Keesing's Contemporary Archives*, vol. 18 (May 29–June 5, 1971), at 24621–24.

83. Howard M. Epstein, ed., *Revolt in the Congo, 1960–1964* (New York: Facts on File, Inc., 1965), at 6–16.

84. Id. at 12–13.

85. Georges Abi-Saad, *The United Nations Operation in the Congo, 1960–1964* (New York: Oxford University Press, 1978), at 10–12.

86. Epstein, at 14–15.

87. Id. at 36.

88. Richard D. Mahoney, *The Kennedy Policy in the Congo, 1961–1963* (Ann Arbor: University Microfilms International, 1981), at 242–45.

89. Abi-Saad, at 16–18, 32–37.

90. Id. at 124–31.

91. Mahoney, at 175–81.

92. Id. at 1–40.

93. Id. at 53–61a.

94. Id. at 425–28.

95. Id. at 437.

96. Abi-Saad, at 181–91.

97. Epstein, at 154–56.

98. Mahoney, at 164.

99. Epstein, at 12–13.
100. Edgar O'Ballance, *The War in the Yemen* (Hamden, Conn.: Archon Books, 1971), at 68–69.
101. Saeed M. Badeeb, *The Saudi-Egyptian Conflict over North Yemen, 1962–1970* (Boulder, Colo.: Westview Press, 1986), at 36–37.
102. Id. at 34–35; O'Ballance, *War in the Yemen,* at 84.
103. O'Ballance, *War in the Yemen,* at 84–85.
104. Id. at 84–85; *1962 Yearbook of the United Nations* (New York: Columbia University Press, 1964), at 149.
105. O'Ballance, *War in the Yemen,* at 82–83.
106. Id. at 86–87.
107. Id. at 87–88.
108. Badeeb, at 61–64.
109. Robert D. Burrowes, *The Yemen Arab Republic* (Boulder, Colo.: Westview Press, 1987), at 22–26.
110. Id.; O'Ballance, *War in the Yemen,* at 127, 130.
111. O'Ballance, *War in the Yemen,* at 185–86; Badeeb, at 85.
112. O'Ballance, *War in the Yemen,* at 187.
113. Id. at 188, 200.
114. Badeeb, at 85–87.
115. O'Ballance, *War in the Yemen,* at 73, 95.
116. Burrowes, at 27.
117. O'Ballance, *War in the Yemen,* at 75, 76.
118. *1962 UN Yearbook,* at 148–49.
119. Badeeb, at 73, 87 n. 6.
120. Burrowes, at 27.
121. Badeeb, at 72–85.
122. *Keesing's Contemporary Archives,* vol. 14 (May 16–23, 1964), at 20071.
123. D. Bruce Jackson, *Castro, the Kremlin, and Communism in Latin America* (Baltimore: The Johns Hopkins University Press, 1969), at 104–6.
124. *Keesing's Contemporary Archives,* vol. 14 (October 3–10, 1964), at 20336.
125. Jackson, at 104–6.
126. *Keesing's Contemporary Archives,* vol. 16 (July 1–8, 1967), at 22119–20.
127. Martz, at 50–51; *1967 Yearbook of the United Nations* (New York: United Nations Office of Public Information, 1969), at 157–58.
128. *1967 UN Yearbook,* at 157.
129. John Akehurst, *We Won a War* (Salisbury: Michael Russell, 1982), at 13–16.
130. Id. at 19–23, 34–38, 120.
131. Id. at 19–23, 29.
132. Id. at 159–73; *Keesing's Contemporary Archives,* vol. 22 (May 7–14, 1976), at 27716.
133. *1965 Yearbook of the United Nations* (New York: Columbia University Press, 1967), at 227–30; *1966 Yearbook of the United Nations* (New York: United Nations Office of Public Information, 1968), at 187–90; *1967 UN Yearbook,* at 269–72; *1968 Yearbook of the United Nations* (New York: United Nations Office of Public Information, 1971), at 296–98; *1969 Yearbook of the United Nations* (New York: United Nations Office of Public Information, 1972), at 244; *1970 Yearbook of the United Nations* (New York: United Nations Office of Public Information, 1972), at 289–90.
134. *1971 Yearbook of the United Nations* (New York: United Nations Office of Public Information, 1974), at 211–12.
135. Kaye Whiteman, *Chad* (London: Minority Rights Group, 1988), at 1–9; Michael P. Kelley, *A State in Disarray* (Boulder, Colo.: Westview Press, 1986), at 10–11; Keith Somerville, *Foreign Military Intervention in Africa* (New York: St. Martin's Press, 1990), at 62–63.

136. Whiteman, at 7–9; Kelley, at 84–95.

137. Kelley, at 27–38; Somerville, at 62; Mary-Jane Deeb, *Libya's Foreign Policy in North Africa* (Boulder, Colo.: Westview Press, 1991), at 132.

138. Benyamin Neuberger, *Involvement, Invasion, and Withdrawal: Qadhdhāfi's Libya and Chad, 1969–1981* (Tel Aviv: Shiloah Center for Middle Eastern and African Studies, Tel Aviv University, 1982), at 31–34; Somerville, at 63–64.

139. Neuberger, at 34–35; Deeb, at 129.

140. Neuberger, at 35–42.

141. Neuberger, at 43–47; Deeb, at 130–31; *Keesing's Contemporary Archives*, vol. 26 (February 1, 1980), at 30064–67.

142. Neuberger, at 48–50; Deeb, at 131–32.

143. *Keesing's Contemporary Archives*, vol. 28 (September 3, 1982), at 31677–78; Somerville, at 65–69; Neuberger, at 51–58.

144. Kelley, at 19–20, 104–6, 121–22; Deeb, at 154–56; Somerville, at 67–71.

145. Somerville, at 71–82; *Keesing's Record of World Events*, vol. 34 (May 1988) at 35876.

146. *Keesing's Record of World Events*, vol. 34 (June 1988), at 35939; (November 1988), at 36256; vol. 35 (August 1989), at 36841; *Territorial Dispute (Libyan Arab Jamahiriya v. Chad)*, 1994 *International Court of Justice Reports* 6 (February 3); *Agreement Between the Great Socialist People's Libyan Arab Jamahiriya and the Republic of Chad Concerning the Practical Modalities for the Implementation of the Judgment Delivered by the International Court of Justice on 3 February 1994*, April 4, 1994, *International Legal Materials*, vol. 33 (1994), at 619; Security Council Resolution 910, April 14, 1994; Security Council Resolution 915, May 4, 1994.

147. *Keesing's Record of World Events*, vol. 36 (December 1990), at 37907; vol. 37 (October 1991), at 38519; vol. 38 (January 1992), at 38710.

148. *Keesing's Contemporary Archives*, vol. 26 (February 1, 1980), at 30066–67; Somerville, at 64–66.

149. Somerville, at 65–66.

150. *Keesing's Contemporary Archives*, vol. 27 (February 6, 1981), at 30695.

151. Somerville, at 66.

152. *Keesing's Contemporary Archives*, vol. 27 (October 30, 1981), at 31159.

153. Id.

154. Neuberger, at 53–54.

155. Somerville, at 68.

156. Id.; Jean-Pierre Cot, "The Role of the Inter-African Peace-Keeping Force in Chad, 1981–1982," in Antonio Cassese, ed., *The Current Legal Regulation of the Use of Force* (Dordrecht: Martinus Nijhoff Publishers, 1986), at 167, 171–76.

157. Somerville, at 70–82.

158. Id. at 82.

159. Id. at 73, 75.

160. *1983 Yearbook of the United Nations* (New York: United Nations Department of Public Information, 1987), at 180–83.

161. Deeb, at 132, 159; Somerville, at 67.

162. Clinton Bailey, *Jordan's Palestinian Challenge, 1948–1983* (Boulder, Colo.: Westview Press, 1984), at 27–57.

163. Naomi Joy Weinberger, *Syrian Intervention in Lebanon* (New York: Oxford University Press, 1986), at 118–21.

164. Id. at 129–30.

165. Id. at 130.

166. Id.; Bailey, at 58.

167. Bailey, at 58; Weinberger, at 280.

168. Marvin Kalb and Bernard Kalb, *Kissinger* (Boston: Little, Brown and Company, 1974), at 198–208.
169. Id.
170. Weinberger, at 304–5.
171. Bailey, at 58–62.
172. Tony Avirgan and Martha Honey, *War in Uganda* (Westport, Conn.: Lawrence Hill & Company, 1982), at 33–35.
173. Id. at 35.
174. Id. at 35–36.
175. Id. at 36; *Keesing's Contemporary Archives*, vol. 18 (October 28–November 4, 1972), at 25543–45.
176. Avirgan and Honey, at 36; *Keesing's Contemporary Archives*, vol. 18 (October 28–November 4, 1972), at 25543–45.
177. Alex Vines, *RENAMO* (Bloomington: Indiana University Press, 1991), at 11–17.
178. Id. at 17–20.
179. Id. at 20–23.
180. Id. at 23–29; Chester A. Crocker, *High Noon in Southern Africa* (New York: W. W. Norton & Company, 1992), at 248.
181. Vines, at 28–31.
182. Id. at 73–119.
183. Id. at 120–32; *Keesing's Record of World Events*, vol. 38 (October 1992), at 39129; (December 1992), at 39227; vol. 39 (February 1993), at 39303.
184. Vines, at 27, 42–52, 126–27.
185. Id. at 127.
186. Id. at 61–67.
187. Id. at 53–60.
188. John A. Marcum, *The Angolan Revolution* (Cambridge, Mass.: The MIT Press, 1978), vol. 2, at 245–48, 252–53, 257–60.
189. Id. at 255, 258–59.
190. Id. at 258.
191. Id. at 266–71.
192. Id. at 264–66.
193. Id. at 272–75.
194. Id. at 273–75.
195. Id. at 259.
196. Id. at 272–78.
197. Id. at 259–60.
198. Id. at 262.
199. *Keesing's Contemporary Archives*, vol. 22 (December 22–31, 1975), at 27500.
200. *1976 Yearbook of the United Nations* (New York: United Nations Office of Public Information, 1979), at 178–79.
201. Id. at 177–78.
202. Herbert Ekwe-Ekwe, *Conflict and Intervention in Africa* (New York: St. Martin's Press, 1990), at 112–14.
203. Id. at 115–18; George E. Moose, "French Military Policy in Africa," in William J. Foltz and Henry S. Bienen, *Arms and the African* (New Haven: Yale University Press, 1985), at 68–70.
204. Ekwe-Ekwe, at 113–14.
205. Moose, at 68–70.
206. Ekwe-Ekwe, at 127.
207. Id. at 115–16.

208. *Keesing's Contemporary Archives*, vol. 23 (June 3, 1977), at 28376.
209. Moose, at 69.
210. Ekwe-Ekwe, at 122, 126.
211. *Keesing's Contemporary Archives*, vol. 23 (June 17, 1977), at 28399–400.
212. Deeb, at 128.
213. Id.
214. *Keesing's Contemporary Archives*, vol. 26 (May 23, 1980), at 30262–64.
215. Hiram A. Ruiz, *Uprooted Liberians: Casualties of a Brutal War* (Washington, D.C.: American Council for Nationalities Service, 1992), at 4–10; *New York Times*, September 30, 1990, §1, page 3, column 4; October 3, 1990, page 20, column 1; October 28, 1990, §1, page 17, column 1.
216. Ruiz, at 10, 23–26.
217. "Liberia: Mediators Hold Breath on Ceasefire Agreement," Inter Press Service, July 26, 1993, available in LEXIS, Nexis Library, Inpres File; *New York Times*, July 18, 1993, §1, page 6, column 1; "Liberian Warlords to Explain Disarmament Holdup," Reuters World Service, June 1, 1994, available in LEXIS, Nexis Library, Curnws File.
218. *The Guardian*, August 26, 1995, page 15; *New York Times*, August 20, 1995, §1, page 17; *New York Times*, September 1, 1995, §A, page 1.
219. *New York Times*, January 16, 1996, §A, page 2; February 1, 1996, §A, page 9.
220. Security Council Resolution 788, November 19, 1992.
221. Security Council Resolution 813, March 26, 1993.
222. Security Council Resolution 866, September 22, 1993; *Eleventh Progress Report of the Secretary-General on the United Nations Observers Mission in Liberia*, U.N. Doc. S/1995/473, June 10, 1995; *Twelfth Progress Report of the Secretary-General on the United Nations Observers Mission in Liberia*, U.N. Doc. S/1995/781, September 9, 1995.
223. Security Council Resolution 1014, September 15, 1994.
224. "Liberia," Inter Press Service, July 26, 1993.
225. "U.S. Still Backs African Troops in Liberia—Cohen," Reuters, Limited, November 12, 1992, available in LEXIS, Nexis Library, Reuters North American Wire File.
226. *Christian Science Monitor*, December 1, 1992, page 5.

## Chapter 7

1. Richard H. Immerman, *The CIA in Guatemala* (Austin: University of Texas Press, 1982), at 101–9.
2. Id. at 138–43, 154.
3. Id. at 157–60.
4. Id. at 161.
5. Id. at 161–68, 173–77.
6. *1954 Yearbook of the United Nations* (New York: Columbia University Press, 1955), at 96–99.
7. Immerman, at 171–72.
8. Immerman, at 173.
9. Mary Jeanne Reid Martz, *The Central American Soccer War: Historical Patterns and Internal Dynamics of OAS Settlement Procedures* (Athens: Ohio University Center for International Studies, 1978), at 57–58.
10. Immerman, at 144–49.
11. Martz, at 58.
12. Immerman, at 4–6.

13. János Radványi, *Hungary and the Superpowers: The 1956 Revolution and Realpolitik* (Stanford: Hoover Institution Press, 1972), at 6–7.
14. Id. at 7.
15. Id.
16. Id.
17. Id. at 12.
18. Id. at 12–13.
19. Id. at 13.
20. Id.
21. *Keesing's Contemporary Archives*, vol. 10 (November 10–17, 1956), at 15192–93.
22. Radványi, at 13.
23. *Keesing's Contemporary Archives*, vol. 10 (November 10–17, 1956), at 15193.
24. *1956 Yearbook of the United Nations* (New York: Columbia University Press, 1957), at 67–96.
25. Id. at 89.
26. Id. at 83–89, 94–96.
27. Id. at 82–89, 94–95; *1957 Yearbook of the United Nations* (New York: Columbia University Press, 1958), at 66–67; *1958 Yearbook of the United Nations* (New York: Columbia University Press, 1959), at 70–71; *1959 Yearbook of the United Nations* (New York: Columbia University Press, 1960), at 50–51.
28. *1957 UN Yearbook*, at 67.
29. *1958 UN Yearbook*, at 70–71.
30. Radványi, at 88–93, 140–50.
31. Id. at 11–12.
32. *Department of State Bulletin*, vol. 36 (March 18, 1957), at 441–42.
33. *1957 UN Yearbook*, at 60–62.
34. Trumbull Higgins, *The Perfect Failure* (New York: W. W. Norton & Company, 1987), at 47–51.
35. Id.
36. Id. at 50–57.
37. Id. at 57, 61–64.
38. Id. at 81–82, 85.
39. Id. at 126.
40. Id. at 61–62, 90, 127.
41. Id. at 126.
42. Id. at 129–31.
43. Id. at 131–32.
44. Id. at 135–50.
45. Richard E. Welch, Jr., *Response to Revolution* (Chapel Hill: The University of North Carolina Press, 1985), at 91.
46. *1960 Yearbook of the United Nations* (New York: United Nations Office of Public Information, 1961), at 160.
47. Id. at 160–61.
48. Id. at 160–62.
49. Id. at 163.
50. Id. at 160–62.
51. See, e.g., *New York Times*, April 17, 1961, page 17, column 4 (Venezuela); April 20, 1961, page 11, column 4 (Yugoslavia and UAR, offering unspecified help); April 23, 1961, page 26, columns 1–2 (Argentina and Brazil).
52. Id., April 20, 1961, page 12.

53. Elie Abel, *The Missile Crisis* (New York: J. B. Lippincott Company, 1966), at 28–32.
54. Id. at 48, 51–52, 60.
55. Id. at 35–36, 48, 60.
56. Abram Chayes, *The Cuban Missile Crisis* (New York: Oxford University Press, 1974), at 8–11.
57. Abel, at 60–63.
58. Foregoing taken from id. at 69, 73, 80–81, 87–89; Chayes, at 15–16, 30–32, 44–45; Lester H. Brune, *The Missile Crisis of October 1962* (Claremont, Calif.: Regina Books, 1985), at 48–51.
59. Abel, at 94.
60. Id. at 121–23.
61. Chayes, at 68.
62. *Keesing's Contemporary Archives*, vol. 13 (November 3–10, 1962), at 19062.
63. Id.
64. Brune, at 60; Chayes, at 74.
65. *1962 Yearbook of the United Nations* (New York: Columbia University Press, 1964), at 104–8.
66. Abel, at 141–42.
67. Id. at 161.
68. Id. at 171–72.
69. Id. at 173–99.
70. Id. at 201–8; Brune, at 67–71; Michael R. Beschloss, *The Crisis Years: Kennedy and Khrushchev, 1960–1963* (New York: Edward Burlingame Books, 1991), at 535–37.
71. Brune, at 71–72.
72. *1962 UN Yearbook*, at 108.
73. Abel, at 136–38.
74. *Keesing's Contemporary Archives*, vol. 13 (November 17–24, 1962), at 19090.
75. Abel, at 149.
76. *1962 UN Yearbook*, at 108, 111.
77. *Keesing's Contemporary Archives*, vol. 14 (April 18–25, 1964), at 20024.
78. Abraham F. Lowenthal, *The Dominican Intervention* (Cambridge: Harvard University Press, 1972), at 36–54.
79. Id. at 54–60.
80. Id. at 60–61.
81. Id. at 74–97.
82. Id. at 70–79, 140–41.
83. Id. at 96–103.
84. *Keesing's Contemporary Archives*, vol. 15 (June 26–July 3, 1965), at 20814–17.
85. Lowenthal, at 104.
86. *Department of State Bulletin*, vol. 52 (May 17, 1965), at 738.
87. Lowenthal, at 106–12.
88. Bruce Palmer, Jr., *Intervention in the Caribbean* (Lexington: The University Press of Kentucky, 1989), at 4–6.
89. *Department of State Bulletin*, vol. 52 (May 17, 1965), at 742–43.
90. Id. at 744–48.
91. Id. at 739–41.
92. Palmer, at 34–35.
93. Lowenthal, at 118.
94. Id.
95. Palmer, at 37.

96. Lowenthal, at 124.
97. Id. at 123–30.
98. Palmer, at 46–47.
99. Id. at 47–48.
100. Id. at 51.
101. *Department of State Bulletin*, vol. 52 (May 31, 1965), at 857–63.
102. Id. at 862.
103. Palmer, at 71.
104. Id. at 69–71.
105. Id. at 72.
106. Id. at 77.
107. Id. at 51–60.
108. *Department of State Bulletin*, vol. 52 (June 21, 1965), at 1018.
109. Palmer, at 58.
110. Id. at 86–138.
111. Id. at 82–83.
112. Id. at 100–118.
113. Martz, at 62–64.
114. *1965 Yearbook of the United Nations* (New York: Columbia University Press, 1967), at 140–52.
115. *General Assembly Official Records*, 20th Session, meeting 1335 (September 24, 1965), at 5 (Soviet Union); meeting 1337 (September 27, 1965), at 9 (Czechoslovakia); meeting 1338 (September 27, 1965), at 8 (Chile); meeting 1340 (September 28, 1965), at 4 (Ecuador) and 6 (Dahomey); meeting 1344 (September 30, 1965), at 4 (Albania); meeting 1346 (October 1, 1965), at 8 (Mexico); meeting 1349 (October 5, 1965), at 7 (Mongolia); meeting 1352 (October 7, 1965), at 3 (Ukrainian SSR); meeting 1356 (October 11, 1965), at 6 (Congo—Brazzaville); meeting 1358 (October 12, 1965), at 15 (Poland); meeting 1363 (October 15, 1965), at 3 (Bulgaria) and 10 (Cuba).
116. H. Gordon Skilling, *Czechoslovakia's Interrupted Revolution* (Princeton: Princeton University Press, 1976), at 180–292, 617–50.
117. Id. at 292–330, 650–75.
118. Id. at 713–15.
119. Id. at 718–30.
120. Id. at 716–18, 729.
121. *New York Times*, August 22, 1968, page 1, column 3.
122. *The Times*, August 24, 1968, page 7e.
123. Richard M. Goodman, "The Invasion of Czechoslovakia: 1968," *International Lawyer*, vol. 4 (October 1969), at 42, 43–44.
124. *General Assembly Official Records*, 23d Session, meeting 1677 (October 2, 1968), at 14 (Sweden); meeting 1679 (October 3, 1968), at 2 (Haiti); meeting 1680 (October 3, 1968), at 1 (Indonesia); meeting 1681 (October 4, 1968), at 5 (Netherlands), 9 (Pakistan), and 13 (Venezuela); meeting 1682 (October 4, 1968), at 1 (Japan) and 8 (El Salvador); meeting 1684 (October 7, 1968), at 5 (Greece) and 11 (Finland); meeting 1685 (October 8, 1968), at 9 (Chile); meeting 1686 (October 8, 1968), at 7 (Israel) and 14 (Iceland); meeting 1687 (October 9, 1968), at 1 (Italy), 5 (Canada), and 9 (Australia); meeting 1688 (October 9, 1968), at 7 (Luxembourg) and 10 (Norway); meeting 1689 (October 10, 1968), at 2 (Belgium) and 6 (Thailand); meeting 1690 (October 10, 1968), at 11 (Mauritania); meeting 1691 (October 11, 1968), at 4 (Albania); meeting 1692 (October 11, 1968), at 10 (Bolivia) and 19 (Honduras); meeting 1694 (October 14, 1968), at 3 (Botswana) and 6 (New Zealand); meeting 1696 (October 15, 1968), at 1 (Philippines), 8 (Dahomey), and 21 (Kenya); meeting 1697 (October 16, 1968), at 12 (Argentina); meeting 1701

(October 21, 1968), at 5 (Malaysia); meeting 1702 (October 22, 1968), at 9 (Barbados); meeting 1703 (October 22, 1968), at 1 (Republic of China), 4 (Democratic Republic of the Congo), and 10 (Burundi); meeting 1705 (October 23, 1968), at 15 (Paraguay) and 18 (Nicaragua).

125. Goodman, at 44.

126. *1968 Yearbook of the United Nations* (New York: United Nations Office of Public Information, 1971), at 300–303.

127. *Keesing's Contemporary Archives*, vol. 25 (November 16, 1979), at 29933–34.

128. Id.

129. George E. Moose, "French Military Policy in Africa," in William J. Foltz and Henry S. Bienen, *Arms and the African* (New Haven: Yale University Press, 1985), at 80–82.

130. Fernando R. Tesón, *Humanitarian Intervention: An Inquiry into Law and Morality* (Dobbs Ferry, N.Y.: Transnational Publishers, Inc., 1988), at 177.

131. Moose, at 82–84.

132. Tesón, at 175–78.

133. Robert A. Pastor, *Condemned to Repetition* (Princeton: Princeton University Press, 1987), at 216–17.

134. Roy Gutman, *Banana Diplomacy* (New York: Simon and Schuster, 1988), at 43, 45–48.

135. Id. at 52–56; Pastor, at 237–38.

136. Pastor, at 223–33.

137. Id. at 236–37; Gutman, at 55–57.

138. Gutman, at 72–87; Pastor, at 236.

139. Pastor, at 238–40.

140. Gutman, at 150–51.

141. Id. at 140–41.

142. Id. at 157–58, 170–73, 194–200.

143. Id. at 200–203, 266, 304, 328–29.

144. Id. at 324–34.

145. Id. at 337–60; Jack Child, *The Central American Peace Process, 1983–1991* (Boulder, Colo.: Lynne Rienner Publishers, 1992), at 46–47, 53–55.

146. Gutman, at 150.

147. See *Case Concerning Military and Paramilitary Activities In and Against Nicaragua (Nicaragua v. United States)*, 1986, *International Court of Justice Reports*, at 14, 70–72.

148. Id. at 324.

149. Child, at 15–47.

150. Id. at 61–95.

151. *1983 Yearbook of the United Nations* (New York: United Nations Department of Public Information, 1987), at 200–9; *1984 Yearbook of the United Nations* (New York: United Nations Department of Public Information, 1988), at 203–4, 207–12.

152. *1984 UN Yearbook*, at 207–9.

153. Gutman, at 201–2.

154. *1985 Yearbook of the United Nations* (Dordrecht: Martinus Nijhoff Publishers, 1989), at 210–19.

155. *Case Concerning Military and Paramilitary Activities In and Against Nicaragua (Nicaragua v. United States)*, 1986 ICJ Reports, at 14.

156. *1986 Yearbook of the United Nations* (Dordrecht: Martinus Nijhoff Publishers, 1990), at 180–98.

157. *1987 Yearbook of the United Nations* (Dordrecht: Martinus Nijhoff Publishers, 1992), at 190–93.

158. Mahnaz Ispahani, "India's Role in Sri Lanka's Ethnic Conflict," in Ariel E. Levite, Bruce W. Jentleson, and Larry Berman, eds., *Foreign Military Intervention* (New York: Columbia University Press, 1992), at 209, 211–15.

159. Id. at 215–18.

160. Id. at 218–19; "The Indian Supply Drop into Sri Lanka: Nonmilitary Humanitarian Aid and the Troubling Idea of Intervention," *Connecticut Journal of International Law*, vol. 3 (Spring 1988), at 417, 424–25.

161. Ispahani, at 220–21.

162. Id. at 221–32.

163. Rajesh Kadian, *India's Sri Lanka Fiasco* (New Delhi, Bombay: Vision Books, 1990), at 84–85.

164. Id. at 10.

165. Ispahani, at 219, 221; *Department of State Bulletin*, vol. 88 (January 1988), at 41–42.

166. Ispahani, at 229.

167. Scott Davidson, *Grenada* (Brookfield, Mass.: Avebury, 1987), at 4–13.

168. Id. at 17–38.

169. Id. at 44–46, 55–57.

170. Id. at 57–73.

171. Id. at 73–75.

172. Id. at 79–85, 174–75; John Norton Moore, "Grenada and the International Double Standard," *American Journal of International Law*, vol. 78 (January 1984), at 145, 152; *Christian Science Monitor*, June 12, 1985, page 9.

173. Davidson, at 86–88.

174. Id. at 90–119.

175. Id. at 160.

176. Id. at 138–47; *1983 UN Yearbook*, at 211–15.

177. *1984 UN Yearbook*, at 376.

178. Jennifer Miller, "International Intervention—The United States Invasion of Panama," *Harvard International Law Journal*, vol. 31 (Spring 1990), at 633–35; John Quigley, "The Legality of the United States Invasion of Panama," *Yale Journal of International Law*, vol. 15 (Summer 1990), at 276, 278–81; Abraham D. Sofaer, "The Legality of the United States Action in Panama," *Columbia Journal of Transnational Law*, vol. 29 (1991), at 281, 291.

179. Miller, at 635, 641.

180. Quigley, at 291, 294, 299–300.

181. *New York Times*, December 24, 1989, §1, page 8, column 2.

182. Id., December 30, 1989, page 6, column 1.

183. Louis Henkin, "The Invasion of Panama Under International Law: A Gross Violation," *Columbia Journal of Transnational Law*, vol. 29 (1991), at 293, 312.

## Chapter 8

1. John Damis, *Conflict in Northwest Africa* (Stanford: Hoover Institution Press, 1983), at 38–40.

2. Id. at 14–25.

3. Id. at 30.

4. Id. at 53–54.

5. Id. at 30.

6. Id. at 55–56.

7. Id. at 34–38, 57–58.

8. *Western Sahara*, 1975 *International Court of Justice Reports*, at 12, 68, ¶162.

9. Damis, at 60, 67.

10. *1975 Yearbook of the United Nations* (New York: United Nations Office of Public Information, 1978), at 188–89.

11. Damis, at 73–75.
12. Id. at 71, 73.
13. Id. at 96–98.
14. *Keesing's Record of World Events*, vol. 34 (June 1988), at 35995–96.
15. Id. (September 1988), at 36131; vol. 36 (January 1990), at 37220–21; vol. 37 (September 1991), at 38456–57; vol. 39 (Reference Section, 1993), at R146.
16. Id., vol. 39 (March 1993), at 39393; "U.N. Says W. Sahara Voting Process Delayed Again," Reuters World Service, June 17, 1994, available in LEXIS, Nexis Library, Curnws File; "U.N. Denies Accusing Morocco of Delaying Vote," Reuters World Service, June 18, 1994, available in LEXIS, Nexis Library, Curnws File; Security Council Resolution 1033, December 19, 1995; *Secretary-General's Report on Western Sahara*, U.N. Doc. S/1996/43, January 19, 1996.
17. *Keesing's Contemporary Archives*, vol. 29 (April 1983), at 32101–2, 32111.
18. *Keesing's Record of World Events*, vol. 36 (January 1990), at 37220–21.
19. Id., vol. 34 (June 1988), at 35996–97.
20. Damis, at 114–19.
21. Id. at 119–27.
22. Id. at 108–13.
23. *Keesing's Record of World Events*, vol. 34 (June 1988), at 35995–96.
24. Damis, at 127–31.
25. Id. at 122.
26. *Keesing's Record of World Events*, vol. 34 (June 1988), at 35995–96.
27. Finngeir Hiorth, *Timor: Past and Present* (Queensland, Australia: James Cook University of North Queensland, 1985), at 21–27.
28. Id. at 24–25, 30–34, 36; James Dunn, *Timor: A People Betrayed* (Auckland, New Zealand: The Jacaranda Press, 1983), at 297–99.
29. Hiorth, at 32.
30. *1975 UN Yearbook*, at 859.
31. Id. at 43–45.
32. Id. at 865–66.
33. *1976 Yearbook of the United Nations* (New York: United Nations Office of Public Information, 1979), at 752–54.
34. *1978 Yearbook of the United Nations* (New York: United Nations Office of Public Information, 1981), at 869.
35. *1987 Yearbook of the United Nations* (Dordrecht: Martinus Nijhoff Publishers, 1992), at 1028.
36. Hiorth, at 58.
37. Id. at 36.
38. Dunn, at 277.
39. *Department of State Bulletin*, vol. 77 (September 5, 1977), at 324–26.
40. *Keesing's Contemporary Archives*, vol. 24 (July 7, 1978), at 29075.
41. *Keesing's Record of World Events*, vol. 35 (December 1989), at 37124.
42. *The Times*, April 12, 1985, page 5a.
43. Dunn, at 362.
44. *Keesing's Record of World Events*, vol. 34 (May 1988), at 35903; vol. 35 (January 1989), at 36395.
45. *The Times*, April 29, 1993; *1991 Yearbook of the United Nations* (Dordrecht: Martinus Nijhoff Publishers, 1992), at 819; *Case Concerning East Timor (Portugal v. Australia)*, 1995 *International Court of Justice Reports* (June 30, 1995), at 90.
46. Hiorth, at 36.

## Chapter 9

1. Sir Clarmont Skrine, *World War in Iran* (London: Constable, 1962), at 109–10.
2. Id. at 231–35.
3. George Lenczowski, *Russia and the West in Iran, 1918–1948* (Ithaca: Cornell University Press, 1949), at 288, 295.
4. Id. at 286–96.
5. *The Times*, March 4, 1946, page 4a.
6. Lenczowski, at 297.
7. Id.
8. Id. at 297–98.
9. Skrine, at 236.
10. *The Times*, March 18, 1946, page 4a.
11. Id., March 28, 1946, page 4b.
12. Id., April 5, 1946, page 5b.
13. Lenczowski, at 298–300.
14. Id. at 300–303.
15. Id. at 301.
16. Id. at 308–12.
17. Id. at 304–6.
18. *Corfu Channel Case (United Kingdom v. Albania)*, 1949 *International Court of Justice Reports* (April 9), at 1, 4, 12–15, 34–35.
19. W. Michael Reisman, "Article 2(4): The Use of Force in Contemporary International Law," American Society of International Law, Washington, D.C., 1986, in *Proceedings of the 78th Annual Meeting*, at 74, 83.
20. Tom Little, *South Arabia: Arena of Conflict* (New York: Praeger, 1968), at 19.
21. Id. at 20.
22. Id. at 20–21.
23. Id. at 37–39; Edgar O'Ballance, *The War in the Yemen* (Hamden, Conn.: Archon Books, 1971), at 49–50.
24. Naomi Schweisow, "Mediation," in Evan Luard, ed., *The International Regulation of Frontier Disputes* (New York: Praeger, 1970), at 141, 144–45.
25. Id. at 145–47.
26. Id. at 147.
27. *Keesing's Contemporary Archives*, vol. 10 (November 12–19, 1955), at 14534–35.
28. *1955 Yearbook of the United Nations* (New York: Columbia University Press, 1956), at 80.
29. Id.
30. Schweisow, at 147–48; John B. Allcock, ed., *Border and Territorial Disputes*, 3d ed. (Harlow, Essex: Longman, 1992) (hereafter *Border Disputes 3d*), at 399.
31. Roger M. Smith, *Cambodia's Foreign Policy* (Ithaca: Cornell University Press, 1965), at 50.
32. Id. at 140–41.
33. Id. at 141–51.
34. Little, at 41–46.
35. Id. at 45–46.
36. *1954 Yearbook of the United Nations* (New York: Columbia University Press, 1955), at 309.
37. Little, at 49–52.
38. *1957 Yearbook of the United Nations* (New York: Columbia University Press, 1958), at 59–60.
39. Little, at 44, 48.

40. Id. at 48–49.

41. Abd el-Fattah I. S. Baddour, *Sudanese-Egyptian Relations* (The Hague: Martinus Nijhoff, 1960), at 194–200; *1958 Yearbook of the United Nations* (New York: Columbia University Press, 1959), at 82–83; *Keesing's Contemporary Archives*, vol. 11 (March 15–22, 1958), at 16075.

42. Mary Jeanne Reid Martz, *The Central American Soccer War: Historical Patterns and Internal Dynamics of OAS Settlement Procedures* (Athens: Ohio University Center for International Studies, 1978), at 67–69; *Keesing's Contemporary Archives*, vol. 11 (June 1–8, 1957), at 15574; *New York Times*, May 6, 1957, page 1, column 2; May 11, 1957, page 9, column 6; June 12, 1957, page 3, column 5; June 24, 1957, page 5, column 4; November 19, 1960, page 1, column 8; March 14, 1961, page 26, column 1.

43. S.M.M. Qureshi, "Pakhtunistan: The Frontier Dispute Between Afghanistan and Pakistan," *Pacific Affairs*, vol. 39 (Spring–Summer 1966), at 99.

44. Id.

45. *Keesing's Contemporary Archives*, vol. 13 (June 24–July 1, 1961), at 18172.

46. *New York Times*, September 8, 1961, page 4, column 6.

47. Id., October 6, 1961, page 3, column 5.

48. Neville Maxwell, *India's China War* (London: Jonathan Cape, 1970), at 1–74.

49. Id. at 80, 97–102, 126–29.

50. Id. at 97–98, 122–25, 211–17.

51. Id. at 107–11.

52. Id. at 115–20.

53. Id. at 221–23, 232–40, 291–92.

54. Id. at 236–37, 243, 255.

55. Id. at 294–96.

56. Id. at 300–304.

57. Id.

58. Id. at 325–28.

59. Id. at 313, 324.

60. Id. at 336–39.

61. Id. at 340–42.

62. Id. at 343–46, 351–53.

63. Id. at 357–58.

64. Id. at 358–71, 393–408.

65. Id. at 417–18.

66. Id. at 427–28.

67. *Border Disputes 3d*, at 435–37.

68. Maxwell, at 371–72.

69. Id. at 372–73.

70. Id.

71. Id. at 374–76.

72. Id. at 364, 378, 384–85.

73. Steven A. Hoffman, *India and the China Crisis* (Berkeley and Los Angeles: University of California Press, 1990), at 166–67, 216.

74. Maxwell, at 365.

75. *Asian Recorder*, vol. 8 (November 26–December 2, 1962), at 4915–16; (December 10–16, 1962), at 4932.

76. Maxwell, at 364–65.

77. Id. at 365–67.

78. *Keesing's Contemporary Archives*, vol. 14 (March 7–14, 1964), at 19939–42; vol. 15 (January 1–9, 1965), at 20507–8; vol. 17 (August 8–15, 1970), at 24125; vol. 18 (July 15–22, 1972), at 25372.

79. Id., vol. 14 (March 7–14, 1964), at 19939–42.

80. "The Congo Crisis 1964: A Case Study in Humanitarian Intervention," *Virginia Journal of International Law*, vol. 12 (March 1972), at 261–62.

81. *Keesing's Contemporary Archives*, vol. 15 (February 6–13, 1965), at 20563–64.

82. "Congo Crisis," at 262–63, 267 n. 31.

83. Howard M. Epstein, ed., *Revolt in the Congo, 1960–1964* (New York: Facts on File, Inc., 1965), at 163.

84. Id. at 164–65.

85. Thomas M. Franck and Nigel S. Rodley, "After Bangladesh: The Law of Humanitarian Intervention by Military Force," *American Journal of International Law*, vol. 67 (April 1973), at 275, 288–89.

86. *Keesing's Contemporary Archives*, vol. 15 (February 6–13, 1965), at 20565–66.

87. *1964 Yearbook of the United Nations* (New York: Columbia University Press, 1966), at 95–97.

88. Id. at 97–99.

89. Id. at 99–101.

90. "Congo Crisis," at 269–73.

91. Richard Wich, *Sino-Soviet Crisis Politics* (Cambridge: Harvard University Council on East Asian Studies, 1980), at 97; Tai Sung An, *The Sino-Soviet Territorial Dispute* (Philadelphia: The Westminster Press, 1973), at 1–45.

92. Wich, at 173–80; Tai Sung An, at 105–6.

93. Wich, at 192–213.

94. Tai Sung An, at 72–79.

95. Wich, at 163–70.

96. Id. at 110–12.

97. Id. at 101, 173–76.

98. Id. at 178–79.

99. Id. at 75–100, 268–83; Tai Sung An, at 91–101.

100. *The Times*, March 21, 1969, page 6a.

101. Alastair White, *El Salvador* (New York: Praeger, 1973), at 181–90; James Dunkerly, *The Long War* (London: Junction Books, 1982), at 82.

102. Dunkerly, at 82–83; Martz, at 74.

103. Martz, at 74–81.

104. *1969 United Nations Yearbook* (New York: United Nations Office of Public Information, 1972), at 183.

105. Martz, at 93.

106. Robin Bidwell, *The Two Yemens* (Boulder, Colo.: Westview Press, 1983), at 255–61; *Keesing's Contemporary Archives*, vol. 19 (January 1–7, 1973), at 25654–55.

107. *Keesing's Contemporary Archives*, vol. 19 (September 10–16, 1973), at 26086.

108. *1973 Yearbook of the United Nations* (New York: United Nations Office of Public Information, 1976), at 250–52, 946–48.

109. *Keesing's Contemporary Archives*, vol. 20 (March 4–10, 1974), at 26388–89.

110. *1974 Yearbook of the United Nations* (New York: United Nations Office of Public Information, 1977), at 187–88.

111. *Keesing's Contemporary Archives*, vol. 20 (March 4–10, 1974), at 26388–89; *1974 UN Yearbook*, at 188, 1085.

112. Alan J. Day, ed., *Border and Territorial Disputes*, 2d ed. (Detroit: Gale Research Company, 1987), at 105–10.

113. *Border Disputes 3d*, at 532–36.

114. *1984 Yearbook of the United Nations* (New York: United Nations Department of Public Information, 1986), at 221.

115. Id. at 222–23.
116. Thomas E. Behuniak, "The Seizure and Recovery of the S.S. Mayaguez: A Legal Analysis of United States Claims, Part 1," *Military Law Review*, vol. 82 (Fall 1978), at 41, 44–82.
117. Id. at 160–61.
118. Id. at 52–54.
119. Id. at 164–66.
120. *Keesing's Contemporary Archives*, vol. 21 (July 21–27, 1975), at 27239.
121. *Facts on File World News Digest*, May 17, 1975, at 332 D1.
122. Id.
123. *Asian Recorder*, vol. 21 (June 18–24, 1975), at 12635.
124. *New York Times*, May 16, 1975, page 16.
125. Id.
126. Chaim Herzog, *The Arab-Israeli Wars* (New York: Vintage Books, 1984), at 327–36.
127. *1976 Yearbook of the United Nations* (New York: United Nations Office of Public Information, 1979), at 315–20.
128. *African Recorder*, vol. 15 (July 15–28, 1976), at 4305; *New York Times*, July 6, 1976, page 3.
129. John Worrall, "Mounting Dangers for Latest U.S. 'Ally' in Africa," *U.S. News & World Report*, August 2, 1976, at 49.
130. Herbert Ekwe-Ekwe, *Conflict and Intervention in Africa* (New York: St. Martin's Press, 1990), at 115–19.
131. George E. Moose, "French Military Policy in Africa," in William J. Foltz and Henry S. Bienen, *Arms and the African* (New Haven: Yale University Press, 1985), at 70–72; *Keesing's Contemporary Archives*, vol. 24 (August 11, 1978), at 29125–31.
132. Moose, at 71–72.
133. Ekwe-Ekwe, at 127.
134. Id. at 118–19.
135. Moose, at 70–71.
136. Ekwe-Ekwe, at 127.
137. Id. at 127–28.
138. Mary-Jane Deeb, *Libya's Foreign Policy in North Africa* (Boulder, Colo.: Westview Press, 1991), at 91–95.
139. Id. at 92–94, 95–98.
140. Id. at 98.
141. Id. at 106–9.
142. Id. at 109; *Keesing's Contemporary Archives*, vol. 23 (December 9, 1977), at 28710–11.
143. *Keesing's Contemporary Archives*, vol. 23 (December 9, 1977), at 28710–11.
144. *Keesing's Contemporary Archives*, vol. 24 (November 10, 1978), at 29305.
145. King C. Chen, *China's War with Vietnam, 1979* (Stanford: Hoover Institution Press, 1987), at 1–68; Pao-Min Chang, *The Sino-Vietnamese Territorial Dispute* (New York: Praeger, 1986), at 20–48.
146. Chen, at 85.
147. Pao-Min Chang, at 47–51.
148. Chen, at 85–89.
149. Id. at 89–93.
150. Id. at 105–14.
151. *Border Disputes 3d*, at 467–72; Steven J. Hood, *Dragons Entangled* (Armonk, N.Y.: M. E. Sharpe, Inc., 1992), at 64–65, 74–75, 79.
152. Id. at 107–8, 109–10; *Keesing's Contemporary Archives*, vol. 25 (October 12, 1979), at 29872–73.
153. Chen, at 135–36; *Keesing's Contemporary Archives*, vol. 25 (October 12, 1979), at 29872–73.

154. Chen, at 112.
155. Id. at 109.
156. Bidwell, at 317–20; Manfred W. Wenner, *The Yemen Arab Republic* (Boulder, Colo.: Westview Press, 1991), at 151–52; *Keesing's Contemporary Archives*, vol. 26 (April 18, 1980), at 30197–99.
157. Bidwell, at 317–19.
158. *Keesing's Contemporary Archives*, vol. 26 (April 18, 1980), at 30197–99.
159. Paul B. Ryan, *The Iranian Rescue Mission* (Annapolis: Naval Institute Press, 1985), at 9.
160. Gary Sick, *All Fall Down* (New York: Random House, 1985), at 209–79.
161. Ryan, at 1–2, 19, 125.
162. Id. at 3, 12–13, 49; Sick, at 287–88, 292–96.
163. Ryan, at 99–100; Sick, at 287, 293; *Keesing's Contemporary Archives*, vol. 26 (October 24, 1980), at 30534.
164. *Border Disputes 3d*, at 588–90.
165. *Keesing's Contemporary Archives*, vol. 27 (March 13, 1981), at 30763–64.
166. Id.; *Keesing's Record of World Events*, vol. 37 (May 1991), at 38256.
167. *Border Disputes 3d*, at 227–29.
168. Dan McKinnon, *Bullseye One Reactor* (San Diego: House of Hits, 1987), at 60–68; Amos Perlmutter, Michael Handel, Uri Bar-Joseph, *Two Minutes Over Baghdad* (London: Vallentine, Mitchell & Company, Ltd., 1982), at 148–49; Uri Shoham, "The Israeli Aerial Raid upon the Iraqi Nuclear Reactor and the Right of Self-Defense," *Military Law Review*, vol. 109 (Summer 1985), at 191, 207–13.
169. McKinnon, at 96–100, 103–7; Shoham, at 213–17.
170. Shoham, at 221–22.
171. Id. at 191, 223; McKinnon, at 105.
172. Perlmutter et al., at 175.
173. McKinnon, at 190–95; *Keesing's Contemporary Archives*, vol. 29 (January 1983), at 31908–9; *1981 Yearbook of the United Nations* (New York: United Nations Department of Public Information, 1985), at 275–83; *1982 Yearbook of the United Nations* (New York: United Nations Department of Public Information, 1986), at 906.
174. *1981 UN Yearbook*, at 275–81.
175. *Keesing's Contemporary Archives*, vol. 29 (January 1983), at 31908–9.
176. Brian L. Davis, *Qaddafi, Terrorism, and the Origins of the U.S. Attack on Libya* (New York: Praeger, 1990), at 14, 47, 103–4; Steven R. Ratner, "The Gulf of Sidra Incident of 1981: The Lawfulness of Peacetime Aerial Engagements," in W. Michael Reisman and Andrew R. Willard, eds., *International Incidents* (Princeton: Princeton University Press, 1988), at 181, 186–87, 197.
177. Ratner, at 196–99; *Keesing's Contemporary Archives*, vol. 27 (November 13, 1981), at 31182; *1981 UN Yearbook*, at 360–61.
178. *Keesing's Contemporary Archives*, vol. 29 (December 1983), at 32592.
179. Antonio Cassese, *Terrorism, Politics, and the Law* (Princeton: Princeton University Press, 1989), at 23–39, 52.
180. Id. at 60–62.
181. Gregory V. Gooding, "Incident—Fighting Terrorism in the 1980s: The Interception of the *Achille Lauro* Hijackers," *Yale Journal of International Law*, vol. 12 (Winter 1987), at 158, 168–69.
182. Id. at 169–75.
183. Id. at 175–76.
184. *1986 Yearbook of the United Nations* (Dordrecht: Martinus Nijhoff Publishers, 1990), at 309–12.
185. Davis, at 48–51, 65–81, 88–91.
186. Id. at 104–5.

187. Id. at 105–7; *Keesing's Record of World Events*, vol. 32 (June 1986), at 34455.
188. *1986 UN Yearbook*, at 249–51.
189. Davis, at 85–87, 115–23.
190. Id. at 119–20.
191. Id. at 126–27.
192. Id. at 133–43.
193. Id. at 145–57.
194. Id. at 151; *1986 UN Yearbook*, at 253–58.

## Chapter 11

1. This observation suggests the accuracy of the statement that "it is wrong for anyone to have wars in North or South America (except the United States Marines)." See Walter Carruthers Sellar and Robert Julian Yeatman, *1066 and All That* (London: Methuen & Company, 1930), at 94.

2. Oscar Schacter, "The Lawful Resort to Unilateral Use of Force," *Yale Journal of International Law*, vol. 10 (Spring 1985), at 291, 291–94.

3. W. Michael Reisman, "Article 2(4): The Use of Force in Contemporary International Law," American Society of International Law, Washington, D.C., 1986, in *Proceedings of the 78th Annual Meeting*, at 75; Reisman, "Criteria for the Lawful Use of Force in International Law," *Yale Journal of International Law*, vol. 10 (Spring 1985), at 279; Reisman, "Allocating Competences to Use Coercion in the Post–Cold War World: Practices, Conditions, and Prospects" in Lori Fisler Damrosch and David J. Scheffer, eds., *Law and Force in the New International Order* (Boulder, Colo.: Westview Press, 1991), at 26.

4. Anthony Clark Arend, "International Law and the Recourse to Force: A Shift in Paradigms," *Stanford Journal of International Law*, vol. 27 (Fall 1990), at 1.

5. See, e.g., Reisman, "Allocating Competences," at 44–47; Reisman, "Coercion and Self-Determination: Construing Charter Article 2(4)," *American Journal of International Law*, vol. 78 (July 1984), at 642.

6. Fernando R. Tesón, *Humanitarian Intervention: An Inquiry into Law and Morality* (Dobbs Ferry, N.Y.: Transnational Publishers, Inc., 1988), at 155–200.

# BIBLIOGRAPHY

## Treaties


*Agreement Between the Great Socialist People's Libyan Arab Jamahiriya and the Republic of Chad Concerning the Practical Modalities for the Implementation of the Judgment Delivered by the International Court of Justice on 3 February 1994.* April 4, 1994. *International Legal Materials*, vol. 33 (1994), at 619.

*Charter of the United Nations.* 59 Stat. 1031, T.S. No. 993 (1945).

*Covenant of the League of Nations. Hudson International Legislation*, vol. 1 (1931), at 1.

*Inter-American Treaty of Reciprocal Assistance.* 62 Stat. 1681 (1947).

*Peace Treaty Between the Allied Powers and Turkey.* Lausanne, July 24, 1923, Article 20. In Fred L. Israel, ed., *Major Peace Treaties of Modern History, 1648–1967.* New York: Chelsea House Publishers, 1967.

*Statute of the International Court of Justice.* 59 Stat. 1055, T.S. No. 993 (1945).

*Treaty on Pacific Settlement of International Disputes.* 1 TIAS 230. 32 Stat. 1779, T.S. No. 392 (1899).

*Treaty Providing for the Renunciation of War as an Instrument of National Policy.* 46 Stat. 2343, T.S. No. 796 (1928; entered into force for the United States July 24, 1929).


## United Nations Documents


*Eleventh Progress Report of the Secretary-General on the United Nations Observers Mission in Liberia.* U.N. Doc. S/1995/473, June 10, 1995.

*Further Report of the Secretary-General on the Implementation of Security Council Resolution 598 (1987).* U.N. Doc. S/23273, December 9, 1991.

*General Assembly Official Records.* 16th Session. Annexes (XVI) 88 and 22 (a) at 26, Doc. A/L.368 (November 24, 1961).

*General Assembly Official Records.* 16th Session, meeting 1066, November 27, 1961; 20th Session, various meetings, September 24, 1965–October 15, 1965; 23d Session, various meetings, October 2, 1968–October 23, 1968.

General Assembly Resolution 3314 (XXIX), December 14, 1974.
*Secretary-General's Report on Western Sahara.* U.N. Doc. S/1996/43, January 19, 1996.
*Security Council Official Records.* Various meetings, February 13, 1946–December 4, 1971.
Security Council Resolution. Annex. *Report of the Secretary-General Pursuant to Paragraph 2 of Security Council Resolution 808 (1993).* U.N. Doc. S/25704, 1993.
Security Council Resolutions. Various numbers, August 2, 1990–December 19, 1995.
*Twelfth Progress Report of the Secretary-General on the United Nations Observers Mission in Liberia.* U.N. Doc. S/1995/781, September 9, 1995.
United Nations Documents. Various numbers, 1948–1996.

## Cases

*Case Concerning East Timor (Portugal v. Australia).* 1995 *International Court of Justice Reports,* at 90.
*Case Concerning Military and Paramilitary Activities In and Against Nicaragua (Nicaragua v. United States).* 1986 *International Court of Justice Reports,* at 14.
*Case of the S.S. Lotus (France v. Turkey). Permanent Court of International Justice Reports,* Ser. A, No. 10 (1927).
*Corfu Channel Case (United Kingdom v. Albania).* 1949 *International Court of Justice Reports,* at 1.
*Territorial Dispute (Libyan Arab Jamahiriya v. Chad).* 1994 *International Court of Justice Reports,* at 6.
*Western Sahara.* 1975 *International Court of Justice Reports,* at 12.

## Books

Abel, Elie. *The Missile Crisis.* New York: J. B. Lippincott Company, 1966.
Abi-Saad, Georges. *The United Nations Operation in the Congo, 1960–1964.* New York: Oxford University Press, 1978.
Abrahamian, Ervand. *Iran: Between Two Revolutions.* Princeton: Princeton University Press, 1982.
Akehurst, John. *We Won a War.* Salisbury: Michael Russell, 1982.
Allcock, John B., ed. *Border and Territorial Disputes.* 3d ed. Harlow, Essex: Longman, 1992.
Ameringer, Charles D. *Don Pepe.* Albuquerque: University of New Mexico Press, 1978.
Anglin, Douglas G., and Timothy M. Shaw. *Zambia's Foreign Policy: Studies in Diplomacy and Dependence.* Boulder, Colo.: Westview Press, 1979.
Attalides, Michael. *Cyprus.* New York: St. Martin's Press, 1979.
Avirgan, Tony, and Martha Honey. *War in Uganda.* Westport, Conn.: Lawrence Hill & Company, 1982.
Baddour, Abd el-Fattah I. S. *Sudanese-Egyptian Relations.* The Hague: Martinus Nijhoff, 1960.
Badeeb, Saeed M. *The Saudi-Egyptian Conflict over North Yemen, 1962–1970.* Boulder, Colo.: Westview Press, 1986.

Bailey, Clinton. *Jordan's Palestinian Challenge, 1948–1983*. Boulder, Colo.; Westview Press, 1984.

Banks, Arthur S., ed. *Political Handbook of the World: 1992*. Binghamton, N.Y.: CSA Publications, 1992.

Barclay, Glen St. J. *A Very Small Insurance Policy*. St. Lucia: University of Queensland Press, 1988.

Beschloss, Michael R. *The Crisis Years: Kennedy and Khrushchev, 1960–1963*. New York: Edward Burlingame Books, 1991.

Bidwell, Robin. *The Two Yemens*. Boulder, Colo.: Westview Press, 1983.

Birdwood, Lord. *Two Nations and Kashmir*. London: R. Hale, 1956.

Brecher, Michael. *Decisions in Israel's Foreign Policy*. New Haven: Yale University Press, 1975.

Brecher, Michael, and Benjamin Geist. *Decisions in Crisis*. Berkeley and Los Angeles: University of California Press, 1980.

Brines, Russell. *The Indo-Pakistani Conflict*. London: Pall Mall Press, 1968.

Brownlie, Ian. *Principles of Public International Law*. 3d ed. Oxford: Clarendon Press, 1979.

Bruce, Neil. *Portugal: The Last Empire*. New York: John Wiley & Sons, 1975.

Brune, Lester H. *The Missile Crisis of October 1962*. Claremont, Calif.: Regina Books, 1985.

Burrowes, Robert D. *The Yemen Arab Republic*. Boulder, Colo.: Westview Press, 1987.

Cassese, Antonio. *Terrorism, Politics, and the Law*. Princeton: Princeton University Press, 1989.

Chayes, Abram. *The Cuban Missile Crisis*. New York: Oxford University Press, 1974.

Chen, King C. *China's War with Vietnam, 1979*. Stanford: Hoover Institution Press, 1987.

Child, Jack. *The Central American Peace Process, 1983–1991*. Boulder, Colo.: Lynne Rienner Publishers, 1992.

Cohen, Mark I., and Laura Hahn. *Morocco: Old Land, New Nation*. New York: Praeger, 1966.

Cottam, Richard. *Nationalism in Iran*. Pittsburgh: University of Pittsburgh Press, 1979.

Crawshaw, Nancy. *The Cyprus Revolt*. London: George Allen & Unwin, 1978.

Crocker, Chester A. *High Noon in Southern Africa*. New York: W. W. Norton & Company, 1992.

D'Amato, Anthony A. *The Concept of Custom in International Law*. Ithaca: Cornell University Press, 1977.

———. *International Law: Process and Prospect*. Dobbs Ferry, N.Y.: Transnational Publishers, Inc., 1987.

Damis, John. *Conflict in Northwest Africa*. Stanford: Hoover Institution Press, 1983.

Davidow, Jeffrey. *Dealing with International Crises: Lessons from Zimbabwe*. Muscatine, Iowa: The Stanley Foundation, 1983.

———. *A Peace in Southern Africa: The Lancaster House Conference on Rhodesia, 1979*. Boulder, Colo.: Westview Press, 1984.

Davidson, Scott. *Grenada*. Brookfield, Mass.: Avebury, 1987.

Davis, Brian L. *Qaddafi, Terrorism, and the Origins of the U.S. Attack on Libya*. New York: Praeger, 1990.

Day, Alan J., ed. *Border and Territorial Disputes*. 2d ed. Detroit: Gale Research Company, 1987.

Deeb, Mary-Jane. *Libya's Foreign Policy in North Africa.* Boulder, Colo.: Westview Press; 1991.

d'Encausse, Hélène Carrère. *The End of the Soviet Empire: The Triumph of the Nations.* New York: Basic Books, 1993.

Dinstein, Yoram. *War, Aggression, and Self-Defence.* Cambridge: Grotius Publications, Ltd., 1988.

Dunkerly, James. *The Long War.* London: Junction Books, 1982.

Dunn, James. *Timor: A People Betrayed.* Auckland, New Zealand: The Jacaranda Press, 1983.

Dupuy, Trevor N., and Paul Martell. *Flawed Victory.* Fairfax, Va.: Hero Books, 1986.

Ehrlich, Thomas. *Cyprus: 1958–1967.* New York: Oxford University Press, 1974.

Eisenhower, Dwight D. *Waging Peace, 1956–1961.* Garden City, N.Y.: Doubleday & Company, 1965.

Ekwe-Ekwe, Herbert. *Conflict and Intervention in Africa.* New York: St. Martin's Press, 1990.

Epstein, Howard M., ed. *Revolt in the Congo, 1960–1964.* New York: Facts on File, Inc., 1965.

Esteves, Sarto. *Politics and Political Leadership in Goa.* New Delhi, Bangalore: Sterling Publishers Private, Ltd., 1986.

Franck, Thomas M. *The Power of Legitimacy Among Nations.* New York: Oxford University Press, 1990.

Freedman, Lawrence, and Efraim Karsh. *The Gulf Conflict, 1990–1991.* Princeton: Princeton University Press, 1993.

Gaitonde, P. D. *The Liberation of Goa.* New York: St. Martin's Press, 1987.

Ganguly, Sumit. *The Origins of War in South Asia.* Boulder, Colo.: Westview Press, 1986.

George, Alexander L., and Richard Smoke. *Deterrence in American Foreign Policy: Theory and Practice.* New York: Columbia University Press, 1974.

Gorman, Robert F. *Political Conflict on the Horn of Africa.* New York: Praeger, 1981.

Grunfeld, A. Tom. *The Making of Modern Tibet.* London: Zed Books, Ltd., 1987.

Gutman, Roy. *Banana Diplomacy.* New York: Simon and Schuster, 1988.

Hammer, Ellen J. *The Struggle for Indochina, 1940–1955.* Stanford: Stanford University Press, 1966.

Hart, H.L.A. *The Concept of Law.* New York: Oxford University Press, 1961.

Heikal, Mohamed. *The Road to Ramadan.* New York: Quadrangle/New York Times Book Company, 1975.

Henriksen, Thomas H. *Revolution and Counterrevolution.* Westport, Conn.: Greenwood Press, 1983.

Herzog, Chaim. *The Arab-Israeli Wars.* New York: Vintage Books, 1984.

Higgins, Trumbull. *The Perfect Failure.* New York: W. W. Norton & Company, 1987.

Hiorth, Finngeir. *Timor: Past and Present.* Townsville, Queensland: James Cook University of North Queensland, 1985.

Hitchens, Christopher. *Cyprus.* New York: Quartet Books, 1984.

Hof, Frederic C. *Galilee Divided.* Boulder, Colo.: Westview Press, 1985.

Hoffman, Steven A. *India and the China Crisis.* Berkeley and Los Angeles: University of California Press, 1990.

Hood, Steven J. *Dragons Entangled.* Armonk, N.Y.: M. E. Sharpe, Inc., 1992.

Horne, Alistair. *A Savage War of Peace.* New York: Penguin Books, 1987.

Hoyt, Edwin P. *The Day the Chinese Attacked.* New York: McGraw-Hill, 1990.
Immerman, Richard H. *The CIA in Guatemala.* Austin: University of Texas Press, 1982.
International Commission of Jurists. *The Events in East Pakistan.* Geneva: International Commission of Jurists, 1972.
Jackson, D. Bruce. *Castro, the Kremlin, and Communism in Latin America.* Baltimore: The Johns Hopkins University Press, 1969.
Jackson, Robert. *South Asian Crisis.* New York: Praeger, 1975.
Jaster, Robert S. *Adelphi Papers 253: The 1988 Peace Accords and the Future of South-Western Africa.* London: Brassey's Defence Publishers, 1990.
Kadian, Rajesh. *India's Sri Lanka Fiasco.* New Delhi, Bombay: Vision Books, 1990.
Kagan, Donald. *On the Origins of War and the Preservation of Peace.* New York: Doubleday, 1995.
Kalb, Marvin, and Bernard Kalb. *Kissinger.* Boston: Little, Brown and Company, 1974.
Kattenburg, Paul M. *The Vietnam Trauma in American Foreign Policy.* (New Brunswick, N.J.: Transaction Books, 1980.
Kelley, Michael P. *A State in Disarray.* Boulder, Colo.: Westview Press, 1986.
Kiernan, Ben. *How Pol Pot Came to Power.* London: Verson, 1985.
Kimche, David, and Jon Kimche. *A Clash of Destinies.* New York: Praeger, 1960.
Kinney, Douglas. *National Interest/National Honor.* New York: Praeger, 1989.
Klintworth, Gary. *Vietnam's Intervention in Cambodia in International Law.* Canberra: Australian Government Publishing Service, 1989.
Landau, Rom. *Moroccan Drama: 1900–1955.* San Francisco: American Academy of Asian Studies, 1956.
Lenczowski, George. *Russia and the West in Iran, 1918–1948.* Ithaca: Cornell University Press, 1949.
Ling, Dwight L. *Tunisia: From Protectorate to Republic.* Bloomington: Indiana University Press, 1967.
Little, Tom. *South Arabia: Arena of Conflict.* New York: Praeger, 1968.
Longrigg, Stephen H. *Syria and Lebanon Under French Mandate.* New York: Oxford University Press, 1958.
Lowe, Peter. *The Origins of the Korean War.* New York: Longman, 1986.
Lowenthal, Abraham F. *The Dominican Intervention.* Cambridge: Harvard University Press, 1972.
Mackie, J.A.C. *Konfrontasi.* New York: Oxford University Press, 1974.
Mahoney, Richard D. *The Kennedy Policy in the Congo, 1961–1963.* Ann Arbor: University Microfilms International, 1981.
Marcum, John A. *The Angolan Revolution.* Vol. 1. Cambridge, Mass.: The MIT Press, 1969.
———. *The Angolan Revolution.* Vol. 2. Cambridge, Mass.: The MIT Press, 1978.
Martin, David, and Phyllis Johnson. *The Struggle for Zimbabwe.* Boston: Faber and Faber, 1981.
Martz, Mary Jeanne Reid. *The Central American Soccer War: Historical Patterns and Internal Dynamics of OAS Settlement Procedures.* Athens: Ohio University Center for International Studies, 1978.
Maxwell, Neville. *India's China War.* London: Jonathan Cape, 1970.
McKinnon, Dan. *Bullseye One Reactor.* San Diego: House of Hits, 1987.
Middlebrook, Martin. *Operation Corporate.* London: Viking, 1985.

Murphy, John F. *The United Nations and the Control of International Violence.* Totowa, N.J.: Allanheld, Osmun, 1982.
Neff, Donald. *Warriors at Suez.* New York: Simon and Schuster, 1981.
Neuberger, Benyamin. *Involvement, Invasion, and Withdrawal: Qadhdhāfi's Libya and Chad, 1969–1981.* Tel Aviv: Center for Middle Eastern and African Studies, Tel Aviv University, 1982.
O'Ballance, Edgar. *The Greek Civil War, 1944–1949.* New York: Praeger, 1966.
———. *The Gulf War.* London: Brassey's Defence Publishers, 1988.
———. *The War in the Yemen.* Hamden, Conn.: Archon Books, 1971.
Paget, Julian. *Last Post: Aden 1964–1967.* London: Faber and Faber, 1969.
Palmer, Bruce, Jr. *Intervention in the Caribbean.* Lexington: The University Press of Kentucky, 1989.
Pao-Min Chang. *The Sino-Vietnamese Territorial Dispute.* New York: Praeger, 1986.
Pastor, Robert A. *Condemned to Repetition.* Princeton: Princeton University Press, 1987.
Patrick, Richard A. *Political Geography and the Cyprus Conflict, 1963–1971.* Waterloo, Ontario: Department of Geography, Faculty of Environmental Studies, University of Waterloo, 1976.
Pelletiere, Stephen C. *The Iran-Iraq War.* New York: Praeger, 1992.
Perlmutter, Amos; Michael Handel; Uri Bar-Joseph. *Two Minutes Over Baghdad.* London: Vallentine, Mitchell & Company, Ltd., 1982.
Poole, Peter A. *Eight Presidents and Indochina.* Huntington, N.Y.: R. E. Krieger, 1978.
Radványi, János. *Hungary and the Superpowers: The 1956 Revolution and Realpolitik.* Stanford: Hoover Institution Press, 1972.
Reid, Anthony J. S. *The Indonesian National Revolution, 1945–1950.* Hawthorn, Victoria: Longman, 1974.
Ruiz, Hiram A. *Uprooted Liberians: Casualties of a Brutal War.* Washington, D.C.: American Council for Nationalities Service, 1992.
Ryan, Paul B. *The Iranian Rescue Mission.* Annapolis: Naval Institute Press, 1985.
Schiff, Ze'ev. *A History of the Israeli Army.* New York: Macmillan, 1985.
Schiff, Ze'ev, and Ehud Ya'ari. *Israel's Lebanon War.* New York: Simon and Schuster, 1984.
Schwarzenberger, Georg, and E. D. Brown. *A Manual of International Law.* 6th ed. Milton, U.K.: Professional Books, Ltd., 1976.
*Sekou Toure.* London: Panaf Books, 1978.
Sellar, Walter Carruthers, and Robert Julian Yeatman. *1066 and All That.* London: Methuen & Company, 1930.
Shawcross, William. *Sideshow.* New York: Simon and Schuster, 1979.
Sick, Gary. *All Fall Down.* New York: Random House, 1985.
Sisson, Richard, and Leo E. Rose. *War and Secession.* Berkeley and Los Angeles: University of California Press, 1990.
Skilling, H. Gordon. *Czechoslovakia's Interrupted Revolution.* Princeton: Princeton University Press, 1976.
Skrine, Sir Clarmont. *World War in Iran.* London: Constable, 1962.
Smith, R. B. *An International History of the Vietnam War.* Vol. 3, *The Making of a Limited War, 1965–1966.* New York: St.Martin's Press, 1991.
———. *An International History of the Vietnam War.* Vol. 1, *Revolution Versus Containment, 1955–1961.* New York: St. Martin's Press, 1983.

———. *An International History of the Vietnam War*, Vol. 2, *The Kennedy Strategy*. New York: St. Martin's Press, 1985.
Smith, Roger M. *Cambodia's Foreign Policy*. Ithaca: Cornell University Press, 1965.
Somerville, Keith. *Foreign Military Intervention in Africa*. New York: St. Martin's Press, 1990.
Strack, Harry R. *Sanctions: The Case of Rhodesia*. Syracuse: Syracuse University Press, 1978.
Stuart-Fox, Martin. *Laos*. Boulder, Colo.: Lynne Rienner Publishers, 1986.
Tai Sung An. *The Sino-Soviet Territorial Dispute*. Philadelphia: The Westminster Press, 1973.
Tesón, Fernando R. *Humanitarian Intervention: An Inquiry into Law and Morality*. Dobbs Ferry, N.Y.: Transnational Publishers, Inc., 1988.
Thomas, Hugh. *Suez*. New York: Harper & Row, 1967.
Tran Dinn Tho. *The Cambodian Incursion*. Washington, D.C.: U.S. Army Center of Military History, 1978.
Turley, William S. *The Second Indochina War: A Short Political and Military History*. Boulder, Colo.: Westview Press, 1986.
Urban, Mark. *War in Afghanistan*. New York: St. Martin's Press, 1990.
Vines, Alex. *RENAMO*. Bloomington: Indiana University Press, 1991.
Weber, Max. *Law in Economy and Society*. Ed. Max Rheinstein; trans. Edward Shils and Max Rheinstein. Cambridge: Harvard University Press, 1954.
Weinberger, Naomi Joy. *Syrian Intervention in Lebanon*. New York: Oxford University Press, 1986.
Welch, Richard E., Jr. *Response to Revolution*. Chapel Hill: University of North Carolina Press, 1985.
Wenner, Manfred W. *The Yemen Arab Republic*. Boulder, Colo.: Westview Press, 1991.
Whelan, Richard. *Drawing the Line*. Boston: Little, Brown and Company, 1990.
White, Alastair. *El Salvador*. New York: Praeger, 1973.
Whiteman, Kaye. *Chad*. London: Minority Rights Group, 1988.
Wich, Richard. *Sino-Soviet Crisis Politics*. Cambridge: Harvard University Council on East Asian Studies, 1980.
Zabih, Sepehr. *The Mossadegh Era*. Chicago: Lake View Press, 1982.
Zagoria, Donald S. *The Sino-Soviet Conflict, 1956–1961*. New York: Atheneum, 1969.

## Articles

"Air Attacks on Neutral Shipping in the Persian Gulf: The Legality of the Iraqi Exclusion Zone and Iranian Reprisals." *Boston College International and Comparative Law Review*, vol. 8 (Summer 1985), at 517.
Arend, Anthony Clark. "International Law and the Recourse to Force: A Shift in Paradigms." *Stanford Journal of International Law*, vol. 27 (Fall 1990), at 1.
Behuniak, Thomas E. "The Seizure and Recovery of the S.S. Mayaguez: A Legal Analysis of United States Claims, Part 1." *Military Law Review*, vol. 82 (Fall 1978), at 41.
Boczek, Boleslaw A. "The Law of Maritime Warfare and Neutrality in the Gulf

War." In Christopher C. Joyner, ed., *The Persian Gulf War* (Westport, Conn.: Greenwood Press, 1990), at 173.

———. "Law of Warfare at Sea and Neutrality: Lessons from the Gulf War." *Ocean Development and International Law,* vol. 20, no. 3 (1989), at 239.

Bothe, Michael. "Neutrality at Sea." In Ige F. Dekker and Harry H. G. Post, eds., *The Gulf War of 1980–1988* (Dordrecht: Martinus Nijhoff Publishers, 1992), at 204.

Buszynski, Leszek. "The Soviet Union and Vietnamese Withdrawal from Cambodia." In Gary Klintworth, ed., *Vietnam's Withdrawal from Cambodia: Regional Issues and Realignments* (Canberra: Australian National University, 1990), at 32.

Caron, David D. "Choice and Duty in Foreign Affairs." In Christopher C. Joyner, ed., *The Persian Gulf War* (Westport, Conn.: Greenwood Press, 1990), at 153.

Claude, Inis L., Jr. "UN Efforts at Settlement of the Falkland Islands Crisis." In Alberto R. Coll and Anthony C. Arend, eds., *The Falklands War* (Boston: George Allen & Unwin, 1985), at 118.

Coll, Alberto R. "Philosophical and Legal Dimensions of the Use of Force in the Falklands War." In Alberto R. Coll and Anthony C. Arend, eds., *The Falklands War* (Boston: George Allen & Unwin, 1985), at 34.

"The Congo Crisis 1964: A Case Study in Humanitarian Intervention." *Virginia Journal of International Law,* vol. 12 (March 1972), at 261.

Cot, Jean-Pierre. "The Role of the Inter-African Peace-Keeping Force in Chad, 1981–1982." In Antonio Cassese, ed., *The Current Legal Regulation of the Use of Force* (Dordrecht: Martinus Nijhoff Publishers, 1986).

D'Amato, Anthony. "Trashing Customary International Law." *American Journal of International Law,* vol. 81 (1987), at 101.

Dekker, Ige F. "Criminal Responsibility and the Gulf War of 1980–1988: The Crime of Aggression." In Ige F. Dekker and Harry H. G. Post, eds., *The Gulf War of 1980–1988* (Dordrecht: Martinus Nijhoff Publishers, 1992), at 249.

Falk, Richard A. "International Law and the United States Role in the Vietnam War." In Richard A. Falk, ed., *The Vietnam War and International Law* (Princeton: Princeton University Press, 1968), vol. 1, at 445.

Feldman, Shai. "Israel's Involvement in Lebanon: 1975–1985." In Ariel E. Levite, Bruce W. Jentleson, and Larry Berman, eds., *Foreign Military Intervention* (New York: Columbia University Press, 1992), at 129.

Fisher, Roger. "Bringing Law to Bear on Governments." *Harvard Law Review,* vol. 74 (1961), at 1130.

Fraleigh, Arnold. "The Algerian Revolution as a Case Study in International Law." In Richard A. Falk, ed., *The International Law of Civil War* (Baltimore: The Johns Hopkins University Press, 1971), at 179.

Franck, Thomas M. "Dulce et Decorum Est: The Strategic Role of Principles in the Falklands War." *American Journal of International Law,* vol. 77 (1983), at 109.

———. "Some Observations on the ICJ's Procedural and Substantive Innovations." *American Journal of International Law,* vol. 81 (1987), at 116.

———. "Who Killed Article 2(4)? or: Changing Norms Governing the Use of Force by States." *American Journal of International Law,* vol. 64 (1970), at 809.

Franck, Thomas M., and Nigel S. Rodley. "After Bangladesh: The Law of Humanitarian Intervention by Military Force." *American Journal of International Law,* vol. 67 (April 1973), at 275.

Fried, John H. E. "United States Military Intervention in Cambodia in Light of

International Law." In Richard A. Falk, ed., *The Vietnam War and International Law* (Princeton: Princeton University Press, 1972), vol. 3, at 100.
Gioia, A., and N. Ronzitti. "The Law of Neutrality: Third States' Commercial Rights and Duties." In Ige F. Dekker and Harry H. G. Post, eds., *The Gulf War of 1980–1988* (Dordrecht: Martinus Nijhoff Publishers, 1992), at 221.
Gompert, David C. "American Diplomacy and the Haig Mission: An Insider's Perspective." In Alberto R. Coll and Anthony C. Arend, eds., *The Falklands War* (Boston: George Allen & Unwin, 1985), at 106.
Gooding, Gregory V. "Incident—Fighting Terrorism in the 1980s: The Interception of the *Achille Lauro* Hijackers." *Yale Journal of International Law,* vol. 12 (Winter 1987), at 158.
Goodman, Richard M. "The Invasion of Czechoslovakia: 1968." *International Lawyer,* vol. 4 (October 1969), at 42.
Grunawalt, Richard. "The Rights of Neutrals and Belligerents" (January 26, 1988). In "Conference Report: The Persian/Arabian Gulf Tanker War—International Law or International Chaos," *Ocean Development and International Law,* vol. 19, no. 4 (1988), at 302.
Henkin, Louis, "Commentary" (January 26, 1988). In "Conference Report: The Persian/Arabian Gulf Tanker War—International Law or International Chaos," *Ocean Development and International Law,* vol. 19, no. 4 (1988), at 308.
———. "International Law: Politics, Values, and Functions." *Recueil des Cours,* vol. 216 (Dordrecht: Martinus Nijhoff Publishers, 1990), at 9.
———. "The Invasion of Panama Under International Law: A Gross Violation." *Columbia Journal of Transnational Law,* vol. 29 (1991), at 293.
Hooglund, Eric. "Strategic and Political Objectives in the Gulf War: Iran's View." In Christopher C. Joyner, ed., *The Persian Gulf War* (Westport, Conn.: Greenwood Press, 1990), at 39.
"The Indian Supply Drop into Sri Lanka: Nonmilitary Humanitarian Aid and the Troubling Idea of Intervention." *Connecticut Journal of International Law,* vol. 3 (Spring 1988), at 417.
Ispahani, Mahnaz. "India's Role in Sri Lanka's Ethnic Conflict." In Ariel E. Levite, Bruce W. Jentleson, and Larry Berman, eds., *Foreign Military Intervention* (New York: Columbia University Press, 1992), at 209.
Isselé, Jean Pierre. "The Arab Deterrent Force in Lebanon, 1976–1983." In Antonio Cassese, ed., *The Current Legal Regulation of the Use of Force* (Dordrecht: Martinus Nijhoff Publishers, 1986), at 179.
Janis, Mark W. "Neutrality." In Horace B. Robertson, ed., *International Law Studies, 1991: The Law of Naval Operations* (Newport: Naval War College Press, 1991), at 148.
Kechichian, Joseph H. "The Gulf Cooperation Council and the Gulf War." In Christopher C. Joyner, ed., *The Persian Gulf War* (Westport, Conn.: Greenwood Press, 1990), at 91.
Kwakwa, Edward. "South Africa's May 1986 Military Incursions into Neighboring African States." *Yale Journal of International Law,* vol. 12 (Summer 1987), at 421.
Leifer, Michael. "Cambodia in Regional and Global Politics." In Gary Klintworth, ed., *Vietnam's Withdrawal from Cambodia: Regional Issues and Realignments* (Canberra: Australian National University, 1990), at 4.
Marr, Phebe. "The Iran-Iraq War: The View from Iraq." In Christopher C. Joyner, ed., *The Persian Gulf War* (Westport, Conn.: Greenwood Press, 1990), at 59.

McDougal, Myres S. "Law and Minimum World Public Order: Armed Conflict in Larger Context." *UCLA Pacific Basin Law Journal*, vol. 3 (1984), at 21.

Miller, Jennifer. "International Intervention—The United States Invasion of Panama." *Harvard International Law Journal*, vol. 31 (Spring 1990), at 633.

Moore, John Norton. "Grenada and the International Double Standard." *American Journal of International Law*, vol. 78 (January 1984), at 145.

Moose, George E. "French Military Policy in Africa." In William J. Foltz and Henry S. Bienen, eds., *Arms and the African* (New Haven: Yale University Press, 1985), at 59.

Olmert, Yossi. "Syria in Lebanon." In Ariel E. Levite, Bruce W. Jentleson, and Larry Berman, eds., *Foreign Military Intervention* (New York: Columbia University Press, 1992), at 95.

Perrera, Srilal. "The OAS and the Inter-American System: History, Law, and Diplomacy." In Alberto R. Coll and Anthony C. Arend, eds., *The Falklands War* (Boston: George Allen & Unwin, 1985), at 132.

Pimlott, John. "The Gulf Crisis and World Politics." In John Pimlott and Stephen Badsey, eds., *The Gulf War Assessed* (London: Arms and Armour, 1992), at 35.

Quigley, John. "The Legality of the United States Invasion of Panama." *Yale Journal of International Law*, vol. 15 (Summer 1990), at 276.

Qureshi, S.M.M. "Pakhtunistan: The Frontier Dispute Between Afghanistan and Pakistan." *Pacific Affairs*, vol. 39 (Spring–Summer 1966).

Rajan, M. S., and T. Israel. "The United Nations and the Conflict in Vietnam," In Richard A. Falk, ed., *The Vietnam War and International Law*, vol. 4, *The Concluding Phase* (Princeton: Princeton University Press, 1976), at 114.

Ramazani, R. K. "Who Started the Iran-Iraq War? A Commentary." *Virginia Journal of International Law*, vol. 33 (Fall 1992), at 69.

Ratner, Steven R. "The Gulf of Sidra Incident of 1981: The Lawfulness of Peacetime Aerial Engagements." In W. Michael Reisman and Andrew R. Willard, eds., *International Incidents* (Princeton: Princeton University Press, 1988), at 181.

Reisman, W. Michael. "Allocating Competences to Use Coercion in the Post–Cold War World: Practices, Conditions, and Prospects." In Lori Fisler Damrosch and David J. Scheffer, eds., *Law and Force in the New International Order* (Boulder, Colo.: Westview Press, 1991), at 26.

———. "Coercion and Self-Determination: Construing Charter Article 2(4)." *American Journal of International Law*, vol. 78 (July 1984), at 642.

———. "Criteria for the Lawful Use of Force in International Law." *Yale Journal of International Law*, vol. 10 (Spring 1985), at 279.

Rubin, Alfred P. "Historical and Legal Background of the Falkland/Malvinas Dispute." In Alberto R. Coll and Anthony C. Arend, eds., *The Falklands War* (Boston: George Allen & Unwin, 1985), at 9.

Russo, Francis V., Jr. "Neutrality at Sea in Transition: State Practice in the Gulf War as Emerging International Customary Law." *Ocean Development and International Law*, vol. 19, no. 5 (1988), at 381.

Saikal, Amin. "The Regional Politics of the Afghan Crisis." In Amin Saikal and William Maley, *The Soviet Withdrawal from Afghanistan* (Cambridge: Cambridge University Press, 1989), at 52.

Schachter, Oscar. "The Lawful Resort to Unilateral Use of Force." *Yale Journal of International Law*, vol. 10 (Spring 1985), at 291.

Schwebel, Stephen M. "The Effect of Resolutions of the U.N. General Assembly on Customary International Law." 1979 *Proceedings of the American Society of International Law* (Washington, D.C., 1979), at 301, 302.

Schweisow, Naomi. "Mediation." In Evan Luard, ed., *The International Regulation of Frontier Disputes* (New York: Praeger, 1970), at 141.

Shoham, Uri. "The Israeli Aerial Raid upon the Iraqi Nuclear Reactor and the Right of Self-Defense." *Military Law Review*, vol. 109 (Summer 1985), at 191.

Sofaer, Abraham D. "The Legality of the United States Action in Panama." *Columbia Journal of Transnational Law*, vol. 29 (1991), at 281.

Weisburd, Arthur M. "Customary International Law: The Problem of Treaties." *Vanderbilt Journal of Transnational Law*, vol. 21 (1988), at 1.

———. "The Effect of Treaties and Other Formal International Acts on the Customary Law of Human Rights." *Georgia Journal of International Law*, vol. 25 (1996), at 99.

Weller, Marc. "The Use of Force and Collective Security." In Ige F. Dekker and Harry H. G. Post, eds., *The Gulf War of 1980–1988* (Dordrecht: Martinus Nijhoff Publishers, 1992), at 71.

Worrall, John. "Mounting Dangers for Latest U.S. 'Ally' in Africa." *U.S. News & World Report*, August 2, 1976, at 49.

Wright, Quincy. "The Goa Incident." *American Journal of International Law*, vol. 56 (July 1962), at 617.

## Speeches, Presentations, Remarks

Dinstein, Yoram. Remarks. American Society of International Law, Washington, D.C., 1990. In *Proceedings of the 81st Annual Meeting*, at 266.

Magraw, Daniel B., Jr. Remarks. American Society of International Law, Washington, D.C., 1990. In *Proceedings of the 81st Annual Meeting*, at 270.

Morrison, Fred L. Remarks. American Society of International Law, Washington, D.C., 1990. In *Proceedings of the 81st Annual Meeting*, at 260.

Reisman, W. Michael. "Article 2(4): The Use of Force in Contemporary International Law." American Society of International Law, Washington, D.C., 1986. In *Proceedings of the 78th Annual Meeting*, at 75.

———. "International Lawmaking: A Process of Communication" (Harold D. Lasswell Memorial Lecture). American Society of International Law, Washington, D.C., 1983. In *Proceedings of the 75th Anniversary Convocation*, at 101.

Schachter, Oscar. Remarks. American Society of International Law, Washington, D.C., 1990. In *Proceedings of the 81st Annual Meeting*, at 159.

## Newspapers

*Christian Science Monitor*. June 12, 1985; December 1, 1992.

*Le Figaro*. May 27, 1954.

*Financial Times*. February 29, 1996.

*The Guardian*. April 7, 1993; July 6, 1994; August 26, 1995.

*Houston Chronicle*. April 24, 1994.
*The Independent*. July 29, 1994.
*Los Angeles Times*. November 11, 1990; May 17, 1994; October 14, 1995.
*Le Monde*. Various issues, 1947–1948.
*New York Times*. Various issues, 1946–1996.
*Orlando Sentinel Tribune*. September 2, 1991.
*The Times* (London). Various issues, 1946–1993.

## News Digests

*African Recorder*. Vol. 15 (1976).
*Asian Recorder*. Various volumes, 1956–1972.
*Facts on File*. Volume 21 (January 19–25, 1961; April 6–12, 1961).
*Facts on File World News Digest*. May 17, 1975.
*Keesing's Contemporary Archives*. Volumes 8, 10–32 (1951–1986).
*Keesing's Record of World Events*. Volumes 32, 34–39 (1986–1993).

## Government Publications

*Department of State Bulletin*. Various volumes, 1957–1988.
"The Legality of United States Participation in the Defense of Viet-Nam." *Department of State Bulletin*, vol. 54 (March 28, 1966), at 474.

## Wire Service Reports

"Fate of Angola Hangs in the Balance." Agence France Presse, June 4, 1994. Available in LEXIS, Nexis Library, Curnws File.
"Liberia: Mediators Hold Breath on Ceasefire Agreement." Inter Press Service, July 26, 1993. Available in LEXIS, Nexis Library, Inpres File.
"Liberian Warlords to Explain Disarmament Holdup." Reuters World Service, June 1, 1994. Available in LEXIS, Nexis Library, Curnws File.
"U.N. Denies Accusing Morocco of Delaying Vote." Reuters World Service, June 18, 1994. Available in LEXIS, Nexis Library, Curnws File.
"U.N. Says W. Sahara Voting Process Delayed Again." Reuters World Service, June 17, 1994. Available in LEXIS, Nexis Library, Curnws File.
"U.S. Still Backs African Troops in Liberia-Cohen." Reuters Limited, November 12, 1992. Available in LEXIS, Nexis Library, Reuters North American Wire File.

# Index

A. Mark Weisburd is Professor of Law at the University of North Carolina, Chapel Hill.